THE '63 STEELERS

WRITING SPORTS SERIES

Richard "Pete" Peterson, Editor

The Cleveland Indians
   Franklin Lewis

The Cincinnati Reds
   Lee Allen

The Chicago White Sox
   Warren Brown

Dreaming Baseball
   James T. Farrell

My Greatest Day in Football
   Murray Goodman and Leonard Lewin

The Detroit Tigers
   Frederick G. Lieb

The Philadelphia Phillies
   Frederick G. Lieb

The Washington Senators
   Shirley Povich

The '63 Steelers: A Renegade Team's Chase for Glory
   Rudy Dicks

THE '63 STEELERS

A RENEGADE TEAM'S CHASE FOR GLORY

RUDY DICKS

THE KENT STATE UNIVERSITY PRESS Kent, Ohio

©2012 by The Kent State University Press, Kent, Ohio 44242
All rights reserved
Library of Congress Catalog Card Number 2012013505
ISBN 978-1-60635-143-7
Manufactured in the United States of America

Every effort has been made to obtain permission from those persons
interviewed by the author who are quoted in the book.

LIBRARY OF CONGRESS CATALOGING-IN-PUBLICATION DATA
Dicks, Rudy.
The '63 Steelers : a renegade team's chase for glory / Rudy Dicks.
p. cm. — (Writing sports series)
Includes bibliographical references and index.
ISBN 978-1-60635-143-7 (pbk. : alk. paper) ∞
1. Pittsburgh Steelers (Football team)—History.
I. Title. II. Title: 1963 Steelers. III. Title: Nineteen sixty three Steelers.
GV956.P57D5 2012
796.332'640974886—dc23
2012013505

16 15 14 13 12   5 4 3 2 1

For the 1963 Pittsburgh Steelers . . .

. . . and for Sheldon J. Dicks, who set an example for
how to be as tough as Red Mack,
as compassionate as Art Rooney, and
as confident as Bobby Layne . . .

. . . and for Lillian W. Dicks,
for nurturing in her sons
a love for reading and writing

You may glory in a team triumphant, but you fall in love with a team in defeat. Losing after great striving is the story of man, who was born to sorrow, whose sweetest songs tell of saddest thought, and who, if he is a hero, does nothing in life as becomingly as leaving it.
—Roger Kahn, *The Boys of Summer*

The noblest battles of all are those fought in vain.
—Edmond Rostand, *Cyrano de Bergerac*

CONTENTS

PREFACE

I grew up in the late fifties and early sixties in a ranch-style house at the corner of Rosewae Drive and Skywae Drive in a city that the *Saturday Evening Post* labeled "Crime Town USA" and that also came to be known as "Murder Town."[1]

Some days my mother would hide the front section of our hometown paper, the *Youngstown Vindicator,* so that my brothers and I would not be exposed to the gory headlines and stories about guys with funny nicknames getting blown up in cars and their body parts being scattered across the neighbor's yard. I didn't find out about her protectiveness until years later, but I wouldn't have minded anyway, as long as she didn't take away the sports section. The only bombs I cared about as a kid were the ones quarterbacks threw.

That '63 *Post* story said that there had been seventy-five bombings in Youngstown over a decade's time, which, if accurate, means that the only person busier than the wise guys in town was my mother stashing away sections of the afternoon paper. But the world of Cadillac Charlie, the Crab, Tar Baby, and the "bug" (the numbers game) was far from ours in northeast Ohio. My view from the crest of the hill on Rosewae was filled with more innocence than Lake Wobegon: dads mowing the lawn, moms working in the garden, kids riding bikes, and the fireworks in the distance from Idora Park, where my dad would take my mom on Sunday nights in the summer to listen and dance to Stan Kenton, Buddy Rich, and Woody Herman. You could phone us by dialing SWeetbriar 23065 or send us a letter using a new number introduced in the summer of '63, something called a zip code, which replaced our old postal code, number 11.

There were much scarier places, I knew, such as the Deep South, Europe, and Africa, because I had seen them up close, bigger than life, when my dad took us downtown to the Palace, Paramount, and Warner theaters, which showed *To Kill a Mockingbird, The Guns of Navarone,* and *Lawrence of Arabia.* Good thing, I told myself, that we lived someplace safe.

The next-door neighbors had a son in high school who played catch with me, coaxed me to show off my basketball-dribbling skills in front of his friend, and one afternoon tried to teach me to play the guitar. Because of his hairstyle, he reminded me of Edd "Kookie" Byrnes from *77 Sunset Strip,* and I was sure that he owned a black leather jacket; maybe he even snuck Marlboro cigarettes like they showed on TV ads. After our family moved away a few years later, I turned on my transistor radio one morning and heard his voice booming out, singing the Isley Brothers' "Nobody But Me." It was Dick Belley, and for nearly half a century his version would remain as popular as it was in '67. Music fans remember Dick Belley as a member of the Human Beinz, who played at Idora Park regularly, but I remember him as a decent older boy who took the time to befriend a kid.

We played Wiffle ball in the backyard, and kickball and kick-the-can in a cul-de-sac, and we loaded kids into our station wagon to go to the drive-in with a cooler full of pop, but my favorite spot of all was the one right in front of me every time I stepped out the front door: a stretch of green lawn that looked as lush to me as any fairway at Augusta would to a golf fan. It was the biggest yard in the neighborhood, and the best for tackle football, and it was where the neighborhood kids always played.

When we weren't playing football, we were watching it on TV. Growing up in Youngstown, what was more intimidating than any mobsters was being a Pittsburgh Steelers fan and finding yourself outnumbered by Cleveland Browns fans. Youngstown's equidistant location between Cleveland and Pittsburgh was convenient for the mob's itinerary, but it didn't mean loyalties were divided equally between the teams. Even I started out, tentatively, as a Browns fan. Without cable TV, the Internet, or *Monday Night Football,* my exposure to other teams was limited to the daily newspaper and football magazines.

One late November Sunday morning when I was seven, I asked my dad if we would be rooting for the Browns that afternoon. My father was born and raised on the Iron Range in Minnesota, so he had more allegiance to the University of Minnesota, Bronislau "Bronko" Nagurski, and the Duluth

Eskimos barnstorming team than he did to the Browns. He paused and then told me about the man who played quarterback for the Steelers, the Browns' opponent that day. "His name is Bobby Layne," my dad said, "and he believes he can do anything."

I wasn't convinced, especially considering the Browns were 6–2 and the Steelers 3–4–1, and my doubts were justified as Cleveland clung to a 20–14 lead in the final minutes. But then the man who would be dubbed "Last-Minute Layne" in the *Pittsburgh Post-Gazette* the next day began working his two-minute magic as my dad and I watched on our black-and-white TV.[2] Two pass completions, a penalty, and a run put the Steelers on the Browns' 17, and with only forty seconds left, Layne hit Gern Nagler under the goalpost with a touchdown pass.

Pennsylvania governor David L. Lawrence was the preeminent fan among the estimated 10,000 Steelers diehards who made the three-hour trip from Pittsburgh to Municipal Stadium on the shores of Lake Erie, and his reaction was duly noted by the *Post-Gazette:* "The governor cast aside dignity for a brief moment in the press box by throwing his hat high in the air and announcing to one and all: 'That was the greatest play of all time.'"[3]

A bit of an exaggeration, even for a politician, because the only great plays for Pittsburgh in the previous twenty-six years of the Steelers' existence had been performed downtown at the Nixon Theater. In that time span, the Steelers had experienced only five winning seasons and only once made it to a postseason game. But the heroics were plenty impressive to a seven-year-old, and when Layne kicked the extra point that gave the Steelers a 21–20 victory, he converted me into a Bobby Layne fan and a Pittsburgh Steeler rooter. I would always remember that day, November 22, 1959, but I could never imagine that the afternoon four years later, to the day, would be even more memorable.

Over the next couple of years, my dad took me to Forbes Field to watch the Vince Lombardi Packer teams, which were evolving into a powerhouse; the expansion Cowboys team led by young quarterback Don Meredith and coached by Tom Landry; and the team that I grew to hate, the Browns, powered by Jim Brown. I struggled in my heart—probably as much as the players did on the field—through a 5–6–1 season in 1960, and then a 6–8 record in '61 before the Steelers' second-place finish in '62, at 9–5, allowed me to dream that they could win the Eastern Conference in '63.

On a Friday afternoon, November 22, 1963, I was in school, watching the hands on the clock inch toward 3:15 P.M., and eagerly looking forward to a trip to Forbes Field in less than forty-eight hours to watch the Steelers play the Western Conference leader, the Chicago Bears, when the bell rang, dismissing us for the weekend. I was almost to the door when someone rushed up and announced that President Kennedy had been shot.

My brothers and I attended a very small private school in downtown Youngstown, which, in a spooky coincidence, was named the Kennedy School, after the school's headmistress. We studied current events all year through the newspaper, so we had scrutinized the 1960 Kennedy-Nixon presidential race, especially when the rivals campaigned fiercely in Youngstown, a key industrial city in a pivotal state. We even held our own mock election.

I remember an older schoolmate who cried over news of the assassination. I did not. I wonder now how many eleven-year-olds did. Mostly, I guess, I felt puzzled. We grew up playing with cap guns and watching men shoot pistols and rifles on *Combat!* and *Gunsmoke* and *The Untouchables,* and reading comic books with illustrations of soldiers who had been shot, but we didn't comprehend that guns—real guns with real bullets—were fired on our own streets. We had studied Abraham Lincoln's assassination, but it was the kind of event that seemed isolated and frozen in history, as unlikely to be duplicated in our day as an Indian attack in the neighborhood.

Ten years later, my college professor Dewey Ganzel would tell us in his course on Hemingway that there are two seminal events in a young person's life: when he realizes that other people die, and when he realizes that he himself will one day die. That spring of '63, I started to learn about death.

In the first week of May, my Uncle Shorty, a family doctor who treated us to root beer floats, took us for spins on his sailboat, and played taps on his old Army bugle at bedtime outside the family cabin in Minnesota, died of cancer. I wondered what kind of cruel disease could kill a man who lived his life with such gusto.

One week later, a story in the *Vindicator* reported that Eugene "Big Daddy" Lipscomb, the Steelers' mountain of a defensive tackle, had died from an overdose of heroin at age thirty-one, and I was left baffled by how a 290-pound man as quick as a cougar could be felled by a needle, the same instrument we faced every fall when given flu shots, the kind my deceased uncle had administered.

Yet another week later, news came that Ernie Davis, the marvel of a running back from Syracuse, a Heisman Trophy winner, and the first overall pick in the 1962 draft, had died from leukemia. How is it, I wondered, that an athlete so fast and powerful could outrun everything except this curious disease? We caught colds and suffered through scarlet fever and strep throat and the mumps, but as lousy as we felt, these illnesses did not kill us. How awful could a disease be that it could kill a grown man who could dart through tacklers and leave them clawing at his jersey in vain?

One month later, my Uncle Rudy, the man I was named after, suffered a fatal heart attack in his home in Hibbing, Minnesota. I traveled with my mother and two brothers all night by train from Youngstown to St. Paul, Minnesota, and then by car another 150 miles north. On the morning of the funeral I rode in a car in a slow procession filled with men in military uniforms looking somber and pained, while a soldier beat an ominous rhythm on a drum throughout the entire route.

I cried for my uncles, but not for Big Daddy or Ernie Davis or the president. Yet they had the kind of impact on an eleven-year-old kid that would last a lifetime.

The morning after the Kennedy assassination brought a clear sky and unseasonably mild weather, allowing my friends and me to play tackle football in our yard. Life went on; I had learned that by gazing at my uncle's casket in a Minnesota cemetery. On any other Saturday afternoon in the fall my dad and I would watch college football, but on that day we watched Walter Cronkite and broadcasters with grim faces talking about a funeral and a murder suspect. My dad stared at the TV screen and said, "I wonder if they'll play the game."

I glanced at him but kept silent. I wondered to myself, "How could they not play the game? The Chicago Bears are coming to Pittsburgh, and we have tickets."

Years later, I would look back at my resolve to see that game, and I would not fault myself for being insensitive or immature. I was eleven, and a young boy lives his hopes and dreams through his favorite team, not through politicians or statesmen. And I was far from alone in my thinking. A total of 334,892 fans would show up for the seven games on the NFL schedule that Sunday, only four involving teams still in a race for a division title, as mine was. It wasn't until I grew older that I began to resent what I considered the self-righteous sermonizing by coaches who compared losing to death. Surely those coaches never realized that the ones most likely to agree with them were eleven-year-old football fans.

The Steelers were in fourth place in the Eastern Conference at 6–3–1 that weekend but mathematically, and improbably, still in the race with three other teams when my dad and I set off for what the *Chicago Tribune* called "dingy, antiquated Forbes Field." "What a depressing place that is for a football game," Giants coach Allie Sherman had commented before meeting the Steelers at the cozier, cleaner, more attractive Pitt Stadium in the second week of the season.[4]

Forbes Field had once been a showcase for sports—about half a century earlier. In '63 it was like an antebellum mansion in desperate need of repair. But it had the character, if not the charm, of a true ballpark. It had a tall scoreboard in left like Fenway, ivy on the brick walls like Wrigley, an outfield as big as Montana—deep enough to stash the batting cage against the center field wall—and a right-field grandstand that reminded me of Tiger Stadium. It was dirty, stinky, worn down, and beat up, and the seats were crummy for watching football, but I adored Forbes Field like no other ballpark I have ever seen.

The crowd was a sellout of 36,465 fans, but it was subdued for the 2:05 P.M. kickoff, with temperatures near 40 and a clear sky that would turn gloomy and cloudy. "It was the most eerie game," said Art Rooney Jr., son of the founder and owner of the Steelers. Gradually, the crowd came alive as the Steelers battled 9–1 Chicago to a standstill and then took a 17–14 lead 6:25 into the fourth quarter.[5]

The Steelers' shot at an upset looked even better after a penalty and a sack left the Bears with second-and-36 at their own 22-yard line with five-and-a-half minutes to go in the settling dusk. But then came a play that would forever remain vivid in my mind. Quarterback Bill Wade hit former Pitt All-America Mike Ditka, described by one reporter as "an earthquake of a man," and for a few seconds it seemed as if worlds had collided and the field trembled and the rickety wooden stands we sat in shook.[6]

"Mike grabbed it with those big paws of his and was immediately pounced on by a half dozen Steelers," wrote *Pittsburgh Post-Gazette* columnist Al Abrams. "He must have had eight guys on his back," said Lou Cordileone, the Steelers' right defensive tackle. "He should have been stopped five times," defensive end and kicker Lou Michaels said. Steelers defensive back Dick Haley said of the scene: "It looked like a bunch of kids trying to flag down a runaway truck."[7]

Ditka shook off and bowled over tacklers, and suddenly the only thing between Ditka and the end zone, and the end of the Steelers' hopes—and my dreams—was the damp, chilly air of a late November afternoon as the tight end lumbered into Pittsburgh territory with safety Clendon Thomas in desperate pursuit, trailed by teammate Willie Daniel.

"The big Bear drove forward and broke clear as the late afternoon light piercing the Forbes Field stands dramatically spotlighted this monumental image," photojournalist Robert Riger wrote.[8] In those suspended seconds, I squirmed next to my dad and felt as if I were in one of those dreams where your feet are stuck in slow motion and your scream is muted and distorted like a 45 rpm record played at a lower speed. Two days after the president was shot, stopping Ditka and clinging to the hope of a championship was all I cared about, and years later I forgave myself for thinking and behaving like an eleven-year-old that day.

What I remember most about watching the funeral the next day, with school canceled, was not the sight of world leaders and grieving citizens. No, it was the sight of the kid along the procession route saluting as the hearse and horses passed, with soldiers marching and a drum thumping, just like at my uncle's funeral, but this time echoing the sound of an entire nation's heart pounding in pain. What I thought at that instant was, "That kid lost his father. His dad is dead." Then it all became clear to me. Then I understood.

It took years, but slowly I came to realize the difference between losing a game and losing a loved one, between victory inside chalked lines on a scuffed up green field and what really matters in life.

ACKNOWLEDGMENTS

One of the most gratifying experiences in life is finding a person who grasps your vision, no matter what kind of dreams, aspirations, or goals you have. My hope in constructing this book was to pay tribute to a football team that gave a kid a season of thrills whose memories would reverberate into adulthood.

The saga of the 1963 Pittsburgh Steelers is not your typical storybook sports tale that concludes with cheers and championship banners, so without the encouragement of Richard "Pete" Peterson, the odds of this book being published would have been even longer than those of the '63 Steelers becoming NFL champs.

Pete Peterson is as gritty as a steelworker in an open-hearth furnace, but he has an appreciation of adversity and empathy for the underdog befitting a kid who grew up on the South Side of Pittsburgh rooting for the woeful Pirates and Steelers of the 1950s. When I presented my project to Peterson, then editor of the Writing Sports Series for the Kent State University Press, he envisioned my book as a prequel to Roy Blount Jr.'s masterful "About Three Bricks Shy of a Load: A Highly Irregular Lowdown on the Year the Pittsburgh Steelers Were Super but Missed the Bowl." Peterson's conceptualization was both inspiring and intimidating. Linking me to a writer of Blount's gifts, however tangentially, was a bit like inserting Johnny Unitas's name into the same sentence with a fledgling quarterback prospect.

I am grateful to the gracious staff at Kent State University Press for embracing the project and giving it a rigorous examination, and I thank them—notably Joyce Harrison, Mary Young, Susan Cash, Will Underwood, and Christine Brooks—for their continuous help and support. Without their adventurous spirit and bold thinking, there might not be a place for idiosyncratic books that take risks and explore neglected territory.

Among the team that makes the author look good, no one is more critical to the success of the finished product than the copy editor. Copy editors are a bit like offensive linemen in football. Linemen do the dirty work, often in anonymity, if not obscurity, but their contributions are indispensable. They are typically thoughtful and insightful, and they make the person who gets the recognition look good. I am most fortunate to have Sonia Fulop apply meticulous, painstaking attention and care to the structure, style, accuracy, and coherence of my manuscript, and fashion it into a polished book. To indulge in one more sports analogy, she is truly All-Pro as a copy editor.

I would like to offer special thanks to Frank Atkinson, Judi Ballman, Jim Bradshaw, Preston Carpenter, Lou Cordileone, Willie and Ruth Daniel, Ed Fay, Dick Haley, Sam Huff, Brady Keys, Red Mack, Tommy McDonald, Lou Michaels, Art Rooney Jr., Andy Russell, George Tarasovic, Clendon Thomas, Y. A. Tittle, and Joe Walton for sharing their time and memories of a time when pro football was, in truth, a different game.

Thanks also to Saleem Choudhry and Jon Kendle of the Pro Football Hall of Fame, Lynne Molyneaux of the Steelers, Gil Pietrzak of the Carnegie Library of Pittsburgh—Main, Jeff Kallin of Clemson University, David Seals of the Greater Pittsburgh Arts Council, the University of Pittsburgh Athletic Department, Brenda Wright of the Paley Library at Temple University, Chris Willis of NFL Films, Bryan Winfrey of Arizona State University, Roy McHugh, Lee Kim, Carl Kidwiler, George Gaadt, and Andrew O'Toole. Plus, a big cheer to personnel at libraries from Dallas to Philadelphia who provided microfilm from 1963 or copies of game stories.

Finally, I want to salute all the newspapermen who chronicled a unique season in history—in particular, Pat Livingston, Al Abrams, Jack Sell, and Jimmy Miller, all of whom covered the Steelers. Any reader cannot help but be impressed by the high quality of journalism of the era: the storytelling of Myron Cope, McHugh, and Arthur Daley; the passionate essays of Sandy Grady and Red Smith; and the reportage of Milton Gross, William N. Wallace, and Alvin Rosensweet, just to name a few of the newspapermen from the time who distinguished themselves.

AUTHOR'S NOTE

I relied on the official play-by-play accounts from individual games, along with descriptions in game stories from as many different newspapers and wire services available, in reconstructing the Steeler games from the 1963 season. I found a couple occasions where there appeared to be a discrepancy of a single yard in citing yardage gained or lost, or the yard line where a ball was spotted, but these situations were isolated.

GAME 1

VERSUS PHILADELPHIA EAGLES
AT FRANKLIN FIELD
SEPTEMBER 15

In his book *The Physics of Football,* Timothy Gay provides some scientific explanations for how and why a football moves the way it does when kicked or thrown. Gay played football at the California Institute of Technology and earned his PhD in atomic physics from the University of Chicago. He uses scientific terms like "launch speed," "air drag," and "angular momentum" to illustrate the flight of an oblong-shaped ball.[1]

When it comes to explaining how a football travels when the toe of a placekicker connects with the ball, Lou Michaels has a more basic explanation. His education came from four years at the University of Kentucky, where he was a two-time All-America lineman and a fourth-place finisher in the Heisman Trophy voting, and from a thirteen-year career in the NFL, where he was a left-footed kicker and defensive end with the Los Angeles Rams, Pittsburgh Steelers, Baltimore Colts, and Green Bay Packers.

In 1962, his second season with the Steelers, Michaels set an NFL record by making twenty-six field goals, helping Pittsburgh to a second-place finish in the Eastern Conference, twice kicking four field goals in a game, and twice kicking field goals in the final thirty seconds to put the Steelers in front. "Mr. Michaels has been nothing short of being the Steelers' Mr. Wonderful this year," *Pittsburgh Post-Gazette* sports editor and columnist Al Abrams gushed. But the path of any kick, Michaels knew, can be as unpredictable as any of the bounces a football takes. His explanation may not be very scientific, but it's as true to this day as it was when Jim Thorpe was drop-kicking footballs from the 50-yard line and players were wearing leather helmets. "You kick a field goal," Michaels said, and "it can hit the crossbar, it can go through the bar, or it can go away from the bar."[2]

In 1963, Michaels would get one less attempt at a field goal, and he would make five fewer kicks. He would miss all five attempts in a single game—and yet the Steelers would win that afternoon. He made no excuses, but he was "fighting a placekicking jinx all season," one Steelers beat writer wrote.[3] Michaels was also the starting left defensive end, playing every down when healthy, but no one—least of all his opponents—ever took pity because he never had the luxury of kicking with fresh legs, and he never sought any sympathy.

The path of a football team over a season can come to resemble the unpredictable arc of a football. The '63 Steelers would run parallel to Michaels's season as a kicker. They would be right in sync in some games, and they would veer off course in others. They would misfire and wait for another chance to redeem themselves, like a kicker who blows an easy attempt. They would keep the crowd in suspense in the final minutes, the fans holding their breath on each play from scrimmage the way they might as a 50-yard field goal attempt floated toward the goalposts. The '63 Steelers would serve as a prime example of how narrow a difference there can be between victory and defeat—like a football clanging off the crossbar, just inches from the mark—and how cruel the bounces can be, as if fate were conspiring to mock all the calculations, theories, equations, and other scientific arguments about launch speed. Thirty years and not one appearance in a championship game by the Steelers wasn't a jinx; it was a curse.

As the start of the '63 regular season drew near, the players were voicing the kind of confidence their coach had expressed the year before. "This is it, buddy. This is the year we're going to win the championship for Art Rooney," middle linebacker Myron Pottios declared the Tuesday before the opener at a welcome-home clambake for the team at Allegheny Elks No. 339.[4]

"We all have that feeling we're going to win," Michaels said. "If we don't get jammed up with injuries again, we should cop the Eastern Division title."[5] Michaels played at Kentucky in the fifties under Blanton Collier, who succeeded Paul Brown as head coach of the Cleveland Browns after the '62 season and would guide them to the 1964 championship. Collier called Michaels "the toughest, most durable player I've ever coached."[6]

That toughness was cultivated in Michaels's hometown of Swoyersville, Pennsylvania, a speck of a town between Scranton and Wilkes-Barre, an area once rich in anthracite coal. Michaels grew up the youngest in a family of seven boys and one girl. "We struggled at first," he said. "If it wasn't for football, I have no idea what I'd have done."[7]

Work in the mines, no doubt, like his father, Walter Majka, who came to America from Poland when he was nineteen and, according to legend, was so strong he could lift a loading car in the mines and carry it from one track to another. Lou's two oldest brothers also worked in the mines. Another son, Eddie, joined the Marines and was killed at Guadalcanal.[8]

A job in the mines was the inevitable destiny awaiting many of the young men in the region, and so a lifetime of working underground beckoned another resident of the coal country, Vladimir Palahniuk, the third of five children of Ukrainian immigrants raised in the Lattimer Mines section of Hazel Township. But the middle child had attributes other than a strong back, and he would use them to his advantage to escape the mines. "The deadliness of his deep-set stare, the shine of his high cheekbones and the honest witness of his dipsy-doodled nose, his tousled, lusterless black hair and belligerent muscular stance give him the edge on virtually all movie villains."[9] Vladimir tried working in the mines, dropped out of college, changed his name, and by 1954 was making $150,000 a year as Jack Palance.

Michaels's father died at age fifty-four, after working thirty-five years in the mines. Lou, bearing the Anglicized form of his father's surname, was eleven at the time. The son's best talents lay in tackling and blocking, but he performed well in the classroom as well, and after two years at the local high school, he enrolled in Staunton Military Academy in Virginia, where he became the school's first four-sport letterman. But there was no doubt where he was determined to go. "If I thought I could have made pro ball without going to college, I'd have signed with the pros right away," he said.[10] In 1954 he began his college career at Kentucky, where opponents "found it virtually useless to run plays at him." The brother whom Lou revered, Walt Jr., then a linebacker with the Cleveland Browns, encouraged his younger sibling to expand his skills, so Lou developed into a punter with a 40-yard-plus average, a deep kickoff man, and "virtually an automatic machine on conversions."[11] Michaels became a two-time first-team All-America. "There's no question that Michaels must be regarded as one of the greatest football players to ever play in the Southeastern Conference," wrote Baltimore columnist John Steadman.[12]

The Los Angeles Rams took Michaels in the first round, the fourth overall player selected, in the 1958 draft. In the second round they took Clendon Thomas, an All-America running back from Oklahoma. Rams management grew disenchanted with Michaels because of his "playboy proclivities," and once they drafted punter/kicker Danny Villanueva after the 1959 season, Michaels's value to them declined. They traded him to Pittsburgh for offensive tackle Frank Varrichione, a former first-round pick, before the '61 season. "I was fascinated by the Hollywood atmosphere and I wanted to see and do everything so I could tell the people back home all about it," Michaels said. "I was a pro football star and a marked man for bad publicity. It got so nothing I did was right."[13]

Michaels resumed his dual role of playing defensive end and kicking in Pittsburgh, making fifteen of twenty-six field goals his first year before his record season in '62. And he fit right in with the long-standing tradition of Steelers players who savored their beer and whiskey and who would no sooner shy away from a fistfight than a Wild West sheriff would back off from a gun duel. He had a couple of scrapes in Los Angeles and Pittsburgh, and in October 1964, after being traded to the Baltimore Colts, he drove his car into a telephone pole late one night. It wasn't quite as colorful an accident as Bobby Layne's legendary escapade driving into a parked street car, but it made big enough headlines.

The Steelers finished the 1963 preseason with a 3–2 record, including a 22–7 victory over Detroit in the penultimate game, the difference coming on five field goals by Michaels, and they concluded the exhibition season with a satisfying 16–7 win over archrival Cleveland, a team the *Post-Gazette* dismissed as "the once-powerful Browns." The game was played in Canton, Ohio, the day after the Pro Football Hall of Fame inducted seventeen charter members into the new shrine. Michaels was good on three field goals, which made him nine of seventeen in preseason, with three of the misses coming from 50 yards. Two days later, in a staged photo typical of the newspaper era, the *Post-Gazette* ran a shot of Michaels kicking, with one member of the Steelerettes, the short-lived cheerleading crew, kneeling to hold the ball and three other Steelerettes behind the kicker. It wasn't Hollywood, but for Pittsburgh, it was good fun.[14]

There was growing reason for optimism both for Steelers fans and for Pittsburgh citizens. At the time, Pittsburgh could boast about being "the operating headquarters of the world's biggest steel maker," and residents could take heart in a surge in economic activity in the tristate area during the year.[15] People were working, and jobs seemed secure.

But beneath the glow of prosperity lay a quiver of unrest. On September 9, 1963, the day before the photo of Michaels ran, the *Post-Gazette* started an eight-part series titled "The Negro in Pittsburgh." The front-page headline read: "Racial Ferment Here Mounting Beneath Surface." Reporter Alvin Rosensweet wrote of "a growing dissatisfaction: with government, with a lack of jobs and housing, and a failure to be accepted as part of the community." The Hill District had been a melting pot of immigrants and blacks, the home of Negro League baseball and the Crawford Grill, where Sarah Vaughan, Mary Lou Williams, Erroll Garner, and Dizzy Gillespie played and where Steelers defensive back Johnny Sample would meet his future wife while having lunch with Big Daddy Lipscomb.[16] The Hurricane Lounge was another popular spot that Bobby Layne was said to visit to enjoy jazz and drink. But in the fall of '63, the Hill District was "a place the city forgot," Rosensweet observed.

Politics, business, and entertainment rarely mixed with the world of sports in that era, so the newspaper series did not address the role of athletes in the black community. Art Rooney, owner of the Steelers franchise, in the quiet but unwavering fashion in which he conducted business, had been assimilating black players literally since the beginning of the franchise, and he championed their rights and worked to ensure their welfare. Ray Kemp, a black player who had grown up in the town of Cecil, Pennsylvania, worked in the mines, and starred at Duquesne University, accepted an invitation from Rooney to become a member of the Rooney franchise's first team, then called the Pirates, in 1933. There was only one other black player in the NFL at the time.[17]

In 1956, a former All-America at Michigan joined the Steelers after fulfilling a service commitment and began electrifying fans as a receiver and return man but fractured his pelvis and dislocated a hip in the sixth game, which would end his career. Rooney visited Lowell Perry during his thirteen-week hospital stay and told the rookie, "Lowell, as long as I own the Pittsburgh Steelers, you have a job in my organization." Perry became the receivers coach the next year, then left to complete studies for his law degree. He became the first black to work as an NFL broadcaster, served as a lawyer with the National Labor Relations Board, and became a leading executive with Chrysler.[18]

Perry had also witnessed Rooney's resolve to stand up against inequality. When the Steelers traveled to Jacksonville, Florida, for an exhibition with the Bears in 1956, black players were excluded from a parade for the team and forced to stay at a segregated hotel. When Rooney arrived on a later flight, he addressed the black players and vowed, "I promise you, this will never happen to one of my teams again."[19] When Rooney discovered that the team's black players were likely to be segregated the next year for an exhibition game in Atlanta, he canceled the game.

Kemp would go on to a four-decade career as coach and athletic director. When he visited Pittsburgh in late August 1963, he scolded the *Pittsburgh Courier* for failing to give proper recognition to Rooney "as a pioneer in the fight to integrate professional sports," praise the newspaper routinely bestowed on baseball executive Branch Rickey and Cleveland Browns coach Paul Brown.[20] Buddy Parker, on the other hand, was no candidate to become a leader in the civil rights movement. However, he believed in team unity because it could foster winning. He encouraged the players to get together after games, and his fellow Texan Bobby Layne had laid a foundation for camaraderie. He was a drinking partner of Lipscomb (for whom Layne would buy an entire bottle of V.O. for a single evening) and a friend of John Henry Johnson, and he made a point to include rookies in his entourage. Layne and Big Daddy were gone by '63, but players continued their regular evening get-togethers at a drinking spot in Brentwood called Dante's.

In 1963 Parker was entering his seventh year as coach of the Steelers, with a cumulative 39–34–3 record, and the best he could show for his re-building efforts was a second-place finish. It was time to see results from his brash shuffling and dealing.

Parker's threats to quit had become an annual rite, dating back to his time in Detroit. It took only one regular-season game in 1961, a last-second loss in Dallas in the opener, for Parker to threaten to quit at season's end if the Steelers didn't win the Eastern Conference. They finished fifth, with a 6–8 record, but Parker came back for the 1962 season. He was "disgusted" after a 35–14 loss in Cleveland in the eleventh week of the '62 season, and a victory over the Cards the next Sunday did little, if anything, to encourage him.[21] "I don't think I'll be back in 1963," he said the day after the 19–7 victory, decided by four field goals by Michaels, who missed three others and had one blocked.[22] Parker's contract expired at the end of the season, and speculation that he would quit intensified as the Steelers prepared for the Playoff Bowl.

The 17–10 postseason loss to the Lions appeared to be the closing argument against Parker's return, but the day after the game, he told Al Abrams, "I'm not going to quit. This team, as it is now, is my best since I came to Pittsburgh. We should have beaten Detroit. I think we can win it all next season."[23]

Three days later, Parker met with Art Rooney and they agreed on an indefinite year-to-year extension. It is unknown whether a game-to-game extension was ever discussed, but Parker seemed revived and confident that his team could win it all. "I think we're at the point now where we can play with anybody in the league," he said.[24]

The players shared that confidence as they prepared for the '63 season opener, and they weren't shy about expressing their optimism. "I know we've disappointed the fans over the years, but this one will be different," vowed defensive end and linebacker George Tarasovic, who had been drafted by the Steelers eleven years earlier and had been there for all of Parker's tenure. "I've never seen better spirit on this club. These fellows are fighting mad and they've got the stuff to go all the way. Few experts are giving us a chance. That's all right. We'll fool them."[25]

Fans were as desperate as the players for a winner in '63. Bill Mazeroski's winning home run in game 7 of the 1960 World Series not only created an unforgettable moment in baseball lore but also resurrected the self-esteem of a city burdened by sports failures. Yet the euphoria wore off over the next three summers of mediocrity. The Pirates fell seventeen games behind the first-place Dodgers on September 8, 1963, the day they lost to the Cardinals while honoring the retiring Stan Musial during his final appearance at Forbes Field. The only thing sustaining the interest of Pirates fans was Roberto Clemente's chase for the batting title. By the following week, Clemente would be leading St. Louis shortstop and ex-Pirate Dick Groat by a hair, .3231 to .3227.

One could only fantasize about how the city would erupt if the Steelers reached the NFL title game. When the Pirates clinched the pennant in 1960, the *Post-Gazette*'s Abrams likened the city's anticipation for the city's first World Series in thirty-three years to the delirious joy of a six-year-old lying in bed on Christmas Eve. "It will be hysteria on pinwheels," Abrams wrote in a column. "New Year's Eve, the Fourth of July and Mardi Gras all rolled into one mass celebration won't come close to approximating the excitement generated by the presence of our Pirates against the Yankees in the World Series."[26] Even if a Steelers berth in the NFL Championship Game generated a fraction of that hubbub, the city would be aglow like the brightest open-hearth furnace for years. Football was special in western Pennsylvania.

The University of Pittsburgh held both a glorious niche in college football history and a special place in the hearts of its fans. In fact, "No place embodied the football-as-life perspective of the Keystone State more than the University of Pittsburgh."[27]

Glenn Scobey "Pop" Warner led Pitt to three consecutive undefeated seasons and its first national championship when he took over in 1915, and one of his players, John Bain "Jock" Sutherland, went on to guide the Panthers to a 111–20–12 record over fifteen years and an undisputed national championship.

Pitt had mixed success during the fifties, regaining its stature when John Michelosen arrived and guided the Panthers to a 7–4 season in 1955 and a berth in the Sugar Bowl and followed with a 7–3–1 season and a trip to the Gator Bowl. Pitt continued to produce consensus All-Americas and future pros over the decade: Eldred Kraemer, Joe Schmidt, Joe Walton, John Guzik, and a player who came to symbolize western Pennsylvania grit as well as a no-surrender style of football—Mike Ditka.

Even if Pitt hadn't won a national championship since 1937, its tradition was lofty compared to the Steelers'. But who dared dream that after a 5–5 record in 1962, the '63 Panthers would be battling for the No. 1 spot in college football and competing with the Steelers for the attention of football fans in western Pennsylvania?

Steelers fans were cranky, impatient, and itching to fight, which they did regularly and with unchecked gusto. On any autumn Sunday at Forbes Field, the best place to catch a slugfest wasn't at a Pirates game; it was somewhere in the stands during the fourth quarter of a losing Steelers effort. Pittsburgh fans were unmerciful, and they spared no one in venting their anger and frustration, least of all themselves. Still, fans felt a personal connection to the team, one that felt almost intimate, largely because of the universal respect and fondness for the owner of the team, Art Rooney, who was viewed as a regular guy, a pal from the neighborhood, a gentleman of distinction and yet a man without pretense. The newspapers referred to the Steelers as "Rooney U." and "the Rooney men." The *Pittsburgh Courier* called the team "Rooniversity." Parker had groused that Pittsburgh people did not want an outsider, a Texan at that, as coach, but the papers also called his team "the Parker men." A bit of thinly veiled hometown rooting may have been behind the nicknames, but there was no denying the affection felt by the fans or media commentators in using them.

In late August of '63, however, Rooney sensed no love for his Steelers. On a day that found him alone in his office, with no sign of ticket buyers, he detected a complete lack of interest in a team that showed a lot of promise, even though it was coming off a 17–14 loss to Johnny Unitas and the Colts in the third preseason game. "There doesn't seem to be any football enthusiasm in Pittsburgh," Rooney told *Press* sportswriter Pat Livingston.

"Something seems to have gone out of the town."[28] Meanwhile, business in Philadelphia, the site of the Steelers' regular season opener, was brisk. Within two weeks the Eagles would sell 45,000 season tickets, nearly four times the Steelers' total.

But the Eagles were trying to recover from a 3–10–1 finish in 1962; the Steelers had won six of their last seven games to finish 9–5. Rooney sensed that maybe Parker finally had the right talent to make a run at the Eastern Conference title. "Personally, I feel a lot more confident this year than I have felt for years," Rooney said. Others shared his enthusiasm, but none of them seemed to be the locals. "Everywhere I go people tell me the Steelers and Giants look like the class of the East," he said. "Here in Pittsburgh, nobody seems to know we're in town."[29]

It wasn't an isolated case of disinterest in the Steelers. At the end of November 1959, the Steelers were coming off consecutive road victories over New York and Cleveland when they hosted the Eagles at Forbes Field. Bobby Layne threw four TD passes and kicked a field goal in a 31–0 romp before 22,191 fans. "As a sports town, Pittsburgh ought to hang its head in shame," Livingston wrote in his lead to the game story. "The crowd was a joke, the biggest laugh in the NFL this year!" The two road games had drawn a combined 135,000 fans, and attendance in the league had been averaging "a whopping 46,000." The Steelers and Eagles played in the snow, but 56,854 turned out in Cleveland to watch the Browns lose to San Francisco in "a driving snowstorm," and the Chicago Cardinals, in suffering their eighth loss, drew 48,867 in a 31–7 rout by the Bears.[30]

Ernie Stautner, who had suffered through more than his share of losing since being drafted in 1950—a decade in which the Steelers had a won-lost percentage of .463—lashed out at the fans after a late November 1961 victory over the Cardinals, a game during which Layne had been booed. "This is a lousy sports town," Stautner ranted, "and if Art Rooney had any sense he'd get out of it." Months before the '61 football season began, Stautner had attended a Pirates game and had been shocked to witness the fans boo Elroy Face, two years after the pitcher went 18–1 and a year after he went 10–8 in the championship season. "What's wrong with these people?" Stautner asked. "Do they have an inferiority complex or something?"[31]

Something like that. "The prototypical Steeler fan was the mineworker, the millworker, who drank hard and fought hard and was violently resigned to losing out in life," Roy Blount Jr. wrote after a season of watching the Steelers day after day in 1973. Some citizens even doted on their city, "with a certain strange pride, as a loser's town." But people were used to defending their turf and protecting their own, and so the fans naturally developed a tradition that identified with a team that approached football games as a barroom brawl. "Football is controlled violence," Art Rooney Jr. said, "and the people around here were close to violence."[32]

Pittsburghers tended to be defensive, if not downright touchy, about their cultural identity and local customs. When a reader alerted a *Post-Gazette* columnist about a sign at the airport in Los Angeles advising barefooted people not to use the escalators, Charles P. Danver sniggered in his column, "Ha! And that's the town that sent us the critic who made nasty cracks about our kolbassi!" The offending party was *Los Angeles Times* columnist Jim Murray, who had clearly overstepped the boundaries of propriety. "He can knock the town all he wants," one reader wrote in, "but when he puts the blast on kolbussi the man has to be nuts!"[33] And woe to anyone who dared to poke fun at pierogi.

Offensive tackle Charlie Bradshaw, in his second year in Pittsburgh in 1962 after three seasons in Los Angeles, listened to the boos at Pitt Stadium as Layne was carried off the field in a 1962 game against the Redskins and thought to himself, "This has to be the toughest group of fans in the country."[34] Steelers fans were grumpy, ornery, and disconsolate, and they had to wonder whether they could allow themselves to dream of a championship team in their lifetime.

The Steelers had built a reputation for themselves, and their fans had done likewise. Offensive tackle Frank Varrichione, the Steelers' first-round draft choice in 1955, left Pittsburgh with some regret when he was traded to the Rams for Michaels in the spring of '61. But Varrichione's wife, Mitzi, was delighted with the move to Los Angeles, and it had nothing to do with kielbasa. "I love it here compared to Pittsburgh for many reasons," she told *Los Angeles Times* columnist Sid Ziff. "The people are nicer. No snowballs or beer cans are thrown at the players. The fans are more considerate. They may boo you one minute but the next they're cheering you like mad. In Pittsburgh, you never take your helmet off until you get through the tunnel."[35]

Layne had become a target of the fans' venom, and Parker was convinced he had to make a critical change if his team was going to have a shot at the Eastern Conference crown in '63.[36]

Parker had an unflagging loyalty to Layne, but the fans had been relentless in pressuring the coach to turn to Ed Brown. "All I heard last year was a lot of screaming to put him in there instead of Layne," Rooney said.[37]

Parker would have to sacrifice Layne's intangibles for Brown's healthier body. The former Bears QB had a stronger arm and nearly as much NFL experience, but he was no Bobby Layne, and no one knew that better than Parker. "I think Buddy just recognized there was something lacking without Bobby," Stautner said years later. "Buddy knew we had the players to make a run at the division, but we needed the take-charge guy in the driver's seat. . . . Bobby had the extra something that made the difference in close games."[38] Maybe it was, indeed, Parker's best team since his arrival in Pittsburgh, but who was going to lead it? "There is no doubt that Coach Buddy Parker's eleven is in dire need of an electrifying and inspiring personality," the *Courier* declared in late August.[39]

Instead of relying on Layne's leadership, Parker could take some reassurance in the fact that he could count on Michaels's toe to make a difference in close games. Four of the Steelers' games in '62 had been decided by three or fewer points—two others by four and six points—and Michaels had proved he was a threat from 50 yards out. But there is another thing—two, actually—that can result from a placekick that Michaels didn't mention when addressing the flight of a ball toward the goalposts, and both happened to him in the opener of the '63 season, against the Philadelphia Eagles at Franklin Field.

The Eagles had plummeted from NFL champions in 1960 to last place in 1962, but they were still an explosive team, with two future Hall of Famers—Sonny Jurgensen at quarterback and Tommy McDonald at wide receiver—and Pete Retzlaff at tight end. On defense, the Eagles had Maxie Baughan at linebacker, and Irv Cross and a roughneck named Don Burroughs in the secondary, but one of their big weaknesses in '62 was the placekicking. Bobby Walston made only four of fifteen field goal attempts.

When Parker met with the officials at midfield before the 1:35 P.M. kickoff for the '63 opener, referee Bill Downes stared at the right upright on one set of goalposts. "Holy cow, look at that goalpost," he said. Later, Parker said it was "as crooked as a gooseneck."[40]

Head linesman Dan Tehan joked that Parker ought to let it go because it would work to the advantage of a left-footed kicker like Michaels.

"The hell it does," Parker shot back. "A left-footed kicker hooks the ball. A hook will veer off that way."

"Well," Townes replied, "what do you want to do? If you want the grounds crew to fix it, the game will be delayed for at least 20 minutes."

"Nah. Let it go," Parker said. "How often does the ball hit the upright anyway?"[41]

Even though his team was a three-point favorite over a squad that had won only three games the year before, Parker was wary of starting the season in sold-out Franklin Field. "Don't let anyone kid you," he said at a welcome home dinner earlier in the week. "An enthusiastic crowd means a lot to a football team. An enthusiastic crowd can make a team play over its head."[42]

Pittsburgh took the opening kickoff and drove to the Eagle 45 before three Brown incompletions forced a punt that was downed at the 13. Despite plummeting to last place in '62, the Eagles had the top-ranked passing offense (and the next-to-worst rushing offense), thanks to a gunslinger of a quarterback who finished first in passing yardage and a flanker who was third in receiving yardage, tied for fifth in catches, and led the league in rodomontade, flaunting his skills to teammates and defenders alike.

The receiver, McDonald, was a five-foot-seven, 172-pound fireball who had played on the Bud Wilkinson Oklahoma teams that ran a winning streak to fifty-seven games, earned All-America honors in 1955 and '56, and won the Maxwell Award in '56. He was fast and fearless and had the kind of ability to catch a football that landed him a cover story in *Sports Illustrated* in October 1962: "Football's Best Hands." The headline on the story inside read: "The Magnificent Squirt."

McDonald played with the unabashed glee of a ten-year-old and the daredevil bravado of a cliff diver, leaping and lunging for passes and bouncing off defenders and up from the turf with a big grin and a glare of defiance. He also earned a reputation as an eccentric, leading *Sport* magazine to ask in a feature story, "Is Tommy McDonald Pro Football's Piersall?" But McDonald felt his idiosyncrasies were all exaggerated. "It really gets my dandruff up [*sic*]," he explained, "when some writer says, 'Is Tommy McDonald a kook?' or 'Is Tommy McDonald flakey?'"[43]

Jurgensen, at quarterback, looked at the start of the NFL season like a hunter awaiting deer season: he just couldn't wait to pull the trigger. On first down, he hit McDonald with a 43-yard pass, down to the Steeler 44. After two incompletions Jurgensen hit Retzlaff with a 27-yard pass to the 17. Jurgy, as he was called, picked up a first down on a quarterback sneak on fourth-and-1 at the 8, and after Brady Keys dropped Tim Brown for a 6-yard loss, McDonald beat Glenn Glass by three steps in the right corner of the end zone and hauled in a 13-yard touchdown pass.

Jurgensen also led the league in interceptions the previous year, and after the Steelers punted, he threw his first of 1963 when Haley picked him off and returned the ball to the Steeler 42. Neither team could mount a drive before the quarter ended, but Ed Brown, who loved to throw deep almost as much as Jurgensen, got the Steelers moving with short passes—to tight end Preston Carpenter for 9 yards, to wide receiver Buddy Dial for 10, to fullback Tom "the Bomb" Tracy for 21, to the Eagle 32. The drive stalled there, so Michaels came on to kick a 38-yard field goal to make it 7–3 with 3:51 elapsed in the second quarter.

Keys fumbled a punt and Lee Roy Caffey recovered for the Eagles on the Steeler 44, but Tim Brown fumbled the handoff on the next play and Tarasovic, the six-foot-four, 245-pound linebacker, grabbed it on the 48. Stalled at the Eagle 44, two yards shy of a first down, Michaels came in again. A year before, on the same field, not far from his hometown, Michaels had kicked four field goals to help Pittsburgh to a 26–17 victory. "Hitting 'em sweet and true under pressure is what counts," he said after that game.[44] With 6:04 left before halftime, Michaels kicked "an astounding 50-yarder" to make it 7–6.[45]

Jurgensen hit McDonald slanting over the middle for a 22-yard gain to the Steeler 42, but on third-and-11 he lost 7 yards attempting to pass, leaving King Hill to punt down to the 8. In the final minute of the half, on third-and-10 from his 30, Brown fired a 27-yard pass to Dial that put the ball on the Eagle 43, giving Michaels a shot at another 50-yarder. This time the kick fell short. Whether it was the impact of the hometown crowd that Parker had feared or an Eagles team undergoing a rejuvenation, the favored Steelers had all they could handle in trailing 7–6 at the half.

John Henry Johnson fumbled on the Steelers' first drive of the second half, and Baughan recovered on Pittsburgh's 41. After a holding penalty, Jurgensen hit Tim Brown with a 42-yard pass to make it first-and-goal at the 6, and on second down he found end Ralph "Catfish" Smith over the middle for a 6-yard TD pass to make it 14–6 with 7:09 left in the third quarter.

Ed Brown stuck to his short game on the next drive, hitting Dial for 9 yards, Carpenter for 9, and Dial again for 10. On third-and-5 at the Eagle 23, Brown was dropped for a 7-yard loss, leaving Michaels a chance at a 37-yard field goal. The year before, he had made 62 percent of his kicks, the third-best figure in the league, but this time he missed.

On the next play, Eagles fullback Theron Sapp fumbled, and defensive end Big John Baker recovered at the 17. The Eagles held, leaving Pittsburgh with fourth-and-3 at the 10, and Michaels came on to kick a 17-yard field goal on the first play of the fourth quarter to make it 14–9.

On third-and-9 from his 25, Jurgensen dropped back to pass, and tackle Lou Cordileone dumped him for a loss of 9 yards. Hill got off a 62-yard punt on which Keys tried to make an over-the-shoulder catch but couldn't hang on. He retrieved the ball and darted up the right sideline, past end Dick Lucas, but rookie linebacker Ralph Heck and Caffey had a good angle and appeared to have the Steelers' return man hemmed in. Keys squirted past them as Steelers linebacker Bob Schmitz hustled in and bumped the two Eagles off track. Keys raced down the sideline and was in the clear as he crossed the Eagles' 10-yard line, where he slipped and fell, untouched, like a skater losing balance and toppling forward. "Crawling, wriggling and squirming," Keys reached the 2 before he was downed.[46] Johnson gained a yard and then leaped over from the 1 to put the Steelers ahead for the first time, 15–14, and Michaels lined up for the point after.

There is one other result that can occur during a placekick apart from the three that Michaels listed, a consequence that not even a perfectly executed kick can circumvent. A year later, Michaels would tell the story about how he was kicking for his high school freshman football team and made good on six of seven extra points in one game. Proud of his accomplishment, he recounted his performance to his brothers when he got home. But they wanted to know what had happened on the missed kick. It had been blocked. The older boys jumped all over their kid brother.

"Know what they told me? They said it was my fault it was blocked because I should have gotten back an extra yard and kicked faster," Michaels said.[47]

It's not the kind of advice Timothy Gay suggests. A kicker sticks to footwork as precise and regimented as that of the Rockettes. Cross, a third-year defensive back out of Northwestern, broke through and blocked the extra point attempt with his arm. The Steelers still had a one-point lead, but the Eagles had proved to be dangerous, and McDonald lurked as a lethal threat.

As a kid growing up in New Mexico, McDonald had a manic energy. In school, he would walk across the desks on his hands, and he was constantly working on catching any object—nails, pennies, rubber balls. "Instead of passing things at the table, we'd pitch them," McDonald recalled. "Mom made us draw the line at mashed potatoes."[48] In any event, his practice paid off. "He'll catch a ball he has no business catching," said Redskins coach Bill McPeak.[49]

After the kickoff, Jurgensen took the Eagles down to the Steeler 35, with 27 yards coming on a pass to Retzlaff, but Clendon Thomas intercepted the next throw and returned the ball to the Eagle 46. Michaels might have been able to try yet another long field goal, but Brown had to punt after he was dropped for a 4-yard loss on third-and-8 at the 44.

Lined up in the shotgun on third-and-5 at his 25, Jurgensen faced heavy pressure from the Steelers' left side. With his neck arched back and Michaels's right arm bearing down on his face, Jurgensen fired away, 50 yards in the air. McDonald, with two steps on Glass, made an over-the-shoulder catch, avoided Glass's diving attempt at a tackle inside the 10, and darted into the end zone for a 75-yard touchdown. Rookie Mike Clark's conversion put the Eagles ahead, 21–15, with 4:05 left in the game.

Clark's ensuing kickoff sailed deep into the end zone for a touchback, which would have left the Steelers 80 yards away from the touchdown they needed to tie the game, and the extra point that would win it. But there was a flag on the play: offside, Philadelphia.

Forced to kick again, from the 35, Clark drove the ball to the 9-yard line, where Thomas returned it 41 yards to midfield. Now the Steelers had only 50 yards to go for the winning TD, and plenty of time to do it. On third-and-7, Brown hit second-year end John Burrell on a down-and-out for a 14-yard gain to the 33, and then the Steeler quarterback hooked up with Dial for a 28-yard pickup and a first-and-goal at the 5. But Brown was sacked for a 6-yard loss, and his pass to Dial was broken up by defensive back Ben Scotti, leaving Pittsburgh with third-and-goal at the 11. Brown hit Johnson, sneaking over the middle, for a touchdown, and all that was left to put the Steelers ahead with two-and-a-half minutes to play was the point after.

In *The Physics of Football*, Gay raises the question of what a kicker can do to improve his accuracy. "First, physics (and common sense) says: Hit the ball square," he writes. "Assume that you're kicking the ball straight ahead and that the force of your foot on the ball is perpendicular to the surface of the ball where contact is initially made. This means that the impulse delivered to the ball must be within three-eighths of an inch of the ball's centerline, or equator."[50]

But there is no mention in Gay's book about crooked uprights, no discussion about how perverse fate can be to a team struggling for success. In 1963 the two goalposts were still planted on the goal line; they would not be moved to the back of the end zone until the 1974 season. Making a point after was basically a 9-yard field goal attempt. The virtual "automatic machine on conversions" lined up for the kick and swung his left leg . . . and a *thump!* sounded as the ball struck the warped wooden upright and bounced back onto the field. The game was tied, 21–21, with 2:40 left, thanks to two failed Steelers conversions.

Jurgensen had time, but he couldn't work any magic with McDonald. His third-and-2 pass from his own 43 was incomplete. Hill punted, and Keys, perhaps thinking of duplicating his near touchdown, fielded the ball on his 2 and was stopped at the 5. Brown played it conservatively, calling for runs on four of the next five plays, but two passes to Carpenter moved the ball to the Steeler 45. The final gun sounded after Brown hit Dial with a 25-yard pass down to the Eagle 30-yard line, with Pittsburgh unable to get the field goal unit lined up for an attempt at a game-winning kick. Asked whether he would have hit the game-winner, Michaels replied, "Of course not. It would have only hit the goal post again. It wasn't my day. I always knew there would be a day like this, a nightmare, but I didn't know it would happen in front of my hometown friends."[51]

Michaels made no excuses and didn't gripe about bad breaks. Asked whether Cross's block on the first missed conversion forced him to overcompensate on the next point after, Michaels said, "No, sir. I just missed it."[52]

The volatile Parker, so quick to ignite over mistakes, consoled Michaels. "The game's over, Lou," the coach said. "Forget about it. Look, we got a bad game out of our system, and we got away with it without losing. We should feel grateful."[53]

After just one game, it was premature to talk of omens or jinxes or destiny, or to suggest that once again, this wouldn't be the Steelers' year, that they had missed their best shot the previous season and were doomed to suffer through more bad luck, another string of losing seasons. After all, how often do goalposts have a crooked upright? And there was no time for the Steelers to feel sorry about their luck, because bearing down on them the following Sunday were the defending Eastern Conference champion New York Giants, who already looked capable of repeating. Not far south of Philly, Y. A. Tittle threw for three touchdowns and ran for another to rally the Giants from a 21–3 deficit to a 37–28 victory over the Colts in Baltimore.

But there was something much bigger, much more important, for the Steelers to feel grateful for than salvaging a tie with the Eagles, although the scene went virtually unnoticed before a packed stadium. On a field that sanctimonious coaches used as a pulpit to elevate a game to an issue of life and death, a real mortality scenario arose.

Four years earlier, in another game between the Steelers and Eagles at Franklin Field, a critical incident occurred that affected the future of the NFL. Bert Bell, for fourteen years the commissioner of the NFL and a close friend of Art Rooney, collapsed from a heart attack while attending the game and died. Alvin "Pete" Rozelle succeeded Bell, and the following season, the NFL would hold the Bert Bell Benefit Bowl, known informally as the Playoff Bowl. The Steelers would play in the third year.

But on this cloudy and cool mid-September day, "Death was cheated . . . on Franklin Field before 58,205 onlookers, unaware of the drama developing before them," Herb Good wrote in the *Philadelphia Inquirer*. "Only quick, skilled work by team doctors and trainers saved John Reger, Pittsburgh Steelers' linebacker, from choking to death."[54]

On the last play of the first quarter, Reger was knocked unconscious and went into convulsions after tackling the fullback Sapp. "Reger's face was blue-black from his inability to breathe after swallowing his tongue, those who rushed to his aid said."[55]

James Nixon, the Eagles' physician, looked at Reger writhing on the ground and ran off in search of a knife he could use to make an emergency tracheotomy if no other means of providing air to the player could be found. Steelers trainer Roger McGill performed artificial respiration, and then John Best, the team physician, forced a pair of scissors between Reger's teeth. The scissors got caught in Reger's mouth, and as the instrument was pulled out, several teeth were dislodged, leaving an opening. Best "forced his finger into the stricken player's mouth and withdrew Reger's tongue."[56] Reger was taken by ambulance to nearby University Hospital, where he spent several days recuperating.

Around the league, Jimmy Brown scored three touchdowns to help the Browns beat the Redskins, 37–14. But "the most astonishing performance" on the opening weekend of the NFL season, according to United Press International, came from the Chicago Bears' restructured defense, which intercepted four Bart Starr passes in a 10–3 victory over the defending champion Green Bay Packers.[57] It was way too far off to look ahead, but the Steelers had to face both teams in November, and after one game they had offered scant proof that they would be able to handle either.

?ESEASON

AN INTRODUCTION

In the mind of head coach Raymond "Buddy" Parker, 1962 was going to be the season the Pittsburgh Steelers put an end to a thirty-year stretch of futility, a hapless period of time during which the franchise had achieved only six winning seasons and never made it to a championship game. The forty-nine-year-old Parker was in his sixth season in Pittsburgh since coming over from Detroit, where he had won three conference titles and two world championships, and he had failed to fulfill his vow to bring owner Art Rooney a championship within five years. "I am coming to Pittsburgh with one objective, to give the Steelers a winner," he said upon his appointment by Rooney in late August of 1957.[1] The best he had done in five years was go 7–4–1 in '58, but even after two straight losing seasons, Parker felt that 1962 was going to be different. "This is the year," Parker told Bobby Layne as the team flew to Detroit for the season opener. "I think we can win it."[2]

Layne had spent his entire life defying the clock, whether he was ordering another round after closing time in a nightclub on the eve of a game or watching seconds tick off the stadium clock in the final minute of a game with his team down by a touchdown and 80 yards from the opponent's end zone. But now time was running out on Layne, the master of the two-minute drill, the invincible quarterback who had led the Lions to two championships and helped them reach two other title games. Three decades later, *Sports Illustrated* would put Layne, wearing his helmet without the face mask he had scorned throughout his career, on its cover in the fall of 1995 with the headline "The Toughest Quarterback Ever." Layne needed one more touchdown pass to break Sammy Baugh's career record of 187, but he was thirty-six, and fourteen seasons of injuries, a disdain for football equipment, and a passion for hearty living in bars and nightclubs had taken a toll. The opener turned into a disastrous homecoming for Parker and Layne. The Steelers were routed 45–7 and then floundered through the first half of the fourteen-game season, going 3–4.

Layne was playing in '62 with a debilitating hematoma—blood clotted from hemorrhaging—on the right side of his body. Art Rooney Jr., son of the Steelers' owner, remembered the clot being "like a watermelon."[3] Relying on tape and painkillers, Layne proved he still had not only the guts but also the magic in his arm as he led a game-winning drive against frisky second-year quarterback Fran Tarkenton and the Vikings in game 8.[4] "What a desperate feeling to stand there and watch our defensive team try to hold Layne," Tarkenton said afterward. "You hear Layne's arm is going dead. It didn't look like it today."[5]

The Steelers then beat St. Louis, but against the Redskins Layne was blindsided and helped off the field to a chorus of boos at Forbes Field. It would not be the last time a Steeler quarterback destined for the Hall of Fame would be jeered while lurching off the field in agony. Ed Brown, obtained from Chicago in the off-season, took over as quarterback, rallied the Steelers to a 23–21 victory, and led them to three wins in the last four games to finish in second place at 9–5 and qualify for the short-lived Playoff Bowl, a consolation game for runner-up teams. Parker's estimation of the team hadn't been so far off after all. The '62 Steelers were a team that Bucko Kilroy, acknowledged as one of the toughest men ever to play in the NFL as well as one of its best scouts, dubbed "Destiny's Derelicts."[6] They were a team of rejects, drinkers, and brawlers, low on skill but high on pain tolerance, and no one ever questioned their guts or desire to win.

The '63 Steelers had the same blue-collar cast, with a couple of critical omissions. Layne, at the coercion of Parker, retired in the spring. Eugene "Big Daddy" Lipscomb, a three-time Pro Bowl defensive tackle, was found dead in May.

The '63 squad also had talent—not nearly as much as the Steeler teams of the seventies would boast, but enough that the pack of vagabonds would find itself clawing for a berth in an NFL title game a decade before a dynasty would arise in Pittsburgh. The '63 Steelers had a player who writer Myron Cope mused "may be the toughest guy ever to have come down the NFL pike." Ernie Stautner was from a different era and mind-set, one in which "going to war" meant firing rifles, not passes, in a critical showdown. Stautner had served in the Marines in World War II before attending college. He was listed as six foot two, 230 pounds, but he played defensive end with a ferocity that distilled football to a Darwinian equation. "Toughest Steeler ever," said Andy Russell, a rookie linebacker in '63. "One of the super-tough guys," said Frank Atkinson, a rookie defensive tackle out of Stanford that year. "Ernie thought the game was all about beating the crap out of the guy across from you."[7]

Stautner didn't have a reputation as a dirty player, but as a competitor he was out for blood. "You got to be a man who wants to hurt somebody," Stautner told Cope. "You know where I'm going for? The quarterback's face. It hurts in the face. I want him to know I'm coming the next time. I want him to be scared. Those quarterbacks can't tell me they don't scare, because I've seen it in the corners of their eyes." Said teammate Lou Cordileone, "Ernie Stautner was one determined sunuvabitch."[8]

Pain and injury? If a roll of tape couldn't fix it, a strong will could. Russell would become a link to the glory years, but he was only a rookie when Stautner indoctrinated him to the concept of playing with pain—or playing with wounds.

"He comes into the huddle; his thumb's broken back," Russell said.

He's not showing off. I just happened to see it. I was right across from him. The bone's sticking out. I wasn't used to seeing bones in the huddle. He's got a compound fracture. He takes his thumb and he jams it down. He says, "What's the defense?" Holy shit! This guy isn't going to leave the game for one friggin' play, and he's got a compound fracture? Finally we make 'em punt four or five plays later. We come off the field and I figure, now he's got to go to the hospital. This could get infected. He's got an open wound. He says, "More tape. Give me more." That was Ernie Stautner. There's nobody that would do that—stay out there with a compound fracture.[9]

The Playoff Bowl, instituted in 1960, was a post-championship matchup of the second-place teams in the Eastern and Western conferences. It was a meaningless game, ridiculed by Vince Lombardi, who called it a "hinky-dink football game, held in a hinky-dink town, played by hinky-dink players."[10] Yet with nothing at stake but pride and an officially sanctioned opportunity to exact vengeance and cause a bit of mayhem, the initial games were played with a viciousness to rival any championship game—or street fight.

The Lions' victory over the Eagles in the Playoff Bowl following the '61 season left Philadelphia quarterback Sonny Jurgensen with a separated shoulder, tackle J. D. Smith with a broken leg, fullback Ted Dean with a broken foot, and defensive end Leo Sugar with torn knee ligaments, a career-ending injury.

The Steeler-Lion matchup in Miami after the '62 season was just as savage. "It's a cinch that Fidel Castro heard the ruckus 90 miles away and mobilized his beach defenses," wrote Sandy Grady of the *Philadelphia Evening Bulletin*.[11] Detroit escaped with a 17–10 win when the Lions held off Layne after he entered the game with seven minutes left and drove Pittsburgh from its own 20 to the Detroit 21. Steeler offensive tackle Dan James was originally thought to have chipped a bone in his ankle during the game, but X-rays showed it was "only" badly sprained. Defensive back Willie Daniel was hospitalized with a broken jaw and severe concussion after colliding with receiver Pat Studstill. John Henry Johnson needed eight stitches to close a cut above his eye and sustained a concussion after getting kicked in the face while fighting Wayne Walker. Johnson was so woozy after one play that he walked toward the Lions' huddle and had to be redirected the other way. "What a game that was. It was brutal," Cordileone, a defensive tackle, said forty-five years later.[12] "My, my, it sure was kinda rough out there for a while today," Lipscomb said with a sigh in the locker room.[13]

What drove two teams to play a meaningless exhibition as if it were the fifteenth round of a heavyweight title fight? It wasn't the money, for sure. "In those days, I think we got $400 to play in that game," Cordileone said. "The winners, I think, got $800."[14] There wasn't enough money in the NFL to inspire players of that era to sacrifice their bodies for victory. They had to work in the off-season to support their families or prepare for a vocation once their NFL career skidded to a halt. Offensive tackle Charlie Bradshaw attended law school. Quarterback Terry Nofsinger earned a master's degree in business. Defensive tackle Joe Krupa was a schoolteacher.

So why the hatred and brutality? Why would two teams fight so desperately and throw their bodies around so recklessly with nothing at stake and only a meager payoff? What drove them to compete and excel, and merely to survive, was something that ran deep inside their souls, and it flowed as easily as the blood that ran like rainwater from their faces and hands. Cordileone pointed back to the opener, the Lions' 45–7 rout. "They kicked our ass," he said. "That's why we were so fuckin' pissed off. That's why we went after them."[15]

Packers offensive tackle Forrest Gregg, praised by his coach, Lombardi, as "a picture ballplayer," remembered a game early in his career when he faced Lipscomb. Gregg had been advised by his line coach, Lou Rymkus, that the only way a lineman could make it in the NFL was to hold. Gregg tried that tactic on Lipscomb on every play until the then-Colts tackle approached him between plays and said, "Hey, Forrest, I've got a deal for you. If you quit holding me, then I won't kill you." At that time, Gregg said, "Not many players were earning fortunes, but they took their football seriously."[16]

Of course, it wasn't all that unusual for the Steelers to interrupt their games for a bit of brawling and bare-knuckle fighting. At a December 3, 1961, game at Forbes Field, the Steelers were going down, 35–24, to the defending world champion, the Eagles, when the amateur gladiators took center stage. Two players from each team would wind up being sent to the hospital: Pittsburgh's Charlie Bradshaw and Philly's offensive guard Stan Campbell, with dislocated shoulders; the Steelers' end and linebacker George Tarasovic, with torn ligaments in his right knee; and Eagles defensive back Irv Cross, with a concussion.[17] A player from each team was ejected: Lipscomb, for punching center Howard Keys in the jaw in the final minute, and J. D. Smith for taking a swing at Big Daddy. Meanwhile, Pittsburgh's 185-pound defensive back Brady Keys was "socking" 235-pound linebacker Bob Pellegrini, and Krupa was wrestling with Eagles defensive tackle Jess Richardson.[18] What was at stake for the Eagles was possession of first place in the Eastern Conference, against the Giants. The Steelers, who would finish 6–8, were scrapping to reach .500, but mostly they were battling, as usual, just for pride and respect and to retain their honor as the clock ticked off another defeat. Some players may have dreaded playing the Steelers, but teams didn't respect them. "I remember as a player with Cleveland we used to make fun of Pittsburgh," Chuck Noll said with a laugh when he was introduced as head coach of the Steelers at the end of the decade. "They'd wear different colored helmets sometimes."[19]

Players did indeed need the meager money available in the NFL at the time, and they had to fight for it—as well as for their pride. Winning players in the January 1959 Pro Bowl got $300 apiece, and Big Daddy Lipscomb had to settle for a smaller loser's share when five-foot-seven quarterback Eddie LeBaron threw a touchdown pass to beat the West squad, which Lipscomb played on as a member of the Colts. When Lipscomb emerged from the locker room and spotted LeBaron after the game, the six-foot-six, 290-pound lineman snarled, "You little SOB. I'll get you next year."[20]

"Next year" never seemed to arrive for the Steelers, just as it seemed unattainable for baseball's Brooklyn Dodgers. "This is a club that has been heir to misfortune ever since it entered the league," sportswriter Tex Maule commented about Pittsburgh. The Steelers had a losing tradition dating back to their inaugural season of 1933, but an unflinching toughness was just as much a part of their heritage. They might not beat you, but they were a sure bet to beat you up. "If we lose," said Russell, "we're going to hurt you." Two members of the '63 team made Layne's list of "Pro Football's 11 Meanest Men": John Henry Johnson and wide receiver Red Mack. If Layne had made a list of twenty-two, surely Johnson and Mack would have had company from the Steelers' roster.[21]

It was a motley mix of individuals, composed like a hot rod from salvaged junkyard parts. Pittsburgh had Daniel, an undrafted speedy cornerback from Mississippi State who made the unlikeliest leap of all to a Buddy Parker team by leaving his high school coaching job and earning a roster spot on the Steelers with a tryout.

The Steelers had an eighth-round draft choice—Atkinson, who played defensive tackle in the pros for two years before walking away from pro football forever for a career in finance—and a sixteenth-round draft pick—Russell, who didn't want to play pro football but would take over a starting spot, leave for two years in the Army, return to Pittsburgh to endure six straight losing seasons, and then conclude his NFL career with two Super Bowl rings.

They had an undersized, slow-of-foot running back, Dick Hoak, who would retire after ten years as the team's No. 2 all-time rushing leader and then spend another thirty-five years as coach of the Steelers running backs. They had a hometown defensive back, Dick Haley, who would play one more season with the team before going on to a stellar career in player personnel, helping to shape the Steelers into a dynasty in the seventies. And they had a defensive tackle, Cordileone, who had been traded straight up for a future Hall of Fame quarterback and, in his fourth year in the NFL, was with his fourth team. He was a New Jersey guy who had hopes of going into business as a mortician after his football career was over.

Jim Brown called them the "Gashouse Gang." They had a reputation for playing all-out on the field, and partying all-out off it. Word was, according to Brown, that the coach loaded up the team bus with beer. "Now I'm not saying that the Steelers are necessarily headed for hell when they die," Brown allowed, but it didn't look as if they were on the road to salvation either.[22]

Clendon Thomas, an All-America at Oklahoma before being drafted by the Rams, wanted to be traded from Los Angeles, but the last place he wanted to go was Pittsburgh. He had heard "all kinds of bad things about the Steelers—that they were a bunch of drunks and rabble-rousers." After the trade, he discovered that the stories had been "embellished to the ridiculous."[23] But enough of the stories were true to maintain the Steelers' reputation as a team that was good to the last drop, whether it was booze or blood.

The '63 Steelers were the Animal House of the NFL.

The Steelers had players no one else wanted or believed in—certainly not enough to think that these men could carry a team to an NFL championship. At least one preseason poll of newspapermen picked the Steelers to finish fourth in the Eastern Conference in '63.[24] *Sports Illustrated* predicted a third-place finish.[25] Veteran sportswriter Joe Falls of the *Detroit Free Press* predicted a fourth-place finish.[26] But by the final weekend of the '63 season, a curious mix of overachievers, castoffs, veterans, and raw young players with more heart than natural talent had put itself on the brink of something special, summed up in one headline in the *New York Times:* "Steelers: A Lot of Discards Seeking a Jackpot."[27]

The race down the stretch between four teams in the Eastern Conference was so crazy a free-for-all that it looked as if the jumble might create "the worst snarl" in NFL history, necessitating a playoff. After the twelfth week, the Giants and Browns were tied for first, at 9–3, a winning percentage of .750. The Steelers, following their third tie of the season, were 6–3–3, a winning percentage of .667, the same as the 8–4 Cardinals. Because the NFL's practice in computing the standings had been to disregard tie games, the Steelers could still win the conference with the best winning percentage if Cleveland lost once and Pittsburgh won its last two games, against Dallas and New York. Frank Ryan, the Browns' quarterback as well as "a mental giant pursuing a doctorate in mathematics," had been asked not long before to calculate the possible finishes and came up with "a stunning total of more than 7,000," *New York Times* columnist Arthur Daley wrote.[28] No matter the math, no one in the NFL had to be told that against the longest odds of all, the most unlikely scenario was that Parker's band of renegades would be fighting for the right to play in the NFL championship game on the last day of the regular season.

As 1963 began, Americans weren't exactly naive about their place in the world. Castro and Khrushchev were as much household names as Ed Sullivan and J. Edgar Hoover, and people were learning to locate Vietnam on a map. Americans had a steady, trusted routine. *Dondi, Pogo,* and *Joe Palooka* appeared daily in the *Pittsburgh Press* comics. André Previn and *Polka, Polka, Polka* records alike—"Hi-Fi or Stereo"—were on sale for eighty-seven cents at Gimbels. Acme markets had T-bone steaks for ninety-five cents a pound. Kellogg's introduced a new cereal called Froot Loops, and *The Fugitive* and *Petticoat Junction* would make their debuts on TV in the fall. The new Corvette Stingrays were zipping down streets.

All in all, not only was life pretty cheery in 1963, but "the American people ha[d] never before had it so good," *U.S. News & World Report* concluded from a nationwide survey. People in general were well off. They had good housing and a healthy amount of time for leisure and vacations. Incomes were at "a record level," and there were "gadgets of all kinds for the home."[29]

But with all the trappings of prosperity and the veneer of success, were people actually happy? Many were not, the magazine said. "Millions keep on the move each year in search of something they don't seem to find."[30] There were problems and trends that could be documented with statistics. The divorce rate was high. Crime in big cities was on the rise. Despite the flush times, plenty of people were in debt. But there was also something that didn't add up, something missing, but it was an elusive worry that was hard to identify, quantify, or articulate.

"We're such an affluent society, we have so much," a newspaperman in Escanaba, Michigan, said, "that what is there left?" An insurance agent in Vermilion, South Dakota, mused, "There is too much money, times are too good. We are losing our basic values." A secretary in Los Angeles felt people lacked spirit and animation, and she faulted the age of automation. "There are too many products: life's too complicated," she said. "We drift. It's a depressing atmosphere." The nation was in a state of flux, and no one seemed to know what to do or think about it. "The national attitude, it seems, is one of some uncertainty rather than one of full confidence," the magazine reported.[31]

Young people across the country were restless and inquisitive. Sex and drinking were becoming more widespread, and parents fretted that kids were getting married too soon. A school official in Jamestown, North Dakota, wondered if kids were growing up too fast. The new generation was starting to assert itself. "Our young people are more insistent on answers to troubling questions," said a Protestant minister in Columbia, South Carolina. "They no longer are quiet, no longer willing to just accept what we older folk tell them."[32]

People brooded about everything from jobs and unions to church membership, and now civil rights had become a big issue, but what to do about the controversy was a dilemma. "We are 100 per cent for integration, of course," said a Jamestown, North Dakota, lawyer, "but 99½ per cent of us don't understand the problem at all." There was a lot of talk about it, the editor of a newspaper in Whitesburg, Kentucky, said, and even if they couldn't grasp what the problem was, people let their worries run unchecked. "The fear here is of mixed marriages," the editor said. "People worry, too, about Negroes demanding jobs downtown."[33]

Not many seemed confident that politicians comprehended the issue either—or that they had the ability to solve any of the other problems plaguing the nation. "I have a feeling that nobody cares whether a Republican or Democrat is elected the next President," said a railroad executive in Chicago. "Both parties eat out of the same bowl."[34]

Football fans were beginning to learn that the sports world was not immune to the temptations and problems of real life. Green Bay's Paul Hornung and Detroit's Alex Karras had been suspended for gambling on NFL games. That punishment was designed as a deterrent to players, of course, not to regular citizens. On the weekend of the 1963 NFL openers, thirty-six state police officers in seventeen cars "swooped down" and made eighteen gambling-related arrests at thirteen establishments in McKeesport, Pennsylvania. "We just scratched the surface," one officer commented. Six more arrests took place outside Uniontown.[35]

The sports world had provided a refuge for diversion and entertainment, but violence, death, and grief were muscling in on the national consciousness. Long before sports viewing became widely popular and accessible twenty-four hours a day, seven days a week, the daily newspaper provided fans with a reliable escape from the onslaught of depressing news. "Agree with me or not," wrote *Pittsburgh Post-Gazette* sports editor Al Abrams in a December 1961 column, "I say sports pages today offer a vicarious, if not welcome relief, in these days of uncertainty, restlessness, turbulence, violence or any other disturbing factor one can name." The places and problems seizing the public's attention at the time, he noted, included Katanga, West Berlin, graft, murder, automation "and even the twist craze."[36]

Most people would have agreed with Abrams. Two years later, Katanga and the twist had faded from the public consciousness, but graft, murder, and automation were as much in vogue as ever. Different spots on the globe were twitching with war, and new social issues were cresting. Barely an hour before NFL games kicked off on the opening Sunday of the '63 season, down in Birmingham, Alabama, a bomb that police estimated had the power of at least fifteen sticks of dynamite went off in a Negro church, killing four girls and inciting riots in which two boys would be shot to death. The four girls had just heard their Sunday school lesson for the day: "The Love that Forgives." The bombing came five days after the desegregation of three of the city's all-white schools.[37]

There were many other incidents of racial intolerance, of course, ranging from the humiliating to the tragic, only there wasn't enough room to squeeze them all into a daily newspaper—at least not on page 1. On the same day that the bombings in Alabama made front-page news, buried on page 8 of the *Post-Gazette* under a one-column headline was an account of an incident that had culminated in the deaths of three Hill District men from an accident believed to have been sparked by a racial insult. The unidentified driver of a passing car yelled a slur at four men in a station wagon, and as the station wagon gave chase, the vehicle collided with an oncoming car on the two-lane Thirty-First Street Bridge. The station wagon caught on fire, and three of the passengers were burned to death.[38]

The world was steadily revealing itself to be more dangerous, more deadly, than people had imagined. Residents of Youngstown, Ohio, were all too familiar with organized crime, but it wasn't until the court testimony of Joe Valachi, "the kindly looking killer with the henna rinse haircut," in late September of '63 that the rest of the nation got its introduction to the Mafia. "Two months ago the world at large had never heard of Cosa Nostra," a wire service reported during the proceedings. "Now Cosa Nostra is a household word."[39]

Two dozen crime families would arise from coast to coast in the United States, as well as Canada. New York and Chicago had the most notorious families, but Cleveland and Pittsburgh could boast major league crime franchises, too. However, when it came to organized crime, Pittsburgh evidently was a bit different from, say, Youngstown—more upper crust. A former associate of Al Capone and Lucky Luciano, speaking in Italy, explained that once the Mafia needed someone to perform a task in Pittsburgh but could find no one to do the job "because the Mafiosi in that city were all well-to-do."[40]

Almost imperceptibly, lifestyles were shifting, traditions fading. The day after the Steelers beat Detroit in an exhibition game, 22–7, on the night the Lions retired Bobby Layne's uniform, the No. 56 trolley from McKeesport to Pittsburgh ended a run that had started in 1895. A week later, the first air-conditioned bus in the area was put into local service.

The world was swirling and seething with changes, day by day, and amid the shadows of calm and strife, the '63 Steelers were aiming to create their own place in history.

GAME 2

Two weeks after the Packers beat the Giants, 16–7, in the 1962 NFL title game before 64,892 fans at Yankee Stadium, the East beat the West, 30–20, in the Pro Bowl in front of a Los Angeles Memorial Coliseum crowd of 61,374. Big Daddy Lipscomb, having completed his second season with the Steelers, was named the outstanding lineman of the game, despite playing on the losing team. "Big Daddy's a happy man," Lipscomb said afterward. "I say it was one of my best games of the year."[1]

Lipscomb was only thirty-one, and every one of the stars on the field that day undoubtedly believed that Big Daddy had plenty of good games—even great games—ahead of him. But it was the last time Big Daddy Lipscomb, six foot six, 290 pounds or more, would terrorize NFL quarterbacks and intimidate offensive tackles. Four months later, on May 10, Lipscomb was found dead in a friend's West Baltimore apartment. The chief medical examiner ruled the cause of death to be an overdose of heroin, but teammates, relatives, and friends considered it preposterous to believe that a man who was terrified to get a shot from a doctor would willingly stick a needle in his own arm. It was widely known among Steelers players and management that Lipscomb would run from a syringe as fast as quarterbacks ran from him. "We had to take tetanus shots, vitamin shots if you wanted 'em," said former teammate Clendon Thomas. "They couldn't get him down to give him his tetanus shots. It would have taken fifteen of us to get him down on the floor, and I'm not sure we could have done it. You couldn't touch him with a needle."[2]

"He didn't overdose," said tight end Preston Carpenter. "Somebody killed him. We know that."[3] Buddy Young, a friend of Lipscomb's as well as a former collegiate and NFL star, said, "I have never known Big Daddy to take any kind of dope. He wouldn't do it."[4]

There weren't many happy times for Eugene Alan Lipscomb while he was growing up. He was eleven years old when a man came to the Detroit rooming house where Lipscomb lived and told him his mother was dead, stabbed forty-seven times by a boyfriend while waiting for a bus. Lipscomb never knew his father. After his mother's death, he was raised by his grandfather, whose idea of discipline was a good whipping.[5]

Big Daddy started working even before his mother was slain. "After she was killed, work was a matter of survival for me," he said. "I had to buy my own clothes and pay room and board to my grandfather. I washed dishes in a café, loaded trucks for a construction gang and helped around a junkyard. One year I ran a lift in a steel mill from midnight until seven in the morning. Then I changed clothes and went to school." Not even a man with the size and strength of Lipscomb could banish from his mind the memories of a childhood spent in purgatory. "I've been scared most of my life," Lipscomb admitted. "You wouldn't think so to look at me."[6]

Lipscomb joined the Marines after high school and learned football playing for a team at Camp Pendleton. The Los Angeles Rams signed him for $4,800, used him sporadically, and then waived him. Baltimore picked him up for $100. He bolstered a defense that helped the Colts win successive championships in 1958 and '59, was voted All-Pro both years, and then was traded to the Steelers before the start of the '61 season. Asked about the trade, Lipscomb told a Baltimore newspaperman, "It makes no difference where I go. I gives 'em hell wherever I play."[7] He was the kind of defensive player—just like Ernie Stautner—who could put fear into an opponent's offense and rattle any quarterback. He was exactly what the Pittsburgh Steelers needed, and he was the kind of battling underdog from a lousy life that Pittsburgh fans would admire and cheer.

Had he lived, Lipscomb was a player who could have pushed the Steelers to the top in 1963. "In my opinion, he was the best defensive lineman in the history of the game," said Johnny Sample, a teammate of Lipscomb's in both Baltimore and Pittsburgh.[8]

Under that Rocky Mountain physique and intimidating scowl was a man with an impish sense of humor and a soft heart toward kids. "He had a heart of pure gold," said former teammate John Nisby. And of all the athletes John F. Kennedy could choose from to form his National Sportsmen for Kennedy Committee in mid-October of 1960, Lipscomb was one who wound up in the group alongside Johnny Unitas and Norm Van Brocklin. But Lipscomb definitely would not have approved of Kennedy, as president, inviting Nikita Khrushchev in September of '63 to consider a joint mission to the moon. No, Big Daddy had dreams that were all his own.[9]

"I'm not kidding. I want to be the first man on the moon," Big Daddy said during training camp in August 1962. "I want to be an astronaut and I sure would like to land up there on the moon. Why, I'd look around, wave the American flag, declare the territory for America and pick up a little glory for Big Daddy, too. . . . You know you just can't send no midgets to the moon."[10]

But if Lipscomb couldn't get his shot at the moon, he was confident he could lift the Steelers to a title, just as he had helped the Colts. Big Daddy, along with everyone else across the country in 1962, had every right to dream, and dream big. "Say, chum," Lipscomb said as he looked at the sky that August day. "I wonder if those cats up there on the moon have a football team. If they do, Big Daddy would have himself a ball. And when those scientists look at the plan[e]t at night and see somebody making tackles all over the surface they'll be able to say, 'There's the man in the moon and it's Big Daddy Lipscomb!'"[11]

As the Steelers prepared to open the '63 season without Lipscomb, one very special player in a different sport, a native of Donora, Pennsylvania, echoed the anxiety of every Steelers fan. Retiring after twenty-two years as a St. Louis Cardinals outfielder and making his final appearance at Forbes Field on Sunday, September 8, Stan "the Man" Musial wondered out loud, "The way the Steelers finished last season they should have something. How much will they miss Big Daddy Lipscomb?"[12]

A lot, the *Pittsburgh Courier* warned. "With Eugene Lipscomb gone, much of the teamwise swank and confidence of the past two seasons is going to be amiss," the newspaper stated. "The big fellow exhuded [sic] 'class,' both for himself and the team simply by striding on the field."[13]

First Bobby Layne left the stage, and then Big Daddy. It was the kind of double whammy that no team seemed capable of overcoming, and certainly not one assembled with vagabonds and players who had no reputation as winners. "The loss of both Layne and Lipscomb, in a single year, shapes [up] as an excessive psychological impediment," the *Courier* stated.[14]

Buddy Parker had a candidate, albeit an unlikely one, to fill Big Daddy's spot. A 1964 Steeler press guide noted that Lou Cordileone had spent "a rather nomadic life in the NFL," an apt as well as poetic description, considering that when he was picked up by the Steelers in '62, the former first-round draft choice of the Giants was playing for his fourth team three years.

Cordileone was a high school star at St. Michael's in Union City, New Jersey, where, as a fullback, he scored five touchdowns and three extra points in a 40–0 win over Ferris in 1955 and went on to set a season scoring record for Hudson County with 128 points. But Cordileone was not cut out for a regimented lifestyle. Years before he became coach and managing general partner of the Oakland Raiders, Al Davis, a Brooklyn native, was offensive line coach at the Citadel, and he tried to recruit Cordileone. The Jersey guy wasn't exactly suited for the military life. "Let me tell you something, coach," Cordileone told Davis. "I'm not going to college to dress in a fuckin' uniform every day. I want to go to college to have fun."[15]

Cordileone did go south, but he chose Clemson, where he became an All-America lineman. When he was selected twelfth overall by the Giants in the 1960 draft, Cordileone envisioned a ten-year career in the NFL, after which he figured he'd go into business, "perhaps as a mortician with his uncle," he explained on the eve of Lou Cordileone Day in Jersey City, February 2, 1960.[16]

But his career veered off course and took a couple of detours, including one that linked him in NFL history to one of the league's greats. A year after getting the keys to his hometown, Cordileone was dealt by the Giants to San Francisco for Y. A. Tittle. Cordileone's reaction to the trade was: "Me for Tittle? Just me?"[17]

Tittle was no less surprised—or appalled. "I was a little bit resentful," the quarterback admitted several decades later. "He may have been a good guard, but I thought I was worth more than a guard that had never even played. I was irritated at the 49ers. I had been to the Pro Bowl four times with the 49ers. I was hurt." The question was, at age thirty-four, could Tittle lead a team to the top? "That's what I had to prove," he said.[18]

For a lineman who had "all the equipment to become one of the best in league history," Cordileone wouldn't wind up with much glory, but he got in plenty of licks on the field and had more than his share of fun off it, according to both him and a few critics.[19] "A little too much sometimes," he admitted, "except on Sunday. But they don't count Sunday, they count what happens during the week a lot, and that's where I used to get in trouble. I was always there on Sunday. I never had a problem on Sunday."[20]

On other days, trouble had a way of finding him, even with no provocation. It didn't take long at the 49ers' training camp for Cordileone to learn that playing for their coach was going to be no fun at all. "I never got along with Red Hickey. He was an asshole," Cordileone said. "He didn't like me, I didn't like him." One night at camp, Cordileone left his room to go to the bathroom ten minutes before bed check and returned twenty minutes later. The next day, Hickey asked Cordileone where he had been at 11 P.M. Hearing the explanation, Hickey replied, "From now on, you shit on your own time, and not on mine."[21]

Cordileone was traded to the Rams after the season, but that stay ended after only a few games. "I got in a beef with [Rams coach Bob] Waterfield," Cordileone said.[22] (If Hickey wasn't much fun to be around, Waterfield was no barrel of laughs either. He earned the nickname "Great Stoneface" for his communication skills with players.[23])

Cordileone got a phone call from his mom informing him that she'd heard on TV that Vince Lombardi had picked him up. "I said, 'I hate to disappoint you, Mom, but I'm going to Pittsburgh,'" Cordileone explained. "What I come to find out from somebody in the office at Pittsburgh [was that] when Buddy Parker saw that Vince Lombardi was picking me up, he said, 'There's gotta be something this kid's got that nobody knows about yet, because Lombardi wouldn't pick him up if he wasn't a good ballplayer.' And he had the last choice. That's how I wound up in Pittsburgh."[24]

Cordileone looked to be as challenging a reclamation project as Parker had faced, but the defensive tackle had landed in the right environment. The Steelers played and partied with his kind of gusto, and Parker didn't worry about bed checks. Cordileone had played on kicking teams in '62, but with Lipscomb gone and the aging Ernie Stautner limited in his playing time as the '63 camp began, the Steelers were desperate for another playmaker on defense, and the budding mortician was looking good. Halfway through the exhibition season, Rooney observed, "That new guy is doing a real good job at tackle. The coaches say he's been playing as well as Lipscomb did."[25]

The Steelers were going to need a grizzly bear of a lineman to cope with the Giants in game 2. Three of New York's backs—Frank Gifford, Hugh McElhenny, and Alex Webster—had a combined career total of 13,090 yards rushing, 9,901 yards receiving, and 174 touchdowns entering the season. Parker had lost Myron Pottios for the '62 season because of a fractured arm, and now he was going to be without his middle linebacker, John Reger, who was still in a Philadelphia hospital, recovering from his collision. Michaels, who had kicked two field goals in a 20–17 victory in New York in '62, was still brooding over his placekicking failures in Philly. (Asked what he was doing to forget his troubles, Michaels explained, "Well, I've got some of the boys out to the house to eat some of my mom's Kolbussi. Win, lose or tie, you gotta eat, you know?"[26])

The Giants had their own injury problems. Tittle, now thirty-six, had hit sixteen of twenty-three passes for 243 yards in the comeback win in Baltimore in the opener, but his hip, chest, and ribs were badly bruised when he was hit by defensive backs Lenny Lyles and Jim Welch while diving into the end zone. The Giants' physician, Francis J. Sweeney, ordered an ambulance to meet the train the team traveled on upon its return to New York and take Tittle and rookie back Charlie Killett to the hospital.

"I don't want to go to the hospital," Tittle said, "and I certainly won't ride there in an ambulance."

"Sit up front with the driver," owner John Mara suggested. "It will be the same as a taxicab. It'll be just like riding shotgun on a stagecoach." Tittle spent two nights in the hospital.[27]

Tittle had the skills that would eventually earn him a spot in the Hall of Fame, but he was driven to keep proving himself year after year. "I never thought I was that good," Tittle said, "and I always felt if I didn't play up to my maximum, there was always somebody on that bench [who] would take my job. I always had pressure. I always had good quarterbacks who were substitutes, and if I didn't watch it . . ."[28]

Tittle had been facing intense competition just to get on the field ever since he began his pro career with Baltimore. He competed against All-America quarterbacks Charles "Chuckin' Charlie" O'Rourke of Boston College and Adrian Burk of Baylor. In San Francisco, he played behind a quarterback, Frankie Albert, who starred not only on the field but in a movie about a glamorous football player. "I got the job finally," Tittle said. "I kept winning the jobs."[29]

The Texas native had been brought to the Giants because Charlie Conerly, who'd played at Ole Miss, turned forty as the '61 season began. As the '63 season opened, backing up Tittle were Ralph Guglielmi of Notre Dame and rookie Glynn Griffing, christened by the Associated Press (AP) "perhaps the greatest in a long line of fine Mississippi quarterbacks" in the aftermath of the Rebels' 17–13 Sugar Bowl victory over Arkansas. Losing coach Frank Broyles declared the six-foot-one 200-pounder from Culkin, Mississippi, "the best college passer I've ever seen."[30]

The Giants signed Griffing, whom they had selected as a "future" in the fourth round of the 1962 draft, immediately after the game.[31] "Now the New York Giants will be looking for Griffing to accomplish similar feats," the Associated Press's Ben Thomas wrote. By season's end, NBC would air a documentary on Griffing's rookie experiences, titled *The Making of a Pro.*[32]

It was a familiar scenario, yet another challenge, for Tittle. "I was always fighting—fighting to stay a step ahead of the other quarterbacks," he said.

"One thing about the quarterback position is, there's no room for two. You can't alternate like you do wide receivers. Quarterbacks stay in all the time, so you either play or you sit, and I wanted to play."[33]

In recent years, the Steelers had repeatedly acquired quarterbacks with rare talent—Johnny Unitas, Len Dawson, Jack Kemp—and discarded them, allowing them to go on to All-Pro and Hall of Fame careers with other teams. The Steelers couldn't shake their image as a loser, and for a long time, neither could the city itself. Once James Parton damned Pittsburgh nearly one hundred years earlier by describing it as "hell with the lid lifted," the city became a wide-open target for jokes and cheap shots. And the Steelers were in the line of fire as well.

The Renaissance that began in Pittsburgh in the mid-forties had started to clear the air and "redd up"—as locals referred to tidying up—downtown, but the biggest source of pride in '63 wasn't the Steelers; it was the two-year-old Civic Arena, the world's first auditorium with a retractable roof. "It has become a sort of symbol of the new Pittsburgh," an editorial in the *Pittsburgh Press* stated in the aftermath of Leonard Bernstein's condemnation of the Arena's acoustics during his performance there on the afternoon the Steelers played the Eagles.[34] Super Bowl trophies wouldn't be displayed in Pittsburgh until the seventies, but in 1963, the Arena served as the showpiece for a city eager to show off something of pride.

Still, the taunts and jibes rankled citizens, and one of the city's foremost advocates, Steelers owner Art Rooney Sr., had to endure the insults toward both his team and his city. Two days after the tie with the Eagles, Rooney addressed the Chamber of Commerce Breakfast Club and pledged not to move the team unless it met with severe financial hardship. "The Steelers are one industry that will not move until the time when it becomes financially impossible for me to keep the team here. It is as simple as that," Rooney said. He also took the opportunity to chide officials and the media for a defeatist attitude toward the city's efforts at self-improvement, citing critical remarks that could undermine efforts to attract new industries and revitalize the downtown. But one regret he voiced seemed to speak more to changes in lifestyles and attitudes than in business, a shift in communities and priorities, and a decline in old-fashioned manners and civility. His unease seemed to presage the discontent that the *U.S. News & World Report* would reveal two months later. "Everyone seems busier and a little less friendly," Rooney said. "We seem to take a more negative attitude toward things."[35]

The world was undergoing drastic changes, and Pittsburgh couldn't avoid being swept up in them. People wanted to hang on to small pleasures and

the normalcy in their lives, even though western Pennsylvania felt the reverberations from thousands of miles away. So, while Bob Schmitz, a third-year
linebacker from Montana State, was working with the first team defense
at the Steelers' Wednesday practice in South Park, with Parker stressing
protection against Tittle's bombs to Del Shofner, WIIC TV was preparing
for its Community Day Parade, a kickoff to the new fall TV season, with
Dan Blocker, Hoss from *Bonanza,* as the grand marshal. Tuesday night had
ushered in a new season of *Combat!* and *McHale's Navy,* plus the premiere
of "a very promising series," *The Fugitive,* starring David Janssen.

Up in Oakland, James Meredith, the first black student to attend the University of Mississippi, received standing ovations at functions at the University
of Pittsburgh, where he told students in a speech, "I think there is another
civil war in the making." Asked if he blamed Alabama governor George Wallace for the bombing in Birmingham the previous Sunday, Meredith replied,
"The truth is all Americans are to blame, including the steel magnates in
Pittsburgh who may own the mills of Birmingham . . . and the Congress . . .
and the professor at the University of Pittsburgh who has failed to acquaint
his students with the realities of the world."[36]

Sports carried on despite death, wars, and tragedies. The sports section
of the newspaper still provided the "vicarious, if not welcome relief" that
Al Abrams had acknowledged two years earlier, and coaches and players
from the high schools to the pros had to carry on.[37] So Parker fretted over
his offense but expressed no doubts that Tittle would play on Sunday. "We
definitely will have to quit messing up our scoring opportunities," Parker
said. "Then we must exert more pressure on the passer."[38]

What Parker should have remembered was Layne's insight when the
Steelers traveled to Yankee Stadium to face the Giants the year before.
"They're too smart to go for the fake and too fast to go around," Layne
said. "Your only chance is to overpower them." Pittsburgh went on to rush
for 259 yards in a 20–17 victory.[39]

Coming to Pittsburgh, it was John Mara who felt nervous. "We've had
some terrible experiences out here," the Giants president said the day before
the game. "It's never been easy."[40] The Giants had won the previous four
meetings in Pittsburgh, but by margins of four, three, two, and five points.
Tittle's uncertain status didn't ease Mara's apprehension.

Before dawn Saturday, the day before the game, Allie Sherman decided
not to play Tittle. "I told him Sunday morning in my hotel room," Sherman
said later, "and it took me an hour to convince him. Naturally, he wanted
to play. He's a real competitor."[41]

Even if he had been healthy enough to play, Tittle would have had a hard time getting on the field that afternoon. "The Steelers won the toss and promptly began knocking the tar out of the Giant defense," wrote one New York tabloid reporter.[42]

So overwhelming was the Steelers' ground game that the Giants ran only three plays from scrimmage in the first quarter, compared to twenty-six for Pittsburgh. The Steelers banged away at the Giant defense on eight straight running plays on the opening series, with John Henry Johnson ripping up the middle for 6 yards, then off right tackle for 7, and Dick Hoak hitting the left side for 3- and 6-yard gains. The Steelers were in field goal range when Hoak ran for 4 yards to the Giants' 39, but linebacker Tom Scott dropped Ed Brown for an 11-yard loss, and the Steeler quarterback punted on fourth-and-17.

The Steelers stopped the Giants cold and started from their 43 after Brady Keys's 7-yard punt return. Parker's offense began methodically grinding out yardage, poking holes in a defensive front—Jim Katcavage, Dick Modzelewski, John LoVetere, and Andy Robustelli—that was showing the wear from a combined thirty-three seasons of NFL play. The Steelers ran the ball for eleven straight plays, and so confident were they in their offensive line that they went for it on fourth-and-1 at the Giant 37, rather than settle for a field goal, and gained 6 yards from Hoak.

On third-and-11 at the 20, Johnson gained 8 yards on a reception, and a penalty against New York gave the Steelers first-and-goal at the 6. Johnson ran the ball to the 2 as the first period ended. On third down, the second play of the second quarter, Hoak burrowed in for a 1-yard touchdown, capping a fifteen-play drive that had covered only 57 yards.

The teams exchanged punts, and Pittsburgh started to put relentless pressure on Tittle's fill-in, Ralph Guglielmi, a seven-year veteran out of Notre Dame. Cordileone had already shown in preseason that he could be a terror on defense. One writer dubbed him Lou "the Lion Hearted," commenting that he "has filled in admirably" for Lipscomb.[43] On second-and-4 from the Giant 39, Michaels batted away Guglielmi's pass. On third down, the former No. 1 draft pick known as "Goog" fumbled when hit by Cordileone, and defensive end John Baker recovered. Baker was nearly as big as Lipscomb but had been faulted for not being aggressive enough. He had the potential to become a force on the defensive line, the *Pittsburgh Courier* suggested, "if he can be supercharged with desire."[44] Baker had excelled in the fourth preseason game after being elbowed by one of the Detroit Lions, leading Rooney to quip afterward, "Maybe we ought to have someone in the runway belt that guy in the nose before every game."[45] The second game of the regular season would prove to be a long, tiresome day for six-foot-three, 260-pound offensive tackle Roosevelt Brown, in his eleventh year, against the six-foot-six, 270-pound Baker. "Big John just ate him up," Michaels said later.[46]

Pittsburgh took over at the 25. Hoak caught a pass on third-and-12 and gained 18 yards, setting up first-and-goal at the 9. On third down from the 2, Johnson lost the ball while vaulting over the line, but Ed Brown recovered at the 4, setting up Michaels for an 11-yard field goal to make it 10–0 with 7:02 left in the half.

After each team went 3-and-out, the Giants started from their 28, and Pittsburgh nearly ran Guglielmi out of the stadium. On first down, Michaels and Joe Krupa dumped him for a 9-yard loss. On second down, Baker batted away a pass, and Michaels nearly caught it. On third-and-19, running back Joe Morrison took a pass 28 yards for a first down at the 47, but after the two-minute warning, Schmitz sacked Guglielmi for a 17-yard loss. Guglielmi hit end Joe Walton for a gain of 8, but then he was smashed by Baker and Ernie Stautner for a loss of 8, leaving New York with fourth-and-28. If Allie Sherman had anything to be grateful for as the half ended with Clendon Thomas intercepting Guglielmi, it had to be that at least Y. A. Tittle wasn't the quarterback on the field taking a beating.

Rarely had a 10–0 halftime lead looked so secure. The Steelers hadn't even let the visitors into Pittsburgh territory in the first half, and it took nearly thirteen minutes into the second quarter for the Giants to complete a pass and earn a first down.

The second half brought only more misery for Guglielmi. Other than a 31-yard gain by John Henry Johnson that took the Steelers to the Giant 45, neither team was able to gain a first down on the first four series. Guglielmi started on his 39, but Michaels dropped him for no gain. King took a pass in the flat and ran 22 yards to the Steeler 29, New York's first threat, but consecutive sacks by Russell and Michaels, plus a holding penalty, pushed the Giants back to their 40. End Aaron Thomas gained 16 yards on a reception, but Don Chandler's 51-yard field goal attempt only reached the Steeler 7, and Thomas returned it 20 yards.

Johnson and Hoak led the Steelers into Giant territory, but Jim Patton intercepted Brown at the Giant 21. Guglielmi gave the ball right back. Glenn Glass intercepted a pass and returned it 29 yards to the Giants' 9 as the third quarter ended. Hoak scored his second TD on a flare pass from the 2-yard line on the third play of the fourth quarter to make it 17–0.

Griffing came on for Guglielmi, and the Steeler defense kept dishing out punishment. Griffing was dropped by Baker for a loss of 9 yards, and then recovered his own fumble, forcing Chandler to punt on fourth-and-20 from the 37. Keys fielded the ball on his 17 and let a herd of blockers plow a path for him as he raced 82 yards before Chandler knocked him out at the 1. Johnson dived over right tackle for a touchdown to make it 24–0.

On the third play after the kickoff, Myron Pottios knocked the ball loose from Griffing and grabbed it in midair, setting up Brown to hit Dial with a 46-yard TD pass to make it 31–0. The Giants got down to the Steeler 13 on Frank Gifford's 64-yard reception, but three throws to wide receiver Del Shofner missed, securing the first regular-season shutout of the Giants in ten years and marking the first time the Steelers had ever blanked them. The Steelers piled up 223 yards rushing, including 123 by Johnson, while holding the Giants to 59 yards on the ground and only one first down rushing. Guglielmi and Griffing were a combined eight of twenty-six passing, with four interceptions.

A crowd of 46,068, the largest ever to see a pro football game in Pittsburgh, "sat in on the execution."[47] Said one Giant player: "They beat the hell out of us."[48]

As sweet as the victory was for the Steelers and their fans, it was especially satisfying to the kid from Jersey. Cordileone, wrote the *New York Times*, "ran around in the Giant backfield as if he were back on the New York team, but with no intention of helping it along."[49]

The *Pittsburgh Press* called it "a hollow victory" without Tittle, but Ernie Stautner responded, "It wouldn't have made any difference, do you think? The way this team played today, nothing would have helped the Giants."[50]

Giants coach Allie Sherman didn't disagree. "They whipped us," he said. "It wasn't a question of Tittle not playing. There were 22 men who didn't play."[51]

Maybe so. Maybe no single player could have made a dent in the Steelers that day. But one week shy of the forty-fifth anniversary of the loss, Yelberton Abraham Tittle, sitting in his office in California, thought back on that afternoon and said, with a nod toward an athlete's code of respect for his opponent and an involuntary flare-up of pride, "If I'd played—don't write this down—it wouldn't have been 31–0."[52]

In place of Tittle, Guglielmi hit only five of fifteen passes for 89 yards, was intercepted twice and thrown for 67 yards in losses, and felt pressure from Cordileone all afternoon. "What a game he played," Guglielmi said. "We tried to go over him, we tried to trap him. We passed, and he knocked the ball down. We tried to fool him with a play pass. Even that didn't work. Nothing worked."[53]

Griffing completed three of eleven passes for 102 yards. It was to be the only NFL season for the college star who had entered the pros to such glowing praise.

From a Giants perspective, wrote Gene Ward of the *New York Daily News*, "It was a dreadful thing to see, the disintegration of what, only a Sunday ago, had been rated one of the NFL's strongest teams and top favorite in the Eastern Division."[54]

The day after the loss, Sherman didn't quite see the game as a disaster. He wasn't so much generous in his praise of the victors as he was critical of his own team. "It was bad, real bad," he said in the Giants' midtown Manhattan offices. "We made everyone on their side look good—Baker, Cordileone, Michaels, all of them." Rather than concede that there was a shift in power in the division, Sherman dismissed the defeat as simply a bad day. "I'm going to take this game and throw it right out this 16th-floor window," he said. "We're going to forget it and get ready for the Eagles just like we do every other team."[55]

But not everybody was going to dismiss the drubbing. Just as the Steelers weren't about to forget the whipping the Lions gave them in the '62 opener, the Giants would hang on to the memory of the 31–0 shutout. The last game on their schedule was at home against Pittsburgh, but at least they could look forward to having Tittle back for the rematch . . . if the game meant anything by then.

"You had to convince yourself pretty hard that 31–0 was just a fluke," Tittle conceded. But with his characteristic modesty, he added, "On the other hand, it's pretty hard to convince yourself that I'm that valuable— thirty-one points, gosh."[56]

There was a familiar show of power—old and new—elsewhere in the league. Jimmy Brown had TD runs of 71 and 62 yards and rolled up a total of 232 yards in Cleveland's 41–24 win in Dallas, and twenty-four-year-old Charley Johnson—"undoubtedly the brightest young quarterback prospect in the NFL," according to UPI—threw three touchdown passes in rallying St. Louis, Pittsburgh's next opponent, to a 28–24 victory over Philly.[57]

After just two weeks, the Eastern Conference race shaped up as a mad scramble, and the Steelers gave every indication that they were going to fight like crazy to win it.

GAME 3

Andy Russell's NFL career was a fluke, a misunderstanding, a mistake. He never should have wound up playing football for a living. Never should have been in position to make seven Pro Bowl appearances and make tackles and sack quarterbacks across a dozen seasons. And he never should have been around to collect two Super Bowl rings.

Not that he didn't have the talent to play in the pros, the proper coaching, the dedication, or the work ethic. He had good speed, size, and athletic gifts. He was an all-state high school player and went on to play at Missouri for Dan Devine, a strict disciplinarian, powerful motivator, and shrewd coach. "I'd never have been a pro if I'd gone somewhere else," Russell later said.[1]

Russell's Missouri teams went 25–4–3 over three years and played in two bowl games at a time when there was no room for mediocre squads in postseason. It was also an era in which college players were still going both ways. Russell started at linebacker and was a backup at fullback his sophomore year, when Missouri earned a berth in the Orange Bowl and beat Navy, 21–14, before 71,218 fans, including President-elect John F. Kennedy. Twice when Navy reached the Missouri 30, Russell intercepted a pass. As a junior, he went both ways and led the team in rushing. He was primarily a linebacker in his senior year and led the team with six interceptions as the Tigers earned a berth against Georgia Tech in the Bluebonnet Bowl, where he picked off two passes. Russell disparaged his blocking ability as a fullback, but he was credited with a key block on the 77-yard TD run by teammate Bill Tobin that gave Missouri a 14–10 victory over the Yellow Jackets.

Russell didn't make All-America; he didn't even make all-conference. Even though he later faulted himself for making too many mistakes and not enough big plays as a collegian, he was a legitimate NFL prospect—except in his family's eyes. His father was a senior executive for the Monsanto Company, and work took the family from New York and Detroit before they settled in St. Louis, Monsanto's headquarters. Russell's parents then moved to Brussels, where his father was to head up the overseas operation of the company.

"You hear about Army brats," Russell said. "I was a corporate brat. My dad had made me promise I'd never play pro football because it would humiliate the family to have a son playing a game for a living. It was an easy promise to make because I'd gone through ROTC. I figured, well, I can't play pro football anyway. I've got [a commitment to] two years of active duty. And I picked Germany because my parents were overseas and I wanted to see them occasionally."[2]

In the early sixties, the NFL draft was still a primitive procedure, far from the refined science it would evolve into, with its obsessive testing and scouting. There were only twelve teams in the league until the NFL added Dallas in 1960 and Minnesota in 1961, and the number of rounds had been cut to twenty from the thirty-round marathons that existed through 1959. The process was raw and erratic, and Parker's interest in the operation grudging and perfunctory.

"In those days they didn't have any camps where they tried you out like they do today," Russell said. "If you were a halfway decent college football player you got a questionnaire from virtually every team. First question was, 'Are you interested in playing pro football?' I wrote, 'No,' and sent it back. . . . One team didn't send me one: the Pittsburgh Steelers. The Pittsburgh Steelers didn't know I wasn't going to play pro football. So they drafted me in the sixteenth round. They called me and I said, 'Well, you wasted a draft choice because I've got to go into the service.'"[3]

The Steelers didn't have many picks to waste in the 1963 draft; Parker had traded away his first seven choices. In those years the draft was often held in the first week of December, right after the conclusion of the season for many colleges, but while the NFL season was still going. Missouri still had a date with Georgia Tech in the Bluebonnet Bowl in Houston. "I go down there and figure this is the last game I'll ever play," Russell said. "I'm OK with that."[4]

The first two rounds of the draft on Monday, December 3, 1962, consumed six hours and eight minutes, with fourteen teams selecting, so it was nearly midnight by the time the Steelers' first pick came around, in round 8.[5] By then, Parker and his staff were long gone from the NFL draft headquarters in Chicago. He and his staff had taken a flight home, leaving scout Will Walls in charge. (Art Rooney also remained.) The final pick wasn't made until 3:30 A.M., but Walls had submitted the Steelers' sixteenth-round pick, who was still practicing for a bowl game scheduled three days before Christmas.[6]

A couple of weeks later, Russell received a phone call in his hotel room in Houston from Walls, a colorful character who had been an end for the New York Giants and an outfielder for the St. Louis Browns and had a bit part in a movie. Walls paid Russell a visit. "Nicest guy," Russell said. "He's really smooth. He's buttering me up. He's trying to sign me." Russell explained that he planned to finish the school year and then report for his military commitment the following January. In between, he intended to get an internship in St. Louis. Instead, Walls suggested, "Why don't you play pro football? It's perfect." The suggestion, Russell said, was "like a lightbulb" going on in his head. He was married but had no money. Walls started to talk contracts and mentioned a signing bonus. "What's a signing bonus?" Russell asked. After Walls explained, Russell asked how much he would get. "A thousand dollars," Walls replied, and the contract would be for ten grand. Russell, a half year away from receiving his degree in economics, negotiated a deal for $12,000 plus a $3,000 signing bonus. "I joke now," Russell said, decades after establishing himself as a highly successful businessman, "but that's the richest I've ever felt in my whole life."[7]

The odds of Russell being around to collect on that contract looked about as good as the possibility of the Steelers winning the NFL championship, at least from what Buddy Parker indicated at an introductory meeting at the Roosevelt Hotel, where the Steelers used to keep their offices. "He hated rookies," Russell said. "His first speech to us was incredible. The rookies are sitting there—maybe twenty guys—not just draft choices but walk-ons. He had each one of us get up and say who we were and where we played college ball. And then he gave this little 'I hate rookies' speech. 'Rookies lose games. I'm gonna get rid of most of you guys. If it was up to me I wouldn't keep any of you, but the Chief [Art Rooney] wants me to keep a couple of you.' I walked out of that room thinking, 'Geez, this is scary.'"[8]

Teams might exercise extra patience with a first-round pick, as the Steelers did with their unproductive No. 1 choice in the '62 draft, Bob Ferguson, but a sixteenth-rounder? Russell was confident that he could make it in the NFL, but he knew that he had a lot to learn and adjustments to make to compete with more experienced pros. And he had limited time to make an impression. "My athletic skills are better," he rationalized. "I'm faster, quicker, and so I thought I should be able to play better than them. But they're smarter. They do things that I didn't know you'd be allowed to do—like they'd run around a block and make the tackle for a loss. So, if I can get as smart and be as tough, I can play in this league."[9]

Russell was identified as "linebacker Andy Nelsen" in one story early on at training camp, but he stood out in the intrasquad scrimmage preceding the exhibition season.[10] It was noted later that the rookie from Missouri "has been a standout from the very start of training camp."[11] He suffered a broken left thumb in the second preseason game, against the Eagles, when he made a great play, but it wasn't enough to damage his status. The Steelers' group of linebackers had been decimated in '62, and Parker had to fortify the position. Russell made the team.

It was a fortuitous decision by Parker. John Reger was lost indefinitely after his collision in the opener in Philly. When Bob Schmitz injured an ankle early in the Giants game in the second week, George Tarasovic shifted to right linebacker, and Russell, wearing No. 36, came in on the left side. The Giants failed to take advantage of a rookie on defense. And with Schmitz hurting, Parker was going to have to count on Russell against St. Louis.

The Cardinals were installed as six-point underdogs. They had won only four games in '62, but they had a dangerous passing attack, led by twenty-four-year-old quarterback Charley Johnson, who had shown signs he just might tear up the league. In his first start the year before, on October 14, he hit nineteen of thirty-three passes for 285 yards and rallied St. Louis from a 14–3 deficit to a 17–17 tie with Washington. He hit twenty-six of forty-one passes for 365 yards and two touchdowns in a 31–28 loss to the Giants, and he threw five touchdown passes and gained 302 yards in the air in a 52–20 win over Dallas. In the '62 season finale, a 45–35 win over Philadelphia, he threw for 386 yards and two more touchdowns.

Johnson had the luxury of throwing to Ulmo Shannon "Sonny" Randle— "the NFL's closest thing to a human butterfly net"—and Bobby Joe Conrad, a pair that had finished second and third, respectively, among leading receivers in '62. The two had combined for 2,112 yards receiving that season—more than the 2,069 yards the entire Steeler team had gained in receptions.[12]

There seemed to be no limits to what Johnson might accomplish. Y. A. Tittle, at thirty-seven, reflected after the season on the prospects of the Cardinals quarterback and said, "I wish I was Charley's age. And had his future. Whooee."[13]

Johnson had picked right up from his '62 surge, guiding the Cards to a

34–7 win over Dallas in the '63 opener. Johnson hit nineteen of thirty-one passes for 219 yards and three TDs—two to Randle, one to Conrad—in a 28–24 victory over Philly in week 2. Randle and Conrad combined for eleven catches for 175 yards.

The Cards' offensive line was anchored by center Bob DeMarco, "a 240-pound animal from Dayton," flanked by guard Ken Gray, of whom coach Wally Lemm said, "I wouldn't trade him for any guard in the league."[14]

But the most important player was Johnson, who appeared "destined to be the cream of the young quarterback crop in the National Football League."[15] Born in Big Spring in west Texas, Johnson was ignored by the recruiters, so he attended a junior college, the Schreiner Institute, in his home state. The school dropped its football program after Johnson's first year, so he went to New Mexico State to play basketball. But he took a shot at football, and with the help of a backfield of future pros, Johnson and the team blossomed, earning two consecutive trips to the Sun Bowl, in which Johnson was named MVP both times.

Johnson attained more honors before the start of his third pro season: his master's degree in chemical engineering. His thesis was titled "Expansion of Laminar Jets of Organic Liquids Issuing from Capillary Tubes." Along with studying his playbook, he was also studying for his PhD.[16]

On defense, the Cards had an aggressive unit reminiscent of the Steelers' crew. At cornerback they had Jimmy Hill, a tackler as vicious as Detroit's Dick "Night Train" Lane and cited by Bobby Layne as one of "Pro Football's 11 Meanest Men." At safety was Larry Wilson, who would cinch a reputation as one of the game's toughest players by playing a game against the Steelers with casts on both hands and still intercepting a pass.[17]

The year before, the Cardinals linebackers had blitzed Pittsburgh on seventy-five out of eighty-six plays. From game films, Parker didn't see as much "red-dogging" in the first two games of the new season but added, "We're preparing for them just as though they were blitzing every play."[18]

St. Louis had been hampered by injuries the year before, and several players were already hurting early in the new season. Johnson had sustained what was reported to be a severe hematoma—the same malady that crippled Bobby Layne in his final season—in the small of his back, but Lemm downplayed the injury. The Cardinals were also burdened by a twelve-game losing streak in Pittsburgh; they hadn't won there since 1948. Still, Parker kept building them up. "They've got to be a great team," he said. "What other team could lose guys like John Crow, Billy Stacy and Prentice Gautt and still run over teams like they do?"[19]

The '63 NFL schedule was only two weeks old, but the seasons in Pittsburgh were quickly changing. The northern lights were visible the night of the victory over New York, a nod to the closing of summer as the overnight low temperature dipped to 36. Television was unveiling its new season, too, as Tuesday night marked the season premiere of *The Jack Benny Program,* with an appearance by Shirley Temple, along with the debut of a "folksy series" called *Petticoat Junction*.

At midweek, the Pirates clinched eighth place in the ten-team National League. On Thursday, Roberto Clemente stumbled in the race for the batting title, going oh for six against the Houston Colts to dip to .315, behind Tommy Davis's .323. On Sunday, the Bucs would lose their finale to the Giants, 4–2, and *Post-Gazette* baseball writer Jack Hernon would type in his dateline for the game story from Candlestick Park: "SAN FRANCISCO (at the end of a dreary season of baseball), Sept 29—." It was left to the Steelers—and maybe the University of Pittsburgh—to salvage some pride among local sports fans.

On Wednesday, the Steelers conducted a combination of offensive and defensive drills at the South Park Fairgrounds. Buoyed by the shutout against New York, Parker vowed, "We plan to give the Cards the same treatment we gave the Giants last Sunday. If our defense gives their quarterback the same intensive rush it gave Guglielmi we could duplicate the result of the Giants' game."[20]

A cold front was barreling in on the Pittsburgh area on Sunday, and the balmy 65-degree temperatures the 28,225 fans at Forbes Field were enjoying at the 2:05 P.M. kickoff would dip down to 53 by 5 P.M., and gusts of wind would reach 30 mph. The clash between the two teams was, fittingly, like elements colliding in a storm front. "If you like football, you should have seen this one," the photojournalist Robert Riger wrote. "There is rarely a game when two teams, offensively and defensively, sustain explosive impact on every play with an all-out effort by every man."[21]

Both teams were threatening to elbow their way—literally, in the no-holds-barred way they played—to the top of the Eastern Conference. The Cardinals couldn't match Pittsburgh's run of futility; they finished first in 1948, back when the team was in Chicago and played in the Western Conference. But the franchise had floundered in or close to the cellar since losing 7–0 in the '48 title game, and this was the year the Cards had hopes of making a breakthrough—which is just what the Steelers were hoping to do themselves.

The Cardinals downed the opening kickoff and started from their 20. Joe

Childress ran for 5 and 12 yards. The Cards then called an end run to the left side by halfback Bill Triplett, who had been used the previous season, his rookie year, as a safety. Right away, Lemm explained later, "We wanted to make them outside conscious."[22] He figured they could get past right linebacker George Tarasovic. Lemm considered the eleven-year veteran slow, but what the coach didn't realize was that Tarasovic had suffered a sprained arch on the first play yet would stay in for the whole game.

"The play wasn't designed to go all the way," Lemm said, but Gray— Lemm's pride on the offensive line—pulled out and decked linebacker Myron Pottios, allowing Triplett to shoot through a gaping hole between Brady Keys and Clendon Thomas.[23] With the two defensive backs giving chase, and Joe Krupa and Russell trailing, Triplett stiff-armed Dick Haley around the Pittsburgh 30 to go in virtually untouched for a 63-yard touchdown just ninety-one seconds into the game.

A 36-yard kickoff return by Thomas from the 12 put the Steelers in good field position at their 48. John Henry Johnson went around right end for 14 yards, and Hoak scooted around left end for 9. Johnson went over left guard for 8 yards and a first down at the St. Louis 16, and an offside penalty moved the ball to the 11. Hoak and Johnson each lost a yard, and a pass slipped off Preston Carpenter's fingers, forcing Parker to settle for a 21-yard field goal by Michaels to make it 7–3.

The teams exchanged punts, and on second-and-9 from the Steeler 36, Thomas intercepted a pass intended for Childress at the 33, where the Steeler defensive back was downed. Ed Brown stuck to the ground, alternating his two backs. Johnson got 8 yards to the 41 and, two plays later, went off right tackle for 6, to the Cards' 49. Hoak ran around left end for 7 yards, but John Henry Johnson lost 7 while trying to go around the left side on the final play of the first quarter. On third-and-12, Brown hit Dial for 11 yards to the 33, shy of the first down, so Michaels kicked a 40-yard field goal to bring the Steelers within 7–6.

The second quarter was a study in defenses that wouldn't budge—as if two opposing pitchers in a baseball game were working on a shutout. "Pittsburgh's defense turned the screws of the vise and gave nothing away," Riger wrote.[24] For the first six series, neither team could gain a single first down. For the first five series, neither team could complete a pass. The quarterbacks were pressured, and the running backs couldn't find any holes. On one third-and-8 situation, Charley Johnson was sacked by John Baker and Krupa for a loss of 9 yards, back to the Cardinal 9. Pittsburgh's good field position at the Cardinal 47 after the punt was quickly nullified when Brown was dumped by tackle Don Owens for a 12-yard loss, and again by Owens for a loss of 10 yards, leaving the Steelers with third-and-32 from their 31. A screen to John Henry Johnson gained only 9 yards, so Brown punted.

Charley Johnson, on third-and-13 from his 22, threw for Randle, but Thomas intercepted for the second time, at the Steeler 48, and returned the ball to the Cardinal 18. On third-and-5, Brown targeted Dial but Wilson stole the ball at the goal line and returned it to the 12 before the two-minute warning was given.

After six punts in the quarter, the Cards finally got a drive moving. Triplett went off left tackle for 8 yards, and Mal Hammack hit the same spot for 9 more. Johnson hit Conrad crossing over the middle for 15 yards to the 45 and then hit the flanker for 14 more, to the Steeler 41, with twenty seconds left before halftime. But Russell broke up a pass over the middle at the last instant, and then the rookie linebacker intercepted a pass intended for Childress and returned it 6 yards to the 41, leaving seven seconds on the clock, time for one incomplete bomb by Ed Brown before the half.

It wasn't unreasonable to figure that neither team would score a touchdown in the second half, and that field goals would determine whether the Cards' 7–6 lead would hold up. At halftime, Ed Brown was two of eight passing for 19 yards, and Charley Johnson was three of thirteen for 28 yards. Even though the pace of the game resembled a sumo match, "the tension was exhausting."[25]

The Steelers took the second-half kickoff but were forced to punt. Starting on their 34, the Cards were stopped for no gain on two runs, but on third down, Childress took a pass in the flat and ran 13 yards to the 47. On second-and-9 at the 48, Randle took a pass 37 yards before Keys stopped him at the 15. Tackle Ernie McMillan was called for holding on the next play, and after rookie halfback Bob Paremore gained 10 yards, Tarasovic dropped Triplett on a reverse for a yard loss on third-and-15 from the 21. Jim Bakken kicked a 28-yard field goal to make it 10–6, halfway through the period, "and some Steeler fans were beginning to think that their heroes were through."[26]

The outlook worsened on the next series when John Henry Johnson lost 2 yards on a pitchout and then gained 9 on a reception. He was forced to the sidelines with a twisted ankle, leaving second-year fullback Bob Ferguson with a big chance to resuscitate a career that had threatened to wind up as a flop.

The Steelers' ignominious history of losing was rivaled only by their tradition of wasting their No. 1 draft picks—when they had a first-round pick, that is. In 1956 the Steelers held the "bonus" choice, the first pick of the draft, which the league awarded on a rotating basis. The Steelers picked Gary Glick of Colorado A&M, passing up a running back from Penn State named Lenny Moore, destined for the Hall of Fame. The next year the Steelers picked quarterback Len Dawson, only to trade him eventually. In '58, '59, and '61, they didn't have a No. 1 pick because Parker had traded each away to San Francisco.

In the 1962 draft, the Steelers selected Ferguson, the two-time unanimous All-America fullback and Heisman runner-up from Ohio State. He had a running style that was blunt and perfectly suited to Parker's offensive strategy. "Fergy just runs right over people," wrote a Chicago sportswriter.[27]

Ferguson was a highly coveted prize. In three seasons at Ohio State, in the years before freshmen were allowed to play, he gained 2,162 yards for a 5.1 average and scored twenty-six touchdowns. He lost only 6 yards as a ball carrier during his collegiate career. As a senior, he became the first black player to win the prestigious Maxwell Trophy.

But Ferguson's rookie year turned out to be disastrous. "Ferguson blundered badly in early trials and soon found himself ostracized."[28] His performance was bad enough, but his lack of commitment turned him into the butt of jokes. During an off-season dinner, receiver Buddy Dial made a crack that the Steelers were saving Ferguson for "the Olympic sleeping team."[29]

When Ferguson first reported to the Steelers, it seemed as if he'd forgotten everything he had learned about football. "Last year Ferguson couldn't catch, he couldn't block and he didn't know his plays," Parker recalled during training camp in '63. "He'd stand around by himself looking like he was lost."[30]

He was. Because of his participation in college all-star games, Ferguson said, he struggled to catch up with the Steeler system. He ran the ball only twenty times and gained only 37 yards as a rookie. But Parker didn't give up on him. At his second training camp, Ferguson looked better in every area of his game. "And he's got a better disposition, a better attitude," the coach said. Ferguson owned up to his failure in his first year and insisted that he was determined to prove himself worthy of a No. 1 pick. "I know I can play professional football," he said. "I have to show them."[31]

John Henry Johnson had gained 46 yards against the Cardinals in the first half, but the total wasn't as important as the runner's willingness to take punishment and keep pounding away against a defense that seemed designed by a chess master. Whatever Ferguson was going to gain against the Cardinal defense, he would have to earn every inch.

After Johnson's reception, St. Louis held Pittsburgh a yard short of a first down. Paremore, a back with 9.3 speed, signaled for a fair catch on Brown's 31-yard punt but fumbled, and offensive end John Powers recovered for the Steelers at the St. Louis 43. Ferguson gained 4 yards, but Brown threw incomplete on third down, setting up a Michaels field goal attempt from the 47. It fell short.

The Steelers weren't moving the ball, but the Cardinals were having just as frustrating a time. After his touchdown run, Triplett picked up only 10 more yards on eleven carries, and Childress would finish with a total of 45 yards on thirteen carries. Charley Johnson's best weapon turned out to be Conrad. The sixth-year back from Texas A&M caught a pass for 13 yards on first down, then caught one for 14 yards on third-and-4 from the 39. A 24-yard catch by Conrad was nullified by a holding call, so on fourth-and-14 from the 49, Jerry Stovall punted into the end zone as the third quarter wound down.

The Cards continued to torment Brown. Defensive end Joe Robb nailed the QB for a 13-yard loss on third-and-10 from the 44 on the first series of the fourth quarter, and Brown followed with a 52-yard punt.

The Steeler defensive line was looking a lot like it did against the Giants, and two players in particular were raising havoc. "Nowhere in the National Football League," wrote *Post-Gazette* columnist Al Abrams, "is there a pair of football players who play with more zest and verve than the Pittsburgh Steelers' 'Larrupin' Lous'—Michaels and Cordileone."[32] They came through at a critical point with time slinking away on the Steelers.

With the Cards facing second-and-5 from their 25, Michaels stuffed Childress for no gain. Then, on third down, Cordileone, ferocious while rushing the passer but otherwise "always with a grin splitting his puss," crashed through and dumped Johnson for a 10-yard loss.[33]

Keys returned Stovall's punt 5 yards to the Steeler 44, and then Hoak and Ferguson began crunching up yardage. Ferguson, "with two men on his back, bulled for 11 yards" to the Cardinal 36.[34] After Hoak gained 3 yards, Ferguson picked up 8 for a first down at the 25. On second-and-9, Dial made "the picture play of the game."[35] Lined up on the right, he made a deep cut across the middle, then leaped, snagged the ball, and landed on his head with the ball secured in his right arm for a 16-yard catch that put Pittsburgh on the 8.

Hoak picked up 2 yards. On second down Robb dumped Brown at the 15 but the defensive end was flagged for being offside, giving the Steelers first-and-goal at the 3. Cardinal assistant coach Chuck Drulis, the man who helped pioneer the safety blitz with Wilson, later called the penalty the turning point of the game. Hoak went off right tackle for 2 yards and then, behind "a punishing block" by Ferguson, rammed into the end zone to put the Steelers ahead, 13–10, with seven minutes left.[36]

Paremore's rookie troubles continued. After the kickoff, he was the twelfth man when the Cards were penalized for having too many men on the field, backing them up at their 10. On the other side of the ball, the kid from Missouri who had wanted no part of a professional football career was looking like a veteran. He held Triplett to a gain of 1, and after Cordileone and Baker dropped Johnson for a 6-yard loss at the 5, Russell held Triplett to a 6-yard reception on third-and-19. Stovall's 34-yard punt set up the Steelers on the St. Louis 45 with 4:36 left in the game.

Hoak and Ferguson got some hard-earned yardage, but a holding call set them back to the Cardinal 48. Dial gained 20 yards with a catch down the right sideline, and Hoak went around right end for 12 yards, setting up Michaels for a 21-yard field goal to make it 16–10 with a minute and forty-five seconds remaining, still plenty of time for a quarterback of Johnson's caliber to drive down the field.

Michaels boomed the kickoff into the end zone. Johnson dropped back on first down from the 20, only to have Cordileone hit his arm and cause a fumble. Michaels, "up to his 18-inch neck in practically every defensive play," recovered on the 12.[37]

Ferguson, "using his 220 pounds like a demolition expert uses a headache ball," picked up 6, 2, and the final 4 yards for the touchdown that sealed the 23–10 victory with fifty-five seconds to go.[38] In only a quarter and a half of play, Ferguson had gained 58 yards on thirteen carries, and Hoak got 85—as usual, the hard way—on twenty-five carries.

The only drama left in the final minute was when one of the "Larrupin' Lous"—Michaels—got in an altercation with Ernie McMillan after hitting the Cards' six-foot-six, 255-pound tackle in the jaw with a forearm. Michaels insisted the blow was legal. "What can you do on defense if you can't hit a guy with your forearm?" he protested.[39]

Informed by a sportswriter that Michaels had accused McMillan of slugging the Steeler lineman, the Cardinal tackle barked, "He was the one who was slugging. I was only defending myself."[40]

Both players were thrown out of the game, an automatic $100 fine. Slugging it out with an offensive tackle didn't worry Michaels, but the prospect of explaining the deduction in his paycheck to his mother did. "She's going to be awfully mad when she gets my check," he said. "She's going to want to know how come I'm punching somebody when it costs a hundred bucks."[41] Worse yet, it looked as if it could mean a week without a shipment of Mom's kielbasa.

The Steelers had witnessed two developments on this day to boost their optimism: the play of Ferguson and Russell. Ferguson looked as if he were grinding out yardage for Ohio State again. Russell was tested often but withstood the pressure and, with Reger out, "proved a fine replacement."[42] With all his superstitions, Parker was not about to tamper with success, even if it meant keeping a rookie in the lineup. "If we won or tied, he wasn't going to change the group," Russell said years later.[43]

A 2–0–1 record was a modest accomplishment measured against the Steelers' ultimate goal, but it wasn't just the best start in Parker's seven years in Pittsburgh; it was the first time the franchise had gone unbeaten after three games since the team went 1–0–2 in the first three weeks in 1940. The only better start came in 1936, the only year the Steelers won their first three games. If Michaels had made one more extra point in the opener, the '63 squad would have been 3–0. Steelers fans had every right to believe that this might be a special year, unless more bad breaks awaited them—like a lingering injury to a key player like John Henry Johnson.

No matter that it was only September, commented *Press* sportswriter Pat Livingston. "Whether the players, or Coach Buddy Parker, like it or not, the Steelers must be regarded as serious contenders today." It wasn't a pretty victory; it was a typical meat grinder of a Steeler game. "You can't look good against those unorthodox defenses," Parker said. "They make anybody look bad."[44]

The Cardinals grumbled about the officiating and were as grudging in their praise of Pittsburgh as they had been stingy on defense. "Sarcasm and bitterness hung like musty ornaments in the rancid St. Louis dressing room." Lemm complained about a call in the first quarter when Hoak lost possession of the ball and Wilson picked it up and headed for the end zone, only to find that the officials had called the play dead. "There was no whistle," the coach said.[45]

Johnson wound up fifteen of twenty-eight for 198 yards, but his three interceptions hurt the team. "Charley Johnson was way off today," Lemm said, "and this cost us the chance of winning."[46]

After Triplett's touchdown run, the Steelers held St. Louis to a field goal over the next fifty-eight minutes and twenty-nine seconds, but Lemm was less than generous in his praise for his opponent. "We knew the Steeler defense was tough," he said, "but they didn't do anything that surprised us."[47]

Ernie Stautner had experienced a lifetime of losing in Pittsburgh and had seen some moments of promise, but this team was different. The spirit, he said, was the best in his fourteen years with the Steelers. The way the team hung on during the afternoon was as revealing to him as the final score. "It's easy to go out there and rip when everything is going your way," he said. "It's something else to play your game when you're behind for 50 minutes and then force them to crack."[48]

But the Cardinals had made an impression on the Steelers. "They're tougher than the Giants," said Pittsburgh guard Ron Stehouwer.[49] And the Cards wouldn't have to wait long for another crack at Parker's team; in two weeks, the Steelers would travel to St. Louis for the rematch.

Meanwhile, 150 miles to the west, the Cleveland Browns, with "the most productive attack in the National Football League," relied on their defense to grind out a 20–6 victory over the Los Angeles Rams.[50] The Browns sat atop the Eastern Conference at 3–0, but detractors were not overwhelmed with Cleveland's wins, which included decisions over Washington and Dallas. The real test would come in six days, on a Saturday night, when the Steelers would travel to Municipal Stadium, on the shores of Lake Erie, with more than 80,000 fans howling wilder than the winds off Canada in January.

GAME 4

It took only two exhibition games for the glow to fade from Buddy Parker's big off-season trade in 1962.

After trading a first-round draft pick to the Chicago Bears for thirty-three-year-old quarterback Ed Brown on April 4, Parker hailed his acquisition as "one of the best quarterbacks in the league." Brown was an ex-Marine, a two-time selection to the Pro Bowl, and "a whiz at finding receivers with deep passes." More important, Brown was "a Parker-type quarterback."[1]

The incumbent Bobby Layne had taken a pounding over fourteen seasons, so Parker not only brought in Brown as insurance but promised the nine-year veteran a shot at winning the starting job. "I know that I'm going to try like hell to win it," Brown vowed before the start of training camp.[2]

Brown got his chance on Saturday night, August 18, the second game on the 1962 preseason schedule, when the Steelers traveled to Cleveland to face the Browns in the second game of the NFL's first doubleheader. Before a crowd of 77,683, the Steelers lost, 33–10, prompting Parker to criticize virtually the whole squad, but singling out one player. "I was especially dissatisfied with Ed Brown's quarterbacking," Parker said.[3]

Brown didn't win the starting job, but his strong performance at the end of the season when Layne was disabled helped validate Parker's confidence in the heir apparent. Moreover, Brown's showing made the coach feel more comfortable that the team would be OK without Layne, then the NFL record-holder for most touchdown passes, pass attempts, completions, and yards gained passing.

The ugly sight of Layne getting booed, as well as injured, in the November 1962 victory over the Redskins had convinced Parker to talk his quarterback into retiring at season's end.[4] Not even a stark contrast in performances by the two quarterbacks in the so-called Runner-Up Bowl in January could dissuade Parker from his conviction that it was time for Layne to quit.

Brown labored in the game, hitting five of twelve passes and throwing a costly interception that led to a Detroit touchdown just before halftime. Despite chants of "We want Layne!" in the stands, Parker held out the future Hall of Famer until halfway through the fourth quarter. It was Layne who put a scare into Detroit as he "pitched with his old-time skill" to rally the Steelers, even though his potential game-tying drive stalled at the Lions' 21.[5] Two days later, Parker admitted that he had "reluctantly suggested" that Layne retire. As for Brown, despite the unimpressive showing, Parker said that the ex-Bear "should be much better next year."[6]

Hall of Fame quarterback Sammy Baugh had watched as Layne broke Baugh's records, and Slingin' Sammy believed that his fellow Texan wasn't ready for retirement. "He still has a good year left," Baugh said at a gathering of the Touchdown Club of Columbus, Ohio, weeks after Parker was ushering Layne out.[7]

But Parker had a close-up of how much pain Layne had endured. "No one really understood what Layne went through as a player," the coach said years later. "It wasn't publicized but he had bursitis in his throwing arm right on from college. I've seen him on the bench while our defense was on the field when he couldn't raise his arm to his nose, but he would go back and win for us." Parker had watched Layne get blasted—by both opponents and jaded fans, whom the coach felt confused an overthrown pass with the quarterback using his discretion to throw the ball away when under too much pressure. Not only did Layne have a remarkable tolerance for physical pain, but he had a skin thicker than an official Duke football. "Layne took more shots than anyone I know," Parker said. "And he took more criticism."[8]

As training camp picked up in the summer of '63, Parker began to regret his decision, and so he asked Layne's friend and former roommate, Ernie Stautner, to approach Layne about coming back for one more year. Layne declined, citing other obligations.[9]

In the preseason opener against the Packers, Brown had "a rather lame passing night," leading Parker to promise that third-year quarterback Terry Nofsinger would see a lot of action against the Eagles the next week.[10] On the first play from scrimmage, Nofsinger hit Red Mack with an 80-yard touchdown pass, but Brown "sparkled" in the 24–13 victory over Philly.[11] A

17–14 loss to the Colts left Parker so dejected about the team, it's a wonder he didn't threaten to quit. "I am really disgusted," he said.[12]

The Steelers lost to the Lions three times in '62—in preseason, the regular-season opener, and the Playoff Bowl—so even a 22–7 exhibition victory in Detroit at the end of August 1963 had to provide Parker with some personal satisfaction. The night was bittersweet, as the Lions honored Layne at halftime and retired his No. 22 jersey. Brown banged up his shoulder during the game, but X-rays were negative. In the preseason finale, a 16–7 victory over the Browns, Brown hit nine of seventeen passes for 155 yards. Any victory over Cleveland was sweet.

Whether or not three victories reassured Parker that his offense was in capable hands, he was committed to Brown. Brown had a stronger arm and nearly as much NFL experience as his predecessor, but he was no Bobby Layne, and no one knew that better than Parker. "I think Buddy just recognized there was something lacking without Bobby," Stautner said years later. "Buddy knew we had the players to make a run at the division, but we needed the take-charge guy in the driver's seat. . . . Bobby had the extra something that made the difference in close games."[13]

The two quarterbacks were opposites in temperament. Layne was gregarious, brash, and charismatic. He would cuss out teammates for missing assignments and threaten opponents who played dirty—or he might take matters into his own hands. "You heard what he did to get Ed Sprinkle one year," Lou Cordileone said. Sprinkle was a defensive end for the Bears from 1944 to 1955. He stood six foot one and weighed only 206 pounds, but he had a reputation as one of the roughest players in the league. Teammates and opponents knew him as "the Claw" for the way he snagged quarterbacks and runners, but his notoriety increased when *Collier's* dubbed him "the Meanest Man in Pro Football" in 1950.[14]

"This is the story I got, and I think it's true," Cordileone said. "He came in and hit Bobby when he shouldn't have hit him. So, one or two plays later, Bobby tells the guys, 'Let the guy in,' and they let him in and he took the ball and he threw it right in his fuckin' jaw and busted his whole face up. In those days they didn't have face masks. Bobby was a competitor, boy, I'll tell ya."[15]

Layne insisted that the only thing about him that was exaggerated more than his nighttime carousing was his reputation for losing his temper and chewing out his own receivers. "I have never once in my life got on a ballplayer for dropping a pass like a lot of people think," he told Myron Cope in an interview. Yet in an article Layne coauthored with Murray Olderman four years earlier, the quarterback recalled how he reacted to rookie end Jimmy Orr, out of the University of Georgia, dropping a long pass in a 17–6 loss to the Giants. "When he came back to the huddle I told him, 'If you drop another pass on me, you Georgia so-and-so, I'll kill you with my own hands.'" Layne added, "I was only speaking figuratively, of course. Jimmy's too good to do away with and he's one of my best friends."[16]

Orr took no offense. "Bobby and I hit it along pretty good," Orr said. "If you went out with him at night, he threw to you during the day."[17]

For Layne, the only thing that could compare to beating the clock with a game-winning drive was drinking the night away with a bunch of teammates at a hot nightspot with a swinging band. He would round up players, vets and rookies alike, blacks and whites, to make the party more fun and build camaraderie.

"Bobby was our man," Cordileone said.

We used to get together and play poker every Thursday night at Bobby's house. He and Ernie rented a house. We used to go over there—me, Bobby, John Henry Johnson, Charlie Bradshaw, once in a while Ernie would play. We'd have five or six guys and we'd sit there all night, till practice the next morning, and play. We used to order food from Dante's, and you couldn't imagine the food that came in there. It was unbelievable. We used to sit and eat and then we'd leave in the morning to go to practice, because the next day—the Friday practice—was very easy. It was just like forty-five minutes, and then we'd go home and that was it. That was the end of it until the game Sunday.[18]

Except for Bobby Layne. For Layne, the week was just beginning.

And when the QB from Lubbock spoke, on the field or off it, players listened. "When Bobby said block, you blocked. When Bobby said drink, you drank," former Lions teammate Yale Lary said.[19] Layne built his reputation on delivering in the clutch, and teammates and coaches knew he was good for his word. "He'd get in a huddle, he'd get down on his knee, he'd say, 'If you sunuvabitches block, we got a touchdown on this play.' And you believed it," said Preston Carpenter, who played tight end for the Steelers from 1960 to 1963. "He was a leader on the field and off the field."[20]

With a little over two minutes left in the 1953 championship game, two days after Christmas, Layne huddled his Detroit teammates with the ball on the Cleveland 33 and the Browns leading, 16–10. He asked receiver Jim Doran if he could beat his man and then called the play. "Okay, men.

Let's run a Nine Up . . . and block them sons of bitches for me." Layne lobbed one of his characteristically wobbly passes to Doran for a 33-yard touchdown pass that gave Detroit a 17–16 win and coach Buddy Parker his second consecutive NFL title.[21]

Brown could not compete with Layne in terms of personality, and he couldn't match the Texan's cachet on the playing field. Layne had led the Lions to two straight championships, lost a third, and pointed Detroit to another title before sustaining a season-ending injury. Brown had led the Bears to the title game in 1956, when they got whipped by the Giants, 47–7. Steeler teammates knew he had talent, but not everyone was convinced he had the intangibles Layne possessed.

"Bobby Layne was like Bart Starr," said wide receiver Red Mack, who played with both. "When he came in the huddle he could call a quarterback sneak on third down-and-15; nobody would question it. But if Ed Brown called it, you'd be saying, 'Wait a minute. We can't run that play.' You knew when Bobby Layne got up to the line of scrimmage that he was going to come up with something that was going to get us 15 yards. You knew that."[22]

Mack got a harsh lesson from Layne one time about following orders from the quarterback. Layne called the play, and once the defense shifted, so did Mack. "They moved into a zone coverage, so I broke the pattern off," he said. "I got back to the huddle, and Bobby Layne chewed my butt out. He told me, 'I don't care if you've got to run all the way to the shithouse. Complete the pattern.' He was the kind of guy that knew it was going to be zone [coverage]. He was going to throw the ball to somebody else. He wasn't going to throw it to me. We didn't have that kind of confidence in Brown. At least I didn't."[23]

Neither did defensive back Brady Keys. "He was not a leader," Keys said. "You could never win with Ed Brown. He wasn't smart—couldn't read defenses, couldn't call audibles. Bobby Layne, he would call audibles and win the game for you. He could read the defense and do those things."[24]

No situation seemed to daunt Layne. He came into games well prepared both from film study and from work on the practice field. Art Rooney Jr. was amazed at how Layne showed up early for practice and stayed late, working with his receivers. If he ever felt pressure, he kept it well hidden. And his confidence was unshakable. "He's always loved a challenge," said former college roommate Rooster Andrews. "And he's just as competitive playing golf or on a fishing trip as he was when he was quarterbacking. Hell, he goes grocery shopping, and he thinks he's the best damned shopper in Safeway."[25]

"He was the baddest-best pro football player of my time," said Alex

Karras, who was a rookie out of Iowa in 1958 when he met Layne at the Lions' training camp. "He feared nobody."[26]

When Layne went out on the town, his free spirit flowed as easily as the liquor. During his career, he enjoyed a reputation as the doggone best party-goer in the NFL, hands down. And when Bobby Layne was hosting the festivities, everyone was invited. "He'd go into a place and say, 'I don't want anybody to buy any drinks while I'm in here,'" Carpenter recalled. "Nobody could buy a drink, even if he didn't know him."[27]

Not long after linebacker Joe Schmidt was drafted by the Lions, Layne found out that the front office had hired a man to investigate the quarterback's nocturnal ramblings. "Bobby came bursting into the room, all aglow," Schmidt recalled at a Touchdown Club gathering.

> "Hey, Joe," he said. "We've got a live one. Let's lead him [on] a chase."
>
> I felt sorry for the man who had to follow Bobby around. Afterward, I learned that he had been a survivor of the Bataan death march. He followed Bobby from bar to bar until he was worn to a nub. Then he made his report to Eddie Anderson, the president of the football team.
>
> "I quit, Mr. Anderson," he said. "Layne is too tough for me. I can't take it. I'd rather go back to Bataan."[28]

Layne's exploits, both in two-minute drills and at after-hours nightclubs, became legendary. Some were embellished and refined into myth. Paul Hornung recalled one rumor that he and Layne were picked up drunk in a doorway in downtown Green Bay, singing together, at 5:30 in the morning. "I didn't know Bobby then," Hornung said, "and if I did, you can bet your life we wouldn't have been picked up in a doorway."[29]

No one had the superhuman recuperative powers of Layne. Asked how he could recover and play a game with not much more than a catnap for rest, Layne replied, "I sleep fast!"[30] "Unbelievable," Cordileone said. "The only guy I've seen in my life to get completely shit faced, lay down, and get up a half hour later like he never had a drink. I mean, he was unbelievable. Booze never bothered him."[31]

At least not enough to keep him from winning football games. On the eve of the Steelers' last game of 1958, a Saturday matinee against the Cardinals in Pittsburgh, Layne was preparing in his usual fashion, so the story goes, with a night on the town. Friday night extended into Saturday morning, and Layne was supposedly spotted leading the band at a private club around 9 A.M. Wherever he'd been, Layne made his way to Pitt Stadium, suited up, trotted gingerly onto an icy field, and hit twenty-three of forty-nine passes for 409 yards and two touchdowns. He also ran for a 17-yard touchdown, and the Steelers finished 7–4–1 with a 38–21 victory. The only thing he did not do on the field that day, evidently, was lead the band at halftime.[32]

The most infamous and oft-told tale about Layne took place off the field in 1961. It didn't happen on the eve of a game, as legend had it; it happened on a Monday night, the day after Layne threw four touchdown passes—tying Baugh's career record—in leading the Steelers to a 30–14 victory in Washington. The front-page headline of Tuesday afternoon's *Press* read, "Trolley Intercepts Bobby Layne's Pass." Years later, Layne would laugh as he recounted how he ran into "that parked swerving streetcar" but, of course, it was No. 22 who, while driving teammate Tom Tracy's car, swerved into a No. 85 Bedford trolley, stopped at Sixth and Wylie, around 2:30 A.M. on a Tuesday. The operator was not hurt, but Layne sustained a cut over his left eyebrow and was taken to the hospital for X-rays. Clearly, he would have been better off with Alex Karras driving.[33] The incident became an everlasting funny story in the arsenal of Layne anecdotes, but it could have turned out badly. Three days later, a man and woman were killed instantly when their automobile collided head on with a trolley in Wilkinsburg.[34] Almost a year to the day later, a teenager commandeered a trolley in Philadelphia on a Sunday and drove it five miles across town without any mishap, clanging the bell and stopping to take on riders, informing them, "I'm not charging any fares tonight, so get aboard."[35]

The entire football world knew of Bobby Layne the legend, but just what Layne was like as a person wasn't clear. "I didn't know him too well as a man," Karras said. "Maybe nobody did."[36]

Layne could throw a baseball nearly as well as he could a football. He loved to drink Cutty Sark and he loved to sing the American traditional song "Ida Red," according to Karras. Layne made a habit of befriending rookie players and, like Karras, they would drink with the quarterback and drive him to bars and nightclubs. One night while Karras was behind the wheel, Layne, "in a drunken stupor," told the lineman about his father's death. According to Layne's biographer, Layne, his parents, and his two sisters had squeezed into their tiny coupe for a short trip, when Layne's father slumped back after apparently suffering a heart attack. Layne, who was sitting in the back seat behind his father, was pinned in the rear of the car. "I'm not sure he ever got over being trapped like that when his father died," said Layne's wife, Carol.[37]

Layne turned silent as Karras drove. "Then he suddenly said he didn't like the dark," Karras said. "He was too scared to sleep, he said." No wonder Layne liked to hang around with Big Daddy Lipscomb and buy scotch for the ferocious lineman with the soft heart.[38]

Brown, by comparison, was more of a loner, although he hung out with his teammates at Dante's and roomed with Lou Cordileone, and then with Dick Haley. "He was really subdued," said Haley. "He was a funny guy," said Mack, who averaged 24.7 yards on his twenty-five receptions during the '63 season. "You couldn't get close to him."[39]

The son of a jeweler and watchmaker, Ed Brown earned the nickname "All-Around Brown" while playing quarterback and kicking and punting for the University of San Francisco. In his senior year he led the Dons to a 9–0 record, but the team was denied a bowl invitation because it refused to drop two black players, Ollie Matson and Burl Toler, from the team for the postseason game, which was a customary concession at the time. Nine players from that team had NFL careers, including Toler and Matson, and three became Hall of Famers: Matson, Gino Marchetti, and Bob St. Clair.

With his thick black hair, cleft chin, and sober gaze, Brown bore a resemblance to the actor Clint Walker, and the bachelor quarterback had a reputation for being popular with women. Any quarterback who succeeded Layne was bound to pale in comparison with the charismatic Texan, but Brown wasn't about to change his style. He knew himself, and he made no apologies for his temperament.

Halfway through the '63 season, days after turning thirty-four, Brown was asked why he wasn't more demonstrative on the field. "There's more to this game of football than showing a lot of fire and fight," Brown replied.

I'm not built like some guys, I guess. I do my job the quiet way.

When you're around as long as I have [been], you learn to take things in stride. Maybe I am too phlegmatic out there. Maybe I don't get mad enough. What good is it to be that way? My job is to run the team the best I know how and to help win games.[40]

As if it weren't daunting enough to succeed a quarterback with Hall of Fame credentials, Brown soon found Layne watching over his shoulder—literally. Three days after the win over the Giants, the Steelers announced that Layne would work in the scouting booth—"the coop atop the roof" of Forbes Field—where he would phone in suggestions to the bench. In the second period of the St. Louis game, he phoned in his observations on the Cardinals' defense. "They're jumping into the gap. Maybe he [Brown] better work on a long count," Layne drawled. Not long after, he phoned Mike Nixon, the backfield coach, and barked, "Tell Brown to get rid of the ball a little faster. He's giving their backs time to move and cover our receivers." Near the end of the quarter, with Buddy Dial speeding into the end zone, Brown hesitated, and safety Larry Wilson recovered in time to make the interception.[41]

It was a working arrangement that was bound to produce friction over the season. "I can remember hearing that Brown was asked to talk to Bobby on the headphones," Andy Russell said, "and he threw the phone down and said, 'You're full of shit,' and walked away. There was a little animosity between the two—or irritation—one quarterback picking on another."[42]

Layne had been acclaimed as a master of late-game heroics. A couple of other quarterbacks in the division drew reverence by earning their masters—degrees, that is—in off-the-field career development. As October broke, Brown had already led the Steelers over the Cards and Charley Johnson, who, not even twenty-five, was hailed as "the erudite St. Louis Cardinal physicist."[43] Next, Brown had to go up against Frank Ryan, who, at twenty-seven, had a master's degree in math and was studying at Rice for his PhD and was regarded as "another quarterback whose intelligence hovers around the genius range." One story in a football magazine featuring the two quarterbacks was titled "Inside Football's Biggest Brains."[44] Brown, in his tenth year, was more likely to be given the tag "journeyman," but, as phlegmatic as he was, was not likely to complain about it.

As the Steelers began gearing up for the Browns, Cordileone, for one, was not awed by Ryan's resume. "He can't play with a slide rule," the defensive tackle sniffed. "Did you ever see a mathematician without a slide rule?"[45]

The Browns seemed to be energized. For the first time since the team's inaugural season of 1946, Paul Brown was not on the Cleveland sidelines calling plays. Art Modell had fired the fifty-four-year-old coach in the second week of January and replaced him with assistant Blanton Collier. On January 10, the same day that Buddy Parker settled on a one-year contract with Art Rooney, and civic leaders unveiled a model of the North Side stadium that was to be built at a cost of $45,170,000 and finished by 1966, Paul Brown made his first comments since being fired. "It did come as a shock and surprise to me," he admitted.[46]

Jim Brown and his teammates were playing as if they had been liberated from the constraints of Paul Brown's coaching. Ryan's emergence had given the team another dimension to their powerful offense. No longer did Cleveland employ a strategy of simply handing off to Jimmy Brown and letting him ramble for 135 or 150 yards. Ryan, after having taken the starting job from Jim Ninowski, ranked as the No. 2 quarterback in the league, behind Y. A. Tittle, with forty-one completions in sixty-four attempts for 674 yards, six touchdowns, and four interceptions in three games. Ed Brown ranked eighth.

Jim Brown, "running as he never ran before," had scored six touchdowns and racked up 489 yards rushing on fifty-seven carries—an average of 8.6 yards a carry—and was 262 yards ahead of the Cards' Joe Childress, in second place. In fact, during the entire '62 season, only twelve backs in the league had done better over fourteen games than Brown had in three.[47]

The Steelers' running attack was clicking, too, and Pittsburgh's domination of the Giants impressed Gene Ward of the *New York Daily News* enough for him to rate John Henry Johnson and Dick Hoak as the top backfield combination in the league.[48] But the ankle Johnson injured against the Cardinals proved to be problematic, and at Wednesday's practice he and linebacker George Tarasovic were limping. Trainer Roger McGill said he expected both to be ready for the Browns, but the next day it was clear that Johnson's swollen ankle would prevent him from playing. "I don't see how he can," Buddy Parker said. "He can hardly walk."[49]

That meant that Bob Ferguson, who had sparked the second-half surge against the Cards, would start. Johnson's absence also meant that if the running game faltered, the pressure would fall on Ed Brown to move the Steelers.

Whatever Ed Brown lacked in personality, the team was making up for it collectively. He may not have been the inspirational type, but neither was Parker. The other thirty-six players on the roster, aside from Brown, found motivation from within or from each other. No team in the NFL quite reflected its plucky population and grimy environment quite so much as the underdog Pittsburgh Steelers, and no one fit the role of overachiever better than Hoak. Hoak was a seventh-round draft pick in 1961 out of Penn State, where he'd played quarterback. He was a local kid, from nearby Jeanette, an overachiever without great athletic gifts, but a guy with a blue-collar worker's mentality. "He digs in there," Parker said. "He's not afraid to hit." Hoak was "an inconspicuous introvert" during the first two weeks of camp in his rookie season, but he had "a flair for doing his job well—if not spectacularly."[50] He stepped in for the injured Tom Tracy in the preseason opener and had fourteen carries for 61 yards—eight fewer than the Colts' team total—and earned a start in the next exhibition game.

Two seasons later, Hoak was an unlikely candidate to rise among the NFL rushing leaders. "Off his physical appearance, he doesn't impress one as a power runner but he runs with as much power as anybody on the team," beat writer Pat Livingston wrote. "He also has a deceptive gait that throws a defender off stride, a quality that he substitutes effectively for speed."[51] All in all, a euphemistic description of an undersized (although listed by the Steelers as five foot eleven, 190 pounds) and slow runner, but one who had earned the respect of teammates and opponents alike for going all-out on every play. "If the Steelers had 37 guys like Hoak, we'd win the championship for sure," center Madison Monroe "Buzz" Nutter said.[52]

Brady Keys, a fourteenth-round pick the year before Hoak arrived, was an unheralded player who turned into a relentless cover man and daring tackler. He wasn't the most gifted defensive back, but he was indispensable to the Steelers. He was a fighter, a toiler who didn't get a lot of praise or recognition, but he was someone who wouldn't quit, and those were qualities Pittsburgh fans could admire. "I'm not a spectacular type of ball player," he admitted. "I never have a bad day and I never have a great day. Therefore, I get no credit at all."[53]

He could have been speaking for all his teammates, but the sum of the scrapyard parts was making the '63 squad click. "There are no stars on this ball club," one anonymous veteran observed, "unless it would be John Henry Johnson. It's a team made up of 37 good, solid athletes who play together. Every one of them has a weakness but, playing together, the team as a unit can cover up every one of those weaknesses."[54]

On Friday the Steelers left by bus for Cleveland. On Saturday afternoon, Zsa Zsa Gabor and her husband, a business acquaintance of the University of Pittsburgh's vice-chancellor, showed up among some 22,000 fans to watch the Panthers beat California, 35–15, at Pitt Stadium. Zsa Zsa left at half-time to catch a flight to New York. That evening, 86,684 fans—the biggest crowd in Cleveland football history—turned out at the lakefront stadium for the 8 P.M. Steeler game. A year earlier, at the exhibition doubleheader, one writer compared the atmosphere to New Year's Eve in Times Square, and a regular-season Steelers-Browns game on a Saturday night had to match—or surpass—that frantic spirit. It was a game that would see the lead change hands seven times and have fans glancing at the clock as if, indeed, the New Year were approaching.[55]

The Steelers took the kickoff and came out throwing. Brown missed Mack deep down the right sideline but, a play later, connected with him on a deep curl for 20 yards at the Steeler 44. Brown was shaken up after running up the middle for 7 yards, so Terry Nofsinger came in and hit Mack down the left sideline for a 27-yard gain to the Cleveland 17. Hoak was stopped at the line, and Ferguson could gain only 5 yards on two carries, so Lou Michaels came on and kicked an 18-yard field goal.

The Browns' mix of running and passing looked unstoppable on their first drive. Jim Brown took a pitch and gained 21 yards on a sweep to the left side. Ryan hit Collins for 12 yards on a slant to the Steeler 49 and, from the 38, connected again for a 21-yard pickup to the 17. Brown gained 9 yards on a sweep to the right side, then burst up the middle, with a block from tackle John Brown, for an 8-yard touchdown to put the Browns ahead, 7–3, with 5:51 left in the first quarter.

Ed Brown returned at quarterback, and the teams exchanged punts. Pittsburgh took over on its 31, and on first down, Brown hooked up with Mack for a 42-yard gain to the Browns' 27. One play later, Brown hit Carpenter, who was Cleveland's No. 1 draft pick in 1956, over the middle for 17 yards to the 9. A pass interference call on Jim Shofner gave the Steelers first-and-goal at the 2, a spot on the field where Pittsburgh sorely needed John Henry Johnson. "He's the only back we have who can jump over the defense on the goal line," Parker said later.[56]

Hoak picked up a yard before getting stuffed by tackles Jim Kanicki and Frank Parker and linebacker Galen Fiss on the last play of the first quarter. On second down, Ferguson was thrown for a yard loss by defensive back Bernie Parrish. On third down at the 2, Ferguson picked up a yard but was stopped by linebacker Vince Costello and tackle Bob Gain. "You gotta get something when you get down there," Parker said later. "You can't go away without anything."[57] Parker sent in Michaels for an 8-yard field goal that made it 7–6.

Cleveland couldn't get a first down, so Collins punted to the Steeler 33. Pittsburgh's running game was plugging away, but Ed Brown was finding his groove on the same field where he had performed so poorly in the exhibition game months after his trade. He hit Dial over the middle for 15 yards, to the Cleveland 38, and after two carries by Ferguson, Brown found his flanker again, for 20 yards to the 16. After an incompletion and an 8-yard loss by Ferguson on a swing pass, Brown fired a 24-yard touchdown pass to Dial. With 8:08 left before the half, the Steelers were up, 13–7, and looking as potent on offense as Cleveland.

After a fast start, Ryan was struggling in a first half that would see him hit only four of eleven passes. He had no more of a reputation than Ed Brown as a runner, but the Cleveland quarterback kept a 70-yard drive alive with scrambles of 25 and 14 yards while missing on three passes, giving Cleveland a first-and-goal at the 6. "That Ryan should be a halfback,"

Parker gushed later.⁵⁸ Ryan had put on a similar show in midseason of '62, when he gained 80 yards on nine carries—more than Jim Brown—to salvage a 14–14 tie with the Eagles. As Ryan looked for breakdowns in the Steeler secondary, Joe Krupa and John Baker dumped him for a 9-yard loss. But on second down, Ryan found Collins open for a 15-yard TD that put Cleveland ahead, 14–13, with 2:51 left in the half.

Ed Brown, "threading the needle all night," came right back.⁵⁹ A roughing-the-passer penalty moved the Steelers to the Cleveland 41. After the two-minute warning, Brown hit Dial with a 41-yard touchdown pass to give the Steelers a 20–14 halftime lead. Jim Brown had 73 yards already, but Ed Brown was ten of sixteen for 181 yards, 100 of them by Dial.

It took only three plays after halftime for Jim Brown to go over the 100-yard mark. On third-and-1 at his 32, Brown erupted on a 49-yard run, going off left tackle and cutting back, breaking a tackle by Keys to reach the Steeler 19. Andy Russell, starting at left linebacker, would remember hitting Brown one time that night and seeing "a bright flash of light" on impact. "In the films you saw him just run over me," Russell said.

That hadn't happened to me too many times where somebody really just flat out ran over me. And I hit him where I was supposed to.

People ask me, "Who was the best running back you ever played against?" Unquestionably, Jim Brown. One thing about Brown, he could run over you or he could make you miss. He could do both. Most guys can only do one or the other. That's a rarity. Every time I thought he was going to run over me, he made me miss. And every time I thought he was going to make me miss, he ran over me. How'd he know?⁶⁰

On second-and-10 from the 19, Brown ran up the middle, and Russell tackled him after a 6-yard gain. On third-and-4, the brainy QB Ryan darted 13 yards up the middle for a touchdown to put Cleveland on top, 21–20.

The Steelers took the kickoff and, starting from their 22, hammered away at Cleveland with the speed—and the stubbornness—of a plow horse. Hoak carried eight times on the drive—over left tackle for 7, over right guard for 3, off right tackle for 4. Then he caught a pass for 14 yards, Mack grabbed one over the middle for 13, and Dial nabbed one for 12, with Parrish making the tackle at the 1-yard line.

Who among the 86,684 dared believe that the Browns could make another goal line stand? On first down, Hoak was stopped by linebacker Mike Lucci, Gain, and end Bill Glass. Then Tom Tracy was stopped by Lucci, Gain, and Kanicki. On third down, Hoak was held to no gain by Costello and Fiss. Parker sent in Michaels to kick his second 8-yard field goal, putting Pittsburgh back on top, 23–21, with 3:46 left in the quarter. It could have been a lead as wide as 31–21, if only the Steelers had a runner to hurtle the Browns' goal line defense. "I never like to alibi about injuries because all teams have them," Parker said later. "However, if John Henry Johnson had been available I'm sure we would have had two scores."[61]

Starting from their 25, the Browns were threatening as the third quarter was closing. Jim Brown went 27 yards on a second-down draw play, to Pittsburgh's 48, and a 27-yard pass to Collins on the next play moved the ball to the 21. But Ryan was thrown for a 10-yard loss by Krupa, and when he rushed out of the pocket on third-and-19, he picked up 15 yards but fumbled. Keys recovered on the 8 as the third quarter ended.

It was an unsung second-year defensive back who gave the Browns a lift in the fourth quarter. Bogged down at his 30, Ed Brown got off a 55-yard punt on which Jim Shorter made a "dazzling" 52-yard return to the Steeler 34.[62] On second-and-10 from the 20, Ryan hit Collins in the end zone to give Cleveland a 28–23 lead. There were still twelve minutes left, however, and Ed Brown was hot.

The Steeler quarterback kept firing away. On third-and-11 from his 24, he hit Hoak for 12 yards to the 36. Hoak lost 4 yards on a sweep but Brown found Dial on a hook on the right side for 15 yards to the 47. From the Cleveland 43, Brown hit Mack for 16 yards to the 27. After Ferguson gained 1 yard and Brown threw two incompletions, Michaels tried a 32-yard field goal. It went wide left.

The ball was placed at the 20, which was then the procedure after a missed field goal, with 7:33 left in the game. The Browns were penalized for holding, and Krupa tackled Ryan for a 2-yard loss on third down, leaving Cleveland with fourth-and-13 at the 17. The Steelers were figuring on getting good field position, around midfield with even a modest return, but Collins, who came into the game averaging only 38 yards a punt, boomed a 73-yarder. With a clipping penalty added on, Pittsburgh was backed up to its 10, and about 80,000 people could predict what Ed Brown had to do. Fiss intercepted Brown on second down, setting up a Ryan 19-yard TD pass to Rich Kreitling to make the final 35–23, Browns, in "one of their greatest performances," a Cleveland sportswriter wrote.[63]

The 4–0 Browns remained alone in first place in the Eastern Conference, and the Steelers would slip behind the Giants and Cards, both of whom would win the next day and wind up tied for second place. Jim Brown chewed up the Steelers for 175 yards on twenty-one carries, but Ryan shared the credit for Cleveland scoring more points than Pittsburgh had allowed in three previous games combined.

Parker took the loss with uncharacteristic calm. Not having Johnson was too big of a disadvantage, he reasoned, without making excuses. "Had we had him, it might have been a different ball game," the coach said.[64] What cheered Parker up was the emergence of Ed Brown as a quarterback who could rally the Steelers time after time. With a running game that totaled only 97 yards—and only 37 on twelve carries by Johnson's fill-in, Ferguson—Ed Brown finished eighteen of thirty-five for 289 yards—nearly twice the yardage of "the mental marvel" on the other side of the field.[65]

The Steeler quarterback, Jimmy Brown said, "turned up throwing like a Sammy Baugh. 'Is this guy ever going to miss?' we asked ourselves."[66] Parker was uncommonly effusive in his praise for his quarterback. "That was as fine an exhibition of passing as I've seen in pro ball," the coach raved. "Anything less than a great game wouldn't have overcome passing like that."[67]

In one night, Ed Brown appeared to have erased whatever doubts had troubled Parker about his quarterback situation and seemed to justify the coach's decision to coax Layne into retirement. Brown's effort not only reassured Parker but gave him the confidence to make a bold prediction. "We'll win it all if we can get our injured boys well," he said.[68]

GAME 5

Lou Cordileone was the Steeler who had earned the distinction of being traded for a future Hall of Fame quarterback, Y. A. Tittle. But it was Clendon Thomas, a former All-America running back, who wound up in Pittsburgh in a trade for Tarzan.

Thomas was a two-way star at Oklahoma who led the nation in scoring in 1956 and played in only one losing game in college—the loss to Notre Dame that snapped the Sooners' forty-seven-game winning streak under Bud Wilkinson. Thomas, "the intense young man . . . who typifies the Oklahoma spirit," was featured on the cover of *Sports Illustrated* that week in 1957, under the headline "Why Oklahoma Is Unbeatable," days before the Irish ended the streak.

Back in high school in Oklahoma City, growing up in a community of oil-field workers, Thomas seemed about as likely to grow up to be Tarzan as become an All-America football player. As a freshman, he was six foot two, 155 pounds—"just a beanpole," he recalled—at Southeast High, which won only two games in Thomas's three varsity years and once got beat 82–6.[1] He was all-state in football, but lightly recruited, although Wilkinson himself paid a visit to the Thomas home. When he wound up a Sooner, Thomas started out on the fifth unit. "I guess they didn't really want me here an awful lot," he said with a smile during his senior year.[2]

The industrial city of Pittsburgh, with its steel mills and factories, seemed a world apart, but the plains of Oklahoma molded the same work ethic and outlook in Thomas and other kids. "For the hardy, lean and tough people who inhabit this country . . . football is a perfect expression of their way of life—hit harder than you are hit, don't cry when you are hurt, win," Tex Maule wrote.[3] Said Thomas: "There were some rough ol' boys in those days, but there always are."[4]

Thomas, the son of an oil-field worker who also starred as a pitcher in an industrial league, could more than hold his own. After those losing seasons in high school, "the gridiron gods . . . smiled at Thomas."[5] A Pittsburgh sportswriter referred to him as the "one-time All-America glamour-boy halfback . . . who brought the state of Oklahoma to its feet with his electrifying runs as a Sooner."[6]

Thomas and Tommy McDonald, the "Touchdown Twins," went on a scoring tear in 1956, a closer race than the home-run chase that Mickey Mantle and Roger Maris would have in 1961. The beanpole had filled out to 188 pounds, and he had speed, power, and good lateral movement. On September 29, 1956, Thomas had a 12-yard touchdown run and an interception as Oklahoma ran its winning streak to thirty-one games with a 36–0 victory over North Carolina. The next week he "couldn't be stopped" as he ran for three touchdowns and 82 yards in a 66–0 rout of Kansas State.[7] The following week, at the Cotton Bowl, the pair "ran almost at will" in a 45–0 decision over Texas, with both players scoring three touchdowns.[8] In a 40–0 romp over "poor old Notre Dame" on October 27, Thomas had two touchdowns, one on a 30-yard interception return of a Paul Hornung pass, and McDonald had two interceptions, one of which he ran back 55 yards for a TD.[9]

Going into the final game of the schedule, against Oklahoma A&M, the two players were tied with sixteen touchdowns apiece. McDonald, a senior, scored once, and Thomas, a junior, scored twice to win the scoring title with 108 points as Oklahoma won its fortieth straight game, 53–0.

On November 30, 1957, two weeks after Notre Dame ended its winning streak in a 7–0 game, the Sooners whipped Oklahoma State, 53–6, as Thomas scored two touchdowns and passed for a third. The two TDs gave him nine for the season and thirty-six for his career, a school record. Thomas finished the day with OU records for most yards rushing in three years (2,120) and most points scored (216).[10]

Thomas made all-conference in his junior and senior years and was a consensus All-America in his final season. For all his running ability, he was also "a ferocious but clean defender" and "deadly at bringing down rival runners."[11]

The Rams picked Thomas in the second round of the draft, the nineteenth overall selection. He played four years in Los Angeles, starting out on offense before shifting to defensive back. The Steelers had gained notoriety for giving away rich young talent, but the Rams were developing an embarrass-ing tradition of their own with personnel moves. They sent away not only Cordileone, Lou Michaels, and Charlie Bradshaw but also Browns quarterback Frank Ryan and Giants receiver Del Shofner. Yet another of their peculiar moves was trying to convert a 195-pound All-America halfback into a tight end. "I'm no tight end," Thomas said.[12] Disappointed with the loss of veteran leadership on the Rams and some unrest in the franchise, Thomas was eager for a trade, preferably to Dallas, because he knew the coach, Tom Landry.

Nearly a continent away, handsome, muscular Mike Henry, a native of Los Angeles and a linebacker with the Steelers, was trying to map out a movie career in 1961. He had a plan to work in California Monday through Friday and then fly to Pittsburgh in time for the Steeler games. "What about practice?" Buddy Parker asked. "What about it?" Henry replied.[13]

At the end of the first week of August 1962, Henry announced he was quitting football for a movie career. "Oglin' Gals Beats Beltin' Behemoths," read the headline on the *Post-Gazette* story. Nearly a month later, after Henry reported late to Steeler camp, Parker swung one more of his deals, swapping a future Tarzan for a future Pro Bowler. Thomas played seven years for the Steelers, picked off fifteen passes in his first two seasons, and made a Pro Bowl appearance. Mike Henry lasted three seasons with the Rams, made three *Tarzan* movies and appeared in a variety of other films and TV shows, and got a bite from a chimpanzee that required twenty stitches and prompted two lawsuits.[14]

Thomas had gotten a fleeting introduction to Pittsburgh in 1957, when he rushed for 86 yards and "bowled over" Panther defensive back and future Steeler Dick Haley on a 13-yard touchdown run that helped Oklahoma gain a season-opening 26–0 win at Pitt Stadium. But, apprehensive about joining what sounded like a bunch of carousers even wilder than the West Coast set, Thomas balked at the trade and went home to Oklahoma. When Steeler as-sistant Buster Ramsey called Thomas, the ex-Sooner said he wasn't going to report to Pittsburgh. But Thomas finally relented, and once he got to know his teammates, he found that accounts of the players' behavior were vastly exaggerated, and he embraced the team, the city, and the Rooney family.[15]

Thomas wasn't as flashy as some runners, but he was as tough as an oil rigger and as disciplined as you would expect a Bud Wilkinson–coached player to be. Even in a 1963 preseason game, he set a high standard, playing flawlessly in the Steelers' 22–7 win in Detroit on August 30. "Thomas was a tiger in Friday's victory," wrote beat writer Pat Livingston. "He had one of those nights when, though he didn't intercept a pass, he could do nothing wrong. He made tackles behind the line of scrimmage, stripped interference, covered his receivers and generally played a great football game."[16]

Thomas wasn't a drinker, but he fit right in with a team that played like a band of marauding Vikings and showed about as much mercy. "We had some really exceptionally talented players," he said.

> We weren't taking a back seat. That didn't mean we matched up physi-
> cally with every team, but with the rules the way they were written in
> those days, we had a black-and-blue defense. People hated to play us.
> We literally punished people. And heaven help you if you'd run into the
> middle of the field. They did not have guts enough to run deep posts
> into the middle.
>
>   It wasn't dirty. It wasn't anything like that. We had a tough football
> team that hit people. So you intimidated people, and Pittsburgh had
> that reputation. They would come in and play us, and then they were
> going to lose next week because we'd beat 'em up so bad.[17]

The day after the Browns game, Buddy Parker wasn't brooding about the loss. Instead, the coach evidenced surprise over St. Louis's victory that afternoon. "Did you see what the Cardinals did to the Vikings?" he said. The Cardinals romped, 56–14, scoring half their points in the fourth quarter to put them in a tie with the Giants for second place at 3–1. Charley Johnson hit sixteen of twenty-five passes for 301 yards and three touchdowns.[18]

The Steelers would be meeting the Cards for the second time in fourteen days, this time at Busch Stadium. Wally Lemm's squad ranked second in the NFL in team offense and defense, and it had the league leader in pass receptions, Bobby Joe Conrad; the No. 3 rusher, Joe Childress; and the third-ranked passer in Johnson. Even more significantly, the Cardinals were a team that could stand toe to toe and slug it out with the Steelers.

The Cards had proved they could take a lot of punishment. Defensive tackle Don Owens "played his heart out," photojournalist Robert Riger wrote, and took "a terrific beating" until the final gun of the Cards' loss at Forbes Field. "The doctor and two trainers led him along the dirt floor of the dark dressing room tunnel, dazed and beaten."[19] The Cards embodied the same combative spirit as the Steelers. Eighth-year linebacker Bill Ko-man explained: "I take out my hostilities on the field."[20]

The Cards had vented frustration after the loss, criticizing the officiating and pointing out bad breaks. Lemm accused Lou Michaels of "doing some funny things"—throwing punches, grabbing face masks, and piling on.[21] The complaining prompted *Press* writer Pat Livingston to label Lemm's squad a "ruthless, cry-baby crew of undisciplined frontrunners . . . the Current Glamour Boys of football," a title that was customarily accorded the New York Giants. Livingston wrote that the Cards took "a sadistic delight in pouring it on" the Vikings, even calling for an onside kick with a 49–14 lead.[22]

Michaels shrugged off the grousing. "They just got hot because we were doing a job on them," he said.[23]

The Cardinals had also gained a confidence that bordered on cockiness. After the loss in Pittsburgh, Johnson was asked if it looked as though the two teams would battle down to the wire for the Eastern crown. "We'll be in it," he sniffed. "I don't know about the Steelers.[24] Said Lemm: "We are contenders."[25]

While the players were off Monday, Parker was busy. In what one writer envisioned as "another case of driftwood turning into teakwood," the coach swung a deal with the Eagles for seldom-used Theron Sapp, the back whose collision with John Reger in the opener KO'd the linebacker. It was a typical Parker move. Sapp had a stellar career in college at Georgia, but he had little track record as a pro. Hampered by a shoulder injury in '62, he carried the ball only twenty-three times. In '61, he rushed only seven times. But Parker was confident in his potential and said that he had wanted to land the six-foot-one, 200-pound back since training camp. "I've got a hunch he's going to be a real football player," Parker said.[26]

Despite fortifying his backfield and watching Ed Brown emerge as a shootout quarterback and a worthy successor to Bobby Layne, Parker was in a "touchy" mood all week.[27] Who knows what was swirling in the mind of a coach with no tolerance for failure, but maybe doubts about his team began creeping in. Maybe '63 was going to fall short the way the '62 season had, as he watched injuries hamper his linebacking corps for the second straight year. Two seasons before, after the Browns edged the Steelers, 30–28, Cleveland coach Paul Brown almost sounded as if he felt sorry for his counterpart. "Parker has all the horses," Brown said, "but the Steelers are a snake-bitten team."[28]

So many hopes, so much infusion of new talent, yet so many disappointing seasons had forged a fatalistic outlook in the fans. The Steelers couldn't catch a break. Reger was still recuperating, and now Bob Schmitz, John Henry Johnson, and Thomas were hurting with foot injuries. Yet every time a key member of an opposing team suffered an injury, it seemed, he got healthy just in time to face the Steelers. "The stars are always ready for the snake-bitten Steelers," Livingston wrote.[29]

This week, two Cardinal starters, defensive back Bill Stacy and former Heisman Trophy winner John David Crow, were healthy enough to rejoin the team, although they were not scheduled to start because their fill-ins had been doing so well. "It puts us at our peak of strength, personnel-wise," Lemm said.[30]

Parker couldn't say the same. A sprained right ankle shelved Michaels during Saturday night's loss. Dick Haley hurt his shoulder, and Dick Hoak bruised his back. Thomas sustained a stone bruise on his right heel while tackling Jim Brown on Cleveland's first play from scrimmage. "The heel isn't discolored or swollen but it sure hurts," Thomas said. "I just couldn't run."[31] The Steelers had X-rays taken on Monday, and they came back negative. Thomas, along with John Henry Johnson, mostly watched Wednesday's practice, but trainer Roger McGill said the safety should be OK by game day.

Parker had been juggling his linebacking corps since the opener. George Tarasovic, who'd hurt his foot in the victory over St. Louis, had "half-limped" through the Browns game, and Schmitz looked to be out Sunday because of a bad ankle.[32] But Johnson was the one Parker stewed over. "He's a slow healer," the coach said. "John Henry's a real football player when he's right, but once he gets hurt it takes him a long time to get ready again."[33]

No one could doubt the fullback's willingness to take hits and absorb punishment as well as dish out the same. Several weeks later, a healthy Johnson would express his resentment over not only the notion that he was shirking his duty but a broader insinuation that seemed ingrained in Parker's beliefs. "I couldn't have played on that ankle even if I had been filled with pain-killing drugs," Johnson said. "Besides, I get tired of certain individuals always taking shots at Negroes when they get injured. Some guys act like we aren't supposed to get hurt like other guys in the league."[34]

In his game story, reporter Pat Livingston wrote in his lead about the lemming, a peculiar mouselike creature that undertakes mass migrations but eventually drowns while trying to cross the sea. Livingston was addressing the squad coached by Wally Lemm, who had led the Houston Oilers to a title in the old AFL just two years earlier. But the reference seemed more appropriate for the Steelers, with their history of letdowns and breakdowns, especially in the Parker years, when the arrival of a coach who had won two titles whipped up hope among the diehard fans.[35]

Twice the Browns had kept the Steelers out of the end zone with goal line stands the week before, forcing Pittsburgh to settle for field goals. But on this day in St. Louis, with clear skies and temperatures in the 70s, Pittsburgh's goal line defense would prove even more impressive than Cleveland's.

The Steelers took the opening kickoff but were forced to punt. Starting from his 26, Charley Johnson misfired twice but hit rookie tight end Jackie Smith for 14 yards and back Bill Triplett for 15, to the Steeler 34. Triplett gained a yard and then burst up the middle for 26 more, setting up first-and-goal at the 7. Andy Russell, starting at linebacker in a personal home-coming, broke up a pass to Conrad on first down. Two carries by Triplett moved the Cards to the 1. On fourth down, Childress tried to ram his way through the center of the line, but linebacker Myron Pottios stopped him short, and Pittsburgh took over.

The Steelers couldn't move the ball, and Brown's 39-yard punt left the Cards in good position after defensive back Pat Fischer returned it 7 yards to the Steeler 37. But Pittsburgh held, forcing Jim Bakken to kick a 44-yard field goal.

Red Mack's 28-yard reception put the Steelers on the Cards' 40, but two incompletions left it up to Lou Michaels, and he hit a 45-yard field goal for a 3–3 tie with 3:25 left in the quarter. The Steelers moved deep enough into St. Louis territory for Michaels to try again from 42 yards on the first series of the second quarter, but lineman Joe Robb blocked the kick.

On first down, Johnson hit Smith with a 53-yard pass, setting up first-and-goal at the 6. Crow rammed up the middle for 5 yards, but Childress was stopped cold. On third down, Johnson's pitchout was off line, and rookie defensive back Jim Bradshaw recovered the ball on the 16.

After Hoak picked up a yard, Mack, "who is built on the lines of a broomstick but is tougher than steel," dashed down the left side and took in Brown's pass, eluding a diving Jimmy Hill at the St. Louis 40 and a desperate lunge by Fischer at the 5 for an 83-yard TD.[36] Pittsburgh led, 10–3, with 4:45 gone in the quarter.

Starting from his 15, Charley Johnson got his team moving, hitting Sonny Randle with a 23-yard pass to put the Cards on the Steeler 36. Childress picked up 8 yards to make it second-and-2 at the 18, but Johnson threw incomplete to Childress, and Brady Keys stopped Childress on a run around left end for 1 yard. Lemm decided to go for it on fourth-and-1 at the 17, but rookie defensive tackle Frank Atkinson stopped Crow for no gain. The Steelers had held again.

Brown hit Dial with a 41-yard pass to move the ball to the St. Louis 43. Pittsburgh could gain only 3 yards, so Michaels drilled a 47-yard field goal to put the Steelers up 13–3 with 1:26 left before halftime.

Charley Johnson wasn't about to run out the clock. He was on his way to a Pro Bowl year—the only one he would enjoy in a fifteen-year NFL career that held such promise. He would lead the league in pass attempts, rank second behind Johnny Unitas in both completions and passing yardage, and finish second to Y. A. Tittle in touchdown passes. But he would also finish second, behind Norm Snead, in interceptions. Starting from his 27, Johnson hit Randle for a gain of 7 yards, but on second down, Pottios intercepted and returned the ball 32 yards to the St. Louis 6. "Pottios was by far the best football player on the field," Johnson said afterward.[37] That impression was growing around the league. In late August, the new coach of the Colts, Don Shula, had paid the Steeler linebacker high praise after an exhibition game. "Pottios is a great football player," Shula said.[38]

Two Hoak carries moved the ball to the 1, setting up a sneak by Brown for a touchdown and a 20–3 halftime lead. Charley Johnson, hitting eight of sixteen passes, was moving the ball, but he had only a field goal to show for it.

Everything seemed to be working for the Steelers—except for Ferguson, who had a mere 13 yards rushing after six carries. But Pittsburgh had kept St. Louis out of the end zone and forced "the baby-faced chemical engineer" into an interception and a pitchout that turned into a fumble.[39] "This game was even more frustrating for me than the one at Pittsburgh," Johnson said later.[40]

The Steelers looked to be on the verge of going 3–1–1 and pushing themselves into sole possession of second place in the Eastern Conference. Cleveland was on the way to grinding out a 35–24 win over the Giants, which would leave New York and St. Louis tied for third at 3–2. With a seventeen-point lead, the Steelers had the luxury of glancing at the scoreboard or listening to the scores announced over the PA system in the stadium.

The Cardinals took the second-half kickoff, and Johnson led them on a Steeler-like march, mixing short passes with the run on a seventeen-play drive. Twelve plays left them with fourth-and-2 on the Steeler 15. Whether he was mule headed or had unwavering confidence in his offensive line, Lemm disdained the field goal once again. Johnson plunged into the line and picked up 5 yards, setting up first-and-goal at the 10.

It still looked as if the Steeler defense was going to stifle Johnson again. The secondary had given up 145 yards passing in the first half but it was getting along without Thomas, sidelined by his injured heel. "We made four perfect defensive plays," defensive coach Buster Ramsey said of the final sequence in the series. Keys broke up a pass to Randle, and Glen Glass broke up one to Conrad. On third down, Johnson threw incomplete to Smith. On fourth down, the Cards tried a halfback pass. "We figured Crow would throw to Conrad," Ramsey said, "and we played that right."[41]

In his book *The Physics of Football*, Timothy Gay plots the trajectories of a kick, a punt, and a pass, but the path of an oblong ball is as unpredictable when it's batted around in the air as when it squirts and tumbles along the ground. Conrad, the intended receiver, fell down on the play. Glass deflected Crow's pass, but it ricocheted right into Smith's hands for a touchdown, making it 20–10. Steelers assistant coach Vern "Torgy" Torgeson almost sounded like a typical fatalistic fan of a snake-bitten team when he observed later, "When they score on plays like that, you're not about to win."[42]

But the Steelers bounced back. Brown hit Gary Ballman with a 33-yard pass on the next drive to set up a 46-yard field goal by Michaels, boosting the Steeler lead to 23–10 with 1:44 left in the third quarter. Brown wasn't matching his form against Cleveland. He had hit several bombs, but he was only four of eleven passing at the half, en route to an eight of twenty-three afternoon, and Ferguson wasn't duplicating his first performance against the Cards. But as heroic as the Steeler defense looked, the lead seemed secure as the quarter ended with a Stovall punt, even though the Steelers had to punt right back. Russell had broken up several passes and roamed over the field making tackles, and he was in the right place again when he recovered Smith's fumble at the Steeler 32 after a 37-yard reception early in the fourth quarter.

The Steelers missed a chance to increase their lead when Michaels missed a 34-yard field goal on the ensuing drive (although some in the press box thought the officials blew the call), but the way the defense was playing, it didn't seem consequential—and certainly not vital—at the time. The Steelers looked as if they had held again after Charley Johnson failed to hit his targets, but a 25-yard pass interference call on third-and-10 moved the Cards to their 45. On first down, however, Johnson was dumped for a 10-yard loss, leaving him with 9:56 to work a small miracle.[43]

The Cardinals almost had enough track stars to field an Olympic team of their own. Besides Bob Paremore, with his 9.3 speed, and Smith, who had won the state hurdles while in high school, Randle had 9.6 speed in the 100. After Johnson picked himself off the ground, he connected with Randle on a 54-yard pass, down to the Steeler 11.

After Triplett lost a yard and Johnson threw incomplete, the Cardinal QB made like Frank Ryan the week before, running up the middle for 9 yards, making it fourth-and-2 at the 3, the third time the Cards were to challenge Pittsburgh near the goal line. Several weeks later, the *Pittsburgh Courier* would rhapsodize about the Steeler defense: "For three seasons, the names of John Reger, Myron Pottios, Joe Krupa, George Tarasovic and

Ernie Stautner have stood for line savagery of the most riotous sort." The crew was living up to its reputation for "rock-and-sock football" on this sunny afternoon. The Cardinals had no better success this time against this grizzled crew: Childress picked up only a yard over right guard, Krupa's territory, and Pittsburgh took over. "Three times the Cards got that close the Steelers' derriers [*sic*] left marks at the goal line," wrote Al Abrams. The Steelers looked like a crew that was defending the Alamo.[44]

The Cardinals had gotten the benefit of a fluke play, but the Steelers were catching breaks too. They couldn't move past the 6 after their goal line stand, but a roughing-the-kicker penalty on Brown's punt gave them new life. Hoak's 18-yard run off-tackle dug them out of a hole, but three plays later, Brown had to punt and got off a feeble 31-yarder that left the Cards on their 40.

A thirteen-point lead seemed safe with only 4:24 left in the game, especially the way the Steelers were playing, and Michaels's 34-yard miss did not loom as a pivotal failure. Johnson was not yet a polished NFL quarterback, and he had receivers who were still raw. Smith, a tenth-round draft pick playing for the injured Taz Anderson, had more of an impact in high school playing clarinet in the band than catching passes. Hampered by injuries, he got into the last game in his junior year, with his team playing in the single wing. "I ran so goofy that the other team couldn't figure out what I was doing," he said.[45]

Clendon Thomas would look back and remember Smith as one of the most talented receivers he faced during his career, but on this day the sixth-year safety mostly watched from the sideline. "Jackie Smith could run away from a lot of people," Thomas said.[46] After Childress went around left end for 5 yards, Smith got open, and Johnson hit him with a 55-yard touchdown pass to make it 23–17 with 3:48 left in the game. Smith would finish the day with nine catches for 212 yards—more yardage than he'd gained in his senior year in college.

Curiously, with the Steelers needing to run out the clock, Brown threw a pass to Dial on first down. It went incomplete. After Hoak picked up 2 yards, Brown threw a 13-yard pass to Mack for a first down on the 35. Ferguson gained 5 yards up the middle, but Mack drew a personal foul for running into a Cardinal defender after the whistle. Instead of having second-and-5 at the 40, the Steelers faced second-and-20 at their 25, and the clock stopped. Brown was sacked for a 6-yard loss, and Hoak, with 2:40 left, gained only 2 yards around right end.

Brown got off a 36-yard punt, giving the Cards the ball on their 43, but some of the 23,715 hometown fans started to leave when Lou Cordileone dropped Johnson for an 18-yard loss, forcing the Cards to use their last time-out with 1:33 left.

With the Steeler goal line 75 yards away and no time-outs, what Wally Lemm needed wasn't more time. What he needed was Bobby Layne at quarterback, or Johnny Unitas. But a baby-faced PhD candidate? Johnson threw an incompletion, and then "the Texas towhead" showed why he was so highly regarded as a future star.[47]

"Pitiful as it was to Steeler fans, one had to admire the artistry of Charley Johnson . . . and the brilliance of his performance when the chips were on the line," Pat Livingston wrote. "In a march that defied credulity, the 24-year-old youngster directed the greatest race against the clock football ever has seen."[48]

Perhaps Livingston had forgotten about Layne's two-minute drills, like the one against the Browns in 1959, or the 80-yard drive, capped by Jim Doran's TD catch, that won the 1953 NFL title for Detroit. Maybe he had forgotten about Unitas moving the Colts into a tie in regulation before Baltimore beat the Giants in sudden death in the '58 title game. No matter. Never had a chemical engineer's performance looked quite so mesmerizing.

The difference between playing the two sides of the ball, Thomas, a former two-way star, explained before the first Cardinal game, is that on defense, "You can't afford a mistake. Make a mistake on defense . . . give up a touchdown, and there's no way you can get it back." And when a passer like Charley Johnson was in a groove, there was no letup from the pressure. "There are times when you feel like you're in the back end of a shooting gallery when those quarterbacks start throwing," Thomas said.[49]

That's the effect a young quarterback like Johnson could induce in a defensive secondary. If only Thomas had been healthy enough to play more than a handful of downs, the Cardinal quarterback might have had to change his strategy. Ramsey put the Steelers in a "prevent defense," designed to give up yardage but use up the clock while discouraging long passes. A day later, Livingston would label it an "idiotic defense."[50] He had just written a feature on the assistant coach for the *Press*'s Sunday magazine titled "The Volatile Mr. Ramsey." Livingston described "the leather-lunged Tennessean" as "this great bull of a man, a shoulder-swaggering megaphone of instructions and warnings . . . as bouncy as a three-month old puppy and as violent as an explosion."

Garrard "Buster" Ramsey handled the defense while Parker concentrated on the offense during the week. Ramsey had a penchant for heckling opponents, and he had a knack for unsettling them. One anonymous Giant player suggested that the NFL ban the coach. "If they don't," the player vowed, "I'm going to belt him good some day."[51]

Ramsey took an ultra-conservative approach on defense. Asked before the season opener why the Steelers didn't more often "red-dog"—the term that became more popular as "blitz"—he replied, "I don't feel defense is the place to gamble on the football field."[52] He was not nearly as daring as Cardinal defensive coordinator Chuck Drulis, who was refining the safety blitz with Larry Wilson, perfecting the timing to rush in to sack the quarterback. It would take little imagination to envision the havoc that Clendon Thomas—or Brady Keys—could have wrought with some surprise blitzes.

Faced with third-and-28 from his 25, Johnson started taking advantage of Ramsey's tactics, while looking as much like an artist as a genius. He hit Childress, coming out of the backfield, and the eighth-year back from Auburn came up less than a yard shy of the first down. The Cards finally converted a shot on fourth down when Johnson hit Conrad for 3 yards and the first down and then picked up 17 on a pass to Smith.

On first down at the Steeler 27, Johnson was dropped for a 2-yard loss and, with thirty seconds left, the Cards were penalized for being offside. Johnson hit Smith with a short pass, leaving the quarterback at the 28-yard line with the clock running out the last twenty seconds. Johnson, backpedaling after taking the snap, spotted Conrad running a post pattern across the 20-yard line, and he fired away.

After watching the films the next day, Buddy Parker explained how Conrad reacted after he caught the pass and found himself surrounded by three defensive backs: Willie Daniel, Dick Haley, and Jim Bradshaw. "They had him in a triangle, a sort of vise," Parker said, "but he got off the hook. Daniel was only a yard behind Conrad but instead of trying to tackle him stuck his foot out and tried to trip him. Had he been knocked down, time would have run out and we'd have won."[53]

Instead, after making the catch, Conrad feinted to his left, ran right, and "breezed into the corner of the end zone."[54] There were five seconds left on the clock. Jim Bakken kicked the point after, and the Cards were 24–23 winners. The lemmings had been successful in their long march and had not self-destructed. Johnson had racked up 428 yards by completing twenty of forty-one passes, the most important ones in the last ninety seconds.

The week after the Steeler loss, Green Bay used a different strategy in St. Louis. Packer defensive assistant coach Norb Hecker had his secondary play man to man. "Unquestionably, Bobby Joe Conrad and Sonny Randle are the two best receivers in the League simply because both men can beat you on every pattern," Hecker said. "On the very deep corners and posts they are in a class by themselves."[55]

Maybe if Clendon Thomas had been healthy and able to play the whole game, he could have added to his league-high interception total of four and picked off Johnson on the final drive. Or maybe broken up a pass. Or at least he could have tackled Conrad short of the goal in the final seconds. Or maybe, as assistant coach Torgy Torgeson suggested when he spoke of the pass deflected to Smith for a "gift" touchdown, it just wasn't meant to be for the Steelers. Certainly not on this day, and maybe not this season.

Parker was in no mood to be philosophical. A tremendous defensive effort had been wasted. "There was [a] bitter smile on Coach Parker's face but he was boiling mad inside. It was obvious that an explosion pended, in the delayed fury of a time bomb."[56] This was no time to pick out any bright spots, as Parker had after the loss in Cleveland. Instead, he "tore through the locker room in an uncontrollable rage," shouting, "It was a disgrace," over and over. "You disgraced me. You disgraced yourselves."[57]

This time, instead of the Cards, it was the Steelers who did the complaining. Keys protested and Parker screamed from the sidelines on the final drive that the officials stopped the clock for no apparent reason after the third-down reception by Childress, giving St. Louis an additional twenty seconds, at least. But there was no disguising the truth that the Steelers had let a certain victory slip out of their hands, just as pathetically and inexplicably as that end zone deflection went for a Cardinal touchdown.[58]

"Agreed that we got some lousy calls and we got some lousy timekeeping," one unnamed player said, "but you can't blame the officials when you blow a 23–10 lead." How do you account for a team whose defense faced first-and-goal situations from the 6-, 7-, and 10-yard lines, and another first-and-10 from the 11, and only gave up a touchdown on a fluke deflection and then yielded two touchdowns in less than four minutes? In Livingston's opinion, there was only one explanation: "They choked up."[59]

The Browns and Bears remained unbeaten and were emerging as early favorites for a showdown in the championship game. Mike Ditka, a former teammate of Haley's at Pitt, caught four touchdown passes to lead Chicago to a 52–14 rout of the Rams in the Coliseum. Jim Brown, "in a fantastic display of power and speed," scored three touchdowns, one on a 72-yard pass from Frank Ryan, as unbeaten Cleveland outmuscled the Giants, 35–24, at Yankee Stadium. Brown earned everything he gained.[60] He called it "the roughest, hardest game" he had played in the NFL, and he earned admiration as much for his willingness to absorb a brutal beating as for his ability to shred a defense.[61] "They beat Jimmy like a dog and whipped him like a pup," someone shouted in the Browns' locker room. "But he showed them."[62]

Charley Johnson had shown them too, and now the Steelers had to wonder whether they were good enough to climb over three teams to win the Eastern Conference. Maybe the final ingredient was still lacking in the Steelers' makeup, some intangible that teams like the Browns and Bears had added. More than once Bobby Layne had noted during his stay in Pittsburgh, "There's just something missing, something we had at Detroit that we don't have here."[63]

Nearing the halfway point of the season, the team had to wonder whether they had enough time left to find that missing ingredient.

GAME 6

VERSUS WASHINGTON REDSKINS
AT PITT STADIUM
OCTOBER 20

By mid-October, the mild, dry fall that Pittsburgh had been enjoying had become too much of a good thing, transforming temperate weather into a genuine drought. The day after the Cardinal loss marked the thirty-second day the region had gone without any appreciable precipitation—not since three days before the opener in Philadelphia.

On Monday, the state of Pennsylvania banned fires and smoking in forests and woodlands because of the dry conditions. On Wednesday, Governor William Scranton issued an emergency proclamation closing all woodlands to the public because of the danger of forest fires. The next day, seven other states closed woodlands. Pennsylvania was one of a handful of states that banned hunting and fishing.

Probably no one was hurting more from the lack of rain than Pittsburgh's so-called Umbrella Man, Sam Cohen, who had a small shop in the Pick-Roosevelt Hotel. Cohen had been selling and repairing umbrellas for fifty years, but it wasn't just the dry spell that was to blame for a lack of business; it was a shift in lifestyles. "Sam's villain is the automobile," a story in the *Pittsburgh Post-Gazette* reported. "That's what took the umbrella business away," Cohen said. "People drive into their garages. They don't walk to church anymore."[1]

The drought extended from Maine to Texas, and by the end of the week, it would only grow worse, with little hope of relief. Hundreds of fires broke out. County health authorities worried about a buildup of heavy smog. It appeared to be the worst drought in Ohio in eighty years. The dry spell in Pittsburgh was called the worst in thirty-five years—and even longer than the championship drought endured by the Steelers.

Buddy Parker had come to Pittsburgh with a pledge to bring the city a championship within five years. Parker had become available to the Steelers when he abruptly quit the Lions as coach in 1957, and he had turned threats of quitting the Steelers into a nearly annual (or even biannual) rite. Two days after the fiasco at Busch Stadium, Al Abrams led his *Post-Gazette* column with a dig at the coach: "This is about the time of year, isn't it, that Buddy Parker announces he's going to quit the Steelers?"[2]

If Parker gave the newspapers just a glance, it would have been hard for him to miss a series of front-page stories "showing ways to win your own personal war of nerves" that ran the week before the opener. Some pressure can work to a person's advantage, "But there is a critical difference between helpful tension and the tension which destroys," according to one article. "A rope drawn taut is a working rope," but one whose fibers begin to fray "under an overload is a rope nearing its breaking point."[3]

Parker had not reached that point—yet. His rage had subsided and his mood had improved considerably by the day after the Cardinal loss, as frustrating as it was, and he expressed confidence that the season wasn't lost. "We blew it," he said. "But, hell, the season's not over yet. It's far from over. We've got a chance to get back in the race. Just wait and see."[4] Two days later, Parker vowed that his 2–2–1 Steelers would stay in the race if they could win the next two games, against Washington and Dallas. "The first and second half are two different seasons," he said. "If we can get through the first half with only two losses, we'll be in the fight all the way."[5]

For the second straight week, the Steelers were facing one of "the bright young men of pro football's movement toward daring and reckless quarterbacking," the Redskins' Norm Snead, a twenty-four-year-old in his third year "who can impale the point of the football on a needle at medium range."[6] Snead had been booed in a 37–24 loss to the Eagles the day Pittsburgh beat St. Louis, but head coach Bill McPeak, a former Steelers assistant coach, insisted, "For my money, he has the potential of being the best quarterback in the National Football League."[7]

What the Steelers would need Sunday against another hotshot passer was a much better performance from their secondary. The game would have a bit of extra meaning for one member of that group. Dick Haley was going to be seeing his old teammates again.

Like a lot of kids who grew up around the steel mills of western Pennsylvania in the fifties, Haley had his mind set on escaping a life of drudgery, grimy jobs, and dangerous work. "Football was a way out for us," said Haley, who grew up in Washington County, where he attended Midway

High School, about an hour south of downtown Pittsburgh. "That was how we were going to make it if we were going to make it."[8]

Haley's father worked in the open hearth at National Steel in Weirton, West Virginia, for forty years. But thanks to his football ability, the son found a way out. After helping his high school win a WPIAL (Western Pennsylvania Interscholastic Athletic League) title, Haley signed to attend Duke. The University of Pittsburgh was determined to change his mind, however, so not only did he get regular visits from an assistant football coach, but the staff got him a summer job at Jessop Steel in nearby Washington, Pennsylvania. Just a couple of months of work there was enough to remind him of what he had been trying to avoid all along. "I decided I didn't want to do that on a full-time basis," Haley said. He had a little extra motivation to succeed in football, as well as additional encouragement to stay close to his roots.[9]

"At that time, when you signed [letters of intent], they weren't binding, so I changed my mind in July or August and decided I was going to stay home." Pitt didn't have to look much farther than its own backyard to stock the squad. "Half of the guys had signed to go other places," Haley said. "The last couple of weeks, Pitt just stayed after them. At the end, everybody said, 'I'm staying home.'"[10]

No wonder Pitt was so keen to keep Haley home. In the first week of October in his junior year, 1957, Haley intercepted a pass to set up the winning score in a 20–14 victory over Southern Cal. On October 19, against Army, "With Dick Haley as their spearhead, the Panthers ran the ball strong out of [a] split T formation." He scored a 53-yard touchdown on "a dazzling catch," but Army prevailed, 29–13.[11]

On November 2, Pitt engaged Syracuse in "a pulsating struggle calculated to make blood pressures climb." Haley scored the first touchdown for the Panthers, a 64-yard run "during which he slipped through the fingers of three Syracuse downfield tacklers." Pitt lost, 24–21, on a field goal, the first one Ben Schwartzwalder had called for in nine years as head coach at Syracuse.[12]

In '58, Haley's senior year, he made a 9-yard touchdown run in a 22–8 loss to Michigan State in mid-October, caught the winning TD pass in a 15–8 victory over West Virginia, and scored on the two-point conversion to enable Pitt to tie Army, the nation's top-rated team, 14–14, in "a bruising contest" in the final week of October.[13] On November 1 he scored on a 14-yard run in a 16–13 loss to Syracuse, and one week later he had two TDs in a 29–26 win over Notre Dame. Haley had a 35-yard catch for a TD in a 14–6 loss to Nebraska as the Panthers slipped to 5–3–1.

Pitt floundered in Haley's senior year, but his talents were recognized with invitations to all-star games. He ran back a kickoff 84 yards for a touchdown in the East's 26–14 victory in the Shrine Game. Along with Nick Pietrosante and Lee Grosscup, two future pros, he was part of the starting backfield in the College All-Star Game, a squad that had a sure-handed receiver from Rice named Buddy Dial at end.

The Washington Redskins drafted Haley in January in the ninth round, the hundredth overall pick, which would have made him an early fourth-round selection after the merger with the AFL and expansion years later. He played two years with the Redskins, returning kickoffs and punts, running, and catching passes besides playing some defense in his rookie year. Then his career hit a snag.

"I'd had some medical problems," Haley said, "and the Redskins were questioning whether they were going to let me play because I had had rheumatic fever when I was nine or ten years old, and that always leaves you with a heart murmur of some type. I took a medical for the Army, and they turned me down because of the heart murmur." The Redskins put Haley on the expansion list for the new Minnesota Vikings franchise, which began play in 1961. "If you wanted to play," Haley said, "you probably could get to play, and I wanted to play." It wasn't until 2005 that Haley underwent heart surgery. "I waited forty-four years to have it, so I thought I made the right decision," he said.[14]

Haley was with the Vikings for four games in the '61 season before Buddy Parker picked him up, along with receiver Bob Schnelker. It took only a few weeks for the pair to become heroes in a win against the second-place Browns in Cleveland. With the Steelers down 13–10 with 3:51 left in the game, Haley picked up a kickoff bobbled by a teammate and returned it 50 yards to the Browns' 38. Two plays later, Schnelker caught a 26-yard touchdown pass from Rudy Bukich. "Castoffs Spark Steelers to Upset, 17–13," read the headline in the *Pittsburgh Post-Gazette.* It was a headline that could have been recycled over and over in 1963.

The five-foot-ten, 185-pound Haley was soft-spoken and looked "more lik[e] a choir boy than a professional football player." His son Todd, who would work his way up the ranks to become a head coach in the NFL, said he never heard his father utter a swear word. "Around this business, that's hard to do," the son said.[15]

Haley also revealed a meditative, analytical side that would likely help him in his future career evaluating college players but was uncommon in a profession that discourages any recognition of vulnerability or failure. After a preseason loss against the Browns in August of 1962, Haley was "a somber study in despair," blaming himself for making wrong guesses that resulted in two Cleveland touchdowns. "Have I been cut yet?" he asked two hours after the game.[16] With Buddy Parker, you never could tell. "I was never 100 percent sure of the job," Haley said years later. "You had to play with your head or you weren't going to stay around the league."[17] Maybe part of his worry was finding a new employer, or maybe it was just an inquisitive football mind fretting about the experience he had failed to use to finish a task. It was a trait that didn't hurt him at all when he joined Art Rooney Jr. in the scouting department and began judging talent. "He's very introspective," Rooney said. "He loved it. He had a real passion."[18]

Playing football was a means of escaping a lifetime of working in the mines or the mills, but it didn't mean striking it rich—not by a long shot in the sixties. But you could do OK for yourself. Haley estimated he made $16,000 in 1964, his last season as a player. "I thought I was pretty well off," he said. "You didn't make a lot of money, but nobody made a lot of money.[19]

Another guy who found a way out grew up only a few miles from Haley: Stanley Robert Vintula Jr., the son of a bandleader. He became known as Bobby Vinton and, like Perry Como, he was from Canonsburg. In a feature story the week before the Redskins game, Vinton said he once considered coal mining as a career. He had attended Duquesne University in Pittsburgh and graduated at the age of twenty with a degree in music and a goal of becoming first oboist with the Pittsburgh Symphony. But then he tried out his singing voice and worked with dance bands that backed visiting musicians like Sammy Davis Jr. and Fabian. Two years after graduation he earned $6,000, but in mid-October of '63, with "Blue Velvet" No. 1 on the record charts, the twenty-four-year-old singer's income was expected to exceed $250,000.[20]

Some of the residents of western Pennsylvania who couldn't sing or catch a football resorted to more creative measures in hopes of getting rich or just getting by—or just to amuse themselves. Four days before the Redskins game, squads of state police and IRS agents teamed up with city police to conduct raids in Pittsburgh and other parts of the county that resulted in the arrests of thirty-one people on gambling charges. The raids boosted the total conducted by state police in Allegheny County for the year to forty-five. Among the items seized at Domenic's Confectionery in Pitcairn were sixty football sheets for betting. Western Pennsylvania football fans might not have had the physical ability of Haley, but they did show an analytical side of their own.[21]

The night after the Cardinal loss, the McKeesport Tigers Booster Club traveled a few miles to downtown Pittsburgh to honor Browns defensive back Ross Fichtner, another hometown kid who'd found his escape out of town. During the evening's festivities he saluted teammate Jim Brown as "the greatest running back of all time."[22] The next day, Buddy Parker finally gave up on a player who, as a star collegian, had seemed destined to earn some comparisons to Brown one day. It was a concession that had to reinforce Parker's distrust of draft choices—even a Heisman runner-up—and his preference for bargain castoffs like Haley. Fullback Bob Ferguson, the Steelers' No. 1 draft pick the year before, was waived and, after clearing waivers, traded to the Minnesota Vikings. Ferguson, who had been serenaded with chants of "We want Ferguson!" by the Forbes Field crowd the previous December, was officially a bust, all the more disappointing because he had shown flashes of promise in preseason and in the first Cardinals game when he subbed for John Henry Johnson. If ever Parker had a right to think he was snakebitten, it was while saying goodbye to a two-time All-America who had averaged 5.1 yards rushing for Woody Hayes but couldn't find his way in the NFL.[23] "I felt that this boy never lived up to my expectations as a top fullback in pro football," Parker said. "He made mistakes and couldn't seem to rectify them. Maybe a change will be good for him."[24]

With Johnson hobbling, Parker's decision to go with Theron Sapp as his lone fullback constituted his riskiest move since he opened the '62 season with only one spare offensive lineman. But Parker was keen on Sapp. "He has a lot of speed and a lot of spirit," the coach said. "A fullback can go a long way with those."[25]

The immediate challenge Sapp faced was finding a hole in the Washington defense, which had given up only thirty-seven first downs and 719 yards rushing in five games. The Redskins were scuffling at 2–3, but they had arguably the finest defensive line in the league, composed of ends John Paluck and Andy Stynchula, and tackles Bob Toneff and Joe Rutgens. "If there is a brace of more violent creatures in the land, it is not employed on one line," wrote Pat Livingston. Toneff, an eleven-year vet, was a gladiator in the Ernie Stautner mold. Rutgens was only twenty-four but was already earning praise as one of the best tackles in the NFL. A magazine feature on him before his senior year at Illinois was titled "Big Daddy of the Big Ten" and called him "a notable smearer of passers." Paluck was just plain scary, even to someone who had a reputation for being a brutal defensive player himself. "'Mean John,' we called him," said Sam Huff, who became a teammate after being traded from the Giants in '64. "He played tough. In fact, he's one of the few guys I played with I actually was scared of. No one ever messed with Mean John."[26]

But for opponents, the scariest player the Redskins had was Bobby Mitchell, a 9.7 sprinter with more moves than a belly dancer. Mitchell had played in the same backfield with Jim Brown in Cleveland but had been converted to flanker and also returned kickoffs. He had good hands and was a threat to turn a 12-yard catch into a 60-yard touchdown at any time. Even Jim Brown marveled at Mitchell's skills in the open field. "As a long-gain threat I am not even in the same class with Bobby Mitchell," Brown stated. "To my mind he is the greatest breakaway threat in football."[27]

While the Steelers worked out at South Park on Wednesday, John Henry Johnson spent his day at Divine Providence Hospital, undergoing tests with the team physician, John Best, but it appeared doubtful that he would return to action against the Redskins. Days later, Parker would deny that he had "banished" John Henry from practice until the fullback made up his mind to play. "I just told him to go and get some treatment on his leg and not to come back until he was able to run," Parker said.[28]

The night before Johnson's trip to the hospital, the *New York Mirror,* the tabloid that had been started by William Randolph Hearst and ranked second in circulation in the nation to the *New York News,* "published its own obituary." The *Mirror* ceased publication because of circumstances that "have necessitated the discontinuance of so many other good newspapers all over the country."[29] Radio and television, along with dramatic growth in the suburbs, had changed readership in the sixties. Twelve big cities, including Pittsburgh, had cut back to two daily newspapers since World War II, and circulation had dipped, while the number of suburban dailies in fifteen major metropolitan areas rose slightly and their circulation jumped 87 percent.[30]

Even though news of the *Mirror*'s demise made front-page news in the *Post-Gazette,* the death of the paper would have little or no immediate impact on the daily lives of Pittsburghers. But one item in the *Mirror*'s final edition had the potential to do to the Steelers what a spark could do to the parched woods in the countryside.

The *Mirror* reported that John Henry Johnson was in Parker's doghouse, a charge to which the coach replied, "This is news to me. All I know is that Johnson hurt his ankle in the St. Louis game in Forbes Field several weeks ago and hasn't run since then. John Henry, and I've known him a long time, is the slowest healing person I've ever seen. He just doesn't bounce back like some players. But if he is in my doghouse, as that paper says, he better let me know. The nights are getting cold out our way."[31]

Even with Johnson questionable, the Steelers were ten-point favorites against Washington. And fans were responding to the Steelers as if this year were special, as if this were the team that Parker had at last constructed into a winner. The ticket office, so slow in August when Art Rooney wondered where the fans were, was busier than it had been in years, selling tickets for all the remaining games.[32] Among the shirt-sleeved crowd of 41,987 that turned up at Pitt Stadium on an 80-degree afternoon were a thousand nuns from the Pittsburgh diocese, as guests of Rooney. "Spiritual help, it has been said, sometimes is greater than physical support," reporter Jimmy Miller wrote. "And the Steelers can do with an extra helping of both."[33]

It looked as if both were working on the first series as Red Mack caught a pass for 16 yards, Theron Sapp ran off right tackle for 13, and Dick Hoak burst off left tackle for 11 before getting tackled at the Washington 39. But Sapp fumbled on the next play, and Mean John Paluck recovered at the 36. The Steelers forced a punt, and Haley returned it 5 yards to his 41.

A holding call set the Steelers back, but Brown hit Dial with a 33-yard pass, down to the Washington 35. The Steelers' offensive line—Dan James, Mike Sandusky, Buzz Nutter, Ray Lemek, and Charlie Bradshaw—was opening big holes. Sapp ran off right tackle for 14 yards, then went left for 11, making it first-and-goal at the 5. Two more carries brought him within inches of the goal line, and on fourth down, Parker defied the Redskins' defensive line and turned from his conservative play-calling, electing to go for it. Ed Brown, benefiting more from the physical support of his offensive line than from spiritual aid, burrowed through to give Pittsburgh a 7–0 lead.

After Frank Budd returned the kickoff 27 yards to his 36, Snead got the Redskins in Steeler territory with an 18-yard pass to Billy Barnes. On third-and-8 from the 33, Ernie Stautner barreled through and dropped Snead for a 9-yard loss, forcing the Redskins to settle for a 49-yard field goal by Ed Khayat to make it 7–3 with 2:38 left in the period.

Brady Keys, who broke big punt returns in the first two weeks, took the ensuing kickoff on the 13 and raced 58 yards to the Washington 28. Brown hit Mack crossing over the middle for 14 yards and then found Hoak on the left sideline for a gain of 13, giving Pittsburgh first-and-goal at the 3 as the quarter ended.

Sandusky, the left guard, had been obtained by Parker, along with quarterback Earl Morrall, in a 1957 trade with the 49ers for linebacker Marv Matuszak and two No. 1 draft picks. Public relations director Ed Kiely wrote a brief feature on Sandusky titled "A Man Nobody Knows" for a 1961 game program. Evidently that reference was applicable to some of his teammates as well, because former Steeler end Goose McClairen once referred to the six-foot, 230-pound guard as "Mike Salsbury." Kiely characterized Sandusky as "exceedingly shy," but he was also as tough as his counterparts on the defensive line.[34] In a December 1959 game against the Bears, Sandusky sustained what was feared to be a fractured cheekbone early in the second quarter yet didn't come out of the game. (X-rays were negative.) Two weeks after the loss to the Browns, the Steelers' futility at the Cleveland goal line had to feel almost fresh in their minds. But after Pittsburgh was called for backfield in motion, Sandusky simultaneously blocked defensive back Jim Steffen and linebacker Bob Pellegrini to give Hoak a clear path for an 8-yard TD that made it 14–3 on the second play of the second quarter.

The speedy Budd took Michaels's kickoff and returned it to the 37, but he fumbled and Mack recovered. Sapp gained 14 yards over the left side, and Mack made a leaping catch for another 14, giving the Steelers first-and-goal at the 7. Two Sapp carries put the ball on the 1, but again the Steelers were called for backfield in motion, and Hoak could only gain four yards on third down. Faced with fourth-and-2, Parker sent in Michaels to kick a 9-yard field goal for a 17–3 lead with 4:10 elapsed in the quarter. Everything was working smoothly for Pittsburgh, but for the rest of the afternoon, the Steelers had "to root like a pack of hungry hogs" to score.[35]

A two-touchdown lead can disappear even quicker than the 20–3 advantage the Steelers held in St. Louis. The Redskins realized that too, having blown a seventeen-point lead themselves to Philly the week before. Parker knew that despite Snead's struggles, he was too good a quarterback to keep straying off target. "He's going to explode one of these afternoons," the coach had warned during the week. "When he does, I hope it isn't against us."[36]

Fullback Jim Cunningham took Michaels's short kickoff and returned it 23 yards to his 43. Parker was about to witness the realization of his fears. On first down, Snead hit Mitchell on the Steeler 20, and he sprinted into the end zone with what appeared to be a 57-yard touchdown. The play was called back because of a holding penalty, but it was only a fleeting reprieve for Pittsburgh. As troublesome as Tommy McDonald and Bobby Joe Conrad had been during the first five games, Mitchell was going to give the Steelers fits.

In explaining his repertoire of moves, Mitchell explained, "I fake with every part of my body."[37] The Steelers got a look at him from head to toe. One play later, Snead hit Mitchell again, and the flanker went into action, eluding Haley and Willie Daniel, although he used one too many body parts in his fakes this time. "Like a mischievous goblin, Mitchell did some tricky maneuvering to thoroughly confound the Steeler secondary. He whirled by a couple, eluded a couple more and, in his frenzied hip action dropped the ball as he raced down the sidelines." Fortunately for his team, Mitchell recovered his fumble at the Steeler 16, a gain of 59 yards.[38] Dick James ran 15 yards to the 1, and Snead's quarterback sneak made it 17–10 halfway through the quarter. Mitchell, clearly, could change the course of a game in a flash.

Dial wasn't as fast as Mitchell—practically no one was—but he ran precise routes and had terrific moves of his own. The Steelers marched to their 49, and from there Brown connected with Dial on a 43-yard completion, giving Pittsburgh first-and-goal at the 8. Sapp lost 2 yards on two carries, and Mack's 6-yard catch left the Steelers with fourth-and-goal at the 4. Parker sent in Michaels to kick a field goal, which he missed. The Redskins were flagged for being offside, however, moving the ball to the 2, although it remained fourth down.

Maybe Parker was fretting over Michaels's blown kick, or maybe he was thinking back to the goal line stands in Cleveland, where twice he chose to kick field goals at the 1. Maybe he was encouraged by Brown's successful quarterback sneak to cap the opening drive this day. Or perhaps he was swayed by the crowd's boos. He might have been tempted to send in John Henry Johnson, but he didn't. In any event, Parker pulled Michaels and let his team go for the touchdown.

Hoak took the handoff and got dumped by linebacker Rod Breedlove for a 4-yard loss. Washington took over, and after James gained a yard, Snead hit Mitchell with a 48-yard pass to put Washington on the Pittsburgh 45.

James, like Hoak, was an unsung, undersized back at five foot nine and 179 pounds, but he was "a first-class player and when the Redskins send him in motion to the left, away from Mitchell, they have a red hot pass pattern going for them."[39]

On first down at the 36, with 1:45 left in the half, James got loose down the left sideline, caught Snead's pass at the 15, and went into the end zone untouched. Khayat, trying for his seventy-third consecutive extra point, had his kick bounce off the hands of linebacker Myron Pottios and carom over the crossbar to tie it, 17–17, with 1:37 left before halftime. No one watching in the stadium could have appreciated the trajectory and flight of such a kick more than Michaels. If Steeler assistant Torgy Torgeson was reminded of what he'd said when another deflected ball cost Pittsburgh points in St. Louis—"When they score on plays like that, you're not about to win"—he probably kept those sentiments to himself.[40] The nuns, however, might have been pondering the concept of divine intervention.

The Steeler defense had held Washington to 27 yards rushing in the half, but on the opening drive of the second half, James carried nine times—as many as he had the entire '62 season—on a thirteen-play, 77-yard drive, benefited by pass interference and roughing-the-passer penalties, and he picked up the final 5 yards to put Washington ahead for the first time, 24–17. The Redskins had rallied with twenty-one unanswered points.

The Steelers came back with a 73-yard drive of their own, with a 35-yard pass to Dial giving them first-and-goal at the 4. Three carries left the Steelers a half yard short of the goal line, so, on fourth down, Parker went for broke. Brown's pass for Dial was knocked down, but interference was called on defensive back Lonnie Sanders, giving the Steelers another set of downs at the 1. Hoak was stuffed twice going off right tackle but then slipped around right end to tie it again, 24–24, with 2:22 to go in the third quarter.

The fleet Daniel was doing his best to stay with Mitchell. Daniel was as fast as former teammate and cornerback Johnny Sample, but keeping up with Mitchell was a daunting task. "If there's a faster or a quicker man in football, I'll have to see him," Daniel said afterward. "There were a couple times I thought for sure I was going to get an interception, but that guy came out of nowhere either to catch the ball or break up my interception."[41]

Mitchell caught only four passes that day and was kept out of the end zone, but he piled up 173 yards, and 51 came on a catch during the next series that put his team on the Steeler 10. Barnes could pick up only a yard, and two passes went incomplete, setting up a 15-yard field goal by Khayat that pushed Washington ahead, 27–24, twelve seconds into the fourth quarter.

"The defense came off and the offense went on, and we're sitting down and everybody says, 'Aw, shit, we're gonna blow it,'" tackle Lou Cordileone recalled. "I said, 'No, we ain't gonna lose this game. Don't worry about it.'"[42]

The Steelers were threatening at the Washington 31, thanks to a 23-yard catch by Dial, but Brown fumbled on a pass rush, and though tackle Charlie Bradshaw recovered, the play lost 6 yards. Brown lost 7 more yards when Stynchula sacked him at the 44, forcing a punt that went into the end zone.

As if Mitchell, in the open field, and James, coming out of the backfield, weren't big enough threats, Snead had yet another target: imposing rookie tight end Pat Richter, a six-foot-five-and-a-half-inch All-America from Wisconsin. "You can look for Snead to throw to him more often from now on," coach Bill McPeak had said days before the game.[43] "He's a tough guy to cover," said the five-foot-ten Haley. "He's so big there's not much you can do about it if they get the ball up high enough for him."[44]

Snead was on his way to a 309-yard day. He had finished the '62 season tied for third in touchdown passes and with the fifth-highest total in interceptions, and he would wind up '63 as the leader in interceptions thrown, but he had not thrown one on this afternoon. For a third-year quarterback, he had the benefit of a rare kind of experience. He had started every game as a rookie, an unheard-of development in the NFL at the time, when rookie QBs remained on the sideline, holding a clipboard and charting plays. He finished '62 ranked fifth in both completions and passing yardage, higher than two other rising stars, Fran Tarkenton and Charley Johnson.

Snead misfired for Barnes, and fullback Don Bosseler was dumped for a 4-yard loss by Pottios, setting up third-and-16 at the Redskin 16. As Snead dropped back, Haley had his eye on the quarterback while Richter was slanting toward the middle. "I don't know what happened, but Snead seemed to hesitate just a second too long," Haley said.[45] "I was afraid of making my move too soon. But when the ball did come it was a cinch."[46] Haley picked off the pass, evaded a diving Richter, got a key block from Cordileone on Khayat, and beat Snead to the end zone for a 24-yard return that put the Steelers ahead, 31–27, with 3:58 gone in the fourth quarter.

On the ensuing kickoff, Leroy Jackson fumbled, and Steelers rookie Jim Bradshaw recovered at the 22. Dial, who would finish with six receptions for 155 yards, caught a 4-yard TD to make it 38–27. The Steelers had turned the game around—and maybe their season—by scoring fourteen points in under two minutes.

Eight straight pass attempts by Snead brought the Redskins to the Steeler 31, and one play later a 16-yard toss to James gave Washington a first down on the 13. But Michaels broke up a pass at the line of scrimmage, and Snead misfired on his next two attempts before Pottios intercepted on fourth down.

Washington yielded a first down before forcing a punt, but Haley got his second interception on a throw intended for Mitchell, and the Steelers killed the clock. It wasn't a miracle—only a heavy rainfall would have qualified for that—but it was a good indication that the Steelers had the composure to rally and not fold under pressure. They hadn't choked; they hadn't disgraced anyone. They had rebounded from a bad game.

The Giants, meanwhile, beat the Cowboys, the Steelers' next opponent, 37–21, as Y. A. Tittle threw four touchdown passes. The Browns stayed unbeaten by whipping the Eagles, 37–7, behind four Frank Ryan TD passes and Jim Brown's 144 yards rushing. The Packers, the Steelers' opponent in two weeks, battered Charley Johnson and the Cards, 30–7, leaving St. Louis and New York in a tie for second place at 4–2.

The Bears showed they weren't invincible, losing 20–14 to previously winless San Francisco, dropping Chicago into a first-place tie with Green Bay.

The Steelers, at 3–2–1, trailed three teams in the Eastern Conference, but they had survived another week. They were still in the hunt. No one could say they were snakebitten this week.

GAME 7

VERSUS DALLAS COWBOYS
AT FORBES FIELD
OCTOBER 27

Playing football and working in a steel mill used to be two birthrights of a Pittsburgh native. But at one time, brawling probably ranked right alongside them as an inalienable right.

The North Side—or "Nor' Side," as locals pronounced it—where the Rooney family lived, had a long-standing reputation for rowdiness. "North Siders used to meet groups from the other side of the Allegheny and fight in the middle of the bridge, throwing each other off into the water," Roy Blount Jr. wrote in *Three Bricks Shy of a Load.*[1]

When no one came across the bridge, well, it was easy enough to pick a fight among your own. And you never had to go far to find a willing participant. It was the quickest solution to a difference of opinion. "Many North Side kids believed that the way to settle an argument was with your fists or by letting loose with a barrage of filthy language," with the second option, naturally, providing an easy invitation to put up your dukes. People tended to feel "that North Side kids were nothing more than hoodlums," Art Rooney Jr. commented.[2]

Throwing punches—or at least thinking about it—was as integral to the routine of daily life as school and sports, a task unbounded by age, size, or skill. The North Side had upstanding, law-abiding citizens who would become sources of pride to the community, to be sure. "On the other hand," Rooney reflected, "there were also plenty of hooligans, and a lot of them ended up in the pokey."[3]

So it was no surprise that while growing up on the North Side, William Richard "Red" Mack learned early in life the lessons that would help a

175-pound offensive back survive for six seasons in the NFL against players who outweighed him by seventy-five pounds or more, and defensive backs—including teammates—who thought that a roundhouse forearm to the head, delivered like a scythe in a farm field, was more effective than a textbook tackle around the hips. The final score, Mack came to realize, really didn't settle anything.

"From my childhood, living on the North Side," Mack said, "if you won, you fought. If you lost, you fought. You always had to defend yourself. Right or wrong, you had to defend yourself, and I always had that mental attitude. It didn't make any difference if the guy was big or little, you still had to defend yourself, because if you backed down, you're not going to be able to be No. 1. You're not going to be able to achieve your goal."[4]

But there was one confrontation, one endless argument, that Mack could do nothing to settle—not with his fists, not with his wits. His parents split up when he was around eleven, leaving him and his two brothers and two sisters in limbo. "They got divorced, and neither one of them wanted us," he said. "So I was a ward of the court for about four, five months. My grandmother convinced the court that they didn't want to separate us. So they put us all in St. Paul's Orphanage. The funny part about it is, I'm Catholic and my grandparents are Mormon. But she kept us together."[5]

Mack spent four years in the orphanage. "I've been asked this question a thousand times over the years," he said during a high school reunion in 2008. "It was a blessing because I didn't have the turmoil that a lot of kids have with divorces where the mother is against the dad, the dad's against the mother. I didn't have that. So when I went into the orphanage, my mother and dad really weren't part of my life anymore. They came on Sunday once a month to visit. One year, I think the second year I was there, I told [the orphanage], 'I'm not going to visitation with my parents.' They said, 'You have to.' I said, 'I am not going. All they do is argue and fight.' So they made it so that my mother came one month and my dad came the other month. I didn't have to put up with that."[6]

Mack attended Hampton High School in his freshman year, and it was on the football field where he learned that he would have to keep fighting for everything he had been fighting for in his youth if he wanted to become a success. "Ed Fay was the line coach," Mack said. "He pulled me out of practice one day and he said, 'If you ever want to amount to anything or you ever want to go anywhere in football, you're going to have to work at that every day of your life.'"[7]

Mack weighed around 110 pounds the first time he put on a football uniform. When he left for Notre Dame after spending a year at the Bullis School in Potomac, Maryland, he had put on some weight but, more important, he had learned a valuable lesson: "You don't have to be big, you don't have to be the fastest guy in the world, but you've got to be the toughest."[8]

Mack wasn't dreaming about an NFL career in college. He played running back at around 170, 175 pounds at South Bend, and he hurt his left knee in his junior year and his right one in his senior year, which limited his playing time. But in his sophomore year he showed the talent that would lead *Sports Illustrated* to list him as a preseason All-America candidate the next year, and he would also serve as an example of the hazards of getting hit by players thirty or fifty pounds heavier.[9] In mid-October of 1958, Mack ran for 106 yards—and had a 64-yard touchdown run called back because of a holding penalty—in a 9–7 victory over Duke. Two weeks later he ran 9 yards for a touchdown and returned a punt 65 yards for another to help Notre Dame beat Navy, 40–20. The next week, at Pitt Stadium, Mack showed what a threat he could pose as a receiver. He caught a 72-yard pass from future pro George Izo to set up a go-ahead touchdown, and after Pitt took a 29–26 lead with eleven seconds left, Mack put a scare in the Panthers by catching a 47-yard pass that put the Irish on the Pitt 15 as the final gun sounded. A week later, Mack ran for two TDs in a 34–24 win over North Carolina. On November 29, however, in a 20–13 victory over USC, he had to leave the game with an injury.

Mack averaged more than 6 yards a carry in Notre Dame's 6–4 season, but he began his junior year on crutches, the result of a torn muscle in his right calf. By the end of the year, the first under Joe Kuharich, there would be thirteen cases of knee surgeries, including Mack and teammate Myron Pottios. The only thing that could keep Mack from stardom, it seemed, was his health. "With a good knee this fireball will make a lot of people forget a lot of heroes of the past," one preseason magazine predicted.[10] Back in action on October 1, 1960, against Purdue, Mack injured his leg while defending a pass against six-foot-five Manzie Winters and had to be taken off the field on a stretcher, lost for the season. Mack had proved he could run and catch a football, and no one would dare dispute his toughness.

Undergoing two knee operations while playing on 5–5 and 2–8 teams in his final two college seasons didn't do much for Mack's prospects as a pro. With six of their first nine picks traded away in the 1961 draft, including No. 1, the Steelers picked Pottios in the second round, Penn State's Dick Hoak in the seventh, and Mack in the tenth round. "Later on in the season,

I found out Art Rooney got [to make] one draft choice every year," Mack said, "and I was his draft choice." As Ed Fay heard it, Rooney said, "I want that skinny kid from Notre Dame from Nor' Side."[11]

It didn't take long for the skinny kid to be tested. Rooney was a former boxer himself—and a good one—and no one knew better what kids from the North Side were like. The players didn't know how much the rookie could take, and they probably didn't know that Mack had boxed with the club team at Notre Dame and was good enough to become light-heavyweight champ. "A little bit of that street fighting on the North Side helped out," Mack said.[12]

Fred Williamson—who later dubbed himself "the Hammer"—"was a wide receiver my rookie year in training camp," Mack recalled. "A week or so into training camp, they moved him over to defense. Of course, he didn't like that. We were running pass patterns one day—all we had on was shoulder pads—and man, he knocked me down—he just flattened me. I got up off the ground, I hit him upside the head, knocked him out colder than hell. I think I made the roster that day."[13]

If there was any doubt about whether Mack would stick, Bobby Layne let his feelings be known to Buddy Parker. "My roommate at Notre Dame was Myron Pottios," Mack said. "Myron Pottios told me, 'I heard Layne tell Buddy Parker, Buddy, you've gotta keep that sonuvabitch around here because you don't know what's gonna happen with him.'"[14]

Fay remembered another defensive back who took his best shot at Mack. "His first year as a rookie they were practicing up at Slippery Rock," Fay said.

> Bobby Layne was the quarterback, and he called this pass pattern for Red. When he made his cut, Brady Keys leveled him. It took three or four minutes to bring him around. They got him on the sideline and got him ready again.
>
> When he went [back] out, he told Bobby Layne, "Call that same pattern again." Layne said, "We don't want to lose you." Red said, "Call that same pattern again." So he does. Instead of breaking on the route, he went right at Keys and he leveled him like you would not believe. Then they carried Keys off the field. He wouldn't back down for anybody.[15]

Mack got into another scrap, this time with defensive back Billy Butler, after colliding on a pass play in early August. They were practicing at Slippery Rock, but for Mack, it must have felt just like being back on the North Side. Mack was unpolished as a receiver, but he had speed and he had Ed Fay's advice: If he was going to succeed, he would have to work at it every day.

It took only a couple of practices for the rookie to make a big impression on Parker, and three weeks later he got the chance to show Steeler fans that he was something special.

The Steelers held a controlled scrimmage on Alumni Day, the first Saturday in August 1961, drawing 5,000 fans. Defense dominated the scrimmage, but when it was over, "the name of William (Red) Mack . . . was on the lips of everyone."[16] Mack scored twice on 80-yard receptions. The first time, he got behind the secondary; on the second, guarded tightly by rookie Overton Curtis, Mack "managed to make a spectacular leaping steal of the pigskin right out of the defender's mitts, then slipped along the white stripe into payoff territory." One news account described him as "a fleet, fancy dan halfback from Notre Dame," which must have come as a surprise to the man without any privilege who'd looked after his siblings in an orphanage and had to face off against bigger kids most of his life.[17]

There had been "phenoms" in camp before—like C. R. "Cash Register" Roberts and James "Jetstream" Smith—and other teams had them too, like Cleveland "Pussyfoot" Jones, a five-foot-four, 147-pound receiver with the Cowboys.[18] But Mack, along with Hoak and Keys, was a genuine NFL player. The main concern about Mack was whether his knees could hold up to the demands of an NFL season. "Mack can run like a gale and has that change of gait that will paralyze a potential tackler," wrote *Press* sports editor Chester L. Smith. "If he can stand up under what's ahead of him, he just may prove to be one of the best targets Bobby Layne ever had."[19]

Mack eventually became a different kind of target for Layne. Three years after entering the league, Mack had the distinction of making an all-star team of sorts compiled by Layne: "Pro Football's 11 Meanest Men." Listed among guys with reputations for being the roughest players in the league—Sam Huff, Alex Karras, and Mike Ditka—was the 185-pound kid with great hands and two bad knees. Wideouts—or "spread" receivers, as they were known then—earned reputations as the fastest or most dangerous in the league, but rarely if ever were they put in the same category as show-no-mercy tacklers such as Dick "Night Train" Lane.

"He's the meanest spread receiver I've ever known," Layne said of Mack. The problem, the retired quarterback explained, was that too much intensity could distract a player from his assignments and draw penalties. But Mack wasn't always the instigator, Layne conceded. "It's possible he may not go looking for unnecessary fights," Layne said, "but somehow he still seems to find them—or maybe they find him."[20]

Mack wasn't looking for a fight when he ran patterns in practice against Williamson and Keys, and he wasn't looking for one when he and several teammates, members of the Steelers' basketball team that played in the off-season, made a stop after a game in winter. "Red had bought a new car," his old coach Ed Fay recalled, "and on the way back they stopped in a saloon, and they were having some beers." The Steeler players began playing one of the electronic bar games, sliding a hockey puck at bowling pins. "Lou Michaels was on Red's end of the table, and he was hunching all the time over the line, shooting the puck. Red said, 'Hey, Lou, stay behind the line, you're cheating.' And [Michaels] said, 'Don't talk to me like that, you little redheaded'—and used an expletive, you know? And Red said, 'Well, I'm going to tell you, you go over the next time, I'm going to knock you on your ass.' So he does it: Michaels goes over. Red confronts him and knocks him right smack on his ass."[21]

The six-foot-two Michaels was one of the players who had been riding in Mack's car, along with halfback Charlie Scales. Mack announced, "Anybody in my car, let's go, I'm going home," Fay said. "So they all walk out to get in the car. Here comes Michaels out of the saloon and he says, 'Get out of that car or I'll kick that door in.' Red said, 'Don't touch that car. I never had one till now. Don't touch it.' So [Michaels] acted like he was going to kick it in, and Red opened the door, got out," Fay said. "And," said Mack, "I decked him." Then, Fay recalled, Mack said, "Let's go. If you want to go with me, in now. [Michaels] is not getting in my car."[22]

Mack played special teams in his rookie year and caught only eight passes, two for touchdowns, but he showed enough promise that the 1962 Steeler press guide said he could turn into "the perfect replacement for former Steeler end Jim Orr," who had been traded away in the Big Daddy Lipscomb deal.[23] Mack only matched his totals for receptions and touchdowns in '62, but he showcased his big-play potential by averaging 25.4 yards a catch, nearly 6 yards better than Dial's average that season.

In the fifth week of the '63 season, the loss to St. Louis, Mack had shown both his game-breaking skills and the reckless play for which Layne faulted him. Mack had caught an 83-yard touchdown pass, eluding Jimmy Hill, but he had also hampered Pittsburgh's chances of running out the clock in the final minutes when he was called for a 15-yard personal foul, sticking the Steelers in a second-and-20 hole.

It was a case of Mack trying to live up to a standard set back in high school—measuring himself against the best, whether it was Southern Cal, the Cleveland Browns, or whomever he was playing that week. Years later, Mack explained, "I always wanted to be better than that guy or that team. And the only way to achieve that, you had to demonstrate that. Sometimes you were better than they were, and sometimes you got in trouble because they were better than you. You still had to defend yourself."[24]

That day in St. Louis, he was tussling with Pat Fischer, a cornerback whom Mack would later rank as one of the toughest defensive backs he'd played against. "I gave him the shoulder real good, and he got me probably with a knee," Mack explained at the Curbstone Coaches luncheon the day after the loss. "Then when I blocked him near the finish of the game the official ruled a foul."[25]

The following week, Mack caught five passes for 69 yards in the win over the Redskins. After taking Monday off, the Steelers began preparing for the Cowboys, who had been featured on the cover of *Sports Illustrated*'s pro football preview issue, with the heady forecast that a revamped defense made Dallas the favorite to unseat the Giants in the Eastern Conference. Before the season began, coach Tom Landry had boldly predicted in a bylined piece for a football magazine, "I think this is going to be the next great team in pro football."[26] Landry wasn't far off in his estimation, but he was a bit premature. The 1963 Cowboys had gotten off to a 1–5 start that dropped them into last place, and they were coming off a 37–21 loss to the Giants.

The year before, the Cowboys had used a curious combination of quarterbacks that took Paul Brown's shuttling guard system one step further—rotating quarterbacks Eddie LeBaron, the recipient of Lipscomb's threat after the Pro Bowl game, and Don Meredith on alternating plays. It was a system devised by someone Meredith called "a living IBM machine"—the former Giants assistant Landry.[27]

Had the five-foot-seven LeBaron stood six two, he "might have been the greatest quarterback in history."[28] And had he been paired with six-foot-seven rookie quarterback Sonny Gibbs, he might have gone down in NFL history as a costar in the Mutt-and-Jeff offense. Instead, he shared command with Meredith, a two-time All-America at Southern Methodist University who set an NCAA record with a three-year completion record of 60.6 percent.

In 1963, Landry was still juggling quarterbacks, sometimes quarter by quarter, but by the end of the week leading up to the Steelers game, he'd committed himself to Meredith.

Pittsburgh was entering its thirty-ninth day without any appreciable precipitation. On Tuesday, "two fair maidens made obeisance to the God of the Heavens" in a ceremony in a downtown Chinese temple, lighting incense and offering prayers for relief from the drought.[29] The weather was unsettling, but the economy was thriving. Unemployment was at 6.6 percent, the lowest since November of 1957. The steel industry was enjoying "glowing profit reports," with the highest earnings over the first nine months of the year since 1957, but the federal government was making an inquiry into steel pricing practices.[30]

Pittsburgh was a sports town—besides football and baseball, it had the Hornets, a minor league hockey team; the short-lived Pittsburgh Rens of the American Basketball League; and big-time college basketball—but the city was also drawing a variety of top-shelf entertainers, and audiences were showing their appreciation. Comedians were cracking all sorts of jokes, but Pittsburgh was no longer the butt of them. Milton Berle opened his run at the Holiday House on the eve of the Cowboys game to a rave review. "I have never heard such response to any entertainer in any club anywhere," Lee McInerney wrote in the *Post-Gazette.*[31] The Pittsburgh Opera was celebrating its twenty-fifth season. A young actress named Joey Heatherton appeared in town to promote her first film and enthused about the city's beauty.[32]

The Steelers opened as an eight-point favorite over the Cowboys, and their outlook improved when John Henry Johnson, after sitting out three games, looked fit at practice. Buddy Parker said there had been no urgency to use him against Washington because Theron Sapp was running so well, and the coach said he might not know until game day who would start against Dallas. Dick Hoak remained the ironman, trailing only Jim Brown and Jim Taylor among the rushing leaders.[33]

John Reger returned to action for the first time since his collision with Sapp in the opener. Willie Daniel, who underwent knee surgery after being injured on the second day of training camp, had made his first start Sunday, and Clendon Thomas was back at safety. Ernie Stautner, who started at right end against the Redskins, had X-rays of his shoulder and ankle taken after being blasted on a block—a clean one—by Vince Promuto.[34]

"I haven't been hit like that since 1951," Stautner said.[35] The X-rays were negative, and the veteran vowed to be ready for Dallas. "I heal quickly," he said.[36] Indeed. Trainer Roger McGill, after examining the black-and-blue ankle, was amazed at Stautner's recuperative powers. "He has to have the highest threshold of pain of anybody I've ever seen," McGill said.[37] If Parker used Stautner as a standard to measure John Henry Johnson's recovery—or any player's, for that matter—it was an unrealistic comparison.

But questions loomed concerning Lou Michaels. The left defensive end suffered what the club believed to be an allergic reaction to a penicillin shot—"skin eruptions" on his hands and feet—and missed two days of practice. Reserve fullback Tom Tracy resurrected his placekicking skills in practice as Michaels went to Divine Providence Hospital for tests. By Saturday, it appeared that Michaels would be limited to placekicking duties against Dallas.

Only 20,000 were expected to turn out at Forbes Field for the Cowboys, and fans had to wonder whether the Steelers' era at the fifty-four-year-old landmark was rapidly drawing to a close. NFL teams were beginning to pressure Art Rooney to schedule all Steelers games at Pitt Stadium until the proposed North Side stadium could be built. Over two seasons, games scheduled at Pitt Stadium drew an average of 41,000 fans, while Forbes Field games averaged 21,500 (although two of the games at the university site had promotions for discounts for youths).[38] Pitt Stadium was clean and had good sight lines all around the stadium, but Forbes Field had only about 10,000 good seats for viewing a game, Art Rooney Jr. figured. Al Abrams of the *Post-Gazette* put the number at 8,000. Once the new stadium was constructed, the sports editor predicted, "The Steelers' advance sale will boom."[39] But for '63, the team still had three dates left at Forbes Field. "That's a shitty stadium to watch a game at," Lou Cordileone said. "The stands were so far away from everything. Pitt was a nice stadium."[40]

Only 19,047 turned out for the Cowboys, the smallest crowd of the season, but what they saw was "a bronco-ride all the way."[41] After fifty-six minutes of football, and with only six weeks of the season completed, the Steelers would be left "with defeat, despair and humiliation, not to say anything of practical elimination from the race staring them in the face."[42]

What put the Steelers on the brink of erasure from the Eastern Conference race was a masterful performance by the fourth-year QB Meredith. The Cowboys were backed up early in the first quarter when Ed Brown's 45-yard punt rolled to the Dallas 8-yard line, where Mack downed it. Billy Howton, who had entered his eleventh season on the verge of breaking Don Hutson's NFL records for total receptions and yards gained, caught passes of 19, 18, and 21 yards to put Dallas on the Steeler 17. Four carries by Don Perkins advanced the ball to the 5, and from there Meredith capped the fifteen-play drive with a touchdown pass to Frank Clarke with 2:27 left in the quarter.

The Steelers couldn't move the ball, and James Stiger, a rookie halfback from Washington, returned Brown's punt 45 yards down the sideline to the Steeler 33. On first down the Cowboys were penalized for holding, but Meredith found Clarke for 13 yards to open the second quarter, and on the next play he hit six-foot-five, 220-pound end Lee Folkins with a 35-yard TD pass to make it 14–0.

Brown was no match for Meredith. The Steeler quarterback had thrown only four interceptions in the first six games, but he threw three in the second quarter alone. Brown hooked up with Mack for a 36-yard gain to the Dallas 19, but a sideline throw to Dial was picked off by Cornell Green, a second-year defensive back who had played basketball at Utah State, but not football. Green caught the ball at the 10 and returned it 55 yards to the Steeler 35. Rookie tackle Frank Atkinson dropped Meredith on a rollout for a loss of 5, which Perkins regained. Meredith threw incomplete, giving Sam Baker a shot at a 42-yard field goal, but it went wide left.

If Dallas was going to improve on its '62 mark, Landry needed his young, inexperienced defensive players to make an immediate impact. Dallas linebacker Jerry Tubbs was a consensus All-America at Oklahoma and winner of the Walter Camp Award as the outstanding college player of the year, but he was in his seventh pro season and aware that he was giving way to young studs like rookie Lee Roy Jordan, an All-America at Alabama. While introducing the sixth overall pick in the '63 draft during a winter function, Tubbs quipped, "I feel like Eddie Fisher introducing Richard Burton."[43]

It didn't take long for Jordan to establish himself in the league, and he put his skills on display for Pittsburgh. Sapp took a flare pass and raced 22 yards and then picked up another 6 over left tackle to the Dallas 49, but Jordan intercepted a pass for Mack on the 40 and returned it 5 yards.

Defensive end John Baker, six foot six and 270 pounds, sacked Meredith for a loss of 10 yards and then tackled Meredith after a gain of 1 on third down. Sam Baker got off a 51-yard punt, which Dick Haley returned 7 yards to the Steeler 17. Then Brown, undeterred by interceptions on two straight possessions, went for broke: he cut loose and hit Dial at midfield as Green slipped on the coverage. The Steeler receiver cut sharply to the left, and Mack sprinted over to block rookie defensive back Jerry Overton, allowing Dial to scamper for an 83-yard TD. Despite the skin irritations on his hands and feet, Michaels attempted the point after, but it sailed wide left to make the score 14–6 with 5:02 left in the half.

Amos Marsh took Michaels's kickoff at the 12 and returned it to the 32. Marsh ran off right tackle and came up a foot shy of a first down, and on third down, Meredith slipped around left end for a 25-yard gain to the Steeler 32. On second-and-5, Marsh fumbled a pitchout and John Baker recovered at the 38. With less than two minutes before the half, Hoak took a pass in the flat on third-and-8 from the 40, broke tackles, and went 23 yards to the Dallas 37. On first down, Mack leaped for a pass and brought it down, only to be hit from behind by Mike Gaechter in midair, forcing the ball to pop up and into the arms of Jordan, who returned it 14 yards to the 39.

On second down, Stiger took a screen pass, slipped away from two tacklers, and ran 41 yards before Keys made a diving tackle at the Steeler 20. Landry, in a peculiar move, inserted LeBaron for Meredith, and the thirty-three-year-old QB threw a pass into the end zone for Folkins that Haley picked off. The Steelers were fortunate to be down only 14–6 at the half but once again a missed conversion loomed ominously.

Between turnovers, stalled drives, and punts, Dallas and Pittsburgh combined for ten series in the second quarter. In the third quarter, there were only three, and it looked as if things were only going to get worse for Pittsburgh.

Starting from his 20 after the second-half kickoff, Meredith got the Cowboys moving with a balanced attack. Marsh went over right guard for 10 yards, and Howton added 10 with a catch. Marsh went over left tackle for 13 yards, and on the next play, as Meredith eluded the rush, he hit Marsh for 19 yards, down to the Steeler 21.

Amos Bullocks gained 8 yards, and on second-and-2, Meredith hit Howton crossing over the middle for a 13-yard touchdown to make it 21–6 with 4:42 gone in the quarter. Howton's catch tied Hutson's record of 488 career receptions, and two more that day would set a new standard. Meredith was moving on the Steelers at will, while Ed Brown's offense had shown only one flash of firepower.

But then the first rain in nearly seven weeks began to fall, and umbrellas appeared. "It seemed that signaled the end of the Steelers' drought, too," wrote Sam Blair of the *Dallas Morning News.* Or, as *Post-Gazette* columnist Al Abrams wrote, "This was where the Steelers finally awoke to the facts of football life."[44]

Johnson was back in the starting lineup but got only four carries in the game, for 10 yards, before Parker pulled him early in the second quarter. Behind Hoak, who would finish with 58 yards on the ground, and Sapp, who would gain 45, the Steelers began a drive from their 34. Hoak cut over right end for 8 yards then left for 7. Dial made a diving catch at the Dallas 31, inches shy of a first down. Sapp picked up the first down and then broke off right tackle for 12 yards to the 18. Brown was dumped for a 7-yard loss, but on third-and-17 from the 25, he hit Dial in the left corner of the end zone to cut the Cowboys' lead to 21–13, with Tracy, in place of Michaels, making the conversion.

Bullocks returned Michaels's short kickoff to the 23 and then carried for 12 yards and 11 more, as Dallas reached the Steeler 47. Meredith's completion to Clarke netted 16 yards to the 28, and Marsh's run around right end gained 14 yards as the quarter ended. Bullocks lost 3 yards, but a holding call on the Steelers gave Dallas a first down at the 11. Bullocks was tackled for a 2-yard loss, Folkins couldn't handle a pass in the end zone, and Daniel nearly intercepted a third-down throw. Sam Baker, a capable kicker, came on to attempt a 20-yard field goal but the kick veered wide left with two minutes gone in the fourth quarter. Michaels wasn't the only kicker having troubles.

Brown's powerful arm made the Steelers a threat to go deep at any time. More typical of the Steeler offense, though, was a painstaking drive in which they chewed up yardage and time while mixing in short passes and the occasional bomb. On second-and-8 from his 22, Brown heaved a throw that went into and out of Mack's arms at the Dallas 40. Dial made a leaping catch for a 14-yard gain, and Sapp and Hoak each picked up 6 yards. Preston Carpenter, reliable and sure-handed, picked up 9 on a crossing pattern, short of a first down at the Cowboys' 43. Brown threw incomplete and Sapp was stopped cold, leaving it up to Sapp to get the first down on fourth-and-1 with a 4-yard run off left tackle.

Brown went back to Mack with a bomb to the end zone, but again it slipped out of the flanker's hands. The crowd reaction was "almost hostile."[45] A screen to Sapp gained 7 yards, but a sideline throw to Dial for 3 left the Steelers about six inches shy of a first down. Faced with another fourth-down decision, Parker went for it, and Sapp picked up the first down with a 2-yard plunge to the 27. Dial caught a 13-yard pass but slipped and fell, leaving the Steelers at the 14. Brown rifled a pass incomplete to Ballman, and then Hoak juggled a throw in the end zone before it fell to the ground.

On third down at the 14, Brown called on Dial to run a post pattern from the right side. The *Dallas Morning News* called him "the magical Dial." The *Press* referred to him as "that animated gluepot." He was as clutch a receiver as any in the league.[46]

"When he came to the pros, he had all the moves, and he had sneaky speed," Mack said of his teammate years later. "But he ran terrific patterns. That's why he got open all the time. Plus, terrific hands. He was always prepared. He was a student of the game. He knew the game like Bobby Layne knew the game."[47]

Brown drilled a pass over a lunging defender, and Dial caught it inside the 1-yard line and stepped into the end zone to make it 21–20 after Tracy's conversion, with 8:17 left in the game. It took seventeen plays for the Steelers to march 80 yards.

Bullocks returned Michaels's kickoff to the 32, but this time Meredith couldn't move his team. Michaels had rejoined the defense after asking permission from John Best, the team physician, at halftime. Sam Baker punted, and the ball rolled dead at the Pittsburgh 15. There was only 4:16 left, and Pittsburgh "was racing the clock to either victory or oblivion in the gathering gloom," when "the spindly-shanked" Mack pleaded his case to Brown. "Throw the bomb to me," he said. "I think I can outrace that guy."[48] That was the guy Mack had blocked on Dial's first touchdown, Overton, the six-foot-two, 190-pound back from Utah.

Brown's confidence in Mack wasn't shaken by the receiver's trouble holding onto the ball in the previous series. But he wanted Mack to run an outside route, then cut across. "I think I can get there faster on the inside," Mack replied. He took the inside route and "shot out of the pack like a human bullet."[49]

Brown dropped back to the 6-yard line, "wound up and threw and hoped Mack could go out there and get it," he explained later. This time, the ball sailed to the Dallas 45, with Mack streaking for it. "I thought I had overthrown him," Brown said. "I didn't think he would come within 5 yards of the ball." Mack had his defender beaten by three or four steps on the soggy turf when he caught the pass over his shoulder, tucked it in, and sprinted into the end zone. "I had it all the way," he said with a smile.[50]

Afterward, Landry shrugged off the touchdown pass. "Even when everything goes right," he said, "a team's only going to hit on a pass like that one time in 10."[51] Michaels kicked the extra point this time, making it 27–21, Steelers.

Meredith still had 3:51 left to work some magic of his own. For all his gifts as a quarterback, Meredith would be burdened with lofty expectations and undermined by some circumstances beyond his control. Two years later, Dallas would trail the Browns, 24–17, in a late-fall game and have first-and-goal at the Cleveland 1, where Meredith threw for Frank Clarke in the end zone. Linebacker Vince Costello intercepted, before 76,251 fans, and the Browns held on for the victory. Gary Cartwright's story in the next day's *Dallas Morning News* read: "Outlined against a gray November sky, the Four Horsemen rode again. You know them: Pestilence, Death, Famine, and Meredith."[52] Meredith was a target of the media as much as of defensive linemen, but his teammates never questioned his guts, willingness to absorb pain, or desire to win. The same fates that had bedeviled the Steelers for years appeared to have descended on Meredith.

But the former SMU star was still looking sharp in the rain. He hit Howton with two consecutive passes for 11 yards each time, the second one a leaping grab that put Dallas on its 47. Working out of the shotgun, Meredith fumbled when he was hit by Michaels, but offensive tackle Ed Nutting recovered for a loss of 9 yards as the clock stopped for the two-minute warning.

On second-and-19, Meredith was hit as he threw, but he completed a 34-yard pass to Clarke, down to the Steeler 28. It was the same spot from which Charley Johnson had thrown the winning touchdown pass to Bobby Joe Conrad two weeks earlier. On first down, Meredith hit Clarke crossing over the middle for 9 yards, leaving the Cowboys about a foot shy of a first down at the 18. On second down, he aimed for Norman, but the second-year end dropped the ball at the 2 as he was hit by Haley and rookie Jim Bradshaw. On third down, Meredith didn't settle for running for the first down; instead, he threw for Clarke, who had drawn two defenders, in the right corner of the end zone. After twisting his leg, Clendon Thomas was out, just as he had been missing on the Cardinals' game-winning drive. Bradshaw, the ex-quarterback from Chattanooga, was in for him and made a game-saving interception. Bradshaw had a knack for being in the right place to make a key play.

Afterward, Buddy Parker was "spent, semi-collapsed" from the tension.[53] A loss, columnist Al Abrams commented, "would have meant the point of no return."[54] Things were bound to get even harder in the next two weeks, against Green Bay and Cleveland, but they couldn't get much more taxing than the comeback over Dallas. "They're all alike—awfully tough," Parker said.[55]

While the Steelers were rallying, New York was thumping the Browns on their home turf, 33–6, handing Cleveland its first loss and leaving both conference races "tighter than a pair of $5 shoes."[56] Jim Brown was held to 40 yards and was ejected near the end, along with the Giants' Tom Scott, for fighting. The Packers, playing without Bart Starr, sidelined with a hairline fracture in his throwing hand, beat Baltimore, 34–20, keeping Green Bay in a first-place tie with the Bears in the Western Conference.

Aside from the rout of the Giants, the Steelers weren't dominating games. They were more like a racehorse bunched in the pack, still in the race, but no one's favorite. Landry rated the Giants as the team to beat in the Eastern Conference race, followed by the Browns. The Steelers, he said, "could do it, but they've got an awfully tough two weeks ahead of them."[57]

GAME 8

To Raymond Klein "Buddy" Parker, the essence of football lay in fundamentals. The game was X's and O's, good technique, and diligent practice, not a batch of complex equations out of advanced calculus. Parker scoffed at the tactic of Cleveland coach Paul Brown, "once regarded as the miracle man of football," in shuttling guards into a game to give his quarterback the call for the next play. "That 'play messenger' stuff is the bunk," Parker said. "What's so mysterious about football?"[1]

When he made his remarks more than halfway through the 1954 season, Brown was coming off back-to-back NFL championships that his Detroit Lions had won by beating the miracle man's teams in the title games. Parker showed due respect for Brown, despite their conflicting philosophies on calling plays. "He's so far ahead of the rest of us, it's pitiful," Parker said.[2]

Parker won by keeping the game simple, minimizing the playbook, and resisting trick plays. The Lions had approximately twenty basic plays and, with variations, around fifty. "You'll find that straight football with good blocking can do more damage to a defense than a lot of dipsy-doodle back of the line."[3] Overcoaching, he felt, proved to be the downfall of teams. Players were smart enough to improvise and learn more plays, he agreed, "but why bumfoozle them?"[4]

The author of one magazine feature felt that Parker's coaching was a reflection of his personality: uncomplicated, straightforward, nothing fancy. During a game Parker was customarily stoic, chain-smoking (two packs a game, right on the sideline), kneeling beside players while he squinted at the action or diagnosed a play on paper. He moved "in the shambling, relaxed fashion of a bear that has just made a successful raid on a honeycomb."[5] In truth, there was nothing simple about Buddy Parker, and the outward show of composure and restraint belied a complex man whose temperament could plummet into inconsolable despair after a defeat. At times he could be charming, erudite, outgoing. In other instances he could turn sullen, crude, and boorish . . . and self-destructive. There might not have been anything esoteric about the game of football in the fifties—or before or since then, for that matter—but within Buddy Parker lay the mystery and riddle of a man with a superior coaching mind and a psyche with the volatility of a summer storm of lightning and thunder. Private demons roiled inside him, and at times they would burst out with the fury of a fullback breaking loose from the clutches of a desperate tackler.

The worst place for the Steelers to lose was on the road, because the disappointment of failure was compounded by Parker's anger and frustration, and a plane flight could feel like a prison stay. Players on a jet headed home would never know whether a pilot's caution about "experiencing a little turbulence" was referring to the weather conditions or the coach's condition after a loss. Liquor was likely to heal some emotional and physical wounds among the players, but it only fueled Parker's petulance and angst. He made a lot of threats after a defeat, and sometimes he followed up on them. "You wanted to stay out of his way after a game if you lost," Dick Haley said, "because you could be on the next boat [out]. If you didn't win, he was going to get himself pretty well oiled up, and so you wouldn't want to be in his vision on the airplane."[6]

Any coach who's ever scratched plays on a chalkboard suffers after a defeat, but for Parker, losing was an agony that "often led to unstable behavior," a torture as unrelenting as a migraine headache, one that led to a wanton search for consolation. "One common procedure was to lock himself in a room and commune with the spirits," wrote *New York Times* columnist Arthur Daley. "Usually they were as mischievous as leprechauns."[7]

They were more like monsters and goblins. There was a ritual to losing, a ceremonial attempt to exorcise the torment that haunted Parker almost like grief over the loss of a loved one. His distress suggested a need to almost punish himself, as if mentally he were making himself run extra laps, the way coaches disciplined players after a poor practice or game. It was a procedure that Parker had to endure much too often.

"When the team loses, Buddy has a routine that never varies," Parker's wife, Jane, explained in a 1954 article aptly titled "He Dies for Detroit

Every Week." "He flops on an ottoman in the living room and pulls out a pocketknife he's been carrying for thirty years. He raises the knife to his throat slowly and cuts his tie at the knot. Until I hear the material rip, I'm never sure it's the tie, not his throat, that he's cutting. He bends down and slashes his shoelaces with two quick strokes. Then he literally tears his shirt off his back without unbuttoning it." A stillness would pervade the house until Tuesday. The only sound Parker could stand was music, his wife explained, but that provided only a temporary, mindless respite. Friends stayed away. Only one remedy could ease the pain. "Nothing brings him out of his black mood until he wins one," Jane Parker said.[8]

The *Los Angeles Times* characterized Parker in his March 24, 1982, obituary as "often quixotic, rarely colorless, and yet a sound gridiron strategist." He was "ridden with monumental superstitions," and his triskaidekaphobia—fear of the number 13—was so extreme that he shunned any combination of numbers that added up to 13, numbers such as 103, and even the letter C, the third in the alphabet, in combination with the numeral 1. One time during a visit his wife rented a room with the number 319, and Parker refused to go see her. "Do you want to ruin me?" he yelled over the phone. "Three and one and nine equal thirteen. Move out or I'll sleep in the park." Parker collected hairpins and howled if his wife touched them. If anyone threw a hat on a bed, he would dwell on the transgression for months, blaming it for any bad turn of events.[9]

"Maybe I'm saying too much," his wife added, "but he should act like a rational person if he doesn't want me to talk about him."[10] As luck—or bad luck—would have it, the issue of the *Saturday Evening Post* in which the feature on Parker ran was published on November 13.

Parker was a player with the Detroit Lions and Jane was a sixteen-year-old in high school when they began dating. They were both from Kemp, Texas, a town of less than two square miles south of Dallas, with a population of 881, according to the 1950 census. Parker was so shy he sent his sister, Peepsie, to ask Jane for a date. She saw him infrequently, but one day in late May of 1940 she was sitting in front of the drugstore in Kemp, barefoot and in curlers, when Parker came up unannounced, dropped a small box in her lap, and told her he would see her that evening. The box contained a diamond engagement ring.[11]

Parker played three sports in high school, attended a junior college, and then earned a scholarship from Centenary College in Louisiana. Centenary lost only two games during Parker's three seasons and beat Texas in 1934, his senior year. Parker wasn't flashy—although the Associated Press described him as a "slashing Centenary halfback" in the upset over unbeaten Texas that he won with a field goal with forty-five seconds left—but he was tough enough as a blocker and linebacker to win a spot on the Lions.[12]

He was traded to the Chicago Cardinals in 1937 and spent seven seasons there before retiring and becoming an assistant coach with the team, and then, in an unconventional arrangement, a co-coach. In 1950, he took a position as assistant with the Lions and was named head coach at season's end. Detroit finished tied for second in 1951 and then won the NFL title the following two years, beating Cleveland each time. The two teams battled in the championship game for the third consecutive season in '54, but this time the Browns won in a romp, 56–10. The Lions dropped into the cellar the next year but challenged for the 1956 Western Conference crown before losing a showdown with Chicago, quarterbacked by Ed Brown, in the final regular-season game.

The Lions' reputation as winners was matched only by their notoriety for late-night merrymaking. On a team led by Bobby Layne, what else in the world would anyone expect? The problem, of course, was that no one had Layne's ability to ring in every Saturday night as if it were New Year's Eve yet come out the next morning and even play an exhibition as if it were a championship game. The night before Detroit got skunked by Cleveland in the title game, one Lion said, "at midnight there weren't a dozen of our guys in the hotel."[13]

In mid-August of 1957, 600 people showed up for the Lions' annual booster banquet, eager to hear Parker assess his team's chances. What they heard left them speechless. "I can't handle this football team," Parker said. "I'm through with football in Detroit." It was a hasty decision that Parker would later regret.[14]

It didn't take long for Art Rooney to snap Parker up. On August 27, with the season opener drawing near, the Steelers owner gave Parker a five-year contract. The *Post-Gazette* reported that the deal was worth $100,000, a drop-off from the $33,000 annual salary he reportedly would have made with the Lions.[15] But Parker had a lot more coming to him than twenty grand a year. Art Rooney was the target of a lot of gibes and snickers for what some fans interpreted as a halfhearted approach to building a winner, but he put his money where his mouth was—clamped down on a cigar. Why else would the Steelers owner shell out a base salary of $80,000 a year for Buddy Parker, if not in the belief that this was an investment that could finally deliver a winner to Pittsburgh?

It was not until long after Parker had left that Art Rooney Jr. learned from a financial adviser to his father that the irascible coach commanded a salary far above the $30,000 Rooney Jr. assumed was the actual figure. The sum of eighty grand was not just "top dollar," as Rooney said; it was more like colossal, considering that Jim Brown—arguably the best player in the game—was making about $35,000. On top of that, Rooney Jr. learned, Parker got a percentage of the profits and racetrack and stock market earnings. Ultimately for Parker, however, there was no way to put a figure on the financial rewards that would appease the torture of a succession of losing Sunday afternoons.[16]

Rebuilding the Steelers posed no modest challenge, even with Parker's reputation as a sharp mind and strategist. It had been ten years since the Steelers had made their one and only postseason appearance, and in that time they had experienced only one winning season. And if Parker couldn't handle the Lions, how could he control the rowdy, hard-core Steelers? Parker was bound to make a big run on a haberdashery's stock of neckties and suffer through some silent, gloomy days before his squad emerged from mediocrity.

In that era, heavy drinking among football players was no more frowned upon than lighting up a cigarette, but alcohol only heightened whatever anxieties were festering in Parker's head, and one time in Dallas his drinking led to an ugly confrontation that could have turned violent. Former defensive back Johnny Sample and Art Rooney Jr. both wrote about their memories of the incident, although they recalled different principles.

On the afternoon before the Dallas game, the Steelers checked into the airport hotel, which was not segregated, and then had dinner. Some of the Steelers went out to visit with Cowboy players, Sample said. Rooney recalled that some of the black players had gone to a blacks-only nightclub and were late getting back to the hotel. When Parker came out of his room, it was evident he had been drinking, Sample said, "because the smell of whiskey was all over him." Buster Ramsey, an assistant and Parker's "chief henchman," in Sample's words, was "egging Parker on," trainer Doc Sweeney said.[17]

In an era in which straight-laced disciplinarians like Vince Lombardi, George Halas, Howard Wayne "Red" Hickey, and Paul Brown set all the rules, Parker gave his players free rein, as long as they performed on Sunday. Parker didn't exactly make a point of performing bed checks with his players. "I'd say about two times in fifteen years," Bobby Layne drawled. "We never had a curfew," Dick Haley said. "When Bobby was playing, he wasn't staying in, so Parker never had a curfew because he would have had to do something to Bobby Layne."[18]

Sample, who roomed with Brady Keys, returned at midnight, past the 11 P.M. curfew, and was almost asleep when Parker burst into the room, in his shirtsleeves, his hands taped by Sweeney like a boxer's. Ramsey was right behind him. "I came in here to see where you've been," Parker said. "I also came in here just in case you wanted to fight, because I know I'm going to have some trouble from both of you. Now what do you want to do?" Sample figured the best course of action was to calm the coach down. "I want to go to sleep and that's just about what I was doing until you came busting in here like that."[19]

Parker left without saying another word. According to Sweeney, Rooney recalled, Parker and Ramsey blamed Johnson and Lipscomb for keeping the black players out late at the nightclub. Parker was walking up and down the hallway, yelling, "I'm going to punch out that Big Daddy and John Henry, right in the face." Parker ranted for twenty minutes before his hands went numb because Sweeney had deliberately taped them too tightly, and the coach asked the trainer to cut the tape off.[20] If Parker had met up with Lipscomb and Johnson, they might have used the same diplomacy as Sample to mollify Parker. If that didn't work, it's reasonable to conjecture that the coach could have ended up looking a lot like Y. A. Tittle in the classic photo taken at Pitt Stadium in '64, when the Giants quarterback was left kneeling in the end zone, dazed and bloodied, after being drilled by defensive lineman John Baker.

It's entirely likely that both accounts are accurate, and that Parker went stalking several players. But it seems that anyone seeking a fight with, first, Big Daddy Lipscomb and, second, John Henry Johnson, would qualify as downright suicidal.

The playing fields of professional football apparently did little to cultivate a sense of equality in Parker. Lipscomb, Johnson, Sample, and Keys were "gamers," and Parker respected them as athletes. But clearly, Parker was not going to be any kind of spokesman for the civil rights movement that was locked in gear.

"He didn't like black people, which was sad," said Preston Carpenter, who was born in Hayti, Missouri, later moved to Muskogee, Oklahoma, and attended the University of Arkansas. "He hated them. He loved John Henry, but he didn't like black people. It was no big deal for me. I liked all the ballplayers. Jimmy Brown was one of my best friends."[21]

"He could be abusive toward all of his players," Art Rooney Jr. said of Parker, "but abusive toward blacks in a way that was shockingly racial."[22]

Of course, Parker wasn't alone in his feelings. Laws and long-standing discriminatory practices were mired in tradition and resistant to change. But the objections to second-class treatment of minorities that were spreading in the nation were beginning to resonate more in sports too. A chapter of the NAACP tried to get black players (the term "Negro" was used then) from the Steelers and Colts to boycott an exhibition game in Roanoke, Virginia, in mid-August of 1961 because of the segregated-seating policy at Victory Stadium. A weak truce was worked out, and the game went on without a boycott, which would have involved up to twelve black players on the Steelers and as many as seven on the Colts.[23] The Steelers did not encounter opposition to their demand that all their players stay at the same hotel for the game, but two weeks later, when they faced the St. Louis Cardinals in Jacksonville, Florida, the Steelers decided not to risk any chances of encountering a protest against segregated housing.[24] They circumvented the issue by taking a flight to Jacksonville on the morning of the game and returning as soon as it ended, making their temporary quarters at an air base.[25]

At the same time, secretary of the Interior Stewart Udall threatened to bar the Washington Redskins from the new government-owned Municipal Stadium unless the team began using black players. The Redskins were the only team in the NFL that had no black players on its roster, which led to one gibe that the team colors were "burgundy, gold and Caucasian."[26] Redskins owner George Preston Marshall pledged that he would use the team's first two picks in the draft on Negro players, making Ernie Davis the No. 1 selection.[27] Marshall then traded Davis to the Browns for Bobby Mitchell. Ron Hatcher, a teammate of Gary Ballman's at Michigan State, was picked in the eighth round and became the first African American player signed by the Redskins.

In the November 1963 issue of *Ebony*, whose cover story gave an account of the August march on Washington in support of economic and civil rights for black Americans, the magazine ran an NFL preview in which it counted 146 Negro players in pro football in the United States: 100 in the NFL, 46 in the upstart AFL. The *Pittsburgh Courier* faulted some Negro athletes for not speaking out about the civil rights movement, but the newspaper was optimistic about progress in sports. "Future of Negro in Sports World Appears to Be Brighter than Ever," read the headline on Wendell Smith's column in the August 17 issue, eleven days before Martin Luther King Jr. delivered his

"I Have a Dream" speech to approximately a quarter-million people in the nation's capital. "Within the next 25 years, there probably will be a Negro managing a major league baseball team," Smith wrote. "There is also the possibility that a Negro will coach a top professional football team."

Black players had to fight for every inch of progress and, for Sample, that meant literally. After the '61 season ended, Sample hit an impasse in salary negotiations. He wanted a raise of $8,000 from his salary of $14,000 but, he said, Art Rooney balked and offered only $1,500. Several weeks into the '62 training camp, Parker called Sample into his office to persuade him to lower his demands. "I know you had a great year, Sample," the defensive back quoted Parker as saying. "But black athletes just don't deserve that kind of money and I won't pay it."[28]

The two shouted and traded obscenities, but no punches were thrown, and Sample left. Sample eventually got a raise of $6,000, he said, but his career with Parker was doomed, and in midseason of '62 he was released. He wound up with—of all the NFL teams—the Washington Redskins.

Superstition led Parker to employ Wallace "Boots" Lewis as an "assistant," a polite term for an aging black man who was a combination gofer and mascot. Parker had been losing a card game during college, so the story went, when he beckoned Lewis, a custodian, and rubbed his head for good luck. Parker won. While coaching for the Cardinals, he ran into Lewis before a big game in Los Angeles and brought him onto the bench for the game. The Cardinals rallied for a dramatic win, so Parker kept Lewis around and brought him to Pittsburgh after being named Steelers coach. Lewis remained dedicated to Parker right to the end; when Parker left Pittsburgh, so did Boots, despite the Steelers' offer to keep him on.[29]

When it came to getting rid of a player or venting his wrath, Parker didn't discriminate. Once he detected what he felt was the slightest trace of disrespect, disloyalty, or simply failure to produce, Parker would spare no one, rendering the player expendable—immediately.

George Tarasovic had been drafted by the Steelers in the second round out of LSU in 1952. His father, an immigrant like Lou Michaels's dad, had worked in a slate quarry in Czechoslovakia. At six foot four, 245 pounds, Tarasovic was one of the biggest players on the team, and he was strong and nimble enough to switch between linebacker and defensive end. He married a Pittsburgh girl, and they made their home in the community where she'd grown up, about fifteen minutes south of downtown. "I was living in Dormont, and everybody there wanted me to run for justice of the peace," Tarasovic said. "They put me up to run, and I guess Buddy Parker figured I was going to quit at the end of the season. I didn't win, and after Election Day he told me that was it. He figured I was ready to retire, but I wasn't even thinking about that. I wasn't even thinking about winning [the election]."[30]

Tarasovic had been playing while hurt. He went the entire first game against the Cards despite suffering a sprained arch on the first play and then played "practically on one foot" in the loss in Cleveland.[31] Tarasovic had a reputation as a rugged player, but that wasn't enough to save him. He was cut the day after the election, along with Parker crony and ex-Lion Tom Tracy—which showed that sentiment only went so far with the coach. The *Post-Gazette* wrote that the double setbacks made it "a dark day" for Tarasovic and then misspelled his name ("Tarasovich") in the headline.[32] Tarasovic was promptly picked up by Philadelphia, which had a rematch with the Steelers scheduled in week 12.

Not even a proven history of success and a reputation for gutty play could spare a player from Parker's impulsive moves, even when the affront was innocuous and entirely trivial. The Steelers were coming back from an exhibition loss to Cleveland in mid-August of '64 when Lou Cordileone—one of the "Larrupin' Lous" who'd proved unstoppable in the first Giant game the year before—made the unforgivable mistake of not showing proper contrition after a defeat, even if it was only the preseason. That was no excuse, even for a player who had rampaged against opposing offenses the previous season.

"We're on the plane going back and I'm sitting with [Myron] Pottios and he tells a joke, but it is so funny I started laughing and I can't stop laughing," Cordileone said. "One of the coaches came back and says to me, 'Buddy wants to see you when we get back to camp.' He cut me because of that. Yeah, because of that. I couldn't believe it. And I had a pretty decent game against Cleveland. That's how nuts this guy was. How do you get upset when you lose an exhibition game? Why the fuck do you get upset?"[33] Despite the rash move, Cordileone still had respect for what Parker could do with a football team. "Buddy was a little nutty," Cordileone said, "but he was a good coach. He was always on the chalkboard."[34]

The potent mix of defeat and liquor made Parker impulsive. Carpenter remembered a flight back to training camp after a preseason loss when the coach cast his menacing scowl at the players as he sauntered down the aisle. "Parker says, 'OK, I'm gonna trade every one of you sons of bitches. I'm gonna trade all my best ballplayers. I'm gonna get out of here.'"[35] On one occasion, as the story goes, Parker tried to put his entire team on waivers, but the commissioner's office interceded and halted the move.

Impetuous moves made out of spite were bound to backfire, and evidently Parker never learned from the blunder in personnel he made when he first took over as Steeler coach. In his effort to show the team who was boss, he cut the skilled halfback Lynn Chandnois, "just to prove no one was indispensable."[36] The Steelers couldn't afford to lose any talent, and Parker's track record for making shrewd moves would be tainted by reckless ones born of frustration and vindictiveness.

"He could be a tyrant," said Dan Rooney, who took over the running of daily operations during Parker's reign, "especially when he was drinking." But that wasn't necessarily the core of the trouble. "When you'd lose, he would become a madman with the booze," Art Rooney Jr. said. "Parker's bigger problem was not booze. He had a psychological problem of deep depression, shyness and that stuff."[37]

The immediate effect on the team when Parker started housecleaning was the loss of talent. The long-term impact was that "his players never developed the closeness that is essential in a championship team," a quality that Layne had tried so hard to instill in a bunch of outcasts on the cusp of success.[38]

Parker's knowledge of the game was never doubted, however. He studied game film painstakingly, frame by individual frame, sometimes taking two days to analyze one single quarter of play. Despite his conservative approach and commitment to fundamentals, he was an innovator. In '63, the Chicago Bears were challenging the Packers for the Western Conference title under a young defensive coordinator named George Allen. Allen would rise to head coach in Los Angeles and Washington and would adapt Parker's approach in trading for proven veterans, assembling the "Over-the-Hill Gang" with the Redskins and turning them into playoff contenders.[39]

After the Redskins game, Pat Livingston wondered whether anyone had noticed the Steelers using a three-man line for one play. Years later, the 3–4 defense would become synonymous with the Pittsburgh defense. In 1964, Parker would find himself plagued again by injuries to linebackers for the game in Cleveland, an almost hopeless situation when facing Jimmy Brown. But Parker improvised—presumably with Buster Ramsey—using defensive back Clendon Thomas like a linebacker and lining him up at defensive end, "which was absolutely scary," Thomas said. "We were running a 6–1 goal line all evening with some scary stunts." The strategy worked, and the Steelers won, 23–7.[40]

Parker also had the respect—and even admiration—of his peers. "Here's one of the great strategists of pro football," George Halas announced as

Parker entered the Bears' locker room later in the season. "He was truly a great coach," Art Rooney Jr. said. "He was not a teacher; he was a strategy guy."[41]

Parker recognized the value of scouting college talent. Before he got to Detroit, the Lions spent $700 annually on scouting; under Parker, the amount went up to $20,000 a year. Drafting was still a somewhat crude process in the sixties, far from the refined science into which it evolved. Parker and representatives from the Lions and Eagles together came up with the idea for a scouting combine—first known as LESTO, then BLESTO—which tested players thoroughly and shared the information and expenses among several teams. The agency kept going strong, in different configurations, for five decades.[42]

Apart from the tantrums and superstitions, sometimes Parker's behavior could seem inexplicably odd—not just to his wife, but to the players as well. "Quite a character," Andy Russell said. "I remember one time it was a brutally cold day at South Park—near zero and snow on the ground—and Parker drove his car down and pulled it up next to the huddle and sat in his car and rolled the window down and told us what plays to run. He had the heater on. He's smoking a cigar, and smoke would billow out of the car. That wouldn't happen today."[43]

Parker was not a motivational kind of coach. "He didn't motivate anybody," Carpenter said. But Carpenter was a self-starter, and some players needed a kick start. Football—and most grueling sports—requires players to push themselves to ungodly limits and demands a stringent self-discipline, which is why coaches are necessary to goad, prod, and inspire the athletes, besides teach them. Parker made the mistake of treating his players as adults and letting them take care of themselves both on and off the field. "Discipline was almost totally lacking. His training camp was a playground. Curfew was a joke. Stars got away with violations without even a reprimand," said Joe Tucker, the former radio and TV voice of the Steelers.[44]

"I think he felt you were grown men," said Red Mack. "He didn't have to prepare you for the game; you should prepare yourself. But everybody's not like that." Mack wound up playing for the Packers three years later, and he would earn a Super Bowl ring. The environment under Lombardi was a dramatic change from Pittsburgh. "I knew why they were always up there, why they were the team to beat, because of what they did every day at practice," Mack said. "When you went on the field at Green Bay in '66, I knew we were going to win. Because that was instilled in you for hours and hours and hours during the week. You prepared for it. And that's what we didn't have at Pittsburgh."[45]

The Steelers would go on to develop one of the shrewdest scouting departments in the league, with Art Rooney Jr. heading the operation and Dick Haley and Bill Nunn Jr. analyzing talent, and they would use the draft—not trades—to turn the franchise into a dynasty. But if there was one thing that agitated Parker nearly as much as a loss, one thing that came remotely close to scaring him as much as the number 13, it was the prospect of having to rely on a rookie. Toward the end of the '57 season, in his first Steeler draft, Parker traded away six of his first nine picks, including the No. 1 selection. The next year Parker traded away his first seven draft picks. In the 1960 draft, the Steelers selected Jack Spikes No. 1 but traded the next five picks. In '61, Parker dealt his No. 1 and four of the next five picks. In '62, he selected Bob Ferguson No. 1 but swapped his next five picks. And if ever there was a personnel decision Parker regretted, surely it was not trading away the No. 1 pick he used on Ferguson.

In the 1963 draft, the Steelers' first seven choices were gone before they took Frank Atkinson, a tackle from Stanford, in the eighth round. Among the diverse group the Steelers plucked in the draft were Bill Nelsen, a quarterback from USC, in the tenth round; Roy Curry, a quarterback from Jackson State, in the twelfth; Russell, a linebacker from Missouri, in the sixteenth; Jim Bradshaw, a running quarterback from Chattanooga, in the eighteenth; and Jim Traficant, a quarterback from Pitt, in the twentieth and final round. All would make the team, except for Traficant, who would go on to a different career, serving eighteen years in Congress before being expelled following a conviction on bribery and racketeering charges, for which he would serve seven years in prison.

Any draft pick must prove he belongs, but rookies under Parker were suspect before they even laced up their cleats.[46] "He said, for every rookie that was on the team we would lose a ball game," Bradshaw said. "He just wanted veterans."[47]

As injuries whittled down the thirty-seven-man roster in 1963, Parker had few options but to play rookies, unless he wanted to engage in some wholesale trading. The impressive play of first-year men Russell, Atkinson, and Bradshaw made Parker's decision to stick with his own personnel less worrisome.

Coming off the Dallas victory, the Steelers were pegged as ten-and-a-half-point underdogs against the Packers. Lombardi's team had won two consecutive NFL championships and was tied with Chicago for first place in the

Western Conference, but he felt the team was aging and growing vulnerable. The week after the Steelers lost in St. Louis, Green Bay whipped the Cards, 30–7, but Lombardi sounded almost dejected afterward. "They're tougher and we're older," he said.[48] Quarterback Bart Starr suffered a hairline fracture of his throwing hand in a sideline scuffle with defensive back Jimmy Hill, and Lombardi's tank of a fullback seemed like only a replica of his former self.

"This was the big test for Jim Taylor," Lombardi said. "He only played a few minutes in previous games. He just has not been strong enough and I think he will never be the same as he once was. Too much has gone out of him."[49]

Starr was originally thought to be lost for six weeks, but on Monday word came that he might see action against Pittsburgh. That prospect dimmed the following day when the Packers added eight-year veteran quarterback Zeke Bratkowski to back up starter John Roach, in his sixth year out of SMU, Don Meredith's school.

Even though the Packers had played in three straight championship games (the first being a loss to the Eagles in '60), they were not considered "a spectacular team." Starr was mechanically sound and smart, and he had led the league in passing in '62, but he was not grouped with the genius quarterbacks, or with the dashing new breed of QBs like Fran Tarkenton. The Packers didn't have a breakaway threat like Bobby Mitchell, and they were without all-around halfback Paul Hornung, who had been suspended, along with the Lions' Alex Karras, for gambling on pro football games. But their disciplined style of play, if not flashy, was brutally efficient. "They just don't make mistakes—a Lombardi theorem of success."[50]

Parker had reached his goal of getting through the first half of the season with two losses. But to keep pace in the Eastern Conference, the Steelers had to be nearly perfect in the second half. "It was always in your mind, if you had three losses you were not going to get there," Clendon Thomas said.[51]

The Giants had won the Eastern Conference with a 12–2 record the year before and finished first in '61 by going 10–3–1. With Cleveland 6–1, and New York and St. Louis tied at 5–2 halfway through 1963, Giants coach Allie Sherman was anticipating a bumper-cars finish. "It is not beyond reason to feel that in three or four weeks the whole division could be scrambled," Sherman said. "Pittsburgh definitely is not out of it."[52]

Lombardi probably saw a lot of his own team's ferocity and manual-labor attitude in his opponent. "Beware of the Pittsburgh Steelers," he said. "They'll fight you like a bunch of alley cats. If you're not up for them, they'll scratch you right out of the Western Division!"[53]

Between two surging football teams—the Steelers and the Pitt Panthers—and a healthy economy, life was pretty good for residents of western Pennsylvania. U.S. Steel reported third-quarter earnings of $46.4 million, bringing profits for the first nine months to nearly $150 million.

And the future looked even better, paved with prosperity and technological advances. After all, if the country's leaders had the technology and ambition to reach the moon, how could anything limit a family's aspirations? "City's Future Painted in Glowing Colors," read a headline in Tuesday's *Post-Gazette,* "Pittsburgh of 1988 to Be Dreamland of Gracious Living." Twenty-five years down the road, the average Pittsburgh man would make between $12,000 and $15,000 a year, his wife would be working, the level of education would be higher, and Pittsburgh residents would enjoy more leisure time, women from the United Jewish Foundation were told at an annual meeting. Local residents would be able to ride underground rapid transit trains and "giant aluminum hydrofoil crafts [that] flit up and down the river at 80 miles an hour." Citizens could also expect an economic rebirth fueled by research organizations and new industries. But progress would also bring complications, such as "an increased threat to the stability of family life.[54]

The Jetsons, the TV cartoon series about a family living in the twenty-first century, had gone on the air the year before, and it fed fantasies about futuristic life. But it wasn't all fantasy. And even if these potential changes were years away, the repercussions they suggested produced some anxiety.

"Planners sit up nights worrying about what the cities of the year 2000 are going to look like," *Post-Gazette* editor Andrew Bernhard wrote in his column the day after the Steelers' win over the Cowboys. "All you need to understand what is happening is to drive out into the suburbs of Pittsburgh. The urban areas are exploding."[55]

People still relied on newspapers for information. The *Post-Gazette* was the morning paper, the *Pittsburgh Press* the afternoon paper. Each cost seven cents. The *Pittsburgh Courier* was a weekly directed toward the black population. The tendency for many workers in the industry was not to look ahead much further than the next edition. But a few forward thinkers started to feel that newspapers were destined to change too, although some ideas might have seemed as if they came straight out of a *Jetsons* episode.

Tucked inside the *Press* the day after the rout of the Giants in September was an account of the convention of the Interstate Circulation Managers Association held in Pittsburgh. Edward Bennett, circulation director of the *Record* of New Jersey, told his peers that papers must adjust to "the rapidly advancing age around us. . . . The newspaper of the future may well be produced right in the reader's home, according to Mr. Bennett. An electronic device similar to a television set, which would produce page likenesses in the home, could get the paper directly from the press into the reader's hands, Mr. Bennett said."[56]

For the moment, when it came to making changes in the community, old-fashioned newsprint was enough to make an impression on voters. Life in Pittsburgh wasn't all that sunny to some observers in the press, and more than George Tarasovic's political career was at stake in the following week's elections. In a front-page editorial, the *Post-Gazette* warned that Pittsburgh was descending into a reincarnation of Sodom and Gomorrah: "Vice and gambling rampant with the knowledge and consent of key public officials. . . . Democratic party leaders grown lax and complacent because they think the voters will put up with anything . . . That is the current portrait of Pittsburgh and Allegheny County."[57]

The grandstands that filled with frustrated Steeler fans weren't the only places where tempers erupted. On the Friday night before the game in Green Bay, a political rally on the North Side "threatened to explode into a full-blown riot" among the political foes in the campaign, the city firemen, and the Teamsters. The riot squad and members of the K9 Corps were brought in, but chaos was avoided when Joe Marrone's band struck up "The Star-Spangled Banner," "and the battlers pulled their punches and snapped to attention." As the confrontations simmered, the band began playing "I Could Have Danced All Night." Nobody, evidently, was tossed off a bridge and into the river.[58]

Football, on all levels, continued to provide an escape. Pitt was 4–1, having lost only to Roger Staubach and Navy. Crowds of 7,500 to 10,000 were common at high school games and, at least a dozen times, had exceeded 10,000. "The strong hold scholastic football has on fans of this area has never been better exemplified than during the present season," wrote a *Post-Gazette* reporter.[59]

If anything had Buddy Parker sitting up at night worrying, it wasn't population expansion; it was the Packers. He made a point during the week to praise his offensive line: left tackle Dan James, left guard Mike Sandusky, center Buzz Nutter, right guard Ray Lemek, and six-foot-six, 260-pound right tackle Charlie Bradshaw, who attended law school in the off-season. "But we will need more than a good offense to win," the coach said. "Our whole team will have to give its best to bring about a win and keep us in the running for the Eastern title."[60]

Lombardi's approach to football was a lot like Parker's. "The Packers win by the simple process of running over people," writer Bill Wise explained. Leading the charge on the offensive line were center Jim Ringo; left guard Fred "Fuzzy" Thurston, who was dropped by three teams before he found a home in Green Bay; right guard Jerry Kramer; left tackles Bob Skoronski and Norm Masters; and right tackle Forrest Gregg. When it came to offensive lines, "Only the Green Bay Packers can claim a better blocking compact tha[n] the Steelers have," the *Pittsburgh Courier* observed. "It is a pounding, punishing compact."[61]

The game, scheduled for County Stadium in Milwaukee, where the Packers played several times a year, had been sold out for months, but the crowd of 46,293 was tame. "You could tell it right from the beginning when they were introducing the players—there wasn't a lot of enthusiasm," Lombardi said.[62]

The Steelers didn't appear to be their customary selves, either. A sportswriter stopped in the locker room before the game and noted "the choked stillness, the eerie, monastic silence." A normally relaxed group had become "as tense as hawsers in a hurricane."[63]

The Steelers should have gotten a big lift when Gary Ballman took the opening kickoff on the 5 and, with a block from Brady Keys on Willie Wood, raced 93 yards before being hauled down by Earl Gros at the Packer 2, from where Dick Hoak scored on the next play.

"The Bays," as both the hometown and out-of-town papers called them, resembled the Steelers in their loss in Cleveland: They scratched their way into Pittsburgh territory, thanks to the Steelers' bungling, but they couldn't cross the goal line. Dick Haley appeared to have an interception on one throw but couldn't hang onto the ball. Taylor was picking up yardage on Green Bay's first drive in John Henry Johnson fashion, 3 and 4 yards a carry. Roach, filling in for Starr, hit rookie end Marv Fleming for 15 yards and a first down at the Steeler 34. After Taylor lost a yard, Roach gained 11, and Moore another 11 before he lost 4, back to the 17. Two passes fell incomplete, leaving it up to Kramer to kick a 23-yard field goal halfway through the first quarter.

The Steelers reached midfield after a 16-yard catch by Mack and a 5-yard reception by Johnson. On third-and-5 from the 50, Brown hit Hoak for an apparent first down at the Packer 36, but the ball popped out and defensive back Jesse Whittenton snagged it and returned the interception to the 50. "Hoak had a touchdown if he had held onto that ball," Parker said later.[64] The Packers failed to capitalize, though, as Boyd Dowler caught a pass for 26 yards at the Steeler 18 and fumbled after the tackle. Glenn Glass recovered for Pittsburgh.

Green Bay held, and Brown's 29-yard punt left the Packers in good position at the Steeler 49, but Myron Pottios stopped the threat as the second quarter began, intercepting Roach at the 11 and returning the ball to the 21. Three plays later, Hoak fumbled and defensive end Willie Davis recovered at the 41.

Three carries by Taylor and one by Moore put Green Bay on the 14, but penalties for holding and offensive pass interference backed them up. Taylor ran 21 yards down to the 15, but another penalty pushed Green Bay back to the 30. The drive stalled, so Kramer came on to kick a 36-yard field goal that made it 7–6 halfway through the quarter.

A 13-yard reception by Hoak moved the Steelers to their 47, but another fumble, this time by Theron Sapp on a 13-yard catch, was recovered by linebacker Bill Forester on the Packer 40. Moore broke loose for 31 yards to the Steeler 22, and a face mask penalty on Glass moved the ball to the 11. Taylor gained 6 yards on one run but was stopped dead on two others. Kramer was on track for his second straight Pro Bowl season as a guard, and he would finish ninth in field goal accuracy (47%), but he was deadly on target this day. He hit his third field goal, from 12 yards, to make it 9–7 with 2:05 to go before halftime.

After the two-minute warning, with the ball on his 36, Brown seemed in no hurry. He called five runs on the first seven plays, but Pittsburgh got a first down at the Packer 41 with fifty seconds left. Hoak gained 9 yards, giving Michaels a chance at a 40-yard field goal, but it was wide left. Even after dropping the ball and muffing their chances, defense kept the Steelers within two points of the Western Conference coleaders, even though Green Bay had already racked up 147 yards rushing.

Still, Lombardi felt his team's lead against a team that had proved it could rally and strike quickly was precarious. "I've seen pictures [film] of this ball club," he said later. "They're behind 21–0 and, all of a sudden, they're throwing the ball around and they win 24–21. That Dial and Mack are two of the greatest receivers in the league, particularly Dial."[65] The problem for Pittsburgh, however, was that Brown had hit only four of fifteen passes.

Taylor, "the crunching Bayou Bronco," had won the rushing title in 1962, racking up 1,474 yards on the ground—more than 300 more than runner-up John Henry Johnson—and averaging 105.3 yards a game, almost 24 yards more than Johnson, at No. 2.[66] It was understandable that Taylor might have a drop-off in '63, and that five-time rushing leader Jimmy Brown would regain his No. 1 status after being hampered by an injured wrist in '62. But as the second half began, the Packer fullback proved he had a lot more left in him than his coach thought after the Cardinal win, and behind him "Coach Lombardi's world champions settled down to tear their opponent apart piece by piece and yard by yard."[67]

The Packers took the kickoff and let Taylor and Moore bang their way to the Steeler 41. Moore had the unenviable task of filling in for Hornung, but the former Vanderbilt star had "supreme running ability."[68] Moore took a Roach pass and raced 40 yards to the 1. After being stopped once, Taylor plunged over to make it 16–7.

Green Bay forced a punt, and Brown's feeble 24-yard kick went out of bounds at the Packer 37. Roach was only three of ten at halftime—and he was only three of sixteen in the two previous seasons as a Packer backup—but he hit Marv Fleming for 33 yards—matching his total passing yardage for 1962—and pass interference on a throw to Max McGee gave the Pack a first down on the Steeler 17. Taylor and Moore alternated grinding out yardage down to the 2, and Elijah Pitts scored from there to make it 23–7 with 4:11 left in the third quarter.

"There was nothing but holes in that line," Taylor said with a broad smile afterward. "They were on both sides, too—big ones. They were stunting quite a bit, and we caught 'em a couple of times. Made it easier to run to the outside."[69] The next day, the day before the elections, in the Steeler offices, secretary Mary Regan, with a trace of a smile, passed on what she said was a message from an anonymous phone caller: "Tell that Tarasovic it's too bad he wasn't elected justice of the peace last week. Then he might have arrested Jimmy Taylor for speeding on Sunday."[70]

From his own 30, Brown threw for Preston Carpenter, whose brother Lew was a halfback-end with Green Bay, but the pass was picked off by defensive back Hank Gremminger, giving the Packers possession at the 37. Pittsburgh held, but Kramer had a shot at his fourth field goal, from 37 yards, on the second play of the fourth quarter. The kick was good, and the Steelers were down 26–7. Worse yet, they had shown little of the explosiveness Lombardi had raved about. Hoak and Sapp combined to march the Steelers to the Packer 31, but any hope of a miracle dissolved when Hoak fumbled again after being hit by linebacker Ray Nitschke and tackle Henry Jordan, and defensive back Willie Wood recovered at the 30.

The Steelers got the ball right back at their 23 with ten minutes left. Dial, the league's No. 2 receiver, had been held without a reception. "We worked like hell on him," Lombardi said later. "[Jesse] Whittenton and [Herb] Adderley did an outstanding job."⁷¹

Brown hit Dial twice and found Mack two times, to the Packer 33. Mack, who would finish with five catches for 87 yards, got open behind Wood and Whittenton in the left corner of the end zone for a 33-yard TD that made it 26–14 with 5:25 to go, but it was too late. The Packers recovered Michaels's onside kick and rode Taylor and Pitts down to the 1, from where Pitts went in to make the final 33–14. The game was over in two hours and twenty-six minutes.

Taylor finished with 141 yards rushing on thirty carries, and Moore added 88 yards. Except for Ballman's kickoff dash, there was nothing positive for Pittsburgh to take from the loss. Hoak had 77 hard-earned yards on nineteen carries. John Henry Johnson gained only 17 yards on seven attempts and carried the ball only once in the second half. Sapp rushed six times for 29 yards. The Steelers gave up the ball five times: twice on interceptions, three times on fumbles.

"It was as convincing a thrashing as any one pro team could apply to another and left the Steelers all but dead for the 31st year in their quest for an Eastern Conference title," *Post-Gazette* columnist Al Abrams wrote. The "Steelers still have a chance, but one would have to be some kind of nut to bet Confederate money or a 1904 calendar on their chances of reaching the top now."⁷²

Despite the win, Lombardi called his team "a little flat" but "fairly bubbled" about Taylor's performance and praised Roach's work.⁷³ Hoak wasn't too impressed with the defending champs. "I didn't think they were that tough," he said. "All we had to do was hold the ball and we would have beat 'em. We had too many fumbles and interceptions. All you've got to do is hold the ball."⁷⁴

But the Steelers couldn't do that, nor could they take advantage of Starr's incapacitation. They were manhandled by Lombardi football.

Meanwhile, Jimmy Brown, the man the Steelers had to face next, rushed for 223 yards, including a 62-yard touchdown on the fourth play of the game, to lead Cleveland to a 23–17 win over the Eagles, keeping the Browns in first place at 7–1. One could only imagine how eager he would be to get his hands on the ball in Pittsburgh once he saw films of the holes opened up for Taylor.

The Giants dropped the Cards, 38–21, leaving New York alone in second place at 6–2 and St. Louis in third at 5–3. The Steelers trailed in fourth place at 4–3–1, their obituary written by Abrams, and seconded by Green Bay sportswriter Lee Remmel, who couldn't track down Buddy Parker afterward. The coach had reportedly left the dressing room immediately for the team bus outside the stadium, "presumably to brood over the defeat which all but obliterated Pittsburgh's Eastern Division title hopes," Remmel speculated.[75]

Reporter Pat Livingston of the *Press* did catch up with Parker, who "gloomily" assessed the damage: "We were moving better against them than anybody moved on them all season. But we blew everything with those fumbles and interceptions."[76]

Hoak, the last player to leave the Steeler locker room, was asked whether Parker said anything before he left. "He hasn't said anything yet," Hoak replied, "but I expect him to say something."[77]

GAME 9

The day after a fullback supposedly past his prime ran for 141 yards against the Steelers, Buddy Parker and his staff began preparing to face a player who was being hailed as the greatest runner in NFL history. After only eight games, Cleveland's Jimmy Brown was "on his way to establishing a mark which in NFL circles may be regarded with as much awe in future years as Babe Ruth's career home run record."[1]

With 223 yards against Philly, Brown had upped his league-leading rushing total to 1,194 yards, on 163 carries—an average of 7.3 yards per carry—and had scored nine of his twelve touchdowns on the ground. Brown was a sure bet to top his career season rushing total of 1,527 yards, set in his second year in the league, 1958 (in a twelve-game schedule), and he had a good shot at reaching the unheard-of total of 2,000 yards. Brown—"230 pounds of rippling muscle"—was averaging 149 yards a game, and he could hit 2,000 by averaging 135 in the last six games.[2]

"If the homelings have finally fallen apart, up front," the *Pittsburgh Courier* said of Buddy Parker's team, "then the worst thing that could happen to them would be Jim Brown running like a madman."[3]

Brown's yardage total was nearly twice that of the No. 2 rusher, Jim Taylor, who had 639 yards on only seven fewer carries than Brown. Dick Hoak was third with 498 yards on 158 carries, a workload that Parker feared was wearing down his smaller, lighter halfback. John Henry Johnson, who had finished second in the league to Taylor the year before with a career-best 1,141 yards, had gained only 226 on fifty-nine attempts because of the playing time he had missed. Like a heavyweight boxing champion who went unchallenged, Jimmy Brown ruled the NFL as its premier ball carrier.[4] "In an era of passers, line-smashing Jimmy is the idol of the hour," wrote Steve Snider of UPI.[5]

And if Taylor could blister the Steeler defense the way he did, who or what was about to stop Jimmy Brown? "Let's face it," said Giant linebacker Sam Huff, a nemesis of both Brown and Taylor, "there's no linebacker in the league who can stop Jimmy Brown man to man."[6] In their futile efforts to stop Taylor on Sunday, "The Steelers could have used five Huffs," the *Press*'s Pat Livingston wrote.[7] How many would it take to stop Brown?

Huff, as a linebacker at West Virginia, had played against Brown in college before their grudge matches in the NFL. "I hit him so hard I knocked myself out—or he knocked me out. Broke my nose, shattered my teeth," Huff said. "I woke up in the locker room on the trainer's table."[8]

Over the years, practically every position saw the evolution of better players—faster, stronger, bigger, quicker—but for one exception. Defensive back Dick Haley began his role of evaluating talent, joining Art Rooney Jr. in the personnel department, while Brown was still playing, and Haley's observations spanned five decades. "I've been watching football players now for quite a few years," he said, forty-five years after Brown's stellar season. "They never made one like Jim Brown. Never. I have seen every back that's come out since 1965. We haven't had anybody like that—that big and that fast and that quick and strong. I've seen no one that had all those tools."[9]

The Steelers had no counterattack on offense. Parker thought that his team's best bet against the Packers was to control the ball, but if Johnson could pick up only 17 yards against Green Bay, and Theron Sapp could manage only 29, who was going to give Hoak a break and rescue the Steelers' running game?

Beneath his pencil mustache, John Henry Johnson had a gentle smile and the serene look of a man at peace with the world. He didn't smoke and drank sparingly at a time when football players indulged in both. He was nicknamed "Mumbles" for his manner of speaking, and he was capable of the occasional malapropism, such as when a friend was dating a teenager and Johnson commented, "Man, they gonna put you in jail for stationary rape." Johnson also had a sly sense of humor. Ten days after Lou Michaels kicked a 50-yard field goal but twice failed on the point-after in the opener, Johnson told his teammate, "Next game kick the conversions from the 45-yard line. You can make them from there."[10]

Brown was the runner defenses feared, but there was something downright scary about John Henry Johnson, with or without a football, anywhere on the field. His career began in an era when rules were minimal and unsophisticated. Players went after knockouts the way boxers did, and punishment was as natural to the game as changes in the weather. Brown stoically absorbed cheap shots and dirty play and resisted responding with either words or fists. "That way," he said, "my opponent never knows if he is getting under my skin." Taylor went charging right at defenders. "He'd swear at you on the field," Huff said. "He'd kick you, gouge you, spit at you, whatever it took. It was a street fight."[11]

Anytime there was a showdown, Johnson was prepared for all-out war, whether he was outnumbered or going one on one. "He went three ways: offense, defense and to the death," Bobby Layne said.[12] "John Henry was the meanest man I ever saw," said former Browns defensive end Paul Wiggin.[13]

"The rougher they get with John Henry, the rougher he gets with them," one Steeler said. And Johnson wasn't the kind of guy to back down from any confrontation. He was a fearless gladiator any teammate wanted by his side. "If I had to go into a dark alley and I had my pick of one man to go with me," a Steeler lineman said, "I'd want that man to be John Henry Johnson."[14]

Johnson played with a ferocity that stood out even in an era when violence was taken in stride. During a 1955 exhibition against the Chicago Cardinals while he was with the 49ers, Johnson struck Charley Trippi, a member of the Cardinals' "Dream Backfield," in the face, inflicting career-ending injuries. Walter Wolfner, managing director of the Cardinals, vowed later that his team would never again play an exhibition game against the Niners in San Francisco, partly because of the incident. In mid-October, Trippi was still undergoing treatment for a skull fracture and smashed nose.[15]

"It was dirty playing because Trippi was standing 30 yards from the play and Johnson punched at him with his fists and forearms while Trippi was completely away from the action," Wolfner said. Niners coach Norman "Red" Strader reiterated his belief that Johnson executed a "fine, clean block" on Trippi.[16]

During an October 1961 game at the Los Angeles Coliseum, as a Steeler, Johnson's fury erupted again, and he lashed out at Ram linebacker and captain Les Richter because of what Buddy Parker called "dirty play."[17] Writer Myron Cope recalled that Johnson hit Richter in the face. "Pop, my jaw was broken," Richter said. After Ram defensive back Ed Meador intercepted a pass, Johnson ran him out of bounds, where four of the Rams accosted the Steeler fullback. Outnumbered, Johnson grabbed the sideline marker and "began bashing it against the helmets of the Rams."[18]

"If you remember," Parker said, "the marker used to be made of wood. Wouldn't you know it? This year they changed to plastic markers. John Henry was whacking Richter with it, and all Les did was stand there and laugh. We couldn't even win when we played dirty."[19]

It was a league with no mercy. Crack-back blocks and picks were common, and players like Dick "Night Train" Lane had a reputation for clotheslining opponents and making "necktie" tackles. The Steelers played hard, but they had no monopoly on rough play.

Bears defensive end Ed Meadows was involved in a nasty incident on the final regular-season Sunday of 1956, when Parker took his 9–2 Lions to Chicago to face the 8–2–1 Bears in a showdown for the Western Conference title. Tempers erupted from the opening kickoff, with abundant "punching, kneeing, kicking and elbowing." A berth to the championship game was at stake, but "too often the players appeared intent on maiming one another." Meadows drilled Bobby Layne, then the Lion quarterback, in the second quarter, knocking him out of the game with a concussion. Meadows insisted it wasn't a dirty play, but Parker said the Bears end "used everything but a blackjack to get Layne." With Layne out, Chicago won, 38–21, and only the intervention of officials, police, and ushers prevented "a king-sized riot" at game's end.[20] Lions owner Edwin J. Anderson urged the NFL to ban Meadows for life and to fine the Bears and their coaches. Parker threatened to quit, citing "a disastrous trend that is making pro football a slugging match."[21] The game wasn't all about winning; it was about surviving, at all costs. As boxers were warned before a fight by the referee, players needed to protect themselves at all times and never turn their backs on an opponent.

Teams seemed to follow the North Side philosophy Red Mack grew up with: "If you won, you fought; if you lost, you fought."[22] In a November 21, 1954, game in which Layne threw two TD passes and ran for a third in Detroit's 21–17 victory in Green Bay, "a midfield melee" erupted at the end, with the Lions' Lee Creekmur and the Packers' Stretch Elliott slugging it out, and "a good share" of the 20,767 fans pouring onto the field.[23]

If it seemed that Layne was constantly at the epicenter of brawls, it was merely coincidental, although he came to the pros with exposure to the volatile environment of the game. His "sharpshooting passes" led Texas to a 34–14 victory over Oklahoma in October 1947, but there was as much action among the 45,000 fans as there was on the field. "The game was punctuated by fights among the fans and pop-bottle throwing as spectators vented their anger," and several thousand rushed onto the field at the end, which ended with the officials needing to be escorted away in a police car.[24]

It wasn't Layne but quarterbacks—stars, in particular—who were constant targets. If you knock the quarterback out of the game, conventional wisdom said, the better the chance of your team winning. In the same year that Creekmur and Stretch Elliott were punching away, Browns quarterback Otto Graham authored a piece for *Sports Illustrated* titled "Football Is Getting Too Vicious." The article was illustrated with drawings of dirty tactics that were commonplace in football but looked more appropriate for a viewer's guide to watching villains in pro rasslin' matches. Graham predicted dire consequences for the future of pro football if the mayhem was not curtailed.[25]

Evidently, Ed Meadows did not read the article or at least did not heed its cautionary message. Neither did Packer defensive back John Symank. Halfway through the Colts' 1958 title season, Johnny Unitas suffered three broken ribs when he was lying facedown on the ground, and Symank, in the words of sportswriter Tex Maule, "plumped down" on Unitas's back with both knees. The Colts, 56–0 winners, did not protest the way the Lions did when Layne was injured, but Maule objected to "an evil which may eventually cost much of the hard-won popularity of the game."[26]

Compared to some of the ruthless play, John Henry Johnson's particular habits were ungentlemanly, but they were permissible—and even necessary—in the Wild West spirit of the time, and he gave defensive players something to worry about.

"Yeah, you worried about him," Huff said. "You worried about him hitting you in the face with an elbow. You're talkin' about a cheap shot. He put a lot of guys out. He'd hit you with that elbow, he'd break your face mask. There was no rule against it then. It was legal. You didn't do it unless you really wanted to hurt somebody, but he did it all the time. Ho, man, that's the first thing they tell you: 'You go in there, you better be careful, 'cause he's gonna hit you with that elbow.'" But, Huff conceded, "That's part of the game."[27]

"Ol' John Henry's got the meanest elbows in football," Layne once said.[28]

Johnson remembered a game when Lew Carpenter—Preston's brother and a halfback and kick returner with the Lions, Browns, and Packers—tried to grab John Henry's face mask. Johnson warned him, and Carpenter later came by on a punt. "I laid an elbow upside his head," Johnson said. "He ain't seen me yet."[29]

Maybe there was a reason, an explanation, and not just the case of a mean disposition, that led John Henry Johnson to play so hard, so all-out. Maybe at some point when he was growing up, he got the same advice that Red Mack had received: "You don't have to be big, you don't have to be the fastest guy in the world, but you've got to be the toughest."[30]

Brown, Taylor, Johnson, and other NFL runners were eventually targets of cheap shots. And the better the runner, the more inviting a target he became, especially when he was vulnerable and often defenseless in a pileup. The line between vicious and dirty play was often blurred. Taylor called Huff "a great one for piling on" after the Packers' 16–7 victory in the 1962 NFL title game but declined to call the linebacker a "dirty" player. During one pileup, Taylor said, "somebody was in there twisting my head."[31] Huff received so much hate mail and criticism that Giants management invited the media to view the game films, after which one reporter concluded, "Huff played no rougher than any other participant."[32] Brown said that during one drive in the Browns-Giants game on October 13, 1963, his opponents went for his eyes in pileups four or five times. Brown insisted, after confiding in a Cleveland sportswriter, that the latter not report about the incident, but the fullback acknowledged, "I felt they were trying to get me out."[33] No team, evidently, was innocent. The day after Pittsburgh upset Cleveland, 17–13, in 1961, Buddy Dial appeared at the weekly Curbstone Coaches luncheon, at which he told the audience that his team had sustained no serious injuries, "but John Henry Johnson had a few teeth marks on his legs."[34]

There were dissenters against the violence, like Maule and Graham, but no drastic action was taken. "The war against roughness is a continuing war," commissioner Pete Rozelle said. "And so it may be," Gordon Cobbledick, sports editor of the *Cleveland Plain Dealer,* wrote, "but wouldn't you think that after all these years some progress would have been made toward winning it?"[35]

That war would last half a century. In the meantime, pro football players treated life on the field as an occupational hazard, like working in a mine. Athletes like Lou Michaels and Dick Haley were driven to escape a life of dangerous, backbreaking work by standing out in sports. Others, like John Henry Johnson, found motivation deep inside themselves. Maybe it wasn't demons that pushed Johnson, the way they danced inside Parker and tormented Big Daddy Lipscomb, but something stoked his pride and vision and made him soar to success, just like he cannonballed over defensive linemen to scratch out the yard that separated his team from the opponent's end zone.

Johnson was born in Waterproof, Louisiana, the son of a Pullman porter who was killed in a railroad accident when John Henry was only three. When he was nine, his mother sent him along with his older brother and sister to Pittsburg, California. He studied yet struggled in high school because of a lack of sound elementary schooling in Louisiana, but he found his outlet in sports.

"He was not a poor student," said Bob Robinett, the general manager of the Calgary Stampeders, Johnson's first pro team, and a former guidance counselor in California. "But he wanted to *excel*. And finally, knowing that he could not excel in the classroom, he decided he would on the ball field. That's why he's always played so ruggedly."[36]

Johnson enrolled at St. Mary's, a California college, but when the school dropped football, he transferred to Arizona State, where he started to gain national attention. For a game against Hardin-Simmons, his team traveled to El Paso, Texas, where the black players had to stay in a separate hotel. "That made me mad," Johnson said, "so I took it out on the other team."[37]

The Steelers drafted him in the second round in 1953, but he decided to play in Canada when Pittsburgh wouldn't up its offer from $12,000 to $15,000. The next year Johnson signed with the 49ers and finished second in the league in rushing to teammate Joe Perry. In the spring of '57, Parker brought Johnson to the Lions in a trade, but he wasn't around to coach him in the fall, having left for Pittsburgh. Parker traded for Johnson again in 1960, and the six-foot-two, 215-pound fullback averaged 5.3 yards a carry while rushing for 621 yards in his first year in Pittsburgh.

What distinguished Johnson from most backs—and particularly from Brown—was not just his willingness to block (and to hit) but his fondness for it. He also had good hands and was a threat as a receiver. For as much passion and energy as he put into the game, Johnson could not tolerate lackadaisical effort from a teammate. In a '62 game against the Giants, he felt that one teammate had loafed near the goal line and cost the Steelers a touchdown. "I ever see you do that again," Johnson said, "I'll kill you with my bare hands."[38]

While in Detroit during the '59 season, Johnson had been suspended by the team for one game, costing him about $1,200 in salary, for missing a team plane departing from San Francisco and also for "a so-called indifferent attitude toward football."[39] At the time Johnson missed the flight, his ex-wife, who lived in San Francisco with their five children, had a bench warrant issued for his arrest for $850 in back alimony.[40]

In his first game back, Johnson, "booed lustily" in pregame introductions, "left the Lions' doghouse and stole the show with his best performance in two seasons." He caught an 11-yard touchdown pass and "bolted through and around the Los Angeles defense" in Detroit's 23–17 victory.[41] John Henry Johnson had a flair for rising to a big occasion, and he had an understanding of what it meant to be "in the doghouse."

Racism in the early sixties was as inherent a problem in football as it was in the rest of society. Black players who were quarterbacks in college were not smart enough to play the position in the NFL, coaches thought. The notion of hiring a black head coach seemed as outlandish as having hydrofoils racing up and down the rivers of Pittsburgh. On the road, blacks roomed with blacks, whites with whites.

Through the '63 season, Jim Brown could recount only two instances in which he was the object of racial slurs on the field, but he recognized that those offenses were minor compared to bigger societal problems. In fact, "The acceptance of the Negro in sports is really an insignificant development. . . . The problem is a little bigger than a ball game," Brown said. "Can anyone possibly think that it does my heart good to sign twenty autographs in a hotel lobby and then be turned out of the hotel dining room?"[42]

Brown gained fame and, for the period, made good money—an estimated $35,000.[43] But that was not enough to compensate for the indignities he endured. "If anything," he said, "I am more angry than the Negro who can't find work."[44] No doubt Brown would have taken interest in a story that ran in the *Pittsburgh Post-Gazette* three days before the Browns-Steelers game, about a report in which the executive director of the Mayor's Commission on Human Relations called Pittsburgh "a racial tinderbox."[45]

But the playing field was the equalizer. Helmets, long-sleeve jerseys, and bulky equipment could practically conceal a person's color and render him anonymous. A moving target wasn't a human; it was just a number on the front and back. Once an opponent charged, you didn't worry about his color; you struck back for self-preservation.

"I hit the colored guy as hard as I hit the white guy, and I don't think about color when I'm playing," Johnson said. "But," he added, "it might be a subconscious thing. I've always felt I was as good as anyone else, that's for sure."[46]

More likely, Johnson was "always conscious of his second-class citizenship." In 1968, two years after he retired from football, he said, "You don't get the endorsements, advertisements and job preferences like white athletes do. I love football and I had aspirations to coach, but I couldn't get a job."[47]

A week before the debacle in Milwaukee, Parker pulled Johnson after just four carries against the Cowboys. Theron Sapp came in to energize the running game with 45 yards rushing, and his production, it was speculated, could relegate Johnson to the bench.[48]

The Browns game was the last of the season scheduled for Pitt Stadium, home of the University of Pittsburgh Panthers, and a crowd of 54,490 was expected, the first sellout for the Steelers since they began playing at "the DeSoto Street saucer" in 1958. The event was being billed as "the greatest day in local pro football history," with the game telecast nationally and the thirty-seven-year-old Pete Rozelle, in his fourth year as commissioner, scheduled to attend.[49] The pride of nearby Jeanette, Pennsylvania, Dick Hoak, was to be honored at halftime. Four New York papers requested credentials to cover the game. Leo "Horse" Czarnecki, custodian of the field, spread a tarp on it at the end of the week to make sure the grass was protected and would be in top shape. "It's all building up to a terrible tussle," the *Post-Gazette*'s Jack Sell wrote.[50]

It was the perfect stage for John Henry Johnson. "His best games came against the Browns and the Giants, because of Jim Brown, and he hated the Giants," Lou Cordileone said. "You could always bet he was going to have a helluva game against those two clubs. He always did."[51]

The year before, Brown had 93 yards in Cleveland's 41–14 victory; Johnson ran for 94. In '61, Brown had 110 yards in Pittsburgh's 17–13 win; Johnson finished with 105. In '60, Brown ran for 86 yards in a 14–10 Steeler upset; Johnson had 73.

But the big bash in the stadium atop "Heart Attack Hill" didn't seem to be the right time for Johnson to stage a big revival. Who could tell how healthy his ankle was, and who could tell how confident Parker felt about using him? But oh, what a sight it was to see Johnson run when he was fit and fired up.

Some of the most fluid runners in NFL history ran wild in the fifties and early sixties. Backs like Hugh "the King" McElhenny, Willie Galimore and Lenny Moore, with his black high-top cleats taped like spats, zigzagged across the field the way Olympic skaters glided across ice. "In his prime The King had the prettiest moves, the most beautiful high step, the smoothest change of pace that you would ever hope to see," Brown said.[52] Taylor, Alex Webster, and John David Crow, however, relied on raw power. Johnson had a style all his own.

Johnson described his moves as "a combination of jitterbug, twist and Charleston, with a little rumba thrown in."[53] Every joint in his body swiveled as he galloped through defenders, herky jerky, like a man scampering barefoot across a bed of red-hot coals. "He was pigeon-toed and knock-kneed," Cordileone said. "You see him running from behind, you'd laugh your ass off, the way he ran. [But] he was tough."⁵⁴

Carrying the ball "like a cake of wet soap," Johnson "starts fast in a half-crouch, moves at a stuttering pace, twisting and turning while he uses head and shoulder fakes, hurdles tacklers, shuffles sideways, straight arms an eager defender and then cuts loose."⁵⁵ A press box observer once commented, "He runs like he's swimming the Australian crawl."⁵⁶

Brown was among the viewers who enjoyed Johnson's performances. "But the best entertainment," he said, "sometimes happens when John Henry hits smack into the center of the line. Those defensive men stack in there to meet him like mad dogs, every one of them wanting a piece of him. So what happens, sometimes, is that you see John Henry charge head-first into that wild mess of beef, and the next second you see him running backwards right out of it. Watching this, I get the feeling I'm viewing a film that's being run back."⁵⁷

The morning after the loss to Green Bay, the violin-playing comedian Jack Benny had a "hilarious" rehearsal before a Monday night benefit performance with the Pittsburgh Symphony Orchestra at the Syria Mosque, an event designed as "a satire on being a great violinist." Benny, with a grin, said, "Actually, I do play as well as I can. The trouble is that it just isn't good enough."⁵⁸

The Steelers could have said the same about themselves. In the aftermath of the season's most disheartening loss, pro football's most temperamental coach made a curious move: He gave the players an extra day off on Tuesday. "This is a funny team," Parker said. "Man, I've never seen a team like this. It's the only team I ever saw that didn't improve with pressure." The players had been wound up too tight, he concluded. "We were gigging them all week, but it didn't do any good. It seems that any time the pressure's on, they fold up. They choke. Not everybody, of course. Just enough of the guys to wreck the rest of the team. We'll just throw out the ball and let them go on their own. Maybe they'll play up to their capacity if they're loose and relaxed."⁵⁹

It wasn't a completely uncharacteristic move. Parker had lightened up on practices before as the season went on. Besides, he said, the loss to Green Bay was caused more by mental mistakes than physical shortcomings. "They were getting out of position all day," he said.⁶⁰

The day after Election Day, Parker cut veterans George Tarasovic and Tom Tracy and continued his lighthearted approach as he began the first practice of the week. "Let's go out and have some fun," he told the squad.[61]

Though both Brown and Taylor were elite runners, they posed distinct challenges for defenses. "They're completely different kinds of runners," said rookie defensive back Jim Bradshaw.

> I'd prefer tackling Taylor, even though it's a more punishing assignment. Taylor comes right at you. You have no problem getting at him. Your only problem is getting up afterward.
>
> Brown is cuter. He can be coming right at you, but you can't be sure he'll still be there when you make your move. With Taylor, you don't have that uncertainty. You know you can hit him, even if you can't stop him.[62]

With Brown, the trick was to get a hand—or shoulder—on him and then hang on for dear life. "Tacklers hit him glancingly and fall off, almost as though they expected to be dragged along in the dust like a fallen rider with a foot caught in the stirrup," beat writer Pat Livingston wrote.[63]

That was what cornerback Brady Keys aimed to avoid at all costs. As a rookie in '61, Keys attracted a lot of attention in camp for his skills as a running back. He was also a wicked, deadly open-field tackler, a tough single-coverage guy, and a dangerous punt returner. Not to mention that he was a nonstop trash-talker, brash and incapable of being intimidated. He was listed in press guides as being six feet tall, 185 pounds, which was still giving away a lot to a six-foot-two, 228-pound fullback like Brown. Jabbering away at receivers and backs was a favorite tactic of Keys's, but Brown rarely responded to any defender's taunts.

"I used to talk to Jim Brown and beat him up and spit on him and every-thing—get him mad," Keys said. "But I could never get to him. I used to love to fight him, man. That's the best thing in the world—to get him to fight you."[64]

Brown was too smart to take the bait, but others proved susceptible. "Every once in a while, you get under their skin, and once they get mad at you, they fly off the handle," Keys explained. A couple of years later, Browns wideout Paul Warfield said he was considering wearing ear plugs in an upcoming Steeler game so he could tune out Keys's chatter. Keys's tactics had worked. "Man," he responded, "if I thought it would help, I'd take a guitar to Cleveland and sing to Warfield."[65]

It took only one season for Keys to develop another kind of reputation—as "a hatchetman" who was "alienating the pros at a furious pace." One anonymous Eagle player groused, "It's tough enough to survive hard, clean play in this league without having to worry about a guy extracting your teeth with a sucker punch, too."[66]

Keys didn't want to be that tackler dragged in the dust with one foot in the stirrup. So, the strategy he tried against Brown worked: aim low instead of challenging his upper body strength. "I hit him very low," Keys said. "I was a little guy. When they came at me they would always think, 'We can run over him.' I know two guys in this world that could handle Jim Brown, and he just hated it. That was me and Andy Russell. I hit him low every time—every time—right at the ankles. He would fall like a big tree. He would be so mad at me. 'Why don't you challenge me?' I am challenging you. I'm challenging you where you're weakest. You want me to hit you in the chest?"[67]

To fill one of the two openings on the active squad created by the departure of Tarasovic and Tracy, Parker was thinking about moving halfback Joe Womack up from the taxi squad. Without Johnson, Hoak had become the team's workhorse. "I feel sorry for Hoak," Parker said. "He's been carrying more than his share of the load so far. . . . He deserves a rest, but I just haven't had anyone to use in his place."[68]

The Steelers-Browns series was known as "the Turnpike Rivalry," for the highway that connected the cities, and it was one of the most intense in sports. By Friday the game was a sellout—the first in ten years—and extra buses were scheduled to shuttle fans from downtown to the stadium in the university area. A big turnout from Cleveland was helping to swell the crowd into the largest ever to see a pro football game in Pittsburgh, although Pitt Stadium had nowhere near the capacity of the Browns' arena. A newspaper story the day before the game explained that back when Pitt Stadium was built in 1925, "students of human anatomy figured that the average person's posterior spanned 18 inches." Based on that figure, the capacity of the stadium was computed at 57,711. "Since then," the writer noted, local citizens' "bulk has grown heavier and spreads out more." The average spread of the posterior, as determined by architects of stadiums, had increased to twenty-one inches. Therefore, the Steelers, "out of consideration for the comfort of their fans," had decided not to squeeze more than 55,000 into Pitt Stadium on Sunday.[69]

More than fifty buses brought fans from northeast Ohio, one with the sign: "Yea Browns, The Gang From Sophie's Café."[70] One from Parma had a sign reading, "Cleveland Browns Boosters"—until someone transformed it into

"Cleveland Browns Boozers."[71] One Browns fan in the south stands blew taps before the game in the unseasonably mild, overcast weather. In the section usually reserved on Saturdays for Pitt students arose "a statuesque blonde with a wild, upswept coiffure, who can best be described as bosomy," wrote Alvin Rosensweet, the reporter who had written the *Post-Gazette*'s series on the Negro in Pittsburgh two months before. Her name, it turned out, was Irma the Body. "When Irma stood up, she revealed—and revealed is the word—a gold lame dress cut down to here," Rosensweet observed.[72]

Traffic stalled in Oakland the way the Steeler drives had at the Cleveland goal line five weeks earlier. John Henry Johnson had overslept Monday, an off day, and missed the Curbstone Coaches luncheon, and he was running late on Sunday. He arrived at Pitt Stadium—what one sportswriter dubbed "the aging DeSoto Street playpen"—forty-five minutes before kickoff, muttering about the traffic jam.[73] Years later Hoak recalled, "One time John Henry Johnson was a little late for a game. He pulled up to the stadium, left his Cadillac in the street, came into the stadium and said, 'Somebody park it.'"[74] And yet it was Johnson who dubbed his teammate "Hoaky Pokey." (In April 1975, indiscriminant parking would catch up with Johnson. His Cadillac was towed to the city pound because he had allegedly accrued 142 unpaid parking tickets. The *Pittsburgh Press* story about the incident did not specify whether any of them were written on the day of the Browns game a dozen years earlier.[75])

The game, set "in the murk and gloom of a heavy overcast," quickly produced an ominous flashback to the previous meeting. The Steelers took the opening kickoff and drove into Cleveland territory, with Johnson and Hoak picking up yardage. Aided by a face mask penalty, the Steelers reached the 42, where the drive stalled. Lou Michael attempted a 49-yard field goal, but it was wide right.[76]

Pittsburgh stopped Jim Brown for no gain on third-and-6, forcing a punt to the Steeler 32. Hoak and Johnson were popping through holes—Johnson for 7 yards, Hoak for 4, Johnson around left end for 6, over center for 4, then busting over right tackle for 20 and a first down at the Cleveland 27. On third-and-7 at the 24, Hoak gained 15 yards on a trap play, giving the Steelers first-and-goal at the 9. Hoak was forced to the sidelines from a hit at the end of the play, and Theron Sapp came in for him.

Johnson picked up 4 yards, Sapp another 2, and then Johnson went off left tackle for another 2 to the 1-yard line. Faced with fourth down, Parker changed his strategy from five weeks earlier and decided to go for it. After the loss in Cleveland, Parker had lamented Johnson's absence, because the fullback had the ability to leap over the defense at the goal line. Inexplicably, Sapp got the call and was stopped at the line of scrimmage, giving Cleveland possession. The teams exchanged punts, and even though the Steelers had come up empty on two drives, they had held Cleveland to a 0–0 standstill in the first quarter and had controlled the ball, running twenty-two plays to only nine by the visitors.

The teams traded punts at the start of the second quarter, but the Browns gained momentum on their next possession, starting at their 26. Jim Brown picked up 11 yards on a sweep around left end. He gained 13 over right tackle, to his 49 and then added 11 more on a safety valve pass. On third-and-4 at the Steeler 34, Ryan scrambled and was downed about a foot shy of a first down. On fourth down, Brown leaped over the right side for a yard and the first down. Ernie Green and Brown each gained 5 yards, and then Brown rambled for 15 more on a pitchout down to the 4. On first down Ryan hit Gary Collins, crossing in front of Glenn Glass, in the back of the end zone to cap the thirteen-play drive and put Cleveland up 7–0 with 2:31 left in the half.

The Steelers came right back. Hoak gained 13 yards over left tackle, and Ed Brown hit Preston Carpenter with a 19-yard pass, down to the Cleveland 44. Mack caught a 21-yard pass up the middle, but on the next play Dial was flagged for pushing off a defender in the left corner of the end zone, backing up the Steelers to the 38. Brown missed Hoak on two passes, leaving Pittsburgh with fourth-and-24 at the 37. It was 65 degrees and cloudy, but there was no wind. Michaels tried again, this time from 45 yards, but his kick fell short at the 2.

Ryan's 17-yard pass to Rich Kreitling put the Browns in position for Lou Groza to attempt a 50-yard field goal with seconds left in the half, but the kick was wide left.

The Steelers had shown they could move the ball; Hoak and Johnson had 102 yards between them. Jim Brown already had gained 92 yards by himself, but it had taken him fifteen carries to reach that total. Still, everyone in the crowd, from Irma the Body to the gang from Sophie's Café, knew that the fullback could break loose at any time, from anywhere on the field.

Michaels kicked off to open the second half and drove the ball 2 yards into the end zone—probably the best kick he had all day. Charlie Scales, a former Steeler, returned the kick to the 26, but the Steelers forced a punt. From the Steeler 27, Johnson went over center for 5 yards, then off left tackle for 4, and again for 4 more. Ed Brown hit Dial for 16 yards for a first down at the Cleveland 44. Brown missed on two passes and threw incomplete to Mack on third down, but linebacker Vince Costello was called for interference, giving Pittsburgh a first down on the 33.

Dial made a leaping catch for 12 yards, but Paul Wiggin dropped Ed Brown for a 10-yard loss. A pass to Johnson gained 11 yards, leaving Michaels to try a 25-yard field goal on fourth-and-7 from the 18. It went wide left, his third straight miss.

On third-and-6 from the Cleveland 24, Russell and Bob Schmitz blitzed Ryan, forcing an incompletion and a second straight three-and-out series for the visitors. Ed Brown was dumped for a 9-yard loss, but on third-and-19 from his 27, he hit Dial with a 22-yard pass for a first down at the 49. Brown threw incomplete to Carpenter twice, but he got off a 52-yard punt that fell dead at the Browns' 2.

Ryan was five of ten at the half, and his first-down pass to Kreitling sailed out of bounds, the quarterback's third miss in three throws in the third quarter. Then Ryan, the so-called genius, made a curious call: a sweep by Jim Brown. It was a familiar play for Brown, but not when he was lining up in his own end zone.

Later, coach Blanton Collier refused to second-guess the play call. "You should be able to execute a play anywhere on the field," he said. "How dangerous a play is depends on how the breaks fall," Jim Brown said. Schmitz, a third-year linebacker who had been drafted on the fourteenth round out of Montana State, after transferring from Wisconsin, was starting at John Reger's spot on the right side. The Steeler press guide called him "the Quiet Man."[77] After retiring as a player, Schmitz would go on to a thirty-three-year career as a scout, working for Haley with the Steelers and Jets, but his obituary would mention a single play he made on the great Jimmy Brown before a sellout crowd at Pitt Stadium.[78]

More than ten minutes had elapsed in the third quarter when Brown took the pitch and ran to his left, several yards deep in the end zone. "We had a rush call, a red dog defense," Schmitz explained. "I just went right to him. He was on his own. There were no blockers in front of him. He tried to go around end, and I was there."[79]

Brown, going one on one against a defender, had the ability to stiff-arm tacklers, run around them, or mow them down. Schmitz didn't give in, but he had a little help. It wasn't textbook defense; it was more like the Lilliputians dragging down Gulliver.

Brown "was hit glancingly by Schmitz, spun around and fled into the arms of Russell and Clendon Thomas. Somewhere between contact with Schmitz and Russell, the whistle blew the play dead."[80] The way Russell recalled it years later, "Jim started to move forward, dragging Schmitz. Clendon Thomas jumped on his head and he still didn't go down. Finally, the officials ruled the play dead, probably because [Brown] would humiliate us by carrying everyone down the field."[81]

Actually, Schmitz had a grasp on Brown, but the Steeler linebacker was on the turf, and he was clinging to the Cleveland fullback, indeed, like a rider who had fallen off his horse and was hanging on for dear life, his foot caught in the stirrup. Ironically, Russell's description of a player who refused to go down against the Steelers would fit another opponent of rare grit, but that encounter was still a couple of weeks away.

The play was ruled a safety, and though *Press* reporter Pat Livingston called it "a rather chicken-hearted safety at that," it counted, and Collier did not object to the call.[82] "I have no complaint," he said. "I didn't hear the whistle," Brown said, "but I guess it was all right."[83]

Cleveland led, 7–2, but the way the defenses were stiffening, two points could mean the margin of victory.

With the free kick, Collins punted from his 20 to Thomas, who returned the ball from his 32 to the 48. On second down, Costello intercepted a pass intended for Gary Ballman and returned it 15 yards to the Steeler 44. Collins's 14-yard reception gave Cleveland a first down at the 27, but on second-and-14 Green fumbled after breaking loose off left tackle, and Keys recovered at the 18. Ed Brown hit Dial with a 41-yard pass to the Cleveland 39 as the third quarter ended. After that, "there was no stopping Johnson."[84]

Johnson was moving behind guards Mike Sandusky and Ray Lemek, tackles Dan James and Charlie Bradshaw, and center Buzz Nutter. Not every offensive line in the NFL plugged away in anonymity. Jim Brown's success—and his praise for his teammates—brought the Browns' line recognition. Vince Lombardi's power sweeps drew attention to the line that made heroes of Paul Hornung and Jim Taylor. But the guys blocking for Johnson, Hoak, and Sapp had about as much fame as the referees. "They don't even know my name," said James, the left tackle.[85]

Bradshaw was a visible presence because he stood six foot six and weighed 255 pounds—good size for the time. He had grown up as an only child on a small farm in east Texas. His mother, Evilla, was five foot eleven, "and she could plow better than anyone I've ever seen," Bradshaw said. Bradshaw played on the same high school team as future Giant receiver Del Shofner, and they both went on to attend Baylor. Bradshaw was drafted by the Rams but was traded to Pittsburgh in 1961. He blocked efficiently enough to make the Pro Bowl in '63 and '64, and because he did so without leaving his feet and smudging his uniform, fans mockingly called him "Mr. Clean" and took out their frustration in upcoming seasons by singling him out for boos. Opposing linemen knew better. "He and Bob Brown of the Eagles are about the two best I've played against in the Eastern Division," said Giant defensive end Jim Katcavage.[86]

Bradshaw and his linemates were making it easier for John Henry Johnson to move on the field than in pregame traffic. He ran off left tackle for 6 yards, then hit right tackle, Bradshaw's spot, spun around, and picked up 10. He hit the left side again for 5, and after Hoak ran for 5, Johnson gained 3 for a first down at the 10. Johnson "ran into a stone wall" for a yard, then was held to no gain by Ross Fichtner while going around left end, leaving Pittsburgh with third-and-goal from the 9. The way Michaels was kicking, not even a 16-yard field goal looked like a sure thing.[87]

Brown dropped back to pass, with Ballman the intended receiver, as defensive tackle Frank Parker bore down on the quarterback. Dial often drew double coverage, but this time Ballman was the one surrounded.

"The hook area on the left side was open all day, so I sent him into it on that play," Ed Brown said. Linebacker Galen Fiss had Ballman covered in front, "so I looked for Buddy Dial on the right side. He was covered, too."[88]

"There were three Browns with me," Ballman said. "I didn't think I was going to get away from them. But then I saw this opening and broke. I didn't think Brown would be able to get the ball to me because somebody was on top of him."[89]

"Gary kept moving around, something a receiver has to do," Brown said, "and the next time I spotted him down the middle the goal post was in the way. Then he moved back outside a bit and I threw to him just as I was being hit."[90]

Brown spotted him "in a beam of daylight" and "put the pigskin right in his arms."[91] It was only the second catch of Ballman's pro career, and his first TD. Michael's conversion made it 9–7, Steelers, with 3:36 gone in the fourth quarter.

Down by only two, armed with the best runner in the game, and with plenty of time to put Groza within field goal range, Ryan abandoned the ground game. He hit Collins for 7 yards, but a flare to Jim Brown lost 3 as Schmitz and Michaels pounced on the fullback. An incompletion forced Collins to punt, and Keys made a fair catch on his 30 with 9:35 left in the game.

On second-and-7 from the 33, Dial made a kneeling catch for a 23-yard gain to Cleveland's 44. Hoak went off right tackle for 5, Sapp over left tackle for 4, and Johnson over the left side for 6, for a first down on the 29. After Ed Brown lost 4 yards scrambling, Dial got wide open in the left corner of the end zone, but the throw led him too much and the ball went off his fingertips. Ballman gained 11 yards on a catch, leaving the Steelers with fourth-and-3 at the 22—and in need of a field goal, which would force the Browns to drive for a touchdown for the go-ahead points. Michaels lined up for a 29-yard field goal and, with 9:56 left, missed his fourth straight kick.

On third-and-11 from the 19, Ryan hit Jim Brown for a 16-yard reception, but Cleveland was called for holding. Russell and Pottios stopped Brown after a 6-yard reception, forcing Collins to punt 48 yards to the Steeler 38. Parker's squad had 2:29 to kill before claiming a victory over their archrival in front of the biggest crowd to witness a pro football game in Pittsburgh history, 54,497 fans.

John Henry Johnson raced around right end for 18 yards to the Cleveland 44. But Cleveland held, forcing Michaels to try a 45-yard field goal on fourth-and-3. The kick was short and to the left, and Michaels was oh for five. And there was still 1:39 left. "All I could think about was how important those three points were to the team," Michaels said later. "If I made one, it took more than a field goal for the Browns to beat us. If I made two, it would have taken more than a touchdown for them to win."[92]

The Browns hardly looked like the explosive team that overcame the Steelers five weeks earlier. "The big team from the shore of Lake Erie was as dull as the gray skies," commented Tommy Holmes of the *New York Herald Tribune*.[93] After a pass for Collins was almost intercepted by Glass and another missed Jim Brown, Ryan connected with Green for 13 yards and a first down. Cleveland took four last shots at cracking the Steeler defense, and Buster Ramsey's unit brought down the Eastern Conference leaders with a crescendo.

A toss to Brown lost 4 yards. Lou Cordileone batted down a pass. Keys broke up a throw to Ray Renfro at the last instant, with sixty-three seconds left. Thomas broke up a pass to Johnny Brewer, and all Ed Brown had to do to run out the final fifty-nine seconds was fall on the ball three times.

Collins, who had two TD catches in the first meeting, had only three catches this day, for 25 yards. Ryan hit only eleven of twenty-five passes for 93 yards. And Jim Brown had only 7 yards in the second half to finish with 99 total, in a season in which he averaged 133.1 a game. John Henry Johnson had outperformed the league's rushing leader, piling up 131 yards on twenty-seven carries, enabling the Steelers to keep the ball away from Cleveland and giving the kid from Louisiana, the son of a Pullman porter, the satisfaction of knowing that he could run with the best of 'em in the National Football League.

He wasn't the only one who silenced the skeptics. Nine months earlier, on Valentine's Day, the same day it was announced that Bobby Layne had turned down Buddy Parker's offer to make him coach of the quarterbacks, Ernie Stautner had accepted the role of player-coach, a concession to reduced playing time as well as a promotion. The week before the first game with Cleveland, Stautner had cautioned, "Don't underestimate the old man. I haven't played much, but I'll be there when they need me. Everybody's given up on me for the last five or six years, but I keep coming back on them." Ever the team player, Stautner stressed that he wasn't complaining. "I don't care if I don't play," he said, "as long as we win."[94]

On Friday, Stautner and Thomas were listed as uncertain for the game because of leg injuries. But anyone familiar with Stautner's recuperative powers knew that he would be on the field, ready to go, because his teammates needed him. Stautner came off the bench to give a performance against Cleveland that earned him a game ball. "Nobody on the field was any better than Stautner," Pat Livingston wrote, "especially in the last five minutes when the Browns tried everything in the book to keep the 38-year-old patriarch out of their backfield." Buddy Parker was impressed, but not surprised. "I don't know how he does it," the coach said, "but he's always there when the chips are down."[95]

When someone suggested to Lou Cordileone that Stautner was still great for a few minutes, the tackle snorted, "He's great for 60 minutes. He's the greatest in the business."[96]

But it was Schmitz who earned honors as the league's player of the week. "Gee, that's probably the best thing that ever happened to me," he said.[97] Five days later, the *Green Bay Press-Gazette* ran an AP photo of Schmitz, a resident of Chilton, Milwaukee, and a graduate of New Holstein High School, plowing into a tackling dummy—and looking just a little sheepish—to demonstrate how he nabbed Jim Brown in the end zone. The kid who switched to Montana State had made good. Steeler fans might not always remember him, but it's a sure bet that Jimmy Brown never forgot him. "That kid Schmitz . . . was great," veteran John Reger said the day after the game. "He's going to be here for a long time."[98]

In New York, up in the Bronx, where the Giants were whipping the Eagles,

42–14, the crowd erupted when the scoreboard showed the Steelers had beaten the Browns. The Giants were now tied with Cleveland for first place in the Eastern Conference at 7–2. "We're back in the race!" Y. A. Tittle said, and Alex Webster clapped "like a kid with a new toy."[99]

St. Louis beat Washington, 24–20, behind Charley Johnson's three touchdown passes, to stick close at 6–3, and the Steelers were right behind at 5–3–1.

Back in Cleveland, there was "No Joy in Mudville," as a *Post-Gazette* headline stated. "At the Slovenian Club and at the Lithuanian Club . . . a feeling of depression has set in. . . . All across northern Ohio, rigor mortis has set in."[100]

In one week, the Steelers had proved that the obituaries written about them were premature. Even with Lou Michaels slumping, they looked very much alive and kicking, and full of fight.

GAME 10

It was said that in times of difficulty, Buddy Parker "would commune with the spirits," but there is no evidence that he ever consulted a fortune teller, worked a Ouija board, or took up astrology to assemble players for his football teams.[1] Those options might have been no more outlandish than a few notions he did entertain. With all his quirks and idiosyncrasies, he could come off as a moonstruck seer using a divining rod to mine for precious talent from the football earth. The record shows, that for all his ill-conceived trades and hasty cuts, he was a shrewd judge of talent and a riverboat gambler when it came to taking risks on discarded or neglected talent.

In an era of unschooled, sometimes crude drafting, Parker was notoriously leery of untested players. Art Rooney Jr., who went to work in the scouting department under Parker, said that the coach decided to have his scouts start taking pictures of top prospects "because he didn't want any stupid-looking players."[2] Rooney recalled Parker saying, "If I knew how ugly that Bob Ferguson from Ohio State was, I never would have drafted him!"[3]

One myth of the time, Rooney said, was that Michigan State players were "slow to catch on," a notion as illogical as the prevailing prejudice against black college quarterbacks. One scout from the BLESTO scouting combine said of Michigan State players, "You could toss them all into a bag and then throw [head coach] Duffy Daugherty in and their IQs wouldn't add up to a hundred and ten." The perverse thinking did not account, however, for the successful careers of such Michigan State alumni as stalwart Packer defenders Bill Quinlan and Herb Adderley; quarterbacks Earl Morrall, Jim Ninowski, and Al Dorow; and the Steelers' gifted running back Lynn Chandnois.[4]

As Daugherty wrapped up spring drills in 1960 and tried to assess his young team, he was sure of one thing: He had "two superlative halfbacks" in Adderley and Gary Ballman, the latter an all-around athlete from East Detroit who was finishing up his sophomore year.[5] Playing with Adderley and future pro George Saimes cut down on Ballman's opportunities to handle the ball, so his collegiate statistics were modest: 715 yards and nine touchdowns on 170 carries, including runs of 74 yards against Northwestern and 56 yards against Illinois. Daugherty called him "our bread and butter player."[6] Ballman was good enough to land a spot in the East-West Shrine Game and the Hula Bowl, though he played sparingly. He had good size— six foot one, 200 pounds—to go along with his speed, and an unflappable approach to playing the game that scouts probably did not detect.

With their No. 1 pick in the 1962 draft—the fifth overall selection—the Steelers took Bob Ferguson and then waited around until the seventh round because Parker had traded away picks 2 through 6. On the seventh round the Steelers took Jack Collins, a back from Texas, and on the eighth they picked Ballman. Playing in the NFL, said his wife, Judi, "was always one of his dreams."[7]

Two dozen rookies opened training camp ahead of the veterans in the third week of July 1962, and it took only about ten days for Ballman to establish himself as "star of the early drills." Those early workouts, however, came without the pressure and intimidation that veterans would bring to a practice, when jobs, pride, and reputation were on the line. One visitor to the rookie camp was Jack "Goose" McClairen, a gifted offensive end whose six-year career with the Steelers was undermined by knee injuries. McClairen knew how different the climate would become once vets like Myron Pottios and Johnny Sample arrived to go head to head with the twenty-one- and twenty-two-year-olds. "Those kids out there catch a pass and dance and prance like they are performing for a photographer," Mc-Clairen said. "One forearm shiver from a defensive back and that dancin' and prancin' will be done!"[8]

Ballman performed well in the club's intrasquad scrimmage with the veterans and was called an "outstanding flanker back prospect."[9] Sample, a master of intimidation and a harsh critic of even the best receivers in the league, was asked who among the rookies had impressed him. "That kid from Michigan State," Sample replied. "He looks like a good one. He has all the moves and a lot of speed."[10]

Ballman wasn't the kind to back down or let himself be intimidated. "He survived because he thrived on personal challenge," one writer wrote in the twilight of Ballman's career.[11] Halfway through the 1962 regular season, Sample was cut, and after being signed by Washington, he would try to taunt Ballman—as he did every receiver—by threatening to hit his ex-teammate late or pile on him. "You do that, Sample, and I'll punch you right in the mouth," Ballman replied.[12]

Yet for all the good impressions Ballman was making in camp, he was destined to be a spectator on game days, relegated to the "taxi squad." The taxi squad was yet another of Paul Brown's contributions to pro football. Arthur B. "Mickey" McBride, founder of the Cleveland Browns, had made his fortune partly through his taxi cab companies in Cleveland and other cities. To keep players who didn't make the Cleveland roster from joining other teams, Brown arranged for McBride to put them temporarily on his payroll as taxi drivers. The system eventually was regulated by the NFL and allowed players to practice with the team but not dress for games unless formally activated.

But even as Ballman worked out on "the twilight unit of football players," Parker envisioned a star in the making. "Ballman's going to be a real ballplayer," Parker said in the fall of '62. "I wouldn't trade him for a first draft choice."[13]

As '63 opened, Ballman was on the roster but seldom on the field. Yet, on a team that Parker felt had a tendency to tense up under pressure, Ballman set himself apart as much by his brash, confident attitude as by his catching and running with a football. He was unshakable.

"Cool, Daddy," Lou Cordileone said. "He's so cool he burps icicles."[14]

He was also tough and self-assured enough to make a friend out of gruff Mike Ditka when the two later became teammates in Philadelphia. They were roommates and drinking buddies, and they chafed under the unimaginative offense of the inflexible head coach Joe Kuharich, who had coached Ed Brown's unbeaten college team. In his first four seasons in Philadelphia after being traded by Pittsburgh following two Pro Bowl seasons, Ballman averaged thirty-six receptions a year, playing also as a tight end. But halfway through the '63 season, Ballman was still waiting for a chance to duplicate the big plays he had made in college, and he started with his 93-yard kickoff return against Green Bay. "It's a special vision," his widow, Judi, said in 2008, four years after Ballman's death from a massive heart attack at age sixty-three. "He used to say he felt like he had a special insight as to what was happening around him on the field. Just pick a spot and go. He used to say things like, 'I don't know how I caught that pass but I think I willed the ball into my hands.' I guess there would be something to that. He just wanted to win so bad. He was highly competitive."[15]

Even after that year on the taxi squad, it took Parker half a season to work Ballman into the lineup. "He had a lot to learn," Parker said, without a trace of regret.[16]

Ballman worked out as a halfback and flanker before Parker settled on him as a split end. There was nothing Ballman could do but wait for an opportunity. "There's no question last year helped me a lot," he said of his year on the taxi squad, "but it was a disappointment not to make the team. Of course, it was a disappointment making the team and spending all my time on the bench, too."[17]

Ballman had an influential party lobbying on his behalf. "Ed Brown convinced Buddy Parker to play this kid," Cordileone said. "Parker wasn't too 'hep' on this kid. But Ed Brown kept saying that this kid's a helluva receiver. 'You gotta play him.' And he finally started playing him."[18]

Ballman's biggest fan had been with him since college. Gary and Judi Ballman got married in East Lansing. He was twenty-one; she was eighteen. "I was probably the youngest wife in the NFL for several years," she said several decades later. "He was a wonderful husband—loving, caring, deeply religious. What you saw is what you got. He was just a really swell guy."[19]

Fortunately for Ballman, he had a veteran leader looking out for him, too. "Bobby Layne kind of took Gary under his wing," Judi Ballman said. "I think that made life a little easier for Gary than it would for the average rookie because Bobby was always there—No. 1, to get him in trouble with me, but No. 2, [to] kind of really watch over him."[20]

Such was life on the Steelers that players could find nearly as much trouble off the field as on it. Jim Bradshaw, who had been a quarterback at Chattanooga, was trying to make the team as a defensive back in the summer of '63. After a mid-August exhibition victory over the Eagles in Bethlehem, Pennsylvania, Bradshaw was one of a half-dozen players who went out to a bar after the game and hung around until about 3 A.M. Charlie Bradshaw (no relation), a native of Texas who studied to be a lawyer during the off-season, presented one of his teammates with a souvenir.

"Charlie Bradshaw brought Lou Michaels a ten-gallon Texas hat," Jim Bradshaw recalled, "and gave it to Lou after the game."

There were five or six of us. George Tarasovic and Bobby [Layne], and I think Ray Lemek was there. The guy that owned the place wanted to leave. Of course, Bobby didn't want to leave. We got up to leave. Lou had put his hat in a coatroom. And the hat was gone. Lou went back and told the bartender, "I want the hat." Bartender says, "I don't know anything about your damn hat." Lou says, "I want that hat and I want it now, and somebody better go get my hat." And the bartender says, "I don't know anything about the hat."

So they just ripped the bar apart. Just destroyed it. I'd never seen anything like it. Broke glasses and broke the bottles behind the bar. Then off to jail we went. About six-thirty, 7 o'clock, the team was coming back to Pittsburgh, and then to West Liberty [West Virginia, site of the training camp]. Fran Fogarty [the Steelers' business manager] came down and got everybody out.

I'm a rookie; I'm scared to death. You want to keep your nose clean. I said, "Oh, man, I'm never going to make this ball club." But Buddy Parker understood. That's the way Buddy was. No problem. That was the last I ever heard of it.[21]

Bradshaw had been selected on the eighteenth round by Pittsburgh and had also been drafted by the Boston Patriots of the old AFL. He was offered $9,000 by the Steelers and called back several days later, requesting a $500 bonus. A scout replied, "I think we can work that out."[22]

Bradshaw ran an option offense in college, and he knew that if he was going to earn a spot on the Steelers, it would have to be on defense. Bill Nelsen, a quarterback at USC, had been drafted on the tenth round and would compete for the No. 3 spot behind Ed Brown and Terry Nofsinger, a third-year man out of Utah.

Bradshaw became a close friend of defensive back Willie Daniel, who was in his third year, out of Mississippi State. In the Eastern Conference, there was never a letup in the quality of star receivers they faced: the Giants' Del Shofner, "a jet-propelled menace to every defensive back in the NFL"; the Cowboys' Billy Howton, who entered '63 on track to break Don Hutson's all-time records for receptions and yards gained; Washington's Bobby Mitchell, who led the league in catches in '62; Philadelphia's Tommy McDonald; and Bobby Joe Conrad of St. Louis.[23]

Eventually, every defensive back got burned, and the growth of television helped expose their mistakes to the entire sports world. "I'm not sure when this happened," Willie Daniel's wife, Ruth, said.

Willie had looked bad on television the week before, and Jim had really had some good games—lots of publicity. The defense was lined up in the tunnel waiting to be introduced, and Willie knew he would be met with a shower of boos.

He also knew that Jim was busy talking, as usual, and wasn't pay-
ing attention to the names being called. So when the announcer called
Willie's name, Willie turned to Jim and said, "Go, they just called your
name." So Jim goes running out onto the field to that chorus of boos.
He says he'll never forget or forgive! We have gotten many laughs with
Jim about that through the years.[24]

If Bradshaw was a long shot to make the Steelers, Daniel was the most
unlikely candidate of all to earn a roster spot. He grew up in Macon,
Mississippi, close to the Alabama line and just south of Mississippi State,
which he attended. After completing his college career in 1959, Daniel
went undrafted by the NFL. The AFL, desperate for players as it prepared
for its inaugural season, ignored him as well. "How unwanted can a guy
get?" asked *New York Times* columnist Arthur Daley.[25]

Snubbed by pro football, and married with one child, Daniel took a job as
a high school football coach in the town of Cleveland, on the western border
of Mississippi. While he was absorbed in the action during a game, so the
story goes, Daniel felt a tap on his shoulder and turned around. "Wham! Out
of nowhere came a punch, smack on the button."[26] Once Daniel recovered,
he asked his assailant, "Who the hell are you? And what was that all about?"

"I won't stand for you keeping my kid on the bench all night," said the
offended father. "Next time this happens, you'll get the same thing."[27]

The story became good copy for newspapers. "The actual event wasn't
nearly as dramatic as the articles indicate!" Ruth Daniel said. "The 'mad
dad' had some inner liquid strength and came onto the field looking for the
head coach. Willie stopped him and they had words, and maybe a slight
nudge or two. Anyway, it made [for] a good story and was picked up by
all the major newspapers in the cities where the Steelers played."[28]

In any event, if anyone was going to be throwing punches, whether it was
Stretch Elliott, Lou Michaels, or an angry dad, Daniel evidently figured the
NFL couldn't be much more hazardous than the sidelines of a high school
field, so he sought out one of his old college coaches for an NFL contact.
The coach called Art "Pappy" Lewis, an ex-pro and former head coach at
West Virginia who worked as a scout for the Steelers, to arrange a tryout.
Daniel reported for training camp at Slippery Rock, Pennsylvania, but
flopped in the team's first scrimmage. Discouraged and homesick, Daniel
was ready to quit, but Jack Butler talked him out of it.

Butler was coach of the defensive backs. A former seminary student, he
made the Pro Bowl four times and had fifty-two interceptions during his

nine-year career as a defensive back with the Steelers. "This kid reminds me of me," Butler said of Daniel. "He comes up and hits guys." Any comparisons to Butler constituted powerful testimony that Daniel had come to the right team. *New York Times* columnist Arthur Daley characterized Butler as "a ruthless desperado" on the field. "Nice guys get nowhere in this sport," Butler said. "The best ones have a mean streak in them. . . . You have to hit hard and keep hitting hard even if you have to take a 15-yard penalty."[29]

Daniel also had speed to rival the fastest of receivers. He resisted the urge to leave camp, and at practice he chased down Preston Carpenter even though the tight end had a 10-yard lead. Parker took notice. Daniel was as fast as his teammate in the secondary, Sample, who himself was a match for his ex-teammate Lenny Moore, the Colts' running back. "That's the ultimate," wrote Daley.[30]

Daniel survived training camp and opened the season at right cornerback. But it wasn't his speed or his toughness that saved him from Parker's wrath on the way home from a loss. "Willie had a less than stellar game—don't remember which one or what year," Ruth Daniel said, "and Buddy was on the warpath with Willie as his target. Willie hid by laying under one of the seats on the plane with some of the guys covering him with their feet. Buddy never found him so he didn't get cut!"[31]

Football interest in Pittsburgh was at a giddy pitch in the second week of November '63. Along with the Steelers' victory over the Browns, the University of Pittsburgh had run its record to 6–1 the day before by beating Notre Dame, and Penn State had defeated Ohio State. Pitt was ranked fifth in the nation—one spot behind Duffy Daugherty's Michigan State Spartans, who several months before had been dismissed as non-contenders. Evidently the collective IQs on the squad and coaching staff amounted to a lot more than some scouts thought.

"Not since the days in the late 1930's when Pitt, Carnegie Tech and Duquesne all had the city in a dither over football has there been so much excitement generated here over the sport as we noted the past weekend," columnist Al Abrams wrote two days after the win over Cleveland. "And we ask you—wasn't it nice to see a story on the Steelers' win leading off page 1 plus a picture of Pitt Stadium filled to capacity rather than vice raids, political promises, murders and what else have you in the way of world ills?"[32]

Abrams neglected to mention one prominent story on page 1 headlined "Police Quiz Gang in Stab Death," the slaying of an eighteen-year-old football star from Westinghouse High School. But at least murders were down. A story inside Monday's *Post-Gazette* ran with the headline "Pittsburgh No

Longer Haven for Murderers." It cited a national magazine article from the early fifties with the title "You Can Get Away with Murder in Western Pennsylvania," a story inspired by the "frightful" number of unsolved murders in Allegheny County, Pittsburgh in particular. The face of Pittsburgh had changed since Captain Eugene Cook took over as head of homicide in April. All fifteen murder cases since then had been solved.[33]

But guns as toys were still popular. An ad in the paper accompanied by photos and descriptions of items such as a burp gun, a combat bazooka set, and a battery machine gun declared Horne stores to be the "Headquarters for Military Fun Toys." That Monday was Veterans Day, and on Tuesday the *Post-Gazette* paired a photo of the parade in downtown Pittsburgh with one of President Kennedy placing a wreath at the tomb of the Unknown Soldier.

Steeler fans weren't the only ones feeling merry from the weekend's events. Abrams received a thank you note and an autographed photo from Irma the Body, who was about to begin a limited engagement as a burlesque dancer at the Casino, billed as "a Pennsylvania Dutch girl from Lancaster County." Abrams also got a request from Sophie's Café in Cleveland for forty copies of Monday's newspaper.[34]

But the career of one woman who had the credentials to compete with Irma the Body suffered a brief setback. Jayne Mansfield's movie *Promises! Promises!*—"which demonstrates she is top-heavy in everything but talent," wrote reporter-turned-critic Vince Johnson—was banned in Pittsburgh on Wednesday.[35] A judge, the police superintendent, an assistant police superintendent, and an assistant district attorney made the unanimous decision after viewing the cofeature, a film on life in a nudist camp, and then a portion of the Mansfield movie. Only a few days before, *Promises! Promises!* had been shut down in a Cleveland suburb despite the lament of Mansfield's husband, Mickey Hargitay. "It's a shame they did it. After all," he said, "sex is here to stay."[36]

Football was a close rival in terms of entertainment, and not just in Pittsburgh—or Cleveland or New York. Chicago, scheduled to play in Pittsburgh the following week, was primed to host Green Bay in a showdown of 8–1 teams tied for first place in the Western Conference. "The big city is all shook up sportswise," and $5 tickets for the game at 48,600-capacity Wrigley Field were being scalped for fifty bucks.[37] Coach George Halas had four security men, including one with binoculars, patrol Wrigley Field during practice.[38] Several railroad lines were scheduling day-long excursions so that fans could view the game on television beyond the 75-mile blackout radius.

The Bears worked out at Wrigley on Tuesday after watching films of the Steeler-Packer game, and the Bays, as they were called, practiced amid 30 mph gusts of wind in Green Bay. The Steelers, meanwhile, were enjoying two days off for the second week in a row. Parker maintained it was not a reward for the victory over Cleveland but rather was meant to give the players a break from the grind of late-season practices.[39]

The Steelers rated as seven-point favorites over Washington even though they had not won on the road all season. The Redskins, with their erratic play, had cultivated a reputation as "football schizophrenics."[40] Since losing the NFL title game in 1945, the Redskins had only three winning seasons in seventeen years, the last coming in 1955, and had won just a single game in two of the three previous seasons. Mired in a last-place tie with Dallas in the Eastern Division at 2–7 in November 1963, the Redskins were a besieged team, faulted for an unimaginative offense and second-guessed for not giving backup quarterback George Izo a shot. Coach Bill McPeak denied there was dissension on the team.[41]

McPeak was trying to work speedy Frank Budd into the lineup at split end, which could pose a worry to a banged-up Steeler secondary. Brady Keys, with bruised ribs, and Clendon Thomas, with bruised thighs, had taken their lumps from Jim Brown but were deemed ready to practice. "Nothing that a little youth wouldn't cure," Thomas said.[42]

McPeak had other worries besides talk of turmoil on the squad. Bobby Mitchell was slowed by a pulled muscle early in the week. Halfback Dick James, described by *Press* beat writer Pat Livingston as "a pygmyish, 29-year-old father of five," was hobbled, but the Steelers, for sure, expected him to play. James had scored two TDs in the first meeting. "That's one kid who's always ready," Steeler assistant coach Mike Nixon said. "Man, he kills us every time we play him," Parker said.[43]

And the Steelers still had to contend with the Redskins' defensive line—"big, two-fisted bruisers who play for keeps."[44] But that was the kind of challenge that brought out the best in Parker's squad. "We beat the crap out of everybody, but didn't win too many games," Ballman said years later, after his retirement. "Buddy Parker . . . picked up all the bad-assed players on waivers. We were sort of like an early version of the Oakland Raiders."[45]

Parker's main concern was the psyche of his team. The Steelers were still in the hunt, but the focus in the Eastern Division was on the coleaders, Cleveland and New York. Pittsburgh loomed as more of a spoiler, and Parker didn't mind the underdog role. "Frankly, I feel a lot better about going to Washington without the pressure of the pennant race bearing down on us," Parker said. "This is a team that plays better when it's relaxed." That was pretty much Ballman's natural disposition.[46]

On the eve of the game, it was announced that sixty-three-year-old Steeler owner Art Rooney, who had founded the team thirty years earlier, was to be honored at a banquet for Children's Hospital. The late Bert Bell, who had served as NFL commissioner, had founded the Philadelphia Eagles, and at one time was co-owner of the Steelers, once said of Rooney, "He looks only for the good side of every man. He's a person with countless friends and not one enemy."[47] The benefit was scheduled for January 19, 1964—three weeks after the NFL Championship Game.

The AFL, in its fourth year of existence, was battling to establish its legitimacy and was challenging the NFL for a championship showdown. That week, Pete Retzlaff, the Eagles' tight end and president of the NFL Players Association, said that the AFL was three to five years away from reaching the level of play necessary to make itself a worthy challenger to the NFL in a title game.[48]

Pete Rozelle, who had succeeded Bell as commissioner in 1960, curtly quashed the possibility of an NFL-AFL title game. "We have no plans for any games at all with the other league," he said.[49]

As the Steelers went though a light workout on Friday, the day before leaving for D.C., another would-be challenger who worked in Washington, and a long shot as well, was visiting Pittsburgh. Barry Goldwater had not formally declared himself a candidate for president, but the Republican senator from Arizona sounded every bit like one as he spoke at an event sponsored by the Harvard Business School Association of Pittsburgh. The *Post-Gazette* published an editorial about the support for him in western Pennsylvania, on the same page it ran a column by James Reston in which the columnist cited "a vague feeling of doubt and disappointment in the country" about President Kennedy's first term. "He has touched the intellect of the country but not the heart," Reston wrote. "He has informed but not inspired the nation."[50]

A Gallup poll revealed that weekend that Kennedy's approval rating was 59 percent. Reston quoted a carpenter from Cleveland, a man who might have been speaking for a significant constituency when he said: "All I know is that we have work and peace."[51]

· In contrast to the dank overcast of the previous Sunday, the temperature at District of Columbia Stadium reached 72 degrees, and the capacity crowd of 42,219 was graced with sunshine. What they witnessed taking place between a last-place team in disarray and a fourth-place team scrapping for a division title was "the kind of action that would have sent the wildest-eyed movie script writer in captivity to the nuthouse," wrote columnist Al Abrams, in "what has to be one of the wildest pro football games in history."[52] Or at least in the Pittsburgh Steelers' 1963 season.

Frustrated Redskin fans were not in a charitable mood. During pregame introductions, they booed defensive back Claude Crabb, who had led the team in interceptions as a rookie the year before but was part of a defensive backfield that gave up three touchdown passes to St. Louis the week before. Obviously, he didn't have the luxury of Jim Bradshaw running onto the field in his stead. But Crabb won over the crowd on the fourth play from scrimmage when he intercepted a pass intended for Red Mack on a square-out pattern and raced 53 yards down the sideline for a touchdown.[53]

It would have been easy to jump to the conclusion that the Steelers were suffering a letdown after the victory over the Browns. On first down after the kickoff, John Henry Johnson fumbled and Washington's Andy Stynchula recovered on the 25. But the Steeler defense held, and Bob Khayat missed a 28-yard field goal.

The Steelers went 3-and-out, and Washington got the ball back on its 38. A 10-yard reception by Mitchell helped move the ball to the Steeler 39, but on fourth-and-1, Khayat missed again, this time from 46 yards. If there was one soul in the stadium who felt any sympathy, it was likely the guy on the other side of the line of scrimmage, Lou Michaels.

Starting at their 20, the Steelers started to click. Buddy Dial would be held to two catches that afternoon, but he beat Crabb for a 43-yard reception that took Pittsburgh to the Washington 37. Ballman made two catches, for 8 and 10 yards, to give the Steelers first-and-goal at the 9. "He's from Detroit," wrote Jack Walsh of the *Washington Post,* "and as fast as any of the latest models they're turning out." Johnson carried three straight times, for 5, 1, and the final 3 yards, on a sweep, to tie the score, 7–7, with twenty-two seconds left in the quarter.[54]

The teams exchanged punts at the start of the second quarter. Snead hit Richter for 13 yards and Fred Dugan for 9 to reach the Steeler 22, but Joe Krupa recovered Snead's fumble at the 32. Ed Brown missed Dial on two straight passes but hit Johnson for a gain of 20 yards to the Washington 37. Two incompletions left Pittsburgh with fourth-and-6 at the 33, giving Michaels a shot at a 40-yard field goal. In eight previous attempts, he had only hit on a 9-yard attempt. The 40-yarder, with just under four minutes left before halftime, was wide right. On this afternoon, it didn't look as if a field goal was going to be enough to make the difference in the game.

Two consecutive penalties—for backfield in motion and pushing—left the Skins bogged down at their 7, but they weren't about to be trapped in the end zone like Jim Brown. Budd wasn't the only former track star on the team. At the University of Illinois, Mitchell set a world indoor record in the 70-yard low hurdles, and he had entertained thoughts of competing in the Olympics. Mitchell was all the more of a threat to the Steelers because Keys was out of the lineup, having committed the cardinal sin of trying to tackle Jim Brown up high.

In a midseason game at Yankee Stadium the year before, Giants defensive back Erich Barnes had the task of trying to cover Mitchell man to man. The Giants survived, 49–34, but Mitchell caught touchdown passes of 44 and 80 yards. "You blink your eyes and he's gone," Barnes said. Barnes was able to contain Mitchell over most of the second half, but the Redskin receiver knew that it was only a matter of time before he would explode. "No one can cover me man-for-man. It just isn't possible," Mitchell told Barnes.[55]

Budd juggled a pass but held on to move Washington 17 yards to the 24. On third-and-6, Snead hit Mitchell for a 22-yard gain to the 46. Ernie Stautner tackled Snead for a 14-yard loss, but on the next play the Steelers were called offside. After the two-minute warning, on second-and-19 from his 37, Snead fired a 44-yard pass to Mitchell, putting the Redskins on the 19. Washington called time-out with 1:47 left in the half.

As an offensive back at Tennessee, Glenn Glass was hailed as "a blinding runner."[56] But even someone with his speed needed help against Mitchell. Snead found Mitchell in the corner of the end zone, beating Glass, who was called for interference on the play, to put the Redskins ahead, 14–7, with 1:31 to go before halftime. Asked afterward if Mitchell was the toughest receiver he had ever covered, a beleaguered Glass replied, "Are you kidding me?"[57]

The Steelers had no match for Mitchell—and neither did anyone else in the NFL. But Pittsburgh was about to unveil a player who could lurk as an explosive threat. After Johnson ran for 11 yards to the 33, Brown zeroed in on Ballman. Defensive back Dale Hackbart, "looking like a centerfielder," focused on the ball, but Ballman leaped to snatch it away and sprint 67 yards for a touchdown.[58] "Hackbart was in front of me," Ballman explained later, "but somehow he missed it. I jumped and it sort of stuck in one hand. That's a once-in-a-lifetime catch for me."[59]

Another one-in-a-million catch would occur before the season was over, and it would also be a case of a pass just sticking in the hand of a receiver. It would be a pivotal point in the Steelers' season, and it would prove once again how fickle fate could be. "Sometime[s] you get a kick from Up Above,"

Paul Brown said after Cleveland got a break in a victory over Pittsburgh the year before.[60] The Steelers were looking for that kind of kick to fulfill Buddy Parker's title hopes, but it had been as elusive during his tenure as a Lou Michaels boot over the previous six quarters of play.

On this day, Ballman was making up for the lost Sundays from his rookie season. He was on his way to catching eight passes for 161 yards, but that was only part of the impact he was having on the game. "Few in the stands had ever heard of the Steeler rookie before, but by the time the game was over his was the name which was on everybody's lips."[61]

Now it was Pittsburgh's turn to get a break. As the clock wound down, Pat Richter caught a 19-yard pass to midfield. A couple of Steelers, "apparently [John] Baker and Ernie Stautner, took turns whacking quarterback Snead," resulting in a personal foul. Clearly, on this day Pete Rozelle would make no headway in his war on roughness. Completions to Mitchell and fullback Don Bosseler, plus a second personal foul, put Washington on the 13. A third-down screen pass to Bosseler took the Redskins down to the 4 with only seven seconds left. Khayat lined up and kicked a 10-yard field goal but the officials ruled the gun had sounded for the end of the half, and the kick was disallowed.[62]

By halftime, Snead already had 210 yards passing, 129 of them by Mitchell. It looked as if the Redskins had learned from their loss to Pittsburgh four weeks earlier and were eliminating critical mistakes.

The Redskins took the second-half kickoff, and Stautner paused from whacking Snead to recover a fumble by halfback Bill Barnes at the Washington 45. The Steelers' ground game perked up, with Johnson carrying for 3 yards, then 5, and 5 more. Hoak picked up 17 on a draw, down to the 15. Johnson's 4-yard run gave Pittsburgh first-and-goal at the 5, and from there he gained four more before plunging the final yard for the TD that gave Pittsburgh a 21–14 lead with 6:58 gone in the quarter.

Snead hit Dugan for a 14-yard gain, but on the next play Thomas got his fifth interception of the season when he picked off a pass intended for Richter and returned it 32 yards to the Redskin 22. But the Washington defense stiffened, so Parker called on Michaels. He didn't have any real option, but Parker had a little insight into pressure kicks. After all, it was the "slashing Centenary halfback" himself who had provided the winning points in the upset of Texas years earlier by kicking a field goal in the final forty-five seconds. In the days after missing all five attempts against Cleveland, Michaels was groping for a solution to his slump. "All I have to do is boot one through the uprights and I'll be OK again," he said. He connected now, from 27 yards, to give the Steelers a 24–14 advantage, and himself a boost in confidence.[63]

Snead stayed aggressive, hitting Bill Anderson for 13 yards and Mitchell for 12 and 15 yards, but on second-and-3 from the Steeler 24, Dick Haley, the hero of the first Washington game, stole a pass at the 6, his fifth interception of the year. The Steelers methodically marched downfield, 2 or 3 yards at a time, with five carries by Johnson sandwiched around one by Hoak. As the fourth quarter opened, a 17-yard completion to Ballman put Pittsburgh on the Redskin 41. After Hoak lost 8 yards, creating third-and-18 at the 49, Brown hooked up with Ballman for a 31-yard gain. But on the next play, at the 18, Brown fumbled and tackle Bob Toneff recovered at the 26.

Snead wasn't wasting time with his running game. Barnes took a 54-yard pass down to the Steeler 20, and then he threw one himself, a halfback option to Mitchell, all alone in the right corner of the end zone, to bring the Redskins within 24–21 with 4:21 gone in the quarter. Parker's squad appeared to be on the verge of another collapse.

"We should have had at least three more touchdowns," Parker grumbled later. "We gummed up at least that number of chances to put the scores on the board. And that fumble scared the daylights out of me."[64]

Brown didn't panic and come out throwing. Other than two passes of 9 yards apiece to Ballman, the Steelers let Johnson and Hoak carry the load on a fourteen-play drive, challenging Washington's rugged defensive line. But on first-and-10 at the Washington 11, Brown threw three incompletions, leaving it up to Michaels to kick an 18-yard field goal for a 27–21 Steeler lead with 5:16 left in the game.

With halfback Dick James injured, the Redskins had no running game. They would total only 38 yards on the ground and not pick up a first down by rushing (compared to 11 by Pittsburgh). Snead had been intercepted twice, but he kept firing away. Glass broke up a pass intended for Mitchell, but on second-and-9 from the Washington 46 Mitchell eluded his shadow and caught a 33-yard pass down to the Steeler 21. One play later, Snead hit Richter in the left corner of the end zone with Thomas close enough to graze the receiver's helmet. With 2:38 to go, the Steelers were down 28–27.

As Ballman and Thomas lined up for the kickoff, the Steelers called for a return left. Ballman caught the ball on the 8-yard line and "careened down his left sideline."[65] As the Redskins converged, Ballman saw second-year end John Powers "smother Rod Breedlove" and guard Mike Sandusky throw another block.[66] "As I got through the hole, Clendon Thomas was ahead of me," Ballman explained. "I grabbed him and steered him into [Lonnie] Sanders [a teammate at Michigan State] and then cut back. They had me sidelined."[67]

Ballman "weaved his way laterally, like a frightened settler, through a war party of Braves in Tribe territory" and then "veered sharply to the center of the field, where he took off like a cannon shot."[68] It was a chance he had to take. "It's always a risk when you cut back in this league," Ballman said. "You never know what's behind you, but I didn't think I could go any farther along the sideline."[69] It sounded like that "special insight" he described to his wife, Judi: "Just pick a spot and go."

From there, Ballman revved up his Detroit motor, and by the time he reached the Washington 30, he was not to be caught. The Steelers had a 34–28 lead, but Norm Snead, "6 feet 4 inches of pure determination," still had 2:20 to work with, and the Redskins had "one final wheeze" left in them.[70]

Budd returned the kickoff to his 35. Snead hit Bosseler for 12 yards, and fist-swinging between the fullback and Baker "precipitated a near-riot." It was just the nature of the game, Stautner explained: "Baker just lost his head when Bosseler started kicking him."[71]

Snead hit Richter for 13 yards, and yet another personal foul advanced Washington to the Steeler 25 with 1:26 left. It was a déjà vu NFL moment, a flashback to St. Louis. But on first down, Snead's pass to Anderson was broken up by Daniel and Thomas and almost intercepted. A second-down pass was intended for Mitchell, who'd already set a team record with eleven receptions for 218 yards, but Glass tipped the ball away at the last second. However, it was Stautner, "the old man," who saved the Steelers, said losing coach Bill McPeak. "Stautner killed that pass, not Glass," McPeak said. "Nobody else in the league could have charged that kid so fast. He made Snead hurry his throw."[72]

On third down, Snead misfired for Anderson again. On fourth down, with 1:09 left, McPeak was looking for a first down, so he called for a sideline pass to Mitchell. "But Norm Snead thought Pittsburgh was going into a zone defense instead of man-to-man and he changed the play, a 'stop' pass to Richter," the coach explained.[73]

Snead aimed for the six-foot-five-and-a-half-inch Richter, but the rookie was guarded closely by Russell and Haley, and the pass went incomplete. That was it for the Redskins. There would be no repeat of the Charley Johnson–to–Bobby Joe Conrad magic. Snead had thrown forty times, completing twenty-three for 424 yards, but his failure to get his twenty-fourth completion left the Skins losers. The Steelers were not the ones who were snake bitten. "Someone is not living right around here," McPeak said, "and it must be me."[74]

Ballman didn't let himself get carried away with his heroics. Asked the next day at the Curbstone Coaches luncheon if he felt that he had "arrived," he reverted to his irreverent manner. "Sure," he replied. "My car is parked in the lot across the street."[75]

The Steelers were still clinging to hopes for a division title, and they were doing it with battered veterans like Stautner and John Henry Johnson, discards like Haley, and unpolished talents like Ballman. The chase was exhilarating but exhausting. "Wasn't that a game," Parker said in a whisper.[76]

The Giants, meanwhile, cruised to a 48–14 victory over the 49ers behind Y. A. Tittle's four touchdown passes and 284 yards in the air against his old team. The win was the Giants' fifth straight, a streak in which they scored at least thirty-three points in each game. The Giants took over sole possession of first place in the Eastern Conference with an 8–2 record as the Cards beat the Browns, 20–14, leaving the two teams in a tie for second at 7–3.

But the most impressive victory of the day came at Wrigley Field, where the Bears whipped the Packers, 26–7, leaving 9–1 Chicago alone in first place in the Western Conference. The Bears throttled the Packer offense, intercepting Bart Starr's fill-ins five times and snatching up three Green Bay fumbles. It was a dominating performance sure to seize Parker's attention, with the Bears traveling to Forbes Field in a week.

But for one day, the Steelers could savor another comeback, from another in a weekly parade of heroes. Art Rooney, as well aware as anyone that a football game and a horse race can be equally unpredictable, could appreciate a contest that went down to the final seconds. "I like to see my horse coming down to the wire neck-and-neck in the pack," Rooney said, "then win out in a photo finish!"[77] Rooney was about to see his kind of race come to life on the football field.

GAME 11

Half-a-million people were expected to turn out to greet President Kennedy in Chicago on Saturday morning, November 2, 1963, the day he was scheduled to attend the Army–Air Force game at Soldier Field. However, press secretary Pierre Salinger announced at the last minute that the trip would be canceled because the president had to tend to the worsening situation in South Vietnam, a military coup that overturned the government of President Ngo Dinh Diem.[1]

Ten days later, as the Bears prepared for their first-place showdown against the Packers at Wrigley Field, and scalpers prepared for a big payoff, coach George Halas was asked if he would invite President Kennedy to the game. "I'm sure if the president wants to see the game, I can find a seat for him," Halas replied.[2]

College football had been revered by fans for decades, and 1963 would mark the tenth straight year in which attendance rose, this time to a record of more than twenty-two million fans. But pro football was turning into a mania. An Illinois couple getting a divorce became embroiled in "the bitterest fight of all" over custody of Bears season tickets. Packer fans' only hope of getting home tickets was by being bequeathed them in a will. "Such is the phenomenal and growing popularity and hypnosis of the gladiatorial encounter known as professional football," wrote Steve Snider of UPI.[3]

In fact, interest in the pro game had been surging for several years, not unlike the frenzy that accompanied the popularity of Elvis and Sinatra. After fans stormed the field at Yankee Stadium before the finish of a Browns-Giants game in December of '59, forcing players and Browns coach

Paul Brown to flee the field, and delaying the game for twenty minutes, *New York Times* columnist Arthur Daley commented that pro football "has become engulfed by an emotionalism that now approaches hysteria."[4]

And that hysteria knew no bounds. Giants coach Jim Lee Howell, a native of Lonoke, Arkansas, observed: "New York fans are just like the fans in Lonoke, Arkansas, only there are more of 'em here."[5]

In 1934, the NFL had fewer customers than the number of people who awaited Kennedy in Chicago. Ten years later, spectators topped one million. In 1952, the thirty-third year of the NFL's existence, attendance reached two million. In 1962, the total was a record 4,003,421, and that figure was likely to be broken by the end of the '63 season. Television sparked the boom in interest, and the NFL profited handsomely. The fourteen teams split profits of $4,650,000 from TV, and the NFL took in $926,000 for telecast rights to the championship game, with much of the sum directed toward a player pension fund. On an average Sunday in the fall, fifteen million TV sets were tuned in to NFL games. Interest in pro football was about to explode, and no longer did baseball enjoy an unchallenged claim as the national pastime.[6]

Chicago fans had as intense an interest as anyone in the nation over the NFL telecasts scheduled for Sunday, November 24. After manhandling the Packers, the 9–1 Bears could edge out 8–2 Green Bay in the Western Conference race by winning their four remaining games, starting with Pittsburgh. After escaping Washington with a victory, the 6–3–1 Steelers still had a shot at climbing over St. Louis and Cleveland, both 7–3, and past 8–2 New York, but they couldn't afford another loss. The day after his game-winning dash, Gary Ballman was asked at the Curbstone Coaches luncheon whether his team could go 4–0 the rest of the way. "You better call Lloyds of London for the odds on that one," he said. "We have as good a chance to win them all as to lose them all."[7]

The Packers had beaten the Steelers by 19. The Bears beat the Packers by 19. "Does that make Chicago 38 points over Pittsburgh on Sunday?" *Post-Gazette* sportswriter Jack Sell asked. "Go right ahead and think so if you want," Ballman answered. "I don't know how they figure games by points."[8]

Halas wasn't buying into the math either. His euphoria after "one of the greatest triumphs in Bear history" quickly turned to worry as Chicago prepared for a visit to Forbes Field.[9] "Never mind the Packers game. The Steelers should have beaten them," said the coach, who had spent forty-four of his sixty-eight years in professional football.[10] "I'd rather be playing any team in the league than the Steelers. They are tough and punishing."[11]

In the Steelers, Halas could no doubt see a mirror image of his own club. Pittsburgh was the one team whose survival-of-the-fittest mentality could rival the reputation of the "Monsters of the Midway." And a letdown by the Bears seemed only human after the Packers' visit received the buildup of a championship game. "No team can play perfect football two weeks in a row, and it seems too much to expect them to be as supercharged as they were last Sunday," Tex Maule said after the Bears' win.[12]

Halas didn't shrink from the growing attention. In fact, he took the opposite approach of Buddy Parker and welcomed the tension. "No, I'm not afraid of a letdown after the Green Bay game," he said. "The pressure is building up this week. That's the way I like it . . . lots of pressure. Being completely relaxed is no good."[13]

Halas had his Bears playing as if it was still the 1940s, "demonstrating that games can still be won in the old-fashioned way."[14] Bill Wade was an efficient quarterback who led the league in pass attempts and completions in '62 and finished third in passing yardage. Ten games into the '63 season, he ranked second in the league to Y. A. Tittle among passers, relying on Ditka, No. 8 among leaders in receptions, as his prime target.

The Bears finished twelfth out of fourteen teams in rushing in '62 and through the first ten games of '63 ranked eleventh in total offense, with none of their backs among the top ten rushers. After eight games, every team in the league with a winning record had scored 200 points—except Chicago. The Bears would go on to finish tenth in the league in points scored.

Young George Allen had taken over from Clark Shaughnessy as defensive coordinator. His crew was "performing virtual miracles," and it would wind up the season allowing a league-low 144 points, 62 less than the second-best unit, and would rank first in differential between takeaways and giveaways (plus 29).[15]

It was the defense, ranked first in the NFL, that had allowed the Bears to win by scores of 10–3 (twice), 17–7, 16–7, and 6–0. It was the only defense in the NFL that had held opponents to an aggregate rushing total under 1,000 yards (892) after ten games. Aptly enough, it was Roger Leclerc of the Bears who was named AP's player of the week after kicking four field goals in the 26–7 victory over the Packers. Pittsburgh's defense, as tough as its personnel was, ranked only tenth in the league and had given up an average of nearly 138 yards more per game than Chicago's unit.

Doug Atkins, a future Hall of Famer, anchored one end spot, and Ed O'Bradovich the other. Bill George, Larry Morris, and Joe Fortunato formed a rugged trio of linebackers. Parker said that the Bears had the best defensive backfield in the league. One safety, Roosevelt Taylor, was leading the league in interceptions, with seven; the other, Richie Petitbon, would go on to a career as coach, rising to defensive coordinator and, briefly, head coach.

The Bears weren't doing anything flashy. They were winning with sheer physical play. "They beat the hell out of us," Vince Lombardi said after his team's 26–7 loss.[16] Jim Taylor, who had rushed for 141 yards against the Steelers, gained only 23 against the Bears, and the Packers had a total of only 71 on the ground.

Both the Steelers and Bears had a key injury. While Halas had to deal with a season-ending ankle injury to fullback Rick Casares, Parker was facing a second straight game without Brady Keys, who had sat out the Redskins game with bruised ribs. Now Keys was hemorrhaging in the chest cavity.[17]

Before practice at Wrigley Field on Wednesday before the game, Halas made it sound as if the Steelers were more fearsome than the defending champion Packers. "My gosh they have a fine team," he said. "That John Henry Johnson is some runner, and now they've come up with this fast young fellow named Ballman."[18]

The player who was perhaps most eager to face the Bears was the man who knew them best: Ed Brown, who was with Chicago for eight years through 1961. "Beat the Bears?" Brown said right around the time Halas was raving about Pittsburgh. "I want to beat them in the worst way."[19]

Brown still harbored a grudge for having to split playing time with Wade and Zeke Bratkowski after Chicago was routed by the Giants in the 1956 title game, 47–7. "After the 1961 season I was fed up, and asked to be traded," Brown said.[20] In '59 he completed 125 of 247 passes for 1,881 yards and thirteen touchdowns, all personal highs for his pro career in Chicago. His playing time dropped off over the next two years, and in '61 he threw only ninety-eight passes. Then Parker rescued him.

"Certainly this game means more than most," Brown said. "Everybody is a little bitter after being traded, even if you ask for it, and this is one way to get back. Besides, I've got a lot of friends on the Bears, guys I came into the pros with, and I'd like to beat them." Brown spoke evenly, but his coach knew that his feelings ran deep. "He's the type of guy who doesn't say much but I know he wants nothing better than to beat the Bears," Parker said.[21]

Brown's old teammates still respected him, and they knew how dangerous he could be with a football. "Ed Brown was our man, and we loved him," Casares said of the quarterback.[22]

The morning of Friday, November 22, 1963, brought cloudy but mild weather, with temperatures expected to hit the 60s, while out West the first major winter storm of the season was gaining strength. The lead story in the *Post-Gazette* warned that the city was facing a December 8 strike by 1,300 trolley and bus operators. Robert F. Stroud, "the Birdman of Alcatraz," had died at age seventy-three. Joey Bishop, Joan Crawford, and Jack E. Leonard were scheduled to appear at a benefit Sunday night at the Penn Sheraton Ballroom. And a page 1 story described President Kennedy's dedication of the Aerospace Medical Center in San Antonio, Texas, the day before. "The conquest of space must and will go on," the president stated. In the spirit of the time, he said, "doing and daring are required of all who are willing to explore the unknown and test the uncertain in every phase of human endeavor."[23]

As a security precaution, the Steelers held a "secret practice" on Thursday at Forbes Field rather than at South Park. There was no indication that Parker had anyone monitor the surroundings with binoculars, although ten years earlier a bit of paranoia surfaced while he was conducting a Detroit Lions practice. As a railroad switch engine passed on a track by the practice field, the coach noticed the engineer and fireman watching the workout, so Parker stopped practice. "For all I know, George Halas could be sitting in the cab of that locomotive," Parker said.[24]

Art Rooney Jr. remembered being in the Steeler offices Friday afternoon. "Joe Carr was our ticket man. He came running in and he said, 'Some nut just shot President Kennedy. It looks like he's dying.'"[25]

Late in the day, Dan Rooney, who had been listed in the '62 press guide as the team's program director but was running the day-to-day operations, got a phone call from commissioner Pete Rozelle, asking what Rooney thought about playing the Sunday schedule. Dan Rooney told the commissioner it would be a mistake to play the games.[26]

Employees in the Steeler headquarters listened to the news on the radio. Before heading home, Art Rooney Jr. said, "I went down to Saint Mary's Church . . . and you couldn't get in the church. It overflowed. Next day I came in, I tried to go to mass and it was the same thing—just packed."[27]

Kennedy had visited western Pennsylvania at least six times in eight years, dating back to his time as a senator. In mid-October of '62, while campaigning for a gubernatorial candidate, he made stops in Monessen, where he shook hands with steelworkers and railroad workers; in Aliquippa, hometown of the Bears' Mike Ditka; in Emsworth, where he accepted a bouquet of roses for the First Lady from Holy Family Orphanage; and at the George Washington Hotel in Little Washington, as it was known locally, an hour south of downtown Pittsburgh, where he watched Army play Penn

State on TV. Estimates of the turnout in western Pennsylvania ranged from 300,000 to half a million, all of them eager to get a handshake or just a glimpse of the president.[28]

News was slow to spread in downtown Pittsburgh. For nearly an hour after the first bulletin of the assassination in Dallas, it looked like a normal Friday. Then, gradually, shoppers and workers began to gather by radios in cigar stores, restaurants, and newsstands. Steeler defensive lineman Lou Cordileone learned of the shooting when he looked in the show window of a store selling TV sets. A table of diners at the Hilton heard the news from a waiter. Mayor Joseph A. Barr was having lunch in the Pittsburgher Hotel when he was informed of the assassination, and then he returned to his office and listened to the news on his radio. Later, as delivery trucks dropped off newspapers on street corners, people eagerly snatched them up. The news spread swiftly. "The word traveled on those invisible lines of communication that make individuals listening posts and transmitters," the *Pittsburgh Press* reported.[29]

The newspaper offices and the courthouse received a deluge of phone calls seeking more information after "the first flash"—the news bulletin with top priority transmitted on paper scrolls to the newspaper offices—reported that the president had been shot. For people along Smithfield Street in mid-afternoon, the dread of a nation was confirmed by one simple act: the lowering of the post office flag to half-staff by two office workers.[30]

When NFL players got news of Kennedy's assassination, they knew that whatever followed over the next two days was out of their control. All they could do was wait for directions on where to go, and when.

The Packers, trying to recover from their loss in Chicago, had wrapped up a meeting on Friday, and most players were leaving for the day when they began picking up news reports on car radios. Five of the Packers were from Dallas. "I suppose we'll be infamous now," said Bill Forester, a tenth-year linebacker from SMU.[31]

Bill McPeak huddled the Redskins in a silent prayer on the practice field before heading to the locker room. After Sunday's game, the team would send the game ball back to the White House.[32]

Sam Huff was driving across the Triboro Bridge, with teammate Don Chandler in the car, heading home from practice at Yankee Stadium, when he got the news. "Terrible. It was absolutely terrible," he said.[33]

Bob St. Clair, a six-foot-nine, 265-pound offensive tackle for the San Francisco 49ers and a pro for eleven seasons, said: "I cried when I heard Mr. Kennedy had been killed."[34] The biggest and baddest in the sports world wept, and that included Sonny Liston and his wife. "I feel very bad for myself and my race for he was a friend of ours and of the people," Liston said in a statement.[35] It's safe to figure that Big Daddy Lipscomb, too, would have wept unashamedly.

Rozelle conferred with Pierre Salinger, and repeatedly with Dan Rooney, and finally the commissioner and Salinger reached the conclusion that playing the NFL schedule would be beneficial to the country. Rozelle issued a brief statement: "It has been traditional in sports for athletes to perform in times of great personal tragedy. Football was Mr. Kennedy's game. He thrived on competition."[36]

Years later, Rozelle conceded that he made a mistake, but under the circumstances it was understandable and forgivable. "When you look back on it, you can question different things, but your life had to go on, even though some things are totally unreal in how they happen," Dick Haley said. "It was hard for everybody to focus, no question about that. Probably everybody was distracted a little bit in circumstances like that."[37]

The University of Pittsburgh, 7–1 and in the hunt for a major bowl bid, postponed its game with Penn State, a sellout at Pitt Stadium, after several hours of discussions and phone calls Friday afternoon. The Penn State players had already checked in at their Pittsburgh hotel.

Other cancellations and postponements came swiftly. Eastern racetracks shut down. The NBA postponed its Friday night schedule. A fight at Madison Square Garden was called off. Dozens of college football games were postponed, but the NCAA left the decision about whether or not to play up to the individual schools. Less than a fourth of about fifty "major" college football games went on as scheduled.[38]

But life did go on. Detroit Lions stockholders approved the sale of the team to William Clay Ford for $6 million. Montana State fired its football coach. North Carolina State College went ahead with its Friday night game against Wake Forest. The Pittsburgh Hornets of the American Hockey League gave up four goals in the final period and lost to the Hershey Bears, 5–3, Saturday night before a crowd of 6,781 in Hershey, Pennsylvania. The Hornets also had a Sunday night game scheduled against the Springfield Indians. In Boston, the forty-eighth dog show of the Eastern Dog Club began Saturday despite criticism of what had become "a trifling event in the face of a national tragedy. There was a pall over all and the realization that what was happening in the rings was of small moment."[39]

The slaying presented the modern sports world with a dilemma it couldn't have imagined. Up to then, the slayings, tragedies, mayhem, and unspeakable

acts that routinely made the front page of the newspaper were reported sol-·
emnly, and readers gasped and lamented the random cruelties that intruded
on their lives . . . and the games went on. But the assassination of a president
at a time when the nation was swirling with civil rights, Cuba, Vietnam, and
the notion of putting a man on the moon was enough to petrify the soul of
any American. Formulating an appropriate response was a challenge.

Post-Gazette sports editor Al Abrams wrote in his Saturday "Notes" column: "President Kennedy's assassination in Dallas yesterday was horrible,
shocking and beyond belief. But things like this will continue to happen so
long as there are human beings who act like mad dogs because they hate."[40]
Abrams's commentary appeared in the first section of his column, but it
was the eighth item he addressed, preceded by snippets about the nice fall
weather, a mention that Pirate pitcher Bob Friend was visiting Hong Kong,
and a get-well wish to a *Post-Gazette* truck driver who was hospitalized. Most
likely, the column had been written and filed early, before the assassination, and the commentary added later. After his brief remarks on Kennedy,
Abrams returned to news and notes from around the world of sports. The
Press offered no sports commentary on Kennedy the day after his death.

Many columnists expressed their outrage that sports—the NFL, in particular, because the AFL postponed its games—did not come to a complete
standstill at a time of national grieving. For some sportswriters, struggling
to provide a voice and perspective for the fan put them in an awkward,
uncomfortable position. Gordon Cobbledick of the *Cleveland Plain Dealer,*
in his Sunday column about the unchecked rough play in the NFL, wrote in
his lead that it was "appropriate" to address the issue "because it's a time
of shocking violence."[41] His remarks were, no doubt, well intentioned, but
in retrospect there was really nothing in sports to equate with the assault
that had been inflicted on an entire nation.

The NFL would carry on, but it would make one concession. The week
before, a *Chicago Sun-Times* story stated that sales of color TVs were
"booming." The report said that, by conservative estimates, 700,000 color
sets would be sold in '63—twice the previous year's total—and that some
estimates were as high as one million sales for the year. Sales were so good
that, with Christmas approaching, there could be a shortage of sets available for consumers. "The public is buying everything that is offered," Sears,
Roebuck and Co. said. But on Sunday, November 24, no fans were going
to tune in their Motorola, Zenith, or RCA color TVs to an NFL game. The
games were not going to be televised. Yet interest in the Bears game in the
Chicago area did not fade. The *Chicago Tribune* reported that it received

Steelers linebacker Bob Schmitz (67) and defensive back Clendon Thomas (28) chase Eagles back Tim Brown during the third quarter of the 21–21 tie in the '63 season opener. Thomas tackled Brown, who gained 42 yards on the pass from Sonny Jurgensen. (Temple University Libraries, Urban Archives, Philadelphia, PA)

Eagles defensive back Irv Cross (far left, 27) rushes in to block Lou Michaels's extra point attempt during the 21–21 tie in the opening game of the 1963 NFL season. (Temple University Libraries, Urban Archives, Philadelphia, PA)

Good hands and speed made "Red" Mack a deep threat and a target for quarterback Ed Brown throughout the '63 season. (Carnegie Library of Pittsburgh)

Head coach "Buddy" Parker with his staff, from left: Jack Butler, Mike Nixon, Chuck Cherundolo, Thurman "Fum" McGraw, and Dick Plasman, at the South Park Fairgrounds, the team's practice site. This is likely from 1961, Nixon's first year on the staff and Plasman's last. (Carnegie Library of Pittsburgh)

Left: Trainer Roger McGill examines the right arm of Myron Pottios, which the linebacker broke in 1962 and forced him to the sidelines for the season. (Carnegie Library of Pittsburgh)

Right: Lou Cordileone, left, grew up in Jersey City, New Jersey, and John Baker came from Raleigh, North Carolina, but what they had in common was a passion for rushing quarterbacks. (Carnegie Library of Pittsburgh)

Left: Offensive tackle Dan James bangs away at a tackling dummy during training camp. James was a vital yet relatively anonymous player who kept the Steelers' ground game going. "They don't even know my name," he once said of the fans. (Carnegie Library of Pittsburgh)

Right: Ed Brown, the quiet successor to Bobby Layne, kept the Steelers in the race in '63 with his long bombs. (Carnegie Library of Pittsburgh)

Left: The Steelers' 1963 starting backfield: flanker "Buddy" Dial, fullback John Henry Johnson, quarterback Ed Brown, and halfback Dick Hoak. (Carnegie Library of Pittsburgh)

Right: Some survivors from the 1963 Steelers rookie class: quarterback Bill Nelsen, quarterback Jim Traficant, offensive back Roy Curry, defensive back Jim Bradshaw, linebacker Andy Russell, defensive tackle Frank Atkinson, and three unidentified players. Nelsen, Curry, Bradshaw, Russell, and Atkinson defied the odds and made the squad. (Carnegie Library of Pittsburgh)

Dick Haley, a kid from western Pennsylvania, became a two-way star at the University of Pittsburgh before settling in as a defensive back with the Steelers. (The University of Pittsburgh: Athletic Media Relations)

Lou Cordileone, an All-America lineman at Clemson, was a vagabond NFL player until he found his perfect spot with the Steelers. (Clemson University Sports Information)

Eugene "Big Daddy" Lipscomb on the athletic field at Slippery Rock State Teachers College in July of 1961. Lipscomb was a terror to NFL quarterbacks, but he was a kid at heart and had a soft spot for children. (Carnegie Museum of Art, Pittsburgh; Heinz Family Fund. © 2004 Carnegie Museum of Art, Charles "Teenie" Harris Archive)

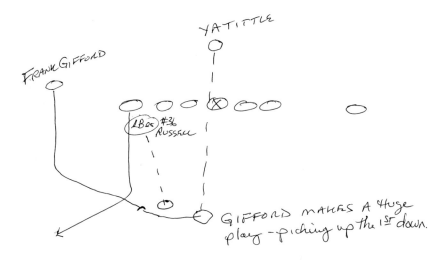

FRANK GIFFORD

YA TITTLE

LB os #36 RUSSELL

GIFFORD MAKES A huge play - picking up the 1st down.

The play that broke the Steelers' backs in the showdown with the Giants in week 14, as diagrammed here by linebacker Andy Russell. Frank Gifford made a one-handed catch of a pass from Y. A. Tittle on third-and-8 early in the third quarter, and the Giants drove in for the score that wiped out the Steelers' momentum.

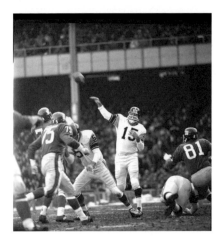

With center Buzz Nutter fending off defensive tackle John LoVetere (76) and defensive end Jim Katcavage (75), Ed Brown fires away during the Steelers' 33–17 loss to the Giants in the 1963 season finale at Yankee Stadium. Brown's scattershot throws in the showdown for the Eastern Division title cost Pittsburgh numerous chances for big gains and possible scores. No. 81 is defensive end Andy Robustelli. (Courtesy of Carl Kidwiler)

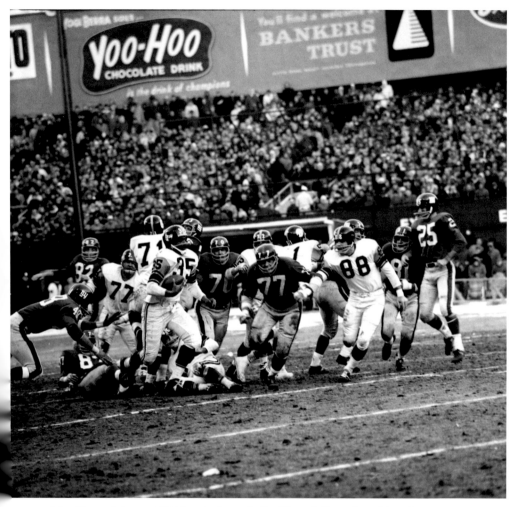

John Henry Johnson (35) bursts through the Giant defense for a big gain as tackle Dick Modzelewski (77) and linebacker Sam Huff (70) give chase during the Steelers' 33–17 loss at Yankee Stadium on December 15, 1963. Other Giants defenders are back Erich Barnes (49), linebacker Jerry Hillebrand (87, on the ground), linebacker Tom Scott (82), end Andy Robustelli (81), and back Dick Pesonen (25). Steelers offensive players are end John Powers (88), tackle Dan James (77), and tackle Charlie Bradshaw (71). Johnson led all rushers in the game with 104 yards on 14 carries. (Courtesy of Carl Kidwiler)

Gary Ballman (85) sprints around Giants linebacker Sam Huff during Pittsburgh's 33–17 loss in game 14 of the '63 season. After a year relegated to the practice squad, Ballman blossomed into an explosive threat both as a kickoff return man and deep receiver. (Courtesy of Carl Kidwiler)

Running back Theron Sapp (33) picks his way behind guard Mike Sandusky (62) during the Steelers' 33–17 loss at Yankee Stadium on December 15, 1963. Sapp earned folk-hero status as a college player for scoring the touchdown that enabled Georgia to beat rival Georgia Tech, but it was his winning touchdown run in Dallas that set up the climactic battle with the Giants in the final game of the '63 season. (Courtesy of Carl Kidwiler)

An unidentified tackler sends Frank Ryan (13) sprawling, as tackle Joe Krupa (75), tackle Lou Cordileone (74), end Lou Michaels (79), and cornerback Glenn Glass (43) converge on the Browns quarterback during the Steelers' 9–7 victory at Pitt Stadium on November 10, 1963. (Courtesy of Carl Kidwiler)

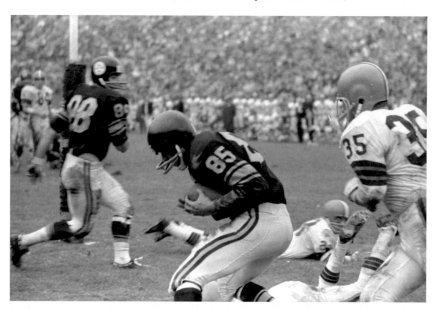

Wide receiver Gary Ballman (85) tucks in the 9-yard touchdown pass from Ed Brown that lifted the Steelers to a 9–7 victory over Cleveland on November 10, 1963. Covering Ballman is linebacker Galen Fiss (35). No. 88 is Steelers end John Powers. (Courtesy of Carl Kidwiler)

A somber-looking Jim Brown, alone on the Cleveland bench, watches the action during the Steelers' 9–7 victory at Pitt Stadium on November 10, 1963. Brown came into the game averaging 149 yards rushing per game but was held to 99 yards on 19 carries and was tackled for a safety, the difference in the final score. (Courtesy of Carl Kidwiler)

Clendon Thomas barrels into Jim Brown in the end zone as Steelers linebacker Bob Schmitz, on the ground, clings to the Cleveland fullback's legs during the third quarter of the November 10, 1963, game at Pitt Stadium. The play was ruled a safety by referee Tommy Bell (7), and Schmitz was credited with the tackle, cutting the Browns' lead to 7–2 in a game they eventually lost, 9–7. Wearing No. 36 is rookie linebacker Andy Russell, and in the background is cornerback Brady Keys (26). On the right side are defensive tackle Lou Cordileone (74) and Cleveland tackle Dick Schafrath (77). (Courtesy of Carl Kidwiler)

Bobby Layne (22), the fiery leader and bon vivant of Buddy Parker's Steelers, rears back to throw long during Pittsburgh's 27–24 loss to the Giants at Yankee Stadium on November 13, 1960. Layne disdained the use of a face mask on his helmet throughout his fifteen-year pro career. (Courtesy of Carl Kidwiler)

Ernie Stautner (70) was an undersized defensive tackle, but he was impervious to pain and played with a ferocity and relentlessness that more than compensated for his size disadvantage. Here he races to chase down Giants fullback Alex Webster during the Steelers' 27–24 loss at Yankee Stadium on November 13, 1960. (Courtesy of Carl Kidwiler)

A bespectacled Buddy Parker, calm but revealing a furrowed brow, watches the action as the Steelers eke out a 20–17 victory over the Giants at Yankee Stadium on October 14, 1962. Flanking Parker on the left are wide receiver Red Mack and assistant coach Chuck Cherundolo. On the right, wearing the cap, is "Boots" Lewis, a former custodian who Parker brought to Pittsburgh as a good luck charm for the team. (Courtesy of Carl Kidwiler)

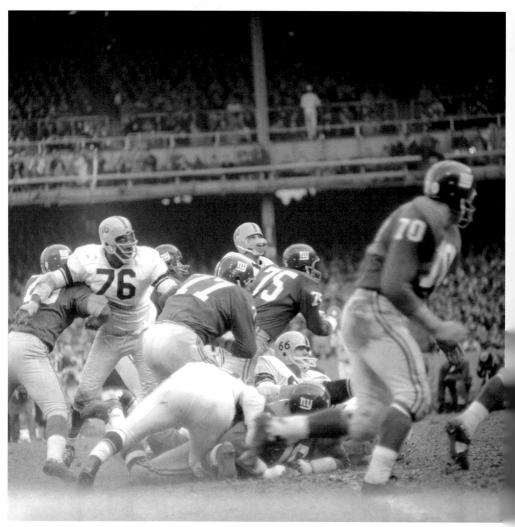

Eugene "Big Daddy" Lipscomb (76), the scourge of quarterbacks around the NFL, but off the field a gentle giant with a troubled soul, battles Giants linemen during Pittsburgh's 42–21 loss at Yankee Stadium on November 19, 1961. Giants players are Dick Modzelewski (77), Jim Katcavage (75), and Sam Huff (70). (Courtesy of Carl Kidwiler)

9,729 telephone calls from fans seeking scores and information during an eight-hour period during and after the game in Pittsburgh. Calls were coming in at a rate of twenty per minute.[42]

Blocking, tackling, and catching passes might have been the last things some players wanted to do, but they had no choice. They would await instructions and perform their duties just as they carried out their assignments when a play was called in the huddle. And most of the players assumed that the games would go on as scheduled.

"We figured, unless there's a drastic change, we're going to play," Lou Michaels said.[43]

Once the decision had been made, players tried to focus on their opponent and somehow block out distracting thoughts. "They said you're gonna play, you're gonna play," Red Mack said. "You just concentrate on the Bears. Once you make the kickoff, you're into the game. It don't make any difference what happened. After the game, you're back like you were before. You're wondering, 'What's going to happen to the country?' It overwhelmed you before the game but during that game it just didn't have anything to do with our play. Not really."[44]

"When game day came around, it was tunnel vision as to how do we beat these Bears," Andy Russell said. "You were thinking of your individual responsibilities."[45]

Fans did not accept the decision with equanimity. Some reacted with outrage. Steeler offices were "bombarded" by fans angered by Rozelle's thinking. One caller threatened to picket the game. Approximately 150 tickets were turned in for refunds Saturday, but as of mid-afternoon, more than 300 tickets had been sold over the counter, bringing the game closer to a sellout.[46]

Dozens of callers phoned the *New York Times,* but most simply wanted to know if the Giants-Cards game was going to be played. "A highly vocal minority" said they were "shocked," "aghast," "ashamed," or "horrified" that the game would be played. One caller said, "Tell Rozelle and [Giants president John] Mara, we couldn't care less about tomorrow's game. It's deplorable that it's being played."[47] The *Milwaukee Journal-Sentinel* reported that it received more than 200 calls of protest. Los Angeles newspaper offices took a "considerable number" of similar calls.[48]

It was a struggle for players to generate enthusiasm for playing, but they had no choice, no say in the matter. "A lot of our players wanted to cancel the game," Y. A. Tittle said. "It was a big letdown. It just seemed like something we shouldn't be doing."[49]

Thirty-eight years later, one Steeler in particular regretted the decision to play the games.

Joe Krupa was a six-foot-one, 240-pound defensive tackle who looked a bit like Popeye and had the same fighting spirit, to boot. The Steeler media guide called him both "a player's player and a coach's player," an unsung grunt whose approach to football made him a perfect fit with guys like Ernie Stautner and Myron Pottios. After his playing career came to an end, he envisioned a career in education, an extension of his off-season job. "I want to teach kids," he said, "young, impressionable kids who can be taught the values of life."[50] As the 1963 season headed into the stretch, Krupa, in his eighth year in the league, was on the way to earning his first Pro Bowl appearance.

Years later, in the hours after 9/11, Krupa thought back to the Bears game, held only forty-eight hours after Kennedy was slain. "Boy, that game should never have been played," he said. Krupa was in good company nearly forty years earlier. The morning of the Bears game, he saw Art Rooney Sr. in church. "He told us, 'There's no way there should be a game today,'" Krupa recalled.[51]

But others thought it was the right call. Twenty-four hours after the assassination, and the day after his twenty-fifth birthday, Charley Johnson of the Cardinals sat in his room in the Hotel Manhattan in New York and declared that it was a positive move to play the next day. "I think people want something to get their minds off the situation," he said. "President Kennedy was too dynamic a person to want us to be stagnant at a time like this."[52] After the Cards won the next day, Johnson admitted, "It was hard to think about football before the game."[53]

Chicago center Mike Pyle, three years out of Yale, wanted to play. "I didn't feel the world had come to a stop. For a period of time on Friday, yes," he said. "But sitting home all weekend, I wouldn't have been as happy as doing what I felt my job was."[54]

But even those who were grief stricken could understand—if not accept—the rationale for going through with the games. Huff, a West Virginia native, had met Kennedy and campaigned for him. "I feel depressed," Huff would say after the game.

I feel as bad about it as anybody. But staying home and moping around wouldn't do any good. Last year, Jimmy Patton's father died the day before the Dallas game. Nobody can say he didn't grieve, but he played the game.

That is our life. The people who don't like it, that's their right. Maybe that's what the President died for.[55]

The NFL schedule provided one meager bit of fortune in the schedule, and it figured in Rozelle's decision to go on with the games. The Cowboys were scheduled to play in Cleveland, not at home in Dallas. "That," Rozelle conceded, "would have presented a different set of problems."[56]

Browns owner Art Modell said he pleaded with the commissioner to cancel the full schedule. "Trust me, don't play those damn games," he recalled telling Rozelle.[57]

People felt the irrational sting of a wound that no one knew how to soothe, and they struck out and flailed in misguided attempts to vent their anguish. As the Cowboys' team bus pulled up to the hotel in Cleveland, bellhops refused to help with the players' bags. Before the game, the public address announcer was instructed to use the word "Cowboys," and not "Dallas," in any references to the visiting team.[58]

Cowboy running back Don Perkins was in his third pro season, out of the University of New Mexico. His college coach, Marv Levy, future coach of the Buffalo Bills, called Perkins "the greatest natural ball carrier I've ever seen."[59] He was coming off a 945-yard season and was en route to his third straight Pro Bowl appearance, but there was no place for anyone associated with Dallas to escape the stigma of a murder. "I just wanted to go hide somewhere," Perkins said.[60]

Modell prepared for the most extreme reactions. He stationed police sharpshooters throughout the 83,000-seat Municipal Stadium and on the roof. "I felt like George Patton," Modell said. "It looked like an armed camp when I got through with it."[61]

And the fans turned out. Whether they were distraught, anxious to find an escape, or desperate to find consolation among 40,000 or 50,000 strangers with a common bond, pro football fans showed up on Sunday. As the headline for a Dick Young story in the *New York Daily News* read, "They Came with Mixed Emotions—but They Came." Yankee Stadium was jammed with 62,992 fans, including Dianne Ebert, a student at Martin Van Buren High School in Little Neck, Long Island. "I think it should have been called off, but I have been looking forward to this game for so long," she said. "It's my only time this year, and I just couldn't stay away."[62]

Others could, like Kenny Byrnes and Jim Fargardo of Manhattan, who had seats in the lower stands. "We've been looking forward to going to this game," Fargardo said. "Anyone can tell you how hard it is to get these tickets. But out of respect for the president, we're not going in. I'll show you," he added, and then he tore up his ticket, and Byrnes did the same.[63]

Red Smith was an angry opponent of the decision to play the games and an unforgiving critic of Rozelle thereafter. His Monday column in the *New York Herald Tribune* opened, "In the civilized world it was a day of mourning. In the National Football League it was the 11th Sunday of the business year. . . ."[64]

Another columnist, the *Philadelphia Evening Bulletin*'s Sandy Grady, who had written with the awe of a fan about the battle between the Steelers and Lions in the Runner-Up Bowl, savaged not only the league but the fans in a commentary oozing with sarcasm and venom. Philadelphia mayor James H. J. Tate had protested the playing of the game against Washington, and Eagles president Frank McNamee refused to attend the event, the first time he had missed a home game in fifteen years.

The total number of fans who attended the seven games was 334,892, according to the Associated Press. Grady called it

a great tribute to the sports fan. The insularity of his dreamland is complete. Even the slow drums of national tragedy cannot be heard in his beautiful cocoon.

In Franklin Field [in Philadelphia] they held a football game that adults would have canceled, in a stadium that should have been empty, before a mob that should have been invisibly mute.

For the first time in his sportswriting career, he said, "I am ashamed of this fatuous dreamland." He concluded, "Even the burlesque house in town had the dignity to shut the doors."[65]

But there was room to empathize with fans who sought a refuge from the unrelenting sense of despair that came through the news nonstop. "There weren't very many channels, no cable," Frank Atkinson recalled. "So all you heard was funeral music and sadness. People needed a break from it, so they went out and bought a ticket to a football game."[66]

Late Friday afternoon, CBS, NBC, and ABC announced the suspension of all entertainment programs on TV and radio. This was uncharted territory for the blossoming age of television. "Uncertainty and bewilderment seemed to characterize the TV networks' reaction to the national disaster," wrote Fred Remington in the *Pittsburgh Press*. "Television, sometimes called an escapist medium, offered no escape," he wrote after a full day of coverage on Saturday. Most radio stations filled air time with "solemn" music.[67]

"I thought the games were a good relief for everybody," Art Rooney Jr. said.[68]

Uncertainty and bewilderment were the justifiable reactions of most people. Whether it was OK to play a football game—or a hockey game, or to hold a dog show, for that matter—was a polarizing dilemma. Dick Young of the *New York Daily News,* who never saw a controversy on which he couldn't pick a side and take a jab, withheld judgment on the issue. "Some men pray aloud, with much pomp and manifestation; some men speak quietly to their God, and some do not pray at all. Yet, they are good men," Young wrote. "And if you ask which is right, I cannot tell you, because I cannot tell you what a man feels in his heart."[69]

Rozelle said he had made his decision on Friday afternoon. While attending the game at Giants Stadium on Sunday, he added, "I realize some feeling has developed since then. The continuous television has deepened the sense of tragedy we feel."[70]

The drama was intensifying that day. Some of the Steeler wives would park their cars at the Roosevelt Hotel and take a cab together to Forbes Field (or Pitt Stadium) and, after the game, return with their husbands to the hotel. "Well, on this particular Sunday when we got in the cab, the driver said, 'Can you believe what has happened?'" Ruth Daniel recalled. "Thinking he was referring to the assassination, we answered appropriately. But as we talked back and forth, we realized that something else had happened. We were not even aware that Lee Harvey Oswald had been shot—and on television at that! Can you imagine in this day and age not to even know about something like that happening until hours later?"[71]

Browns quarterback Frank Ryan, who grew up in Fort Worth, Texas, and was a teammate of Buddy Dial at Rice, was sitting on the bench at Municipal Stadium before the game with the Cowboys when he heard voices on the coaches' headsets. He put on the headset and listened to two voices talking about Oswald getting shot. "I just thought that was bizarre," Ryan said years later. "I wondered what type of conspiracy was going on here."[72]

The Giants Stadium crowd was "unusually quiet." The customary player introductions were omitted. At Metropolitan Stadium in Bloomington, Minnesota, where the Vikings were hosting the Lions, 20,000 copies of "The Star-Spangled Banner" were passed out to fans. The crowd of 28,763 at the site in suburban Minneapolis was the smallest of the day.[73]

The capacity crowd of 45,905 at Milwaukee County Stadium stood in silence for a minute before the kickoff. The Packer Band played "The Star Spangled Banner" and then put away their instruments for the rest of the afternoon.[74] The only halftime entertainment was the Punt, Pass & Kick contest. Vince Lombardi had said there would be no commercial announcements, not even notices on "the flash-o-gram space" on the scoreboard.[75]

In Cleveland, which had stuffed in 80,000-plus fans for the Steeler game, only 55,096 came out on a sunny day. A week earlier, 75,932 had shown up for the Cardinals game. A halftime tribute to retiring star Ray Renfro was called off. Notified of the change of plans, the slick receiver known as "the Rabbit" replied softly, "That doesn't matter. I'll have lots of days. President Kennedy won't have any more."[76]

The weather in New York was appropriately stark—a perfect shade of gloom for the conflicted state of mind of seventy-four players, the coaching staffs, and nearly 63,000 [the actual figure was 62,992] people more aptly described as onlookers than as fans. "The sky was grim and gray and outlined against its somberness all the flags flew half staff around the roof of the Yankee Stadium and you had to wonder what the two teams were doing on the football field playing a game," syndicated columnist Milton Gross wrote. "Then you looked through the stands where 63,800 people sat subdued and, it seemed, ashamed and you had to wonder whether it was disrespect to the memory of the President or the understanding that life and games do go on in the midst of the tragedy or death."[77]

Players struggled with their emotions. "Let me tell you something," the Eagles' Tommy McDonald, a native of New Mexico, said decades later. "The two worst days of my life were when they made us play after JFK was assassinated and when I had to leave the game. I never felt such an emptiness."[78]

"I didn't want to play, right up until the moment they played taps on the field," said Bobby Mitchell of the Redskins. "In losing the President, I felt like I'd lost a brother. Then the game started and I tried my best."[79]

So, too, did players around the country, but for some, their hearts didn't appear to be in it, nor their heads. Once the game began at Giants Stadium, wrote Jim Becker of AP,

the players went through all the motions down there on the green field in the late November haze, but it seemed as if they were moving with the jerky movements of a man whose leg has gone to sleep and is trying to walk it back to life again.

The eye played tricks and slowed everything down. When there were cheers they sounded thin and unreal, as if they came from somewhere else far away.[80]

Huff played, but he admitted, "My heart wasn't in it. That's the only game in my life that I didn't wish to play in."[81]

Nothing was at stake between Washington and Philly, two teams fighting to stay out of last place, but 60,671 fans turned out on a windy day to watch "a strange and, at times, almost listless contest."[82] The last 1,500 tickets were sold just before game time.[83]

The players, Grady wrote, "played like sad marionettes in a sad puppet show."[84]

Pittsburgh was different. What transpired in the melancholy environment at Forbes Field was "a vicious contest of long marches, and lost opportunities," one of the Bears' "most grueling battles of this or any recent season," a brawling tug-of-war speckled with controversy and the boos of riled fans and angry players, the case of a first-place team that came "strolling into town . . . to hunt rabbits . . . but ran into a horde of tigers," and one epic play that would be remembered for decades.[85]

It was sixty minutes of football on the ugliest, most misbegotten of days that a generation would experience, an afternoon that summed up the season of a renegade team scratching and clawing for its ultimate due. Bears quarterback Bill Wade said afterward, "We ran into a team that wanted very, very badly to win."[86]

From a strictly professional perspective, Parker could never have imagined a worse scenario. He had a team that he felt was susceptible to pressure, and he had to get it ready to face the Western Conference leaders. St. Louis coach Wally Lemm had to prepare his team for a chance at snatching a share of first place from New York, but he admitted, "Frankly, I didn't know if they could keep their mind on football."[87] The players on all fourteen teams had to cope not only with their private feelings but also with the conflict of fulfilling their professional obligations on a day when the rest of the country was grieving. Amid all the distractions, the man from Kemp, Texas, about forty miles southeast of Dallas, was experiencing anxiety from something else.

"Buddy Parker was terrified," Rooney said. "We're standing out there on the field before the game. He said, 'People are nutty about their president getting shot, and the only Texan they know is me. Boy, it'd be an easy shot to pick me off.' Buddy was odd that way."[88] (Buddy Dial, John Burrell, and

Charlie Bradshaw were also from Texas, as was Bobby Layne, retired as a player but working in a scouting capacity.)

Forbes Field, like the other stadiums, was subdued, even though the crowd of 34,465 was the largest of the season there. "Boy, I'll tell you, that was a somber, somber crowd," Atkinson said. "It was a packed house."[89]

It was 40 degrees at game time, with the sun peeking through the clouds, and no precipitation. Beginning with the opening kickoff, which Lou Michaels drilled into the end zone, it was no surprise that the Steelers "appeared tense and taut."[90] Wade got the Bears moving, running Willie Galimore for 8 yards, hitting Joe Marconi for 10 yards, and Ditka for 14.

A 15-yard penalty for illegal use of hands pushed the Bears back to their own 45, making it third-and-21. Wade was nearly caught as he dropped back, but he got off a 54-yard pass to end John Farrington, who made it to the 1 before he was stopped by Dick Haley and Clendon Thomas. Galimore took a handoff and darted to the right side, cutting sharply inside defensive back Glenn Glass and into the end zone with 4:51 elapsed. Leclerc kicked the field goals, but rookie tight end Bob Jencks handled the conversions, and his point-after put Chicago up 7–0.

The teams exchanged punts, but late in the quarter the Bears got a break and a first down when Andy Russell was flagged for roughing the punter, former Steeler Bobby Joe Green. On third-and-7 from his 31, Wade threw a pass intended for Galimore, but Haley intercepted and returned it to the Bear 10. "I thought I had thrown it high enough," Wade said. "It looked like a touchdown. Haley made a perfect play."[91]

Hoak was tackled for a 4-yard loss, and a pass to John Henry Johnson gained nothing as the quarter ended. On third down, a call against Chicago for illegal use of hands gave Pittsburgh a first down on the 6. Behind blocks by Preston Carpenter, Johnson, and Ray Lemek, Hoak went off left tackle, "tip-toeing through a path of fallen Bears" to tie the game with Michaels's conversion.[92]

Starting from their 20 after the kickoff, the Bears advanced 15 yards on a penalty against John Reger for tripping. Wade hit Morris for 9 yards and then found Ditka on a crossing pattern for 18 yards, down to the Steeler 32. Offside on Pittsburgh gained another 5 yards.

Johnny Morris, a shifty flanker, had tied Ditka for the team lead in receptions and touchdowns the year before, and in '64 he would lead the league in catches (93) and yards receiving (1,200). Wade had missed Morris with a pass from midfield, but the quarterback tried again for what could have been a 27-yard TD pass. However, Glass had Morris covered at the goal line, and Thomas leaped in front of the receiver to pick off the ball.

Johnson and Hoak ground out enough yardage to get the Steelers to the Bear 49 but, facing fourth-and-1, Brown punted to the 17. Needing 4 yards for a first down from his 31, Wade twice tried to hit Ditka, but Thomas broke up both passes.

Green, who was born in Vernon, Texas, and would finish the year with a 46.5-yard average, boomed a 59-yard punt that backed up the Steelers to their 9. Brown fumbled a handoff on third-and-8 for a loss of 5 yards, forcing him to kick out of the end zone. His feeble punt of 31 yards, after a fair catch, left Chicago 37 yards away from a go-ahead touchdown. After Ronnie Bull gained 11 yards off left tackle, Ditka caught a pass over the middle for 16 yards and then went flat out to make a catch for eight yards that put Chicago on the 1. Bull went around the left side for the touchdown, giving Chicago a 14–7 lead with 1:57 left in the half, and leaving "a suspicion that the Bears were going to have no trouble preserving their full game lead on Green Bay."[93]

But that's when Brown did a pretty good Bobby Layne imitation. The Steelers got good field position after Gary Ballman returned the kickoff 23 yards to the 25, and another 15 were tacked on for a penalty when he was tackled out of bounds. Dial caught a pass and fumbled, but Hoak recovered for a 7-yard gain. Brown underthrew Ballman, but a 13-yard pass to Dial was on target, and the flanker stopped the clock by stepping out of bounds at the Bear 35. Brown overthrew an open Ballman, but Hoak gained 4 yards on a trap play, setting up third-and-6 from the 31.

Roy Curry, a twelfth-round pick activated from the taxi squad, came in for Hoak. Curry's pro career had gotten off to a start similar to Ballman's. Like his second-year teammate, Curry had size (he was six foot one and 205 pounds) and speed and showed hints of stardom. Unlike Ballman, Curry had been a quarterback in college. He was also black. The *Pittsburgh Courier*, which scoured the country to report on talented black football players, had twice named the Jackson State (Mississippi) QB to its All-America team. As training camp opened, the newspaper intensified the expectations for the rookie from Clarksdale, Mississippi. "Experts, who have seen Curry perform, to the last man, will vow that he has the gifts to become extraordinary Steelers' property," the *Courier* reported.[94]

But Curry wasn't going to do it by throwing passes. *Ebony* magazine, in its November issue, ran a football preview that broke down the "tan" players by position, noting, "Conspicuously absent in U.S. professional football are

Negro quarterbacks." All too aware that the rookie was not going to make his mark by taking snaps from center Buzz Nutter, the *Courier* envisioned him developing into "what is known as a Gifford-type operative"—a versatile player who can run, catch passes, and throw an option pass, like the Giants' all-purpose star.[95]

As Brown backed up in the shotgun, Curry lined up on the right side. With John Henry Johnson handling the blitzing linebacker Bill George, the rookie wide receiver veered to the sideline in front of Rosey Taylor, who would finish the season as the NFL leader in interceptions, with nine. Brown fired away. Taylor lunged for the ball, but it sailed past him into Curry's arms at the 8-yard line, and "in three easy strides," the game was tied 14–14 with thirty-one seconds left in the half. It was the first catch of Curry's NFL career, and it would turn out to be the only one.[96]

Maybe Brown's drive shifted the momentum, or maybe Parker's staff made adjustments at halftime. Maybe, at last, the Steelers were getting that lift, that boost, from up above to make up for all the years of misfortune. Whatever it was, the Steelers came out for the second half "an inspired, almost infuriated aggregation."[97]

Two days earlier, Layne, who continued to work for the Steelers from the scouting booth on game days, had commented on reports that Lions coach George Wilson had tried to lure the quarterback out of retirement. Layne had been out pheasant hunting when the phone call came. "I thought he was kidding," Layne said. "Actually, I don't believe he expected me to play very much, only to help out the team's morale a bit."[98]

The Steelers' morale had perked up since the letdown in Green Bay, and Brown had a hand in two straight victories. So if Parker had entertained any thoughts about making a similar invitation to Layne, it's unlikely the coach seriously considered them.

But aside from his two-minute drill before halftime, Brown was struggling against the Bear defense, and he would wind up completing only ten of twenty-five passes. He was judged guilty of "overthrowing Buddy Dial, Preston Carpenter and Gary Ballman on plays that were almost certain touchdowns," Jack Sell would write days later.[99]

The Bears had been ruthless against every quarterback. Brown's TD pass was only the eighth the Bears had given up all season, and they had come into the game with a league-leading twenty-eight interceptions. But Pittsburgh's ground game was grinding it out. John Henry Johnson would finish with 86 yards on twenty-one attempts, and Hoak would have 72 on nineteen carries, constituting the second-best day against the Bear defense all year.

The Steeler defense was every bit as rugged as the Bears' unit. "The play of Joe Krupa, for example, was a vision," the *Press*'s Pat Livingston wrote.[100] No player was a more representative image of Pittsburgh than the six-foot-two, 235-pound tackle from the South Side of Chicago: "a steady, reliable sort, the bespectacled son of Polish immigrants." His high school coach had talked him out of going to Notre Dame and steered him to Purdue. The second-round pick of the Steelers in '56, Krupa felt "downhearted and homesick" in training camp and had his bags packed to sneak out of camp for good late one night with a teammate, but he fell asleep and had a change of heart in the morning.[101] He was as tireless and anonymous as a worker in an open-hearth furnace, but to those who appreciated the grunts in the trenches of football, he was "Joe Krupa, the indestructible tackle."[102]

Forced to pass because Chicago could only dent the Steeler defense for 87 yards on the ground, Wade would wind up with an advantage over Brown in passing yardage, 264 to 134, but he also threw three interceptions—and was lucky to avoid a fourth.

For all their pounding away at the Bears, "Pittsburgh had a right to curse the fates on this day"—and that was the sympathetic view of a Chicago writer. There were wasted scoring opportunities, a couple questionable calls, and a bad bounce.[103]

Chicago stopped Pittsburgh cold on the opening drive of the second half, forcing a punt, but a roughing-the-kicker penalty on rookie Bears tackle Steve Barnett gave the Steelers a first down. From his 38, Brown hit Dial for a 20-yard pickup to the Chicago 42, and after a 2-yard run by Johnson, Brown connected with Ballman over the middle for 14 yards and a first down at the 26. Two passes to Carpenter missed, and Johnson ran for 5 yards, leaving the Steelers with fourth-and-5 on the 21. Michaels seemed to have broken his kicking slump the week before, but his 29-yard attempt went wide right.

Pittsburgh held and took over on its 28 after Haley returned Green's 55-yard punt 9 yards. Ballman gained 8 yards on a reverse, and then Johnson broke loose over right end and down the sideline for 36 yards and a first down at the Chicago 28. After Hoak gained 2 yards, Brown's pass for Ballman was almost intercepted by Taylor, and his toss to Hoak was off the halfback's fingertips. Michaels lined up for a 34-yard field goal attempt. The kick fell short.

Starting from his 20, Wade hit Farrington for 24 yards, and then Morris for 11 to the Steeler 39. Russell almost intercepted a pass intended for Ditka, but Willie Daniel was flagged for holding Farrington, giving Chicago a first down on the 34, well within field goal distance.

John Reger was another player on the Steeler defense who was playing as if it were a championship game. He had made a remarkable comeback after his near-tragic accident in the opener but, like Daniel, he had taken a circuitous route just to make the team, back in 1955. Reger had grown up in Wheeling, West Virginia, along with one brother and five sisters, and attended a private military school before being recruited by Pitt. He played on the undefeated freshman team, but his college career ended when he sustained a knee injury after two games in his sophomore season. Several years later, he landed a tryout with the Steelers and won a starting job.[104]

With a first down at the Steeler 34 and time winding down in the third quarter, Wade came right back to Farrington, but Reger intercepted on the 21 and picked his way to the 38.

Pittsburgh started to move. Dial made a leaping catch for a 13-yard gain to the Bear 45, and after Hoak gained 6 yards, Brown overthrew Dial at the goal line as the third quarter ended.

On the first play of the fourth quarter, Johnson gained 9 yards with a catch out of the backfield, 5 more over left guard, and, a play later, ran over right tackle for 7 to give his team a first down at the 15. After Dial dropped a bullet at the 7, Hoak caught a pass and got as far as the 8, where Taylor grabbed the halfback's right ankle and hung on for his life, a bit like a defender trying to tackle Jim Brown and clinging to the runner as if he were a horse rider caught in the stirrup and being dragged along. Hoak yanked himself loose, as if his galoshes had been stuck in the mud, and scampered into the end zone.

Seven years earlier, when Parker threatened to quit over the incident in which Bobby Layne was blindsided by Ed Meadows, the coach charged that the NFL was being "run" by Halas and George Preston Marshall.[105] On this day, a few people would tend to agree with that sentiment. Halas biographer Jeff Davis described the Bears owner and coach as "a flesh-and-blood Ursus horribilis: surly, snarly, sinister, and smart." Davis quoted the sportswriter Bill Furlong as having described Halas as a man possessing "all the warmth of breaking bones."[106] He badgered, berated, and cussed out referees in shamelessly profane fashion, often to great effectiveness. After the Steelers' 27–21 loss in Chicago in 1959—a game to which beat writer Pat Livingston devoted six paragraphs to inventory what he considered suspect calls that went in favor of the Bears—Parker remarked, "I'll sure be glad to see Halas retire, then maybe you'll be able to beat the Bears in this town."[107]

Whether the specter of another Halas obscenity-laced tantrum influenced the officials, subconsciously or consciously, is conjecture. After all, they weren't in Halas's hometown on this afternoon. But Hoak's run was called back, the touchdown disallowed. Back judge Tom Kelleher had ruled the ball dead, even though Hoak later said he had not heard a whistle. The call enraged not only the fans but the players. Because of the configuration of Forbes Field, both benches were on the same sideline, putting opponents within shouting distance of each other.

"I remember Ernie Stautner and Red Mack were chewing out George Halas, saying, 'You've got the officials in your pocket, George,'" Hoak said.[108] Russell recalled Stautner, Krupa, Pottios, and Johnson swearing at Halas, making the same accusation.[109]

"You had to blow the whistle on that play," umpire Fritz Graf said after the game. "A guy could get his leg broken on a play like that." Kelleher was not available to comment. He had "set a record for getting out of the dressing room."[110]

Instead of a 21–14 lead, the Steelers had third-and-2 at the 8. Johnson went off left tackle for 2 yards and on fourth down leaped over right guard for a yard and first down at the 5. Johnson managed a yard, but Hoak was stuffed at the line by end Bob Kilcullen and linebacker Bill George. On third down, the Steelers made a peculiar call for that spot on the field: a double reverse to Ballman. That play had gained 8 yards early in the third quarter, but it came with the Steelers on their 28 on first down. This time, Ballman was nailed for no gain by Fortunato. Michaels connected on an 11-yard field goal, giving Pittsburgh a 17–14 lead with 8:35 left in the game. The way the Steeler defense was playing, the lead looked good enough to stand up.

The Bears' shot at tying the game or taking the lead "started inauspiciously, almost disgracefully," on the ensuing kickoff.[111] Five weeks later, in the NFL title game, a fumble recovery on a kickoff would be nullified because a member of the kicking team was offside, leading Red Smith to comment, "There isn't much excuse for a professional to be off-side on a kickoff."[112] As daylight faded at Forbes Field, Charlie Bivins, pressed into action because Casares had sustained a separation of his right ankle, fumbled on the return and the Steelers' John Burrell recovered on the Bear 18. But once again fortune seemed to be conspiring against Parker's squad. The Steelers were called for being offside and had to kick over, this time with Bivins on the bench. Bull returned the kick to the 23.

Bull picked up 5 yards, and Wade hit Morris for another 5, then Ditka for 14. The Steelers' chances of holding their lead looked even better after

Morris was called for illegal use of hands against Glass, and Krupa sacked Wade, leaving the Bears with second-and-36 at their 22 with five-and-a-half minutes to go. Wade wanted to call a deep route to Ditka, who had earned All-America honors three years earlier while playing at Pitt Stadium and on this day had family and friends from his nearby hometown of Aliquippa in the stands. Like Stautner, John Henry Johnson, and Mack, Ditka was a man driven to succeed by forces that seemed supernatural. "There's a lot of Ty Cobb in Ditka," the Pittsburgh sportswriter Roy McHugh observed.[112] In their ferocity of play and desire to win, the only difference in the way they ran was that Ditka led with his head rather than with his cleats. "He was all business, both in practice or during a game," one of his college coaches said. "He had that killer instinct."[113]

But Ditka was tired. He had run pass routes on the three previous plays, and he had already caught six passes. So he told Wade, "Bill, I can't go deep. You throw me something short. I'll go down about 14 yards and hook. Then I'll try to run with it." Years later, Ditka would call it "the luckiest run in the world."[114] Halas called it "one of the greatest individual efforts I have seen in 40 years of football."[115]

It started out, simply enough, as a short pass to the left side. Wade faked to a back releasing on the left side and got rid of the ball as Krupa bore down on him from his right. Thomas came in and skidded past Ditka. Reger dove from behind and missed. A trio of Steeler defenders converged, "and with a twisting Herculean effort of explosive strength, Ditka threw off all three men" and broke free, the ball tucked into his left elbow, his helmet hunched below the level of his waist, with a clear field ahead of him "in the ancient home of the baseball Pirates."[116] Ditka lumbered ahead, half limping, like an amateur marathon runner straining for the finish line, until Thomas, in a desperate sprint, dragged down the tight end at the Steeler 15 on the infield portion of the field, with Daniel right behind. The play covered 63 yards. Ditka lay spread eagle and was helped off to the sidelines.

"Lord, I was exhausted," Ditka said later. "I thought I was going to black out." In the locker room afterward, Halas gazed at Ditka and said, "I can't remember the last time I saw such a helluva play."[117]

"It was the greatest run I've ever seen," said Bears defensive coordinator George Allen.[118]

Steeler players and Parker insisted that the play should have been whistled dead, just as Hoak's run had been with Taylor strapped to the Steeler's ankle. "They were identical plays," Parker said. Halas disagreed. "Ditka was churning his legs. Hoak was definitely stopped."[119]

The fates of both teams were at stake. A loss would knock the Steelers out of the Eastern race for good; a defeat would drop the Bears into a tie with Green Bay if the Packers beat the last-place 49ers. On first down, Bull slanted off tackle for 4 yards, and then Marconi juggled but lost a high throw from Wade. On third-and-6 from the 11, Farrington, open in the end zone, dropped a pass. Leclerc kicked an 18-yard field goal to make it 17–17 with 4:31 left in the game.

The Steelers were in good shape after Thomas returned the kickoff 38 yards to the 45, but on third-and-9 Brown threw to Curry, and this time Bennie McRae intercepted at the Bear 41. The Bears needed only 20, 25 yards for a shot at a field goal, but on second-and-7 Reger dropped Marconi for a 9-yard loss on a screen pass, setting up third-and-16 from the 35. There would be no heroics this time: Michaels, Stautner, and Krupa smothered Wade for a loss of 12 yards.

Following Green's 43-yard punt, the Steelers took over on their 32 with two minutes left—the last chance to pull the game out. Linebacker Larry Morris deflected a Brown pass, but Dial caught it for a 21-yard gain to the Bear 44. Hoak gained 2 yards, and with 1:04 left, the Steelers called time-out. Dial caught and then dropped a pass on the Bear 30, but from the 42, Michaels still had a shot at a field goal from 49 yards. On third down, however, Bill George dropped Brown for a 9-yard loss, back to the Steeler 49. The Steelers had no choice but to punt. Taylor dropped the punt but recovered on his 12. All Wade had to do was fall on the ball three or four times and the Bears could escape with a tie—and be grateful for it.

But the fates weren't finished teasing and tormenting the Steelers. The Bears' offense had stuck to conservative play-calling, but "for only some reason understandable only to himself," Wade decided to throw a pass in the left flat to Marconi.[120]

Reger was surprised by the call, but he was ready. "I saw it coming," he said. "I was merely trying to cover my man. I never expected a pass in that situation."[121]

Neither did Wade's coach. The pass "almost caused Coach George Halas to swoon on the sidelines."[122] It was probably too much of a shock to Reger as well. "The ball hit me on the right forearm," he explained, "so I had no chance to intercept."[123]

If Reger had caught the ball, he would have been a bigger hero than Ditka—and would have had about a quarter as far to run. "There was a clear field for Reger and page lines all over the sports world if he had nabbed the ball and scored," Jack Sell wrote.[124]

Halas rushed in guard Roger Davis with instructions to kill the clock, and with two carries time ran out. A tie didn't hurt the Steelers—it kept them alive in the Eastern race, which saw the Giants, Browns, and Cardinals all tied for first place at 8–3 after St. Louis upset New York, 24–17, behind Charley Johnson's two TD passes, and Cleveland beat Dallas, 27–17. A tie not only let the Bears, at 9–1–1, hang onto first place in the Western Division, ahead of the 9–2 Packers but it also left Halas thankful for escaping defeat. "We'll settle for the tie," the coach said.[125]

He had every reason to feel relief. *Chicago Tribune* sportswriter George Strickler said of Halas's team: "Today they were not what the advance notices had proclaimed. They were just lucky." Or embarrassing. "We played like a bunch of jackasses," Morris said.[126]

Parker showed no frustration, no bitterness over the tie, the officials' calls, or the breaks of the game. "You'd think we won," he said with a laugh. "Well, it was almost like winning."[127]

The angriest person in either locker room hadn't suited up that day; it was a Pittsburgh newspaperman upset over the officiating. "I do know the writer chased Halas and yelled, 'You paid the officials,'" Ditka recalled years later. "A couple of us grabbed that guy and ran his ass out of there."[128] The writer, later identified by Myron Cope as one P. Murray Livingston, said the confrontation was overblown, and he returned to apologize, but the *Tribune* reported that he had threatened "to punch Halas in the nose."[129] There is no evidence that the writer had his hands taped as Parker did when he went after Big Daddy Lipscomb and John Henry Johnson in Dallas.

On their flight home, the Bears were still buzzing about Ditka's run. "I have never seen a play so great," Pyle said years later.[130]

A day of mourning lay ahead for the nation. If fans leaving stadiums in the dusk could not deny or ignore how their world had changed so abruptly and irrevocably, some did find a brief distraction, a fleeting escape, at least in one city, before having to resume the task of groping for comfort or some peace of mind. Maybe it was, as Sandy Grady seethed, "a dismally farcical moment for child's games," and maybe the most reverent, thoughtful, and decent thing for any citizen to do was to pause and bow his head for the day.[131] But for some, maybe the only response to tragedy was to find some kind of reminder of what makes a person feel alive and vital, and perhaps they found it at a football stadium.

As the fans filed out of Yankee Stadium, one man said to another, "I wonder if they should have played?"

"I don't know," the second man replied. "I'm not God. Where else were they going to go today?"

"Or maybe they were looking for someplace to go."[132]

By late afternoon, as people made their way home by subways, cars, buses, streetcars, or on foot, it was time to return to a national Götterdämmerung.

"In a way," wrote Arthur Daley of the *New York Times,* "the fans at the Stadium yesterday could not have been blamed for letting their heavy hearts have a stimulating fillip for 2½ hours on a bright, brittle afternoon."[133]

Two seasons earlier, *Pittsburgh Post-Gazette* sports editor Al Abrams had made his remarks about how the sports pages offered a "vicarious" relief amid the turbulence and violence of everyday life. On a grim Sunday four days before Thanksgiving, a real-life spectacle in seven cities across a dazed country put that notion to the test. "While the world rocked and reeled under the impact of weightier and more important happenings in Dallas the past few days," Abrams wrote, "Pittsburgh district fans forgot assassinations and murders for a couple of hours to watch pro football. They saw it at its toughest best as two hard-bitten teams, battling for flag contention, clawed at each other from start to finish."[134]

It was easy to indulge in platitudes and sanctimonious pronouncements about John F. Kennedy's beliefs and "what he would have wanted" in this raw situation. Most likely, what he would have loved to do on a Sunday afternoon in late November would be to watch the Redskins on TV, then round up eight or ten people, grab a football, and pick up sides on a patch of green lawn. Dave Hackett, a family friend, once wrote a tongue-in-cheek set of "Rules for Visiting the Kennedys," and it included one obligatory activity the family insisted on: "It's touch football but it's murder. The only way I know of to get out of playing is not to come at all, or to come with a broken leg."[135]

It sounded as if Ditka would have fit right in at a Kennedy pickup game. He had played with a fury to match the passion of the Steelers. It was not a day to have fun at a kid's game, or to savor athletic achievement. But Ditka was a professional, and he played like one, and he tried to express the right sentiment for his president. "I think everyone felt something," Ditka said. "Not having known the man, however, I think he would not have wanted it postponed. So we go out on the field—and it's business to us—and after the first kickoff, all you think about is the Steelers."[136]

In Milwaukee, where the Packers beat the 49ers, 28–10, Vince Lombardi was asked if he was troubled that they were playing "on this day of world gloom."

"If this had been designated the day of national mourning, instead of tomorrow, I'm certain it would not have been played," he replied. "Really, tho, [sic] there was no reason for postponing today's game. Knowing how Mr. Kennedy's thoughts were on sport, I believe that he would have been the last one in the world to ask the game be called off."[137]

But no one, Lombardi said, was immune to the despair that hung over the nation. "If you have any kind of feeling," he said, "you have to be affected."[138]

In two weeks, the Steelers would travel to the Cotton Bowl in Dallas to face the Cowboys. But first, they would have a rematch with the Philadelphia Eagles.

On Tuesday, the Steelers would still be off, but stores, schools, and government offices would reopen, and people would try to get back to their regular routines, even though they would have "to explore the unknown and test the uncertain," as Kennedy had said the day before his death. And on Tuesday, the New York Daily News ran a front-page photo of Jacqueline Kennedy; her daughter, Caroline; and son, John-John, saluting, with the headline "WE CARRY ON."

GAME 12

Among the rejects and snubbed players Buddy Parker had assembled, no one burned with more passion to prove himself than Gilbert Leroy "Buddy" Dial, born in Ponca City, Oklahoma, and raised in Magnolia, Texas.

As an end at Rice, he caught passes from future pros King Hill and Frank Ryan, was named sophomore lineman of the year in the Southwest Conference, averaged 24 yards a catch as a junior, and was a consensus All-America as a senior, when he was cocaptain and most valuable player for the Owls. The Giants took him in the second round of the 1959 draft with expectations of greatness. Dial was glib, likable, irreverent, and as down home as a slice of cornbread—a person with deep religious faith, and talented enough as a musician and singer to record an album of gospel songs. He also had an uncanny ability to catch a football—so good, in fact, that he drew the envy of Jimmy Brown.

"If I had Aladdin's lamp," Brown said, "I would ask the jinni to give me Buddy Dial's hands, Bobby Mitchell's moves, Lenny Moore's change of pace."[1] Erich Barnes, the Giants' All-Pro defensive back, insisted, "Dial has better moves than Mitchell."[2] The combination of skills made Dial about as good a receiver as there was in the NFL in 1963—and good enough to compete in just about any era.

But no one would ever dare barter with the devil and make a deal for that talent if he had any inkling of the fate that was to befall Buddy Dial, a husband, father, and two-time Pro Bowler who would go on to be elected to the College Football Hall of Fame.

A life as cursed would have killed most men, a former teammate said.[3]

Halfway into the '63 schedule, Dial was off to the best start of his five-year career, ranking second in catches behind Bobby Joe Conrad but first in receiving yardage, ahead of Mitchell. Even though his thirty-six receptions left him trailing Conrad by eight, Dial loomed as a threat to win the NFL receiving title.

In the sixties, insensitivity to people of different origins was both flagrant and subtle. Stereotypes flourished. Black quarterbacks weren't considered smart enough to make it in the NFL. Latin baseball players were subjected to the condescending, quaint approach sportswriters took in mimicking athletes' speech patterns. But a small-town white, too, could end up looking cartoonish. Any story quoting Dial—or virtually anyone with a trace of a southern accent—was liable to make him sound like a talking tumbleweed. "Dadgum if ah wouldn't like to win that title," Dial was quoted as saying "in his cheerful Texas drawl" on the eve of the Packer game. "But ah also want to play on a championship team and we have the chance this year. Ah don't know which one I want more. Maybe ah can have both."[4]

Four games later, in the aftermath of the tie with Chicago, both goals looked like long shots. The Steelers needed each of the three teams tied for first place—New York, Cleveland, and St. Louis—to lose a game. After catching five passes against Chicago on a day when Ed Brown hit only ten of twenty-five attempts, Dial was in a fourth-place tie for receptions with Detroit's Terry Barr, with fifty-one catches. Conrad was in first with fifty-eight, followed by the Giants' Del Shofner with fifty-three and Mitchell with fifty-two. But only Mitchell, with 1,088 yards in receptions, and Dial, with 1,033, had reached the 1,000-yard mark among receivers. The young man from Magnolia, Texas, was in elite company.

Dial, like Tommy McDonald, brought the giddy spirit of a kid to the job of playing professional football. No matter how hard you hit him, you couldn't knock the smile off his face. Opponents not only respected him, but they couldn't help but like him. Cardinal cornerback Jimmy Hill patterned his game after the Lions' Dick "Night Train" Lane, earning a reputation for the kind of tackling that was "worthy of a Pier Six brawl."[5] But with his jocular manner, penchant for pranks, and disarming grin of a child at heart, Dial had the ability to defuse a volatile confrontation with the fiercest opponents.

"You know," Hill said, "that is one guy I couldn't get angry with even if he clipped me from behind." Hill was at Forbes Field the afternoon Dial caught seven passes for 186 yards in a December 1962 victory over the Cards. As

Dial ran a square-in pattern, Hill dashed at him, ready to swipe "a scythelike forearm" at the Steeler end's head.[6] Dial made an 18-yard reception and was tackled by another defensive back as Hill swung and missed.

"Some guys get real mad and are ready to fight after I do that," Hill said, "but not Buddy. He jumps up, smiles at me and says, 'Jimmy, you just took five years off my life.' Now, how can you dislike a guy like that?"[7]

The one thing that did make Dial mad—fighting mad, for years—was getting cut after being drafted by the Giants, which gave him little time to validate his status as the twenty-second overall selection in the 1959 draft. The Giants were more impressed in training camp with a twenty-seventh-round draft pick, an end from Richmond named Joe Biscaha—the 323rd overall selection—than they were with the All-America from Rice. When Giants coach Jim Lee Howell delivered the bad news to Dial two days before the 1959 opener, the rookie replied, "Someday, I'm going to make you look bad."[8] Dial became another of Parker's salvage projects, on the eve of the '59 season opener, a discard ripe with potential and a ravenous appetite to prove his doubters wrong.

In mid-December of '63, Dial was about to get another crack at the Giants. Three days before the regular-season finale in New York, and two weeks before Christmas, the *Pittsburgh Press* ran a photo of a smiling Dial surrounded by his family: his wife, Janice, beside him in their Brentwood home, with three-year-old Darren wearing a football helmet, perched on his father's lap, and one-year-old Kevin sitting in his mother's lap, reaching out to touch his brother's helmet. It would have made the perfect photo to accompany any of the newspaper or magazine ads of the time extolling a happy home life, or it could have been fashioned into a Hallmark Christmas card.

Coaches, players, and amateur sociologists have forever philosophized about how the game of football is just like life. You face adversity. You get knocked down, you get back up. Practice and prepare to do your best. Work hard enough, and the breaks will fall your way. Ultimately, you will be a winner.

It would be convenient if any individual could devise a strategy for facing life every week the way teams prepare game plans for an opponent. It would be reassuring to know that you could map out your route in everyday life and follow it the way Buddy Dial ran his square-in pattern to catch an 18-yard pass against Jimmy Hill. But if there is one valid comparison between football and life, it is that the ball can take the craziest, most unpredictable of bounces, and not even someone with the sure hands of Buddy Dial has any certainty of controlling it, on or off the field.

On the day that picture of blissful family life was taken, Dial couldn't have predicted that after three more seasons, at age twenty-nine, his football career would be over, the result of debilitating injuries. And he couldn't have imagined that he would eventually undergo five operations on his back and become addicted to painkillers. Or that he would lose his wife and that she would win a court battle for half of his monthly disability checks.[9]

And surely not in his worst nightmares could Dial have imagined that the one-year-old boy on his wife's lap that December day would years later be diagnosed with an inoperable brain tumor and, two years after, wind up one of nine victims shot to death by a suicidal gunman.[10]

After being hospitalized for cancer and pneumonia, Dial would die in March 2008 in a Houston hospital at the age of seventy-one.

"He had his struggles, but never once did he express ill will or place blame on anybody other than himself for the choices he made," said a third son, David. "He never regretted playing pro sports, even though it cost him personally, physically and financially."[11]

Dial grew up in a devout Christian family, learning to play guitar and mandolin from his father, a laborer for an oil company. Coming out of Magnolia High School, Dial drew meager interest from recruiters. He wanted to attend Baylor and study for the ministry, but during a visit there he was told he was too small to play college football. "That broke my heart," he said. That evening, Jess Neely, head coach at Rice, called and offered Dial a scholarship. "That's the only dadgum one I was ever offered," Dial said.[12]

Years before he would embarrass the Giants for dumping him, Dial showed all the disinterested colleges they had made a mistake, and he made Baylor pay, too. As a junior, he caught a 10-yard touchdown pass from Ryan in a 20–0 win over Baylor, a victory that clinched the Southwest Conference title for the Owls and earned them the right to meet Navy in the Cotton Bowl. The next year against the intrastate rival, Dial caught a 6-yard TD pass, stopped a Baylor drive by recovering a fumble at the goal line, and thwarted another threat by intercepting a pass at the Rice 14 and returning it 46 yards. Rice won, 33–21. Dial didn't look too small to be playing for anyone.

As Dial went into that Cotton Bowl, he was already being compared to a great Rice pass-catcher, Billy Howton, who would enter the '63 NFL season primed to break Don Hutson's all-time records for passes caught and receiving yardage. Dial was blessed with "deception and glue-fingers."[13]

Two days after his two-way starring role in the victory over Baylor, the NFL held its draft. The Giants had made ballyhooed Utah quarterback Lee

Grosscup their priority, and they pounced on him with their first pick, No. 10 overall. In round 2, twelve picks later, "they gasped in relief because Dial was still alive" and snatched him, too.[14]

Grosscup and Dial, along with two other Giant draft picks, couldn't report to training camp on time because they had been named to the College All-Star squad. The collegians annually played the reigning NFL champion, in this case the Baltimore Colts, who had beaten the Giants in sudden death in the 1958 title game. Dial quickly attracted "quite a coterie of admirers" and caught a 30-yard TD pass from Grosscup in a 7–6 decision over the Chicago Bears in a scrimmage. "Buddy makes wonderful moves to get free," said Pete Pihos, coach of the All-Star ends, "and if the ball is anywhere near him, he'll find a way to catch it."[15]

According to one account, the Giants' rejection of Dial was "blown all out of proportion." His late arrival at Giants camp after the Colts spanked the collegians, 29–0, along with a groin pull and an intestinal virus, slowed the rookie, limiting the time the Giants had to evaluate him. Meanwhile, Biscaha was making an impression on the club. The Giants even tried shifting Dial to defensive back a week before they dumped him, despite his strong record of success as a receiver.[16]

"It was very insulting to me, dadgum it," Dial said. "They had scouted me in college and they knew I could catch a pass and could run patterns. But the only thing the coaching staff could do was to holler at me. I know I didn't get a real chance with them."[17]

The insult burned inside Dial, without any letup. As the Steelers looked toward a showdown with New York in the final week of the '63 season, Dial was reminded of his short stay with the Giants and commented, "I guess they didn't want a rinkydink like me."[18]

Once the Giants cut Dial in '59, Parker grabbed him. The only problem was that Dial was as leery of going to Pittsburgh as Clendon Thomas had been, and the main reason was Bobby Layne. Dial, a teetotaler, had a memorable introduction to the Steeler quarterback at the 1959 All-Star Hula Bowl in Honolulu. "Bobby was drinking his breakfast," Dial said. "Every morning when I came down for breakfast, I'd see Bobby at the bar. And he was always putting others up to pulling tricks on us college kids."[19]

For Layne, music and singing were as natural an accompaniment to his nights on the town as ice in his Scotch. So, naturally, when the college players were invited to a luau and the quarterback accompanied them, Layne suggested that the native combo invite Dial to sing with them. "Well, I'd ask them if they knew a certain song and they'd shake their heads, no," Dial said, "and then they'd ask me if I knew a number and I'd shake my head, no. Finally, someone hollered out: 'Let him do the hula.' It was probably Bobby. And I ended up doing the hula with one of those little Hawaiian girls. Anyway, from that association, I sure felt sorry for Steeler rookies."[20]

At that point, Dial could hardly have imagined that he would wind up one of those rookies. While in Detroit, Layne used Alex Karras as a chauffeur and confederate as they made the rounds during nights on the town. Gary Ballman, in '62, became another first-year player indoctrinated by Layne in the quarterback's pursuit of good times and winning football. Dial led a lifestyle the opposite of Layne's, but they were both Texans, and Dial could sing as well as catch a football. "I didn't want to go to Pittsburgh, for I knew Bobby would run me ragged," Dial said.[21]

Dial might not have realized that meant both on and off the field, right from the start. Weary one day from having taken a flight into Pittsburgh, Dial was watching Steeler practice from the sideline when Layne beckoned to him to run some patterns. Layne sent him long. "Dadgum if he didn't try to throw the ball clear out of the park," Dial said with a chuckle, "and I just caught it with my fingertips. But I did catch it, and from that day on he threw to me." It was a test Layne did routinely with his receivers, and Dial passed with ease. "I didn't worry about Buddy," Layne said. "I had confidence in him when he first came over. The first day Buddy worked out he had all the moves of a pro."[22]

It didn't take long for Dial to show the Giants what a mistake they had made. In the fifth game of the '59 season, against New York, he caught four passes for 146 yards, including a 35-yard touchdown pass from Layne, though the Steelers lost, 21–16. Over four years, going into '63, Dial had caught 159 passes for 3,428 yards—an average of 21.6 yards a catch—and thirty-three touchdowns. Biscaha, meanwhile, lasted one year with the Giants then spent the 1960 season with the Patriots of the AFL before retiring. The Giants could only fantasize about what their passing attack might have been like with Dial alongside Del Shofner, and Y. A. Tittle throwing to them.

Dial was destined to become a principal in a Parker deal that would go down as probably the worst in the coach's career. In a move that shocked Steeler fans, Parker traded Dial at the end of the '63 season to the Cowboys for the draft rights to Texas's All-America tackle Scott Appleton, winner of the Outland Trophy as the nation's outstanding interior lineman. Even by Parker standards, the deal was a risk because the Houston Oilers had picked Appleton sixth overall in the rival AFL's draft, held two days earlier, and owner Kenneth "Bud" Adams, who had made a fortune in the oil business, had plenty to spend on a potential star. You could bet the ranch on that.

The Cowboys spent two hours and thirty-nine minutes in discussion before making their pick. "Buddy Parker was offering us a trade for Buddy Dial," GM Tex Schramm explained, "and we were spending all that time trying to work out that deal."[23] Parker should have spent part of that time recalling the 1960 draft. On November 30, 1959, nearly a week after Adams's Oilers picked Heisman Trophy winner Billy Cannon No. 1 overall, the Los Angeles Rams made the LSU back the first pick of the NFL draft. Pete Rozelle, then the general manager of the Rams, signed Cannon to a series of contracts, but the Oilers signed him too. The case went to court, and half a year later a federal judge ruled that the Rams' contracts were invalid. Cannon became an Oiler, with a contract worth $110,000, about double the Rams' contract.[24]

On February 1, 1964, the Oilers signed Appleton to what was believed to be a four-year $104,000 contract, plus other bonuses worth nearly $50,000, including cattle for his father's ranch. All the Steelers wound up with was another ignominious saga in their history of personnel blunders.[25]

However, Appleton was headed for a star-crossed life with eerie similarities to Dial's. With a lucrative contract, a pretty wife, a Cadillac, and a fine home, "I was on top of the world," Appleton said. "I felt totally invincible." Traded to San Diego after three seasons with Houston, Appleton was making more money in the stock market than he had in football. But the pain from a back injury induced him to take drugs, and he became addicted to uppers and alcohol. After being cut by the Chargers, Appleton took on different jobs just to get by, including one stint as a cook at McDonald's. He also spent time in a sanitarium outside the Texas campus in Austin. "I was the most celebrated player on the national championship team, and here I was in this nuthouse a couple miles from school," he recalled.[26]

Appleton made peace with himself. He stopped drinking and devoted his life to religious studies. "I have a fresh life, and I am feeling the joy," he said in the spring of 1986.[27] Six years later, Appleton died of heart failure. He was fifty years old.

Dial took a pounding as a receiver, but he kept practicing and playing. It was the code of players to do whatever was necessary to keep going even if they were hurt. "So to ensure your performance, it was standard—and totally accepted—to use painkillers," Dial said.[28]

Preston Carpenter roomed with Dial in Pittsburgh, and he remembered the pranks they would play on teammates—like unhinging a door to surprise Lou Michaels—and Carpenter also recalled his roommate's heavy use of painkillers. "He was fragile," Carpenter said. "He was in pain most of the time."[29]

In the penultimate game of the regular season in '63, in Dallas, Dial damaged his knee when he was tackled after catching a pass. But there was no way he was going to miss the finale against the team that had junked him four years earlier, not as long as he could dull the pain. As the week went on, the swelling subsided—"thanks to the enzyme the doctor prescribed," he said.[30]

Dial returned to Pitt Stadium in '64, wearing a Cowboys uniform, to face his old teammates and looked like his old self. "There's nobody better," said Willie Daniel, who covered Dial. He wound up being taken off the field on a stretcher in the fourth quarter after being drilled by Clendon Thomas. Dial was taken by ambulance to Presbyterian Hospital, where he shrugged off the injury as simply a bruise, but it was severe and it happened to the same leg he had injured in the preseason. Dial insisted on leaving the hospital to return home with his team.[31]

Defensive players like Ray Nitschke, Larry Wilson, and Ernie Stautner were renowned for being tough, but Buddy Dial could take a heap of punishment, too—until it overwhelmed him.

Dial's career ended in '66, with a disappointing three-season total of thirty-two catches in Dallas, two years before Appleton retired. Dial had injured his back in Pittsburgh, but his problems worsened in Dallas. He tore a hole in his thigh, which looked, according to one doctor, as if "a firecracker had been inserted" in it "and exploded." He injured his back again but took pain medication and continued to work out even though he was on injured reserve. Looking back after his retirement from football, Dial admitted, "I abused pain medication in such excessive fashion it was unbelievable."[32]

Dial took painkillers to play in a game and sometimes just to get through practice, and he took them so he could play with his kids on weekends because, he said in 1985, "I didn't want them to see their daddy as a cripple." Darvon, Demerol, and Percodan had ravaged his kidneys, reducing their function to 10 percent by that time.[33]

In 1993, the NFL devised a new disability plan, increasing the monthly benefit for Dial, one of the league's first players to be declared permanently disabled. His wife, who had been collecting part of Dial's disability benefits in 1977 from their divorce settlement, petitioned to have half of the new benefit awarded to her. The NFL agreed with her claim, but in 1997 a federal judge ordered that the disability benefits be reinstated to Dial.

Two years later, however, in May 1999, a federal appellate court vacated the order. "It's a defeat for Buddy, but it's not the end of the world," said Dial's attorney, Tom Alexander.[34]

No, the end of the world probably didn't come for Buddy Dial for another two months. On the night of July 28, 1999, Dial's son Kevin, who had been diagnosed with an inoperable brain tumor two years earlier, forwarded an e-mail to a friend. The words were not his own, but the message conveyed his spiritual faith: "Every morning when I open my eyes, I tell myself that it is special. Every day, every minute, every breath truly is a gift from God." The following afternoon, a securities day trader walked into the Atlanta office of the brokerage firm where Kevin Dial worked and shot four people, then walked across the street and shot five more workers in an office before killing himself hours later. Kevin Dial was one of the first four victims. He was thirty-eight years old.[35]

The day after the tie with the Bears, as Washington laid President Kennedy to rest, Pittsburgh and the rest of the nation ground to a halt. The players were off, except for those needing treatment, and the Steeler offices were closed. Clendon Thomas had X-rays of his jaw. Bob Schmitz had hurt his ankle. Myron Pottios had dislocated his left hand early in the game, had it put back in place, and returned to action.

In downtown Pittsburgh, and across the country, government offices, banks, schools, businesses and stores closed down—"virtually every facet of a city's lifeblood." The window of a Fifth Avenue dress shop in downtown Pittsburgh displayed a portrait of Kennedy with the inscription "We mourn, with all." *Post Gazette* entertainment columnist Harold V. Cohen wrote that he had "no heart this morning for the trivia of show business. . . . For nearly 72 hours, the world has stood still under a black crepe hung from the trackless wastes of the moon." There was almost no traffic downtown. Churches were "overflowing" with parishioners. Every kind of store sported "closed" signs. Governor Scranton asked that all citizens pause at the stroke of noon. The Council of Churches of the Pittsburgh Area suggested that church bells toll for ten minutes at noon. In the mills, steelworkers doffed their hardhats and paused in silence.[36]

In the aftermath of President Kennedy's death, in the sports world, attention returned to the games, and there was still grumbling over the refereeing in the Steelers-Bears contest. "It's hard to figure how the officials can blow a quick whistle on Dick Hoak and then a slow whistle on Mike Ditka," one "top college official" was quoted as saying. Jack Sell, Steeler beat writer for the *Post-Gazette,* commented that since former Notre Dame coach Joe Kuharich had taken over the supervision of NFL referees, "officiating seems to be getting worse each week."[37]

On Tuesday, the second day off for the players, the Steelers were scheduled to participate in a league drawing for playoff possibilities among the contending teams if any ties resulted in the final regular-season standings. The Giants, Browns, and Cardinals, all with 8–3 records (a .727 winning percentage), were locked in a tie for first place in the Eastern Conference, with the Steelers 6–3–2 (.667) right behind them. The Bears were alone in first place in the Western Conference at 9–1–1 (.900), trailed by the Packers at 9–2 (.818). Commissioner Pete Rozelle determined that there were ten potential playoff possibilities in the Eastern Conference—including four scenarios in the event of a three-way tie—and one playoff possibility in the Western Conference. Winning percentages, not most victories, determined the conference winners. Because ties were thrown out, the Steelers could finish 9–3–2 (.750) by winning their last three games and finish first if New York, Cleveland, and St. Louis each lost a game, which would leave them all 10–4, a winning percentage of .714. The Cards and Browns were scheduled to face each other so, barring a tie, one part of the equation would come true. The scenario shaped up as a long shot all right, but the Steelers had already defied the odds to get this far.[38]

College football had its own reassessment to make because of postponements after the assassination of the president. On Tuesday, while Pete Rose was named National League rookie of the year, it was announced that the Army-Navy game would be rescheduled for December 7. Pitt athletic director Frank Carver explained that the Panthers' bowl prospects looked shaky, with the Orange and Cotton bowls reduced to outside chances, but the Gator Bowl remained a possibility. Carver reiterated a point on the university's postponement of the scheduled November 23 game with Penn State: "I am certain now that we did the right thing."[39]

The Steelers held a practice at South Park Thanksgiving morning. Even though they were listed as thirteen-point favorites over the Eagles, Buddy Parker fretted. "Those Eagles will be rough on Sunday," he said. Philadelphia quarterback Sonny Jurgensen had been hampered by a shoulder injury for five weeks, but it appeared he would be ready for Pittsburgh. "Doesn't it beat all how everybody gets well just before they play us," Parker said.[40] In the opener against Pittsburgh, Jurgensen was sixteen of twenty-six for 322 yards, three touchdowns, and two interceptions. "The robust redhead from Duke is still the best passer in the NFL and poses a constant threat every time he throws the ball," wrote Pat Livingston of the *Press*.[41]

The Eagles' defense had finally gotten healthy too. Defensive end Bill Quinlan, who had played in only four games because of a pinched nerve in his neck, had returned the previous week and teamed up with Steeler castoff George Tarasovic to give the Eagles "their most aggressive defense of the season."[42]

But the Eagles were swirling in turmoil. There was speculation that head coach Nick Skorich would lose his job and rumors that the team would be put up for sale, for $5 million, within a week or two. The unrest had started back in preseason. Jurgensen and his backup, King Hill, had left training camp because of contract disputes. Jurgensen wanted $30,000, an increase of approximately $5,000 from 1962; King was resisting a cut from the $25,000 he had made.

But the ugliest, most disturbing evidence of the dissension that was wracking the club could be observed behind closed doors in a virtual duel between two players the day after the Kennedy assassination, and the story was not fully detailed until two weeks afterward. It was "the most violent episode in the history of the National Football League," columnist Milton Gross wrote in a vivid account of the incident.[43]

The Eagles, who were opposed to playing in the aftermath of the assassination, met at the Sheraton Motor Inn in Philadelphia to vote on whether or not to donate money to the widow of J. D. Tippit, the Dallas policeman shot and killed before the capture of Lee Harvey Oswald. "The game wouldn't have to be played if it wasn't for Pete Rozelle, that guinea," Gross quoted Quinlan as saying. Rozelle was not of Italian heritage, but defensive back Ben Scotti was, and he objected to the epithet. "Cut it out or there'll be trouble," he said.

Quinlan repeated the slur then backed off, but his roommate, 260-pound center John Mellekas, kept provoking the 184-pound Scotti. "You want to fight?" Scotti said. "I'll fight you right here in front of the team."

"Anywhere you want," Mellekas replied, "but not in here. I'll take you outside."

After the meeting ended, the two went to a private lounge, locked the door, "and went at it." Much later, Scotti told Gross, "He must have thought he was King Kong that night, but when I was through with him they must have thought he was hit by a freight train."

"It must have been a dilly of a fight," the *Philadelphia Inquirer* reported.[44]

Afterward, Mellekas lay unconscious, with a broken nose, black eyes, and "teeth strewn with blood." Scotti stood over him, both hands bleeding extensively from lacerations caused by punching his teammate "into oblivion." Scotti needed fifteen stitches on his left hand, broke his right hand, and nearly severed his right ring finger on Mellekas's teeth.[45]

The slurs triggered the fight, but Scotti's rage ran deeper, far out of bounds. "I let my anger of the whole year and everything else out on him," he said. "I knocked him down and I stood over him and worked him over." Mellekas's head was so swollen, Scotti said, "he could hardly put on his helmet."[46]

Both men were hospitalized. Mellekas was fined but returned to play. Scotti was suspended and, finally, released even though Mellekas apologized and stood up for his teammate. In conclusion, said Scotti, "This is an emotional game, you know."[47]

In a bloody instant, Skorich not only had another controversy to deal with, but from a sheerly pragmatic perspective, he no longer had a healthy defense to confront a team rated two touchdowns better.

Sunday brought windy weather and snow flurries, marking autumn's end and ushering in winter. The newspapers were still filled with news about the reverberations of Kennedy's death. The Warren Commission was beginning its investigation into the assassination. In Dallas, where the Steelers would play the next week, one of the notes amid the wreaths at the site of the slaying read, "God Forgive Us All."[48]

But life went on, with other news signaling the changing times. A government study was about to be released that linked smoking to cancer. The papers were filling up with Christmas ads and holiday recipes. The *Pittsburgh Press* ran a feature with a photo of four shaggy-haired musicians, titled "The Beatles . . . Britain's Latest Craze." The story noted that the group had gone from making about $50 a week to $14,000 by using "three amplified guitars, bellowing voices and a drum that beats hard and fast, like a human heart heading for sudden failure." Steeler fans undoubtedly felt the same sensation after the close calls of the previous three weeks, with more suspense in store. "I've never seen a race this close," Parker said, "and I've been connected with this league for the last 30 years."[49]

The Steelers needed 17,000 fans to set a home attendance record, but a "half-frozen throng" of only 16,721 turned out for the final home game in "that ancient rookery, Forbes Field."[50] Who among them knew—or even cared—that the dilapidated structure in which Johnny "Blood" McNally, Byron "Whizzer" White, and Bobby Layne had performed was about to host a Steeler game for the final time? On this chilly afternoon, there was no crooked upright as there had been in the opener, but the game would seem eerily similar to the one three months earlier.

With less than five minutes left, the Eagles looked poised to salvage something from their misbegotten season and ruin the Steelers. With Hill playing instead of Jurgensen, and with a defense revamped because of the Scotti-Mellekas fight, Philadelphia held a 20–10 lead. After the game, Parker would be sipping a cup of coffee, shaking his head. "We gave them everything," he said. "Nobody but us hurts us."[51]

Layne, phoning down information from the scouting booth, watched as Ed Brown threw for two touchdowns and 243 yards but hit only thirteen of thirty-one passes and had four interceptions. "How can you get so far behind?" he would later ask Parker.[52]

The Steelers had a tendency to do that. The teams chugged through a scoreless first period. On their first possession, the Eagles moved to the Steeler 35 on a 17-yard pass to Pete Retzlaff, but on the next play Tommy McDonald was called for pushing, moving the Eagles back to midfield. On third-and-13 at the Steeler 38, Andy Russell intercepted Hill. Russell fumbled on his return, but rookie teammate Frank Atkinson recovered at the 37.

As the period wound down, Pittsburgh started on its 20 after a Hill punt into the end zone. Brown hit Preston Carpenter for a 23-yard gain on the first play of the second quarter. Brown missed Ballman, but pass interference on Irv Cross put Pittsburgh on the Eagle 30. John Henry Johnson and Hoak crunched yardage to give the Steelers second-and-goal at the 1, but Hoak fumbled for a yard loss and Johnson was stopped cold on third down. Parker played it safe and sent in Lou Michaels for a 10-yard field goal with 6:19 elapsed in the quarter.

But soon "disaster hit."[53] Pittsburgh forced the Eagles to punt, but on third-and-9 Brown missed Dial and middle linebacker Dave Lloyd made the first of his two interceptions and returned the ball 11 yards to the Steeler 24. Years later, defensive back Dick Haley would be asked about the toughest receivers he had ever faced. It wasn't McDonald or Bobby Mitchell or Del Shofner. It was the man one football guide referred to as the Eagles' "blond adonis of an end."[54]

"The most difficult and best guy in the league then, I thought, was Pete Retzlaff," Haley said. "I thought Retzlaff was phenomenal at that time."[55] Retzlaff had the speed to play split end, but Skorich moved him to tight end after Retzlaff sustained a broken arm in '62. On first down, he got behind Haley in the right corner of the end zone and caught Hill's pass to put Philly ahead 7–3.

On the kickoff, Gary Ballman, the hero in Washington, fumbled and rookie linebacker Lee Roy Caffey recovered for the Eagles on the 14. On the first play, Tim Brown made a terrific individual effort, first shaking off John Reger, then slipping away as Clendon Thomas hit him low on the left side and Haley grabbed his shoulders from the right, and finally hurtling sideways 5 yards and over the goal line for the touchdown. It took just forty seconds for the Eagles to grab a 14–3 lead with 4:39 left in the half.

The Eagles forced a punt, and their lead looked secure even after Thomas made an interception at the Steeler 43 with seven seconds left before half-time. Ed Brown took one last shot, heaving a pass down the left sideline for Dial, who was covered by Don Burroughs. At the 2-yard line, "Dial made a miraculous catch of the ball" around the 10, "stumbled like a drunkard into the end zone," and fell flat on his back.[56] Burroughs immediately leaned over and pointed to a spot along the chalk around the 2.

Of all the players in the NFL, Burroughs was perhaps the last one the officials wanted to hear voice any comments about a ruling—or nonruling. After the season-opening tie with Pittsburgh, Burroughs, angered at being denied a fumble recovery by a whistle during the final series of the game, chased the officials across the field and accosted field judge Dan Tehan. The next day, Rozelle suspended the Eagle safety for one game for grab-bing or shoving Tehan and for accidentally striking referee Bill Downes in the face. Burroughs issued a prompt apology.

But on this day, Burroughs's lobbying for the call didn't hurt his team. The officials ruled that Dial had been out of bounds and discounted the touchdown. Instead of cutting their halftime deficit to 14–10, the Steelers remained in a 14–3 hole.

For "a soft-hearted, easy-going Steeler who never lets adversity ruffle his feathers," Dial was pretty upset about the call.[57] "I wasn't out," he said. "Don Burroughs went over and told the man I was, and he listened to Bur-roughs."[58] And all along, the Steelers thought that George Halas was the one who had the power to persuade the officials.

The halftime statistics were closely matched in yards rushing and receiv-ing and first downs. One big disparity favored the Steelers: Philadelphia had been penalized five times for 65 yards, but Pittsburgh had not been flagged. The Steelers held after Philadelphia took the second-half kickoff, but they committed another mistake on their second play from scrimmage. Ed Brown threw right to Lloyd, who returned his second interception 12 yards to the Steeler 20. Defensive end John Baker stuffed Tim Brown for a yard loss, and a pass gained nothing, so rookie Mike Clark kicked a 23-

yard field goal to put Philadelphia ahead 17–3. Mistakes were proving to be the difference in the game.

The Steelers fell into a hole against both St. Louis and Dallas and came back, but they had shown little indication they could rally against Philly. Their stunting on defense forced Hill into delay-of-game penalties when he couldn't call an audible in time, Skorich said, but Parker maintained that at halftime he made "no radical adjustments. The only thing we did was to play a little better."[59]

Pittsburgh wasted a prime opportunity late in the quarter when Ed Brown, on first down at the Eagle 40, threw deep for Dial. Cross broke up the pass but Mike McClellan, filling in for the suspended Scotti, was called for pass interference at the 2. Theron Sapp lost two yards against his old team, and then McClellan atoned for his mistake by intercepting a pass intended for Dial in the end zone. If Buddy Parker had any fantasies about bringing Bobby Layne down from the press box and suiting him up, time was running out on that daydream—and Pittsburgh's season.

The Steelers forced a punt, and took over on their 37. Ed Brown missed Dial, then hit Ballman for 16 yards to Philly's 47 as the third quarter ticked down. On the second play of the fourth quarter, a 13-yard pass to Ballman was nullified when guard Ray Lemek was called for illegal use of hands— Pittsburgh's only penalty of the game—pushing the Steelers back to their 43. New heroes on the team had popped up all season—Dick Haley, Red Mack, Bob Schmitz, Jim Bradshaw—and in recent weeks Steeler fans had come to appreciate that Ballman's "impossibilities . . . [were] quickly becoming routine."[60] On first-and-33 from the Steeler 43, the split end got behind Cross down the left sideline and caught a 57-yard touchdown pass with fifty-seven seconds elapsed in the fourth quarter to bring the Steelers within 17–10. "By now, the Eagles were coming apart," wrote Hugh Brown of the *Evening Bulletin.*[61]

Pottios and Joe Krupa were sparking a defense that prevented the Eagles from gaining a first down in the second half until the final thirty seconds, but the Steelers continued to hurt themselves on offense. Johnson, open in the flat, dropped a pass, and ex-teammate Tarasovic dumped Ed Brown for a 9-yard loss on the Eagle 36. Michaels seemed to be back on track, but he missed a 43-yard field goal attempt, wide left. When Brown threw his fourth interception, to Jimmy Carr, setting up a 40-yard field goal by Clark and a 20–10 Eagle lead with only 4:38 left, it looked as if the Steeler season was doomed. But then "the killer" ensued for Skorich's team.[62]

Clark kicked off, and Ballman, 3 yards deep in the end zone, raced 63 yards to the Eagle 40 before Cross, the last defender, brought him down. Brown, out of the shotgun, hit Carpenter for 14 yards and then picked up 18 more with a throw to Ballman, a catch on which the former taxi squad member broke away from three defenders, giving the Steelers first-and-goal at the 8. Brown hit Carpenter at the goal line, but the tight end couldn't hang onto the ball. Then Brown overthrew Carpenter, but he hit Ballman on third down for the touchdown that brought Pittsburgh within 20–17 with 3:22 to go.

The Eagle offense had fizzled. Hill was en route to a nine-of-twenty-four afternoon with three interceptions. McDonald had caught a pass on the Eagles' first possession but then was shut out. The Eagles were trying to run out the clock, but Lou Cordileone and Krupa stuffed two carries. Hill was forced to punt, and his 56-yard kick rolled dead on the Steeler 22.

The Eagles were on the way to amassing 145 yards on eight penalties, and 37 of the yards came on first down after the punt, another pass interference penalty on McClellan, guarding Dial, a disputed call made right in front of the visitors' bench. Even Dial allowed that "it was a close call." From the 41, Carpenter made a leaping catch on third down for 12 yards to the 29, and then Brown found Dial for 13 more to the 16. There were fifty-eight seconds left. Brown overthrew Carpenter in the end zone on first down. Cross broke up another throw to Dial. On third-and-10, Brown threw incomplete to John Henry Johnson. "I've been throwing the ball too quickly," Brown said later.[63]

That left it up to Michaels, who had suffered the indignity of having one conversion blocked and another striking the upright in the opener in Philly, to attempt a field goal from the 24. Asked later what he was thinking about when he lined up for the kick, Michaels shot back, "I was thinking of two things: Keep my eye on the ball and follow through."[64]

The kick was good. There were forty seconds left. Hill heaved a desperation pass in the final seconds, but Thomas intercepted and returned the ball 25 yards to the Eagle 35 as the clock died.

The Steelers were still in the race. A third tie—the first time in twenty-five years an NFL had had that may—did not hurt them. They could still win the Eastern crown by beating Dallas and the Giants, provided the Browns, winners over St. Louis, lost to either Detroit or Washington. Parker was as content—or relieved—as Halas was the week before, to salvage a tie. "Sure, I settled for the tie," Parker said. "We were lucky to come out of that one alive."[65]

But the locker room was quiet.[66] The Steelers had come precipitously close to letting a thirteen-point underdog end their season. Dial was upset not only with the officiating but with the way his team had played. "That was the worst game I've ever seen us play," he said. "We made more mistakes than we've ever made. We were watching the scoreboard."[67]

Cleveland beat St. Louis, 24–10, knocking the 8–4 Cards from a three-way tie for first place and into a tie for third with 6–3–3 Pittsburgh. Throwing out the Steelers' ties, each team had a .667 percentage. The Steelers needed Cleveland to lose once over the next two weeks, but with Jim Brown scoring two touchdowns and running for 179 yards to break his own single-season rushing record, it looked nearly impossible for the Browns to lose to either 4–7–1 Detroit or 3–9 Washington.

If there was a game to grab the Steelers' attention, it was in Dallas, where the Cowboys built a 27–14 halftime lead over the Giants by intercepting Y. A. Tittle three times in the first half. But Tittle rallied New York in the second half, hitting Del Shofner with a 17-yard TD pass to give the Giants a 34–27 victory and allow them to keep a share of first place. Parker's crew would face the Cowboys in a week.

The Steelers could be grateful just for surviving another Sunday. "It was our worst game of the year," Parker said. "You're always lucky when you get a tie, playing a game like that."[68]

All season long, except for the rout of the Giants in week 2, the Steelers had to claw their way back, rallying for a victory or just a tie. If it was true, as Ernie Stautner said, that the team had choked against Green Bay, it had not folded under the pressure since that afternoon. They caught a couple of breaks and maybe got shortchanged a few times. But they had played all out. That was Steeler football. That was their heritage. That was how they were either going to become champions or fall one step short.

"Nobody is going to give us anything in this league," Lou Cordileone said. "You have to earn it yourself."[69]

GAME 13

Straight from graduation, months after his selection by the Steelers in the NFL draft, Stanford tackle Frank Atkinson took a slow boat to China.

It wasn't actually a boat; it was a freighter. And China wasn't the actual destination, but he did make it to Japan, Korea, Vietnam, and Indonesia during his travels, half by freighter and half by plane. "I visited Seoul after there had been riots. It proved a very interesting three months," Atkinson said during his first training camp. "I like to travel, meet people and have different experiences."[1]

One of those experiences was life as a pro football player. Atkinson didn't even know he had been drafted until he heard the news while listening to a sports report on the radio in his fraternity house. He had assumed that the Cowboys were the only team interested in him because they had phoned several times. The AFL, craving talent to compete with the NFL, didn't bother with Atkinson. "This draft business really has me puzzled," he said.[2] The six-foot-three, 250-pound tackle had the distinction of being the Steelers' top pick in the 1963 draft—because Parker had traded away every one of his first seven picks. Atkinson was picked in the eighth round, the 108th overall pick, eight rounds before fellow rookie Andy Russell.

Russell and Atkinson, both with more interest in an MBA than the NFL, began a friendship that would live on long after their playing careers. For players like Gary Ballman, playing pro football was a dream come true. For Lou Michaels and Dick Haley, it was an exit from a life in the mines or mills. But for Atkinson, it was an adventure like, say, taking a freighter to foreign lands.

"His attitude of playing professional football was a little bit like a guy might say, 'Between my undergrad and my grad school I'm going to spend one year fooling around in Aspen, waiting tables and skiing,'" Russell said. "'I'm going to take a year off.' That's how he viewed playing professional football. It was a frivolous, personal, fun thing to do. He was going to spend one year doing it and then he was going to go to graduate school. He starts his rookie year, he does very well, and he quits, gets his MBA."[3]

What kind of expectations did Atkinson have about playing professionally? "Zero. I was flattered and I was mainly curious," he said. "I didn't really have career aspirations."[4] In fact, at that time Atkinson didn't have many aspirations about anything. "In my senior year I couldn't even have told you what I planned to be doing the next day," he said.[5]

Atkinson had options. He could have chosen a career that paid better, provided more job security, and was less physically demanding—say, with his father's business, the Atkinson Construction Co., which built freeways, bridges, and dams and handled other major projects. The San Francisco 49ers, whose practice field was minutes away from the Atkinson home, were so sure the Stanford senior had no interest in a pro career that they didn't bother to send him a preliminary questionnaire before the draft. Atkinson insisted his father was not a millionaire, but an executive on the 49ers, Lou Spadia, scoffed at the notion the Steelers could sign Atkinson. "Why, Atkinson's old man could buy your ball club," he said.[6]

Atkinson made a career choice, as if making a decision on whether or not to visit a given country: He bypassed the family business. "It just doesn't appeal to me," he said.[7]

It didn't take long for anyone to realize that the Stanford history major was different from most draft picks. "Atkinson is one of the most unusual young grid candidates at Rooney U. in years," beat writer Jack Sell wrote.[8]

The Steelers' defensive line loomed as questionable on the right side, away from Lou Michaels and Joe Krupa. Big Daddy Lipscomb had died, and his likely successor, Lou Cordileone, was a guy who had done almost as much traveling around the NFL as Atkinson had done in the Far East. Ernie Stautner had spent thirteen years in the league, and his role was going to be reduced to that of player and coach. John Baker had been inconsistent. Buddy Parker needed someone to step in immediately and help at right end and tackle, but using a first-year player went against everything Parker preached. "He'd rather get a 10-year veteran off the dust bin than a rookie who was a superstar," Atkinson said.[9]

Atkinson sustained a pinched nerve in his left shoulder in the first contact drill in camp, but trainer Roger McGill fixed him up with a harness for protection, and the rookie returned to drills in a few days. He made an impression in the team's intrasquad scrimmage, and it lasted. The Steelers lost their exhibition opener to the Packers, 27–7, but Atkinson "did the best job of the new players," it was noted.[10]

"I started like our second exhibition game," he said. "Like a minute before kickoff, Buddy Parker said, 'Hey, Frank, you're starting; it's going to be on the left side. First time I'd ever played that. And that was a good game, so I started getting my reps in there.'"[11]

Atkinson was tempted to cut his career even shorter when he saw John Reger in critical condition in the season opener, knocked out and struggling to breathe after a collision. "I'm standing on the sideline saying, 'If this is going the way I think it's going to go, I'm just going back in the locker room right now and take a shower and get out of here,'" Atkinson recalled. "That was the scariest thing I'd ever seen on a football field. There's Reger, he's on the verge of death. He's back in a couple weeks playing. Tough guy."[12]

As the season progressed, Atkinson worked his way into the starting lineup, but he was making other plans as well. UCLA helped him work out an arrangement, around his NFL commitment, to work on his MBA degree. When Atkinson showed up for training camp in '64, he loomed as the successor to Ernie Stautner, who was retiring as a player and becoming a full-time coach. The fourteen-year veteran offered qualified praise for Atkinson. "He improved quite a bit and I have reason to believe he will improve a lot more," Stautner said. "He's a strong kid and he's still filling out. His will power will determine how far he goes. It all will depend on how much he wants to play."[13]

Atkinson had his own timetable, but he figured on playing the '64 season. "I even told the Steelers the second year that this is my last year—sort of the gentlemanly thing to do so they could make plans accordingly," he said. "They didn't like me very much after that. They released me—the night before the opener. If you're not on the squad at the start of the year, you're out of luck."[14]

The Denver Broncos of the AFL obtained the rights to Atkinson, and he played for them that season. "That wasn't so much fun," he said. "I was just waiting for it to get over. I found out how good the game got, and I found out I could play it. Once I was satisfied there, I wasn't quite as interested."[15]

It was a great opportunity, like jumping on and off a freighter, as if he were an explorer riding the rails, but a career in finance was beckoning. Years later, Chuck Noll would arrive as coach, and he would advise players that football was but a stopover before you "get on with your life's work." Atkinson didn't need to be told that it was already time for him to get on with his and "ultimately went into the venture capital business in San Francisco before anyone had even heard of venture capitalists," Russell said. Atkinson left football behind, with no regrets about leaving so soon, so abruptly. "Being a Steeler, I'm really proud of that, and it was really a wonderful experience," he said. "But it was one of those things you wouldn't [trade for] a million bucks. . . . but you wouldn't necessarily want to do it again."[16]

Atkinson's name was relegated to a line in the Steelers' all-time roster, one more entry in Parker's picked-apart carcasses of drafts. Atkinson had performed well enough as a rookie to crack the starting lineup of a coach who shunned rookies. Who knows how far he could have gone if he had devoted his life to football? Of course, Atkinson never had everlasting fame in mind when he signed with the Steelers. Two years after he left football, Atkinson's name popped up coincidentally in a Detroit sports column, whose author commented, "Atkinson's whereabouts today are unknown."[17]

Move forward another ten years, and Atkinson's name was back in a Pittsburgh newspaper. "Remember Frank Atkinson?" the *Post-Gazette*'s Al Abrams asked in a 1976 column, a month after the Steelers beat Dallas in Super Bowl X. "Of course, you don't." Abrams had learned that over the previous two years Atkinson had flown from the Middle East to Khartoum, the capital of Sudan, to watch the Steelers' first two Super Bowl appearances through the satellite station that relayed the game to U.S. forces overseas.[18] Evidently Atkinson's allegiance to his former team ran deeper than his love for the pro game.

Abrams reported that Atkinson, "a man of many distinctions," had been living in Beirut but had relocated to Dusseldorf, Germany, in the wake of the Lebanese Civil War.[19] No wonder his whereabouts were unknown. The tackle who had once lined up with Ernie Stautner, Joe Krupa, and Lou Michaels was a vice president for Triad International Marketing, a company run by Saudi billionaire Adnan Khashoggi, who would go on to become a key figure in the 1980s Iran-Contra affair. Khashoggi had attended Stanford University and was, presumably, a football fan. Atkinson was just getting started in business. He would go on to a variety of other positions, such as working with a private equity investment firm and a firm providing investment banking services to technology companies. A guy who hitchhiked around Asia by freighter wasn't likely to be pinned down in one spot forever.[20]

Parker was hoping for another unheralded gem like Frank Atkinson as the NFL draft got underway in Chicago the day after the 20–20 tie with

Philadelphia. The Steelers had hung onto their No. 1 selection, the tenth overall pick. The draft began at 10:05 A.M. and ended at 7:18 A.M. the next day, Tuesday. Parker, one of five coaches who did not attend, resisted the opportunity to pick Miami quarterback George Mira and instead selected hometown hero Paul Martha of the University of Pittsburgh, one spot ahead of Ohio State halfback Paul Warfield, who went to the Browns and would go on to the Hall of Fame. With Bob Ferguson's exit still a raw wound, Parker had evidently had his fill of Ohio State backs. In the second round, Parker selected Notre Dame end Jim Kelly.

Martha played six seasons with the Steelers, but he lasted as a safety, not as the heir to Buddy Dial's position. Martha had six receptions in his rookie year. Like Atkinson, he would play an additional year with Denver and find his true calling as a high-powered attorney and executive, notably with the 49ers and Pittsburgh Penguins of the NHL.

Parker had little time to enjoy what he envisioned as a draft bonanza; his team was still clinging to an outside shot at a division title, but it couldn't afford a loss or even a tie against the Cowboys. Despite all the heady expectations, Dallas "never got out of its cleat prints" in '63 and dropped to 3–9 after blowing a 27–14 lead against New York and falling, 34–27, as Y. A. Tittle broke Bobby Layne's career record for touchdown passes.[21] After losing at Forbes Field in late October, the Cowboys had gone 2–3 but, tellingly, had given up twenty points in both wins and twenty-seven points or more in all three losses. Landry had fallen way short in his goal of shoring up his defense.

Still, after scrambling for a tie against a last-place team riddled with dissension, Parker was wary of a team that had nothing to lose. "That's about all they have left, knocking us out [of] the race," the coach said. "It hasn't been a very happy season for those fellows, you know. They've had their bad moments and darn few good ones, but they have the personnel to explode anytime they go out on the field. I hope they don't pick this weekend to do it."[22]

A year earlier, Don Meredith had made as bold a prediction as Landry had about the future greatness of the team. "In the next couple of years, maybe sooner, the Cowboys are going to be right at the top year after year. [Landry]'s pretty close right now to what he wants. When he gets it, the Cowboys and the Packers will be playing for the championship."[23]

That scenario was still a few years away. The Dallas defense was spotty in '62, but the offense ranked second in the league in scoring and yardage. They had two powerful backs in fullback Amos Marsh and halfback Don Perkins, who, "with disregard for life and limb, used his 200 pounds like a human projectile."[24] Perkins ranked sixth among rushers, with 612 yards. Billy Howton was in his last days as a receiver, but Frank Clarke—"one of the most dangerous runners in football"—was coming off a year in which he caught fourteen TD passes.[25]

Meredith may have been "the most promising young thrower in pro football," but in no way was he about to be hailed as a brainy counterpart to Charley Johnson or Frank Ryan.[26] "What worries his colleagues is his blithe spirit," *Sports Illustrated* reported. Meredith clearly had more in common with Layne on a football field than he did with any quarterback working on a PhD. In the huddle during one 1961 game, he reportedly told a receiver, "Just run downfield, I'll find you."[27] He was the kind of brash, gunslinging Texas kid Parker knew all too well, and he had nothing to lose in the final two weeks.

The Cowboys had the kind of explosive attack that unnerved Steeler center Buzz Nutter. "They've got a great offensive team, the kind of team that gives us trouble," he said. "Frankly, I'd rather be playing either Chicago or Green Bay than these guys."[28]

Said team president Art Rooney: "They're good enough to knock us out of the box Sunday unless we play up to par."[29]

That week the Pittsburgh Opera was preparing for performances of *Aida,* featuring three members of the Metropolitan Opera, to be held at the Syria Mosque. On Sunday morning, Pat Livingston warned Steeler fans, "It could be a tragic showdown" in Dallas. Although the four-year-old Cowboy franchise had endured "a campaign of horror," Pittsburgh "can point to a long history of similar frustrations and heartbreak."[30] The game had all the makings of melodrama for the Steeler franchise.

Most disturbing, Livingston wrote in echoing Parker's lament, was "the Steelers' inexplicable capacity for freezing up in the games they have to win. This appears to be a team that tightens up when the chips are on the line, a team that fails to play to its potential when it has to win."[31] That was not truly accurate. The Steelers had blown a game in St. Louis, and maybe, indeed, they had choked against Green Bay. But they had not lost since the debacle in Milwaukee, and they had staged two comebacks besides stuffing Cleveland and beating Chicago everywhere but on the scoreboard.

Now they needed help. Either Detroit or Washington had to upset Cleveland, but the Steelers could find some hope in the resurgence by the Lions. Winners of only four games, the Lions had turned from the biggest flops of the NFL to "the bogeyman of both conference races" after tying the Packers on Thanksgiving Day.[32]

There was even a chance, as unlikely as it was, that the Steelers could vault into first place in the Eastern Conference on Sunday if both the Giants and Browns lost. The Steelers would be 7–3–3 (.700), and New York and Cleveland would be 9–4–0 (.692)—and so would St. Louis, with a victory, thus creating a three-way tie for second. "It's all very confusing," Jack Sell wrote.[33] Not entirely. The Steelers knew one thing for sure: They had to beat the Cowboys. Parker's team could not afford another tie.

On Saturday morning, Pearl Harbor Day, as the Steelers took a flight to Dallas, the *Post-Gazette* ran a story headlined "Gloom Shrouds Night Life in Dallas." The "kicker" on the head read: "Horror of Assassination Still Hangs Heavily." An editorial in the paper commented, "It is a monstrous injustice to blame the millions of patriotic and law abiding citizens of Dallas, of Texas, of the whole United States for complicity in the death of the President."

But no one could escape the fact that Dallas was the site where John F. Kennedy was slain. "The bus driver took us on a tour past Dealey Plaza and the whole deal, coming back from the Cotton Bowl after a brief workout," Atkinson recalled. "Eerie."[34]

Art Rooney Jr., along with his father and Fran Fogarty, the business manager, were given a tour around the city by an acquaintance. "People were milling about; it was just quiet," Art Rooney Jr. said. "I was a young adult, and I found it really spooky." The elder Rooney had met Kennedy and was "terribly hurt" by the assassination, his son said. From then on, Art Jr. said, his father would make any excuse not to travel to Dallas unless a trip was unavoidable.[35]

The surreal atmosphere continued. Atkinson remembered the night before the game when the Steelers had their team dinner at the hotel. "In comes Bobby Layne with Mickey Mantle. Mickey Mantle was so drunk he couldn't get his chin off his chest. Talk about seeing an icon crumble before your eyes—boy, that was sad. That was his downfall."[36]

In three weeks, 75,504 fans would jam the Cotton Bowl to watch the No. 1 Texas Longhorns take on Roger Staubach and Navy on New Year's Day in the postseason game that the University of Pittsburgh felt worthy of an invitation. But for the Cowboys' home finale, only 24,136 fans showed up on a sunny but blustery afternoon, with 25 mph winds. The gusts quickly became a factor and would influence strategy, especially a critical decision in the final minutes.

Landry had abandoned the QB shuttle and committed himself to Meredith, but in deference to LeBaron's final home game, the eleven-year veteran was given the start. He hit Pettis Norman with a 32-yard pass to move into

Steeler territory on the Cowboys' first possession, but a holding penalty negated a 24-yard screen pass to Marsh and pushed Dallas back into its own territory. Marsh gained 12 yards on a delay, but an incompletion left Dallas with fourth-and-11 at the Steeler 46. Sam Baker, with the wind at his back, drilled a 53-yard field goal, the third-longest in NFL history at the time.

The Steelers started from their 20, with Johnson and Sapp picking up big chunks of yardage, but Ed Brown fumbled and defensive end George Andrie recovered on the Dallas 37. Meredith took over for LeBaron and, after an incompletion, threw a swing pass to Marsh for 35 yards before Bob Schmitz caught him at the Steeler 24. Bullocks carried four straight times, hammering the middle of the defense, to move Dallas to the 1. Meredith recovered his own fumble on first-and-goal, losing a yard, and after Bullocks was stopped at the line, the quarterback muscled his way over right tackle for the touchdown. LeBaron mishandled the snap on the point after, making it 9–0, Dallas, with 1:01 left in the quarter.

With the aid of the wind, Baker's kickoff sailed out of the end zone for the second straight time, denying Ballman a shot at a long return. The Steelers were starting to bring a trace of validation to Livingston's assessment of them as "a ribald band of head-hunting youngsters who can't play a lick under pressure."[37] If that wasn't entirely true, it was fair to suggest that the Steelers often resembled a boxer who hasn't warmed up properly before entering the ring and quickly finds himself in trouble.

As the second quarter began, the Steelers had the benefit of the wind at their backs. On second-and-9 from his 45, Brown heaved a pass that defensive back Cornell Green tipped, and Buddy Dial, "stumbling and weaving, somehow managed to pick it from the air. The incredible Steeler receiver then danced the remaining 15 yards . . . while Green and Mike Gaechter watched in helpless horror."[38] Lou Michaels kicked the point after to make it 9–7.

The teams went 3-and-out on four of the next five possessions, but Pittsburgh got good field position, at its own 40, after Baker's punt into the wind went only 28 yards in the final minutes before the half. Brown connected with Ballman on first down for 32 yards, down to the Dallas 28.

Preston Carpenter finished the season with seventeen catches, a drop from his thirty-six receptions in his Pro Bowl season of '62, but as a tight end he was vital in the Steeler scheme as a blocker. "I was a good blocker because I played blocking back in the single wing at Arkansas," he explained. "All I did was block. I never ran the football at Arkansas. I never touched the ball."[39]

The Browns drafted him in the first round, the thirteenth overall pick, in the infamous 1956 draft that saw the Steelers take Gary Glick with their lottery bonus pick and then select Mississippi State halfback Art Davis four spots later, allowing Lenny Moore to fall to the Colts in the ninth slot. Cleveland used Carpenter as a running back, and he rushed for 756 yards as a rookie, with a 4.0 average. He also was a return man, averaging 25.4 yards on kickoffs. Cleveland shifted him to split end the next year, but Pittsburgh moved him to tight end. "I was a good blocker for 198 pounds," he said. "I blocked guys 245, 250. I took pride in my blocking."[40] Dial called Carpenter "just about the best blocking end I've seen."[41]

But Carpenter loved to catch the ball. "I wish I had speed," he said. "I could have been another Ray Renfro." Forty-four years after that game in Dallas, Carpenter still sounded like a kid with a dream. "I always wanted an opportunity to catch a touchdown pass and win a ball game," he said.[42] On the play after Ballman's catch, Carpenter, running step for step with defensive back Warren Livingston, caught a 28-yard touchdown in the right corner of the end zone—his lone touchdown of the season. Now Pittsburgh was up, 14–9, with 1:57 before the half.

Meredith sent in LeBaron during the next series, but after reaching the 45 with the aid of a roughing-the-passer penalty, Dallas had to punt. Baker's kick went only 30 yards but left the Steelers with barely half a minute before halftime. On first down from the Steeler 35, Brown hit Dial with a 48-yard completion. Dial got out of bounds at the 17-yard line to stop the clock with two seconds left, and Michaels hit a 24-yard field goal to give Pittsburgh a 17–9 lead.

The Cowboys were proving to be stubborn, but the Steelers had shown good balance in the first half. Brown was six of eight for 171 yards and two touchdowns, and John Henry Johnson and Sapp had 138 yards rushing evenly split between them. But the powerful winds loomed as the pivotal influence on the field.

On the first series of the second half, the Steelers appeared to have forced a punt when Michaels stuffed Meredith for no gain at the Dallas 34 on third-and-4, but the defensive end was called for a face mask penalty, giving the Cowboys a first down on the 49. Dallas advanced to the Steeler 28, but Michaels dropped Bullocks for a 10-yard loss. LeBaron was inserted again, and he threw two incompletions, so Baker kicked a 46-yard field goal into the wind, cutting the Steeler lead to 17–12.

The Steelers picked their way to midfield, but even with the wind at his back Michaels couldn't hit a 56-yard field goal attempt. Gaechter caught the ball on the 8 and returned it to the 24. Marsh gained 21 yards on a delay up the middle before Glenn Glass hauled him down at the Steeler 43. After

Michaels dropped Meredith for a 4-yard loss, Norman made a diving 42-yard catch that gave Dallas a first-and-goal at the 5. After Bullocks picked up a yard, Meredith rolled around left end to put the Cowboys ahead, 19–17, with 3:38 left in the third quarter.

A short kickoff and Ballman's 28-yard return put the Steelers on their 46. Brown was moving his team, but on first down at the Dallas 24, defensive back Don Bishop intercepted a pass at the 2 as the third quarter ticked away. Pittsburgh stopped Meredith on the first series of the fourth quarter, but for the next fifteen minutes the Cowboys could count on their best ally: the wind. Baker boomed a 56-yard punt that Dick Haley returned 1 yard to the 25. The Steelers gained one first down before they had to punt.

A few years later, Ballman would become a teammate of both Mike Ditka and Baker on the Eagles. Loris Hoskins "Sam" Baker liked to sneak out after curfew, Ballman recalled, and kept a makeup kit to disguise himself, often as an old man. One night Baker was leaving his room, in makeup and carrying a cane, and passed Eagle coach Joe Kuharich in the hall. Baker said good evening to the coach and kept right on walking, unrecognized, a six-foot-two, 220-pound man actually in his mid-thirties.[43]

But without question, the nine-year vet from Oregon State had a leg to kick a football. Defensive end John Baker (no relation) dropped Meredith for a 4-yard loss on third-and-1 from the Dallas 29, so Sam Baker came in and unloaded a 58-yard punt that Haley returned 9 yards to his 27. The Steelers got as far as the Dallas 46 before they were forced to punt on fourth-and-7. They needed a break, but even when they got one, it seemed to backfire. The Cowboys were caught with too many men on the field on the punt, so, with the benefit of an extra 5 yards that left Pittsburgh 2 short of a first down, Michaels attempted a 49-yard field goal, into the wind. Bishop blocked the kick, and instead of having possession on the 12, where Brown's punt had landed, the Cowboys took over on their 47. Meredith lost 4 yards and threw two incompletions, but Baker got off a 57-yard punt, into the end zone. The Steelers looked capable of beating the Cowboys, but it didn't look as if they could beat Mother Nature.

Parker's crew was likely down to its last shot. Brown was sacked by Andrie and Larry Stephens for a 4-yard loss, and then his screen pass to Johnson was tipped away by Andrie. On third down, Brown's pass over the middle to Carpenter went incomplete, leaving Pittsburgh with fourth-and-14 at the 16-yard line with four-and-a-half minutes to go, and "things looking black as a coal miner's meeting clothes."[44]

To Cowboy fans, what happened next was a microcosm of their ill-fated season. "Any other club would have been dressing for the victory dance, but the Cowboys have a genuine passion for these situations," Gary Cartwright wrote in the *Dallas Morning News.* Cowboy fans had endured an infinitesimal amount of the heartbreak that Steeler fans had suffered, but the letdowns by the '63 Cowboys had swiftly turned their fans into cynics, waiting for disaster, just as Pittsburgh fans had been resigned to failure for decades. "Any school girl could have told you that, having the odds stacked so impressively in their direction, nothing could help the Cowboys. Not the Turkish cavalry, not Scotland Yard, not Billy Graham, not Mary Worth."[45]

But this season was turning out differently for Steeler fans. From a Pittsburgh fan's perspective, thinking back to the heroics of Bob Schmitz, Red Mack, and Gary Ballman, the Steelers had the Cowboys right where they wanted 'em.

"There was nothing else we could do," Parker said afterward. "We had to keep the ball. We had to score or we were out of it."[46]

Brown lined up to punt. Atkinson, who had been playing special teams all year, was preparing to cover the kick. "There's a funny story," he explained forty-four years later. "I was 10 yards down the field covering the punt, and I had no idea it was a fake. I guess they called the play on the sidelines and not in the huddle on the field. I might have been the only guy on the Steelers that didn't know. I'm 10 yards down the field, and I didn't hear the foot hit the ball. Ed Brown's pass goes flying by me." No call was made by the officials; no flag was thrown. "Well, I sure got away with one in Dallas, I'll tell you that. They just completely missed it."[47]

Brown targeted Mack, but the Cowboys, evidently, weren't suckered by the fake. "He ran a great pattern and made a good fake," Parker said. "We didn't fool them with that pass call, you know. Mack was covered and they had four men on [end] Johnny Burrell, but Red made a great play to get out in the open."[48]

"Mack had only one man to beat," Brown said, "and he did it."[49] Just like he did in the game at Forbes Field against the Cowboys.

Mack caught the pass—his only catch of the day, and his first since the Browns game—down the right sideline and ran 42 yards to the Cowboy 42. On first down, Andrie held Johnson to a yard over left tackle. Sapp gained 8 yards over right end, but on third-and-1, Stephens stopped him at the line. With fourth-and-1 at the 33, Parker sent in the field goal unit but then called time-out.

"Buster Ramsey brought up the wind," Parker explained later. "We were going to kick, but Buster suggested we go for the sticks [the first-down marker].

He figured even if we did kick a field goal against the wind, the Cowboys would come back with the wind behind him and Sam Baker would kick a 55-yarder to beat us. If it weren't for that, I'd have gone for the field goal."[50]

Michaels would have been kicking a 40-yarder—into the wind. "Well, it took me off the spot," he said, "but if he said to kick it, I'd have made it."[51]

In the aftermath of Michael's oh-for-five day against Cleveland a month before, *Post-Gazette* columnist Al Abrams had commented, "Lou Michaels is a man who thinks and broods a lot."[52] But Michaels always took on questions with as straightforward an approach as his steps to a kick, and his confidence did not waver after the game when pressed about whether he had worried about a kick—one single play—that could determine the fate of his team's season. "No, sir, not a bit," he replied. "I knew I wouldn't miss it. You got to think positive. If you think you're not going to make it, you won't."[53]

Parker decided to go for it. John Henry Johnson took the handoff and dived over right guard for two yards to give the Steelers a first down at the 31.

Sapp was in the lineup at halfback because Dick Hoak had pulled a leg muscle in the first half against Philadelphia. On a team dotted with players who had been unlikely candidates to make a living as professional football players—from Russell to Daniel to Reger—perhaps the most improbable of all was Theron Coleman Sapp, who grew up in central Georgia, the youngest of ten children. Sapp's college career at Georgia was in jeopardy after he cracked three vertebrae in his neck while practicing for a high school all-star football game. "If you were my son, you'd never play football again," Sapp remembered the doctor telling him.[54]

Sapp sat out his freshman college year, wearing a cast that covered the upper half of his body. He played sparingly in his sophomore year, then finished third among Southeastern Conference rushers as a junior, and second to LSU's Billy Cannon as a senior in 1958. But it was one game, on November 30, 1957, that immortalized Sapp in Georgia football history. The Bulldogs, in their third consecutive losing season, had lost eight straight to Georgia Tech—a stretch known as "the Drought"—and were mired in a scoreless tie with their rival when Sapp recovered a fumble at midfield. Sapp carried seven times on Georgia's drive, capping the march with his 1-yard touchdown on fourth-and-goal, to give the Bulldogs a 7–0 victory. It was one of six touchdowns he scored as a collegian. Sapp earned the nickname "the Drought Breaker," saw his No. 40 jersey retired, and even had a poem written about him by a fan.

On a blustery day in Dallas, Sapp was closing in on a 100-yard rushing day when he lined up behind Brown on first-and-10 at the 31. Sapp had not scored a touchdown all season. He went around left end for 7 yards before linebacker Dave Edwards stopped him. From the 24, Brown called on Sapp again.

It was Ditka's run against the Steelers that would take on epic proportions that season, but there were other efforts, long forgotten, that could stand out among the highlights. The next play was remarkable in its simplicity, and devastating in its execution.

"Everybody blocked straight ahead," Buzz Nutter explained. "It was a quick handoff to the halfback, who followed the fullback between [Ray] Lemek and [Charlie] Bradshaw."[55] A year earlier at Forbes Field, during one goal line stand by Dallas in a 42–27 victory, linebacker Jerry Tubbs had shrugged off a block by Bradshaw "with little more concern than if he were bumped by a fat lady in a bus" and tackled John Henry Johnson.[56] But on this Sunday Johnson wasn't carrying the ball, and he underscored his passion for blocking by knocking Tubbs "halfway to Lubbock." Sapp zipped through the hole, off right tackle, in a flash, pivoted to his left and ran a few steps laterally, and then darted to the left sideline. "Cutting downfield, behind Dan James and Mike Sandusky now, Sapp hurtled, wriggling free of Defensive Back Mike Gaechter and streaked by Don Bishop into the clear." Tubbs recovered, gave chase, and made a futile attempt at a tackle near the 5-yard line. "It was the greatest blocking I ever saw," Sapp said.[57]

And it was matched by an extraordinary individual effort. It was "a sprint in which he ran over four or five Cowboys and lurched past Tubbs for the winning touchdown, the one that could put Pittsburgh in line for a crack at the franchise's first championship in history."[58] Parker had made the perfect move weeks earlier when he picked up a running back whose nagging injuries had kept him from making the kind of run he did on this day. "I don't think there's a man in football who could have stopped him, once he got his momentum up," the coach said.[59]

Sapp was still getting requests for autographs and interviews fifty years after his game-winning touchdown against Georgia Tech. "There was more to my career than one play, you know," Sapp reminded a sportswriter once.[60]

Indeed. Georgia's drought had lasted only eight years. The Steelers' had lasted three decades. Not only did the touchdown in the Cotton Bowl end up being the lone one of Sapp's '63 season, but it was the last of his pro career. But it was a dandy, and he had every right to be reminded of that once in a while.

The Cowboys still had 1:53 left, but on first down from their 19 Thomas brought down Clarke after a catch at the 34 and then recovered the end's fumble. The Steelers killed the clock to preserve their 24–19 victory.

A familiar-sounding epitaph was being written that afternoon: "It started out like the National Football League success story of 1963 but it turned into a saga of frustration and heartbreak."[61] This time, it wasn't the Steelers but the Cleveland Browns whose obituary was written by United Press International. The Lions, in fourth place in the Western Conference, whipped the Browns, 38–10, denying Cleveland any shot at its first Eastern Division title since 1957 and handing the Browns their fourth defeat in the previous seven games, after a 6–0 start. The Steelers got the break they needed. The Browns and Cards were out. Pittsburgh would face the Giants the next week in a showdown for the Eastern Conference crown and a berth in the title game.

"This is for all the marbles," Giants coach Allie Sherman said.[62]

"We beat 'em the last two." Lou Cordileone said, pointing back to a 1962 victory before the shutout in week 2. "Now they gotta come get us."[63]

Linebacker Sam Huff didn't sound impressed with the upstarts. "If the Steelers can beat us twice in the same season, they deserve the championship," the linebacker said in the aftermath of New York's 44–14 rout of the Redskins. "If we can't beat Pittsburgh in one out of two games, we don't deserve the championship." Teammate Jack Stroud added, "Yer [sic] absolutely right, Sam."[64]

Now Parker's "ribald band of head-hunting youngsters" would face its greatest pressure test of all, and perhaps make NFL history.

GAME 14

Sitting in the rear of a jet while flying over New York City, playing cards with Bobby Layne, John Henry Johnson, and Ernie Stautner, Big Daddy Lipscomb looked out the window and mused, "New York, New York. Sum bitch is so big they had to name it twice."[1]

Any time they played Cleveland in 84,000-seat Municipal Stadium, on the shore of stormy Lake Erie—no matter what the records or standings—the Steelers annually faced bigger crowds and more hostile fans than they did in New York, as well as a greater threat of wicked weather. But the teams from the West and the East coasts were the ones that drew the attention and spawned the glitz.

Los Angeles had stars like Tom Fears, Elroy "Crazy Legs" Hirsch, and Bob Waterfield, who was himself married to a star of equal stature, the movie actress Jane Russell. "The Rams have always been a flamboyant team, perfectly attuned to rabid fans accustomed to getting their showiness in wholesale lots," wrote *New York Times* columnist Arthur Daley. "Maybe it's the Hollywood influence."[2]

New York had a half-dozen newspapers to publicize heroes like Kyle Rote, Sam Huff, and Rosey Grier, and a Hollywood image of its own in Frank Gifford, a native Californian who had his pick of work in TV, movies, and radio. Cleveland, Pittsburgh, and Detroit had soot, sweat, aching backs, and a Puritan work ethic—and don't forget the kielbasa—but little glamour.

Anytime a team went into New York, no matter how talented or successful, it could not deny that a radiance surrounded the city, as thick as smog. Some would resent it; others, at the least, might feel envy. With all the glitter, anyone could feel unnerved by the spell the city cast. Manhattan had the lights of Broadway; Pittsburgh had the glow of the open-hearth furnaces. New York had the most historic sports arena in the world—outside of the Coliseum in Rome; Pittsburgh had that "ancient rookery," Forbes Field, scorned by Giants coach Allie Sherman. "The place players wanted to go to was New York, where you got the ad money, and the television shows, and the extra income," Clendon Thomas said.[3] As the Steelers began preparing for perhaps the biggest game in the franchise's history, it would only be natural to ponder the TV and Hollywood image of the city as well as its football team, and its effect on opponents.

"I seem to recall a bit of intimidation going into Yankee Stadium," Frank Atkinson said. "I had the impression the guys on the Steelers really thought the Giants were lucky as hell. They're in New York City, they're in the media center. Everyone wanted to be a Ram or a Giant for the endorsements and ads and stuff like that, and they felt kind of screwed being in Pittsburgh. And I think that manifested itself somehow in a little intimidation factor going into Yankee Stadium."[4]

"That might have been him and me because we were rookies," Andy Russell said with a smile. "I don't think those old guys that played in the fifties like Ernie Stautner were intimidated by anyone."[5]

The Steelers had every right to feel confident about facing the Giants. Pittsburgh had monopolized the ball in week 2 with a meat-grinder running game that kept the Giants' offense on the sidelines. Even if Y. A. Tittle hadn't sat out the game, how much difference could he have made? "Tittle doesn't play defense, does he?" Ernie Stautner growled. "Well, we scored 31 points on New York the first time out. We'll do it again."[6]

Still, these were the New York Football Giants. From their names, they sounded like workers at a western Pennsylvania steel mill—Katcavage . . . Robustelli . . . Modzelewski—and the defense was "the envy of every defensive platoon in the league, not so much for its talent, but for the unique regard in which it is held by the New York fans."[7] In sports, when you mentioned New York, you always thought of the Yankees, the most successful, most glamorous team of all, and the one that shared the stadium with the Giants. Fame stoked the city, and stars from every industry rubbed shoulders with each other and fed off one another. "That's a showdown town," linebacker Sam Huff said. "They don't have to tell you it's showtime, because you live in New York, and it's Broadway. It's showtime."[8]

In New York, a soft-spoken, unassuming guy from Marshall, Texas, by the name of Yelberton Abraham Tittle could become a celebrity, even if he had about as much hair as Yul Brynner. Tittle posed in a two-page ad for a shirt manufacturer in *Sports Illustrated,* looking as tough as Ray Nitschke, even if he was wearing a crisp white shirt and tie. Dick Lynch posed in an ad for Vitalis, shunning "that greasy kid stuff." Alex Webster, with his son Jimmy, appeared in an ad, modeling suits. Charlie Conerly not only became the face of "the Marlboro Man" but endorsed a word game produced by *Sports Illustrated.* Huff endorsed an aftershave, and *Time* put him on a 1959 cover. CBS made a documentary titled *The Violent World of Sam Huff,* narrated by Walter Cronkite, the newsman who gave viewers the evening news and who had announced the death of President Kennedy to the nation. Channel 11 in Pittsburgh would carry the documentary *The Making of a Pro,* featuring Giant quarterback Glynn Griffing—only a rookie—on Sunday evening, hours after the Steelers-Giants game ended.

Maybe "intimidation" wasn't the right word. Maybe it was more a case of a bunch of outsiders not just having to beat a successful team, but having to prove to the sports world that they really belonged on the same field. Opponents of teams like Notre Dame, the Boston Celtics, and the Yankees battled preternatural forces as well as uniformed men. Winners exude a feeling of self-confidence and live for the opportunity to come through in the clutch, Layne said, and that kind of attitude could make unproven opponents who couldn't handle the pressure wilt. "It's kinda like the New York Yankees," he said. "Those guys win about 30% of their games because they got those pinstripe suits on."[9]

Ruth Daniel, the wife of defensive back Willie Daniel, had the same impression as Atkinson when recalling the Steelers' mind-set. "I remember that they were confident," she said, "but the fact that they were going to New York was a bit daunting, as the Giants enjoyed quite an aura in those days."[10]

Any team that felt a sense of entitlement just because it wore a certain uniform and was carrying on a tradition was vulnerable to a backlash of resentment. It wasn't necessarily envy that drove players, nor was it an inferiority complex. What fired them up was pride, a craving for respect.

But the Giants, undeniably, had a distinguished history. They were a lot more than flash and glimmer. They had put the pelts on the wall. They had not won an NFL championship since 1956, but they had made it to the title game four times in the previous five years, even if they lost all four games—twice to Johnny Unitas and the Colts, and in the past two years to Lombardi's Packers. The Giants hadn't won it all in a while, but they knew how to get to the championship game. And all their opponents knew it.

"The Giants have that attitude," Steeler offensive lineman Ron Stehouwer explained after the shutout of New York. "They act and think like champs. They overwhelm a lot of teams in this league with their buoyancy."[11]

Of all the players on Parker's squad, no one—aside from Stautner—was more immune to intimidation than Buzz Nutter. No one knew better than the tenth-year center what it took to play in a championship game, and no one knew better than him what it took to play the Giants on football's biggest stage—and beat them. Ed Brown and John Henry Johnson had played in title games, and Parker, as coach, had won three division titles and two championships with Detroit. But Nutter had played in what would come to be known as the greatest game ever played. Other players got a feel for greatness by playing with outstanding players. Nutter knew what it was like to line up with immortals. He had hiked the ball to Johnny Unitas, blocked for Lenny Moore, and held off red-dogging linebackers while Ray Berry caught passes.

Nutter grew up in Huntington, West Virginia; played at Virginia Tech; and was drafted by the Washington Redskins on the twelfth round. He was cut, so he spent a year working in a West Virginia steel mill and then won a spot with the Colts in 1954. He was the Colts' center on the afternoon of December 28, 1958, when Baltimore beat the Giants at Yankee Stadium in sudden death. "Nutter was the most outstanding offensive player on the field. He was playing like a man possessed," former Colts defensive tackle Art Donovan said when Nutter passed away in April 2008.[12] The Colts beat the Giants in Baltimore in a return match in '59. Two years later, Nutter came to Pittsburgh along with Big Daddy Lipscomb in a trade for Jimmy Orr.

So, when praise for the Giants blew into town as fiercely as the gusts at the Cotton Bowl days before, Nutter, for one, wasn't about to feel over-whelmed. "How in the world are a bunch of pore ol' mountaineers like us going to beat a team like that?" he said in a voice glazed with his West Virginia roots and packed with sarcasm. "They're the greatest team in the world, aren't they? They have the greatest quarterback, the greatest offen-sive line, the greatest defensive line, the greatest linebackers, the greatest receivers, the greatest secondary, the greatest kicker, the greatest coach."[13]

Those who had helped create and nurture the Giants' mystique were grous-ing about the possibility of an upstart 7–3–3 team unseating the 10–3 Giants with fewer victories than the defending Eastern Conference champs. If the Gi-ants lost, they would finish 10–4 (.714), with two more wins than Pittsburgh, yet the Steelers would finish first, with a better winning percentage at 8–3–3 (.727), because ties were not counted in figuring won-lost percentages; they were simply tossed out. (The Browns and Cards, officially eliminated, could both finish at 10–4 with a victory.) "The entire controversy revolves around the attitude of many New York sports writers," wrote Pat Livingston of the *Press* in midweek.[14] On Monday before the showdown, commissioner Pete Rozelle nimbly sidestepped the issue. He said that the method of computing the NFL standings could be brought up at the January league meetings "if any club is enough concerned to feel that it merits discussion."[15]

Rozelle himself hadn't given the issue "any thought," Livingston quoted the commissioner as saying. Rozelle added, "None of the owners have brought up or discussed such a change. It's been in use for 30 years and we've had similar situations twice before."[16]

In 1935, the Lions, with a rookie fullback on the team named Buddy Parker, won the Western Division with a 7–3–2 record, while the Packers went 8–4. In 1949, the Rams won the division with an 8–2–2 record compared to the Bears' 9–3 mark. "Nobody acted to change the rule after those years," Rozelle said.[17]

Jack Sell of the *Post-Gazette* pointed out that in 1932, the last year the NFL was composed of a single division, the Bears won the title with a 7–1–6 record and a winning percentage of .875, and the Packers finished second at 10–3–1.[18] (Chicago and the Portsmouth Spartans finished the regular season tied for first, each with a winning percentage of .857; the Bears at 6–1–6 and the Spartans at 6–1–4. The Bears beat Portsmouth in a playoff game.)

As nonchalant as Rozelle sounded about the issue, he seemed pleased that a neck-and-neck race was drawing publicity and attention to the NFL in its final week. Whether the novelty of the situation created a germ of an idea about wild-card races in the future, only Rozelle knew. "I think those ties made it pretty interesting," the commissioner said. "I think it's very interesting when a fourth-place team can jump into first place practically overnight, don't you?"[19]

Joe Williams of the Scripps Howard News Service thought that Rozelle's predecessor had more to do with the issue, though the guidelines had been in place years before. "I imagine this was Bert Bell's baby," Williams wrote. "In any case, it reflects the late commissioner's thinking on a commercially vital objective, namely, keep the race alive as long as possible. This purpose is served to a considerable extent by sweeping ties under the carpet."[20] (In 1972, the NFL changed the way it calculated winning percentages.)

The Steelers bristled at any suggestion that their claim on the Eastern Conference crown was sullied. "You mean that somebody thinks that even if we beat the Giants twice, they should still get the title?" said ex-Giant Lou Cordileone. "How ludicrous can you get?"[21]

The Steelers were still dealing with the skeptics who felt Pittsburgh's rout of the Giants wasn't legitimate because Tittle was held out of the game. *Post-Gazette* columnist Al Abrams ran into Huff at a gathering of college All-Americas in New York two days before the Steelers played in Dallas, and the Giants linebacker was full of swagger over the prospect of a rematch.

"There's no team in the league we'd rather meet than the Steelers," Huff told Abrams. "Tittle will be the difference. You guys murdered poor 'Goog' [Ralph Guglielmi] but it will be different with 'Yat.' Wait and see. You fellows make a big deal over that 31–0 score. If I remember right, it was 10–0 going into the last period. When the dykes opened you made 21 more points. That doesn't mean a thing. Wait and see."[22]

After he read the quotes in the newspaper, Cordileone couldn't wait to meet his former team again. "Who in the hell do they think they are?" he barked. "We'll show 'em they're nothing."[23]

Three months after the whitewash, the Steelers still resented any suggestion that they had only beaten the junior varsity quarterback. "I've heard a lot of people say that the score might have been different if Tittle had been in there," Buddy Parker said at Wednesday's practice.

Well, that's a lot of nonsense. The rush we put on that day would have been as harmful to Tittle as it was on Guglielmi.

We would have been in on top of Tittle, and no passer can be true when he has to hurry his throws, especially the long ones which can kill a team. . . . I think they know we intend to give Mr. Tittle one big, fat headache all afternoon. That's the only way to do it. Just don't give Tittle a chance.[24]

No one in the league had as impeccable a reputation for fair play, sportsmanship, and gentlemanly conduct—not to mention humility—as Art Rooney. On Saturday night, the eve of the game, Rooney stood among friends in the most popular bar in Manhattan—Toots Shor's, where the stars of all industries gathered—smoking a cigar, treating the crowd to drinks, and acknowledging the good wishes of admirers. He too was well aware of the carping over his team's number of victories compared to the Giants. "Well," he said, "if we beat them again tomorrow, how can anybody say they deserve the championship and we don't? Both clubs know that everything is at stake in this one game. There shouldn't be any excuses."[25]

The two teams took different approaches at practice that week. Parker stuck to his revised schedule of giving the players Monday and Tuesday off. The team seemed "relaxed and lighthearted" Wednesday as it practiced for an hour in two inches of snow, focusing on offense, and taking time to pose for photos with Ed Brown holding a snowball and drawing plays in the snow.[26] On Thursday, the team stressed defense as it worked out for about an hour and ten minutes in the South Park Fairgrounds.

The Giants, meanwhile, put in their longest day of the season Wednesday at Yankee Stadium, in meetings, watching film, and working on both offense and defense on the field, as if they were cramming for a test. Oddsmakers had made the Giants seven-point favorites, which only put more pressure on them, the Steelers felt.

"They're the defending champs," Ernie Stautner said. "They're on the spot."[27]

But the same kind of revenge that had driven the Steelers, smarting from a 45–7 loss, to battle the Lions in a no-holds-barred postseason exhibition the year before was chomping away at the Giants. Huff wanted to retaliate for his team's 31–0 embarrassment.

Huff grew up in a coal town—No. 9 coal mining camp—run by a mining company near Farmington, West Virginia, near the Pennsylvania border. He was raised in a house that his father rented from the company, a home with no running water and an outhouse for a toilet. Like Dick Haley and Lou Michaels, Huff was determined to escape a life submerged in hardship. His father wanted him to quit school at sixteen but, said Huff, "I didn't want to go in that coal mine. Coal mines and steel mills were tough living." Huff became the first member of his family to graduate from high school and went on to play for nearby West Virginia University. Butting heads with Jimmy Brown, Jim Taylor, and John Henry Johnson made for a tough living too, but it kept Huff out of the mines, and it fired up a passion for winning that hadn't cooled forty-five years later.[28]

"Let me tell you something," Huff said. "You beat me once, the next time we tee it up I'm going to knock your head off. You ain't ever gonna beat me again. You play the game like me and Modzelewski and Grier and Robustelli and Katcavage, and we tee it up again, by God, we're gonna see."[29]

To survive in the NFL, Huff discovered, you had to learn to be mean. "From the minute practice starts until the season ends, you make yourself mean," Huff told the journalist Jimmy Breslin. "The minute I come on the field, I say to myself, 'I'm gonna be the meanest guy on the field. I'm gonna give it to anybody I can get a shot at.' It gets easier to be mean every year and harder to get out of it at the end of the season. Pretty soon there's no in-between: you're mean all year round."[30]

No one could understand and respect that approach to the game better than Ernie Stautner, undersized at six foot two, 230 pounds, but a volcano of a defensive lineman. The 1963 season was Stautner's fourteenth as a pro, and though his age was listed as thirty-eight, some believed he was as old as forty-one. Skeptics had been saying for a few years that he was over the hill, and it was no different in July of 1963. If Stautner was going to make it through one final season, there was only one way to survive.

"I gotta be mean," Stautner said back in camp. "At my size, I can't afford to play any other way. . . . You're gonna see the meanest guy in the league this year." Stautner was routinely giving away twenty or thirty pounds or more to offensive tackles like the Browns' Dick Schafrath, the Giants' Jack Stroud, and the Packers' Bob Skoronski. "Unless I'm meaner than them, unless I can intimidate them, I'd have no chance in the world against them," Stautner said of his opponents.[31]

Ernie Stautner was born in Bavaria, on the edge of the Alps, and he was three when his father brought the family to upper New York State, where he started a farm. Andy Russell's father disapproved of his son playing pro football; Ernie Stautner's father disapproved of his son playing football at all, but the boy was determined to play. He commuted to a high school in Albany; swore his brother, sister, and friends to secrecy about his playing football; hid the newspaper when his name or photo appeared in the sports pages; and made excuses for the cuts and bruises he got from football. By the time Ernie earned all-star honors, his father had relented on his objections.

But people still kept telling Ernie Stautner he couldn't play. He enlisted in the Marines and served during World War II. After his discharge, he offered his services to Notre Dame. Not big enough, Frank Leahy told him. Stautner enrolled at Boston College, where he played for four years. Back in his home state, he approached the Giants. Too small for an NFL lineman, Steve Owen told him. "Man, that got my dander up," Stautner recalled years later. "I said, 'I want to tell you something. I'm big enough to play for your team or anybody's team. And you're going to regret it.'"[32] He sounded just like Buddy Dial several years later. Stautner and Dial were snubbed . . . Nutter cut . . . the Bears lost faith in Ed Brown—they all had something to prove, and at least Buddy Parker believed in them.

The second-round pick of the Steelers in the 1950 draft, Stautner was selected to the first of his nine Pro Bowls two years later. He earned those honors on guts and sheer desire.

"That man ain't human," Baltimore Colts tackle Jim Parker once said. "He's too strong to be human. He keeps coming, coming. Every time he comes back, he's coming harder."[33]

Stautner was symbolic of the Steeler way of playing defense. The Steelers had no intricate system on defense—nothing like Tom Landry was introducing to the Cowboys. Steeler assistant Buster Ramsey, coach of the defense, didn't like his unit to gamble. Parker wasn't much for razzle-dazzle; his teams came at you the same way Stautner did—relentlessly, with no letup.

"This is the toughest ball club physically that we'll ever play," Giant assistant Emlen Tunnell, a future Hall of Fame defensive back, said after returning from Dallas on a scouting mission. "They do nothing fancy. The defense is simple. But they hit, hit, hit."[34]

"That's their history," Allie Sherman said. "They play hard."[35]

For all the luster surrounding the Giants, the Steelers had something else on their side, an intangible that went completely against the grain of a team whose approach to football was to treat each game as a human demolition derby. It was romantic and fanciful and a little spooky. For anyone who wanted to believe that the football gods eventually rewarded the unsung, the workers with bloodied knuckles, scraped cheekbones, and unbowed hearts, the Steelers were a team of destiny.

"There is something eerie about them," sportswriter Joe Williams wrote. "They don't know when they are beaten. . . . They've got something going for them besides mundane mechanics. A sort of mysticism that defies analysis, makes assessment impossible. Ray (Buddy) Parker is not a coach, he's a voodoo doctor who burns candles to a heathen God, revered by his disciples as the 'last gasp.'"[36] Appropriately enough, the story ran in the *Press* on Friday the thirteenth, a hobgoblin of Parker's calendar.

Sherman, by contrast, was much like the former Giant assistant Landry—a human computer. "All week he has been working on blocking, tackling, timing, dull terrestrial commonplaces," Williams continued, "when he should have been reading tea leaves, attending spiritual séances, boning up on witchcraft."

The cast of the '63 Steelers was shaped by the touch of a wizard. Only some kind of sorcerer could compile such a motley grab bag of players and have them challenging for a conference title on the final Sunday of the season. A headline in the December 10 *New York Times* cast an epitaph for their year: "The Steelers: A Lot of Discards Seeking a Jackpot." *Times* reporter William Wallace counted nine starters on offense who had played for other teams, and six on defense. "There are no publicity heroes on this team, no television nor radio announcers, no product endorsers, just dangerous, hungry football players," Wallace wrote.

The Steelers were relatively healthy, but they had lost one vital cog in their defense: cornerback Brady Keys, who had suffered a season-ending injury to his chest when he collided with Jim Brown in November. Still, the defense had coped without him. Bobby Mitchell went wild against the Steelers in D.C., catching eleven passes, but the Eagles' Tommy McDonald was held to one catch, and Billy Howton had been shut out in Dallas. The Giants, however, presented a new set of problems.

The suspense in New York was over whether fullback Alex Webster would be ready after missing almost a month with a pulled thigh muscle. The Giants didn't have a rusher in the top ten. Phil King ranked eleventh and was averaging 3.6 yards a carry. Joe Morrison was averaging 4.8 yards but was tied for fourteenth place in the league. Morrison's value lay in his versatility: He could play flanker, halfback, fullback, tight end, even defensive back, and he could return punts and kicks. "He was the ultimate team player," said Wellington Mara, son of the team's founder, Tim Mara. "He would do anything you asked him."[37]

But that didn't seem like enough. "Without big Red [Webster] at his effective best, the Giants have little but the magic in the arm of the elderly Tittle," Arthur Daley wrote. Without a dependable ground game, the Giant attack "becomes a sporadic, hit-or-miss thing."[38]

Those who harped on Tittle's absence from the lineup in the second week forgot that the Steeler running game racked up 223 yards that day and held New York to just one offensive series in the first quarter. "Tittle still hasn't discovered the secret of throwing touchdown passes while the opposition has the ball," Daley wrote.

But what magic remained in that thirty-seven-year-old arm. Tittle ranked as the No. 1 quarterback, ahead of Johnny Unitas, going into the final Sunday, and he had thrown thirty-three touchdown passes and completed 59.8 percent of his throws. That week he was named most valuable player by the AP, "and people [were] coming at him with money in their fists."[39] Tittle also had the respect of opponents. He even drew the admiration of ex-Steeler defensive back Johnny Sample, who never stepped onto the field against a quarterback he couldn't criticize. "Y. A., I think, was everything you'd want in a smart quarterback," Sample said.[40]

Tittle had capable receivers in Joe Walton and Frank Gifford, but the man who put fear in teams was speedy Del Shofner. "I'd rather cover anyone [other] than Del Shofner," said Cardinal cornerback Jimmy Hill.[41] Two seasons before, as Philadelphia was preparing for a showdown with New

York for the Eastern title, Eagles defensive coach Jerry Williams commented, "Our main problem is stopping Del Shofner. . . . Shofner is the man we're afraid of."[42]

Pittsburgh had a comparable threat in Buddy Dial, who had caught only six fewer passes than Shofner, scored as many touchdowns (eight), and gained more yards receiving than anyone but Bobby Mitchell. But Ed Brown wasn't having the kind of year Y. A. Tittle was enjoying.

"Tittle is famous and in demand," the New York Times commented, while Brown was "the anonymous quarterback."[43] He had been on three Pro Bowl squads while with the Bears and had led them to a Western Conference title in 1956, when he was regarded as "the boy wonder of football."[44] They faced the Giants in the championship game and were thrashed, 47–7, and Brown was knocked out of the game in the fourth quarter with a concussion suffered when he was hit by defensive end Jim Katcavage. Days before the Steelers traveled to New York, Brown wondered, "I guess he's still there, isn't he?"[45]

Brown ranked sixth among NFL quarterbacks, but his completion percentage was a poor 47.1, thirteenth among the fifteen rated passers. He had thrown nineteen touchdown passes and had been intercepted seventeen times, four more than Tittle. His average gain per completion was almost identical to his counterpart's: 8.4 yards versus 8.3. But all that mattered in the final week of the regular season was that Brown had led the Steelers to a point where they could make history. The Steelers had watched as new heroes arose virtually each game. "But more than any other individual player, it has been the 'Question-Mark Quarterback' Ed Brown who has kept the hometown team in contention through eleven exciting weeks of football," Joseph V. Rieland had written two weeks earlier. And Brown did not lack for confidence. "There is no question in his own mind," wrote Pat Livingston during the preseason, "that he's the equal of Tittle."[46]

But Brown had not completed 50 percent of his passes in one game since October 20, against the Redskins. He had struggled over the past three games, during which he had completed only thirty-one of seventy-four passes (42%), thrown a total of five touchdowns and six interceptions, and gained 596 yards. No question, he was erratic, but the self-described "too phlegmatic" quarterback hadn't lost in the past three weeks either.[47]

Dial, for one, admitted that coming into the season, he had doubts about whether the Steelers could win without Layne. "I wondered if Brown would work out as well because he is quiet," Dial said. "But it's his quiet leadership that helps us and he is tremendous at throwing the right pass after spotting a hole. I'd have to say that Ed has been the main factor in our drive this season."[48]

A touchdown had been the widest margin of victory in the Steelers' previous five games, so the outcome of the Giants game loomed as a duel between Lou Michaels and Don Chandler, New York's punter and kicker. Sherman gave the edge to Chandler (nicknamed "Babe"), not because of Michaels's schizophrenic year, but because of the home field advantage, particularly in December.

"Yankee Stadium at this time of year is always full of winds, swirling winds," Sherman said. "They play havoc with a ball that's not kicked just right. But this is our home and Chandler is better acquainted with the wind conditions here than any other kicker in the league." Said Chandler: "Yankee Stadium is the toughest place for kickers in the league."[49]

Michaels was only twenty of thirty-eight on field goal attempts, but his misses, including his "oh-fer" against the Browns, had not lost a game for Pittsburgh. Chandler was sixteen of twenty-six. Both could connect from fifty yards. "When their toe explodes against the cadaver of a porker you can hear the ghostly groans of purgatorial agony in the farthermost reaches of the park," wrote Joe Williams.[50]

Touchdown passes from Tittle or Brown packed more excitement, "but in go-for-broke situations the kick can be as poisonous as a cobra cocktail, as suspenseful as a Fleming mystery." In ninety-one games over thirteen weeks of the '63 season, Williams calculated that a field goal was the difference in twenty-two games—seventeen victories and five ties.[51]

The wind was unpredictable, Chandler said, and was just as tough on a punter. He didn't mention that the wind was bound to be as rough on a passer as on a kicker or punter.

Weather was the other factor that could alter the course of the game. The forecast was for clear but very cold weather on Sunday, and Parker insisted that he preferred a dry, fast field, even though wet conditions might slow Tittle's passing game. "I can't agree with this talk that we'd be better off on a wet field," he said. "On a wet field, football becomes impossible. The defensive backs can't cover the receivers, the runners can't cut and you can't run anything but quick, straight-ahead plays."[52]

A tarp was placed on the Yankee Stadium field Wednesday night. It snowed Thursday morning, but the tarp protected the field, and the Giants were able to work out at 1:30 P.M. for an hour before the tarp was put back on.[53] Piles of snow lay on the perimeter of the field when the Steelers had a run-through on Saturday.

Most athletes, including professional football players, are creatures of habit whose lives run on routine and repetition; that's why Parker stuck to his practice of giving players two days off once he made the change after the Packer game. Players can be almost as superstitious about changes as Parker was—well, not quite. But one season-long Steeler routine was altered during the week before the Giant game.

The Steelers regularly gathered for get-togethers, a practice that Parker encouraged. Bobby Layne organized bowling nights on Mondays and hosted all-night card parties. Some Steelers drank together every week at a restaurant called Dante's, where Layne once held court. Brown, who enjoyed a cocktail every bit as much as Layne and Parker, was a regular, sipping Scotch on crushed ice with a dash of Drambuie. But on the Wednesday before the Giants game, as sportswriter and later, broadcaster, Myron Cope recounted, Brown was a no-show, evidently abstaining before the big game, leaving "his insides [as] dry as a temperance union president's."[54]

Lou Cordileone couldn't convince his roommate to go out.

> I said to Ed Brown, "Come on. We got to go out."
> "No, we can't. I got to be ready."
> "Eddie, yo, fuck, you can't change your routine the last game of the season. C'mon, let's go out. Let's fool around." Nobody went out. I don't think I went out one night. I said, "I'm not going to go out by myself. The hell with you guys."[55]

Cope, no stranger himself to the establishment, said of Brown, "It is not in his nature to lock himself in a room." Furthermore, Cope observed, Brown "contravened the very motto that had carried the Steelers to the brink of the title: 'Stay loose.'"[56]

Brown had his own premonition of how the game would unfold. "Ed was a good friend of mine," Cordileone said. "We're bullshitting the night before the game. We were in the [hotel] room, watching television, and people are coming around, like my family. It was so funny. Ed Brown said, 'Well, I'm going to tell you what's going to happen tomorrow. If we can take the kickoff and go down and Michaels kicks a field goal, we'll win the game. And if he misses the field goal, we're in trouble."[57]

Inside Toots Shor's on Saturday night, while temperatures fell into the mid-teens in Manhattan, Art Rooney was staying loose with the help of a crowd of friends and well-wishers. If sentiment could sway the outcome of the next day's game, the Steelers would have been a prohibitive favorite.

No one was admired and respected more around the NFL than the Steelers owner, and he was long overdue for a championship. "Good-Guy Rooney Deserves Winner," read the headline over one column, and it expressed a universal feeling. "He's still a kind, generous, thoughtful, God-fearing man whose honesty is almost painful," columnist Arthur Daley wrote. Even New York sportswriters found it difficult not to pull for the Steeler patriarch. "How can I root against Art Rooney in the big showdown?" a colleague of Daley's said.[58]

Rooney himself believed that he was on the cusp of ending three decades of frustration and disappointment. "Boys," he said, "I'd like to win this one. It's been a long, long time."[59]

The players stood to make another $5,000 or $6,000 with a berth in the title game, but they were aware of what Sunday's game meant to the Steelers owner. During Saturday's workout at Yankee Stadium, "The Steelers crackled with noisy confidence, tickled by the prospect of kicking the daylights out of all those New York players who pose for Madison Avenue's shirts ads."[60]

On Sunday morning, as he waited for the team bus outside the Belmont Plaza Hotel at Lexington Avenue and Forty-Ninth Street, Buddy Dial stood alongside the Reverend Robert Messenger, who had conducted some religious services for the Steelers during the year.

"You know something?" Dial said to Rev. Messenger. "I want to win this game more than any game I ever played in."

"Of course," Rev. Messenger replied. "It would be a great thing if you could beat the Giants in their own backyard."

"No, not that," Dial said. "I want to win this game just for Mr. Rooney's sake. I'd give all the money I'll make if we win just for the satisfaction of bringing it in for Mr. Rooney. That's what I think of him. Sure, we want this game, but I'll bet that deep in our hearts, none of us want it as bad as he does."[61]

The Steelers were in trouble as soon as they stepped on the field for warm-ups. The turf that had been in such good condition two days earlier had changed overnight. "Yankee Stadium was an ice pond," Clendon Thomas recalled. "It had low spots that had, literally, ice spots in them. Little ponds of ice. It was just atrocious. You couldn't stand up. . . . We didn't have the right shoes. We had left our 'ice shoes' in Pittsburgh. It's like some epoxy on tennis shoes that will let you run on it. It was like 18 degrees. It was somewhere between dry ground and a slick spot, and, of course, those guys are smart. They'll take you down to a slick spot and turn, and down you go."[62]

The Giants had experience playing in frigid conditions. They'd lost the title game to the Packers the year before at Yankee Stadium amid "fierce" winds and a frozen field that Paul Hornung and Jim Taylor said made it "impossible" to cut back on runs. In the heated press box that day, it was still cold enough to freeze the manual typewriters. Despite the unsure footing, Taylor was one among many players who wore regular football cleats.[63]

The Steelers had adjusted to winter conditions before, too. For a mid-December game in Chicago in 1959, Bobby Layne wore black high-top basketball shoes, and Tom Tracy wore sneakers, too, as did some Bears players. The year before, on the eve of the season finale at home against the Cardinals, coach Frank "Pop" Ivy paid a visit to Pitt Stadium where the caretaker of the field, Leo "Horse" Czarnecki, had his crew "attack ice and snow bumps with a sweeper, picks and a blowtorch" to thaw out icy spots on the field. Ivy despaired that the Cards would never be able to stop Layne on that field, and he was right. Layne threw for a team record 409 yards in a 38–21 Steeler victory.[64]

In the battle for the Eastern crown, some Giants stuck to football cleats. Tittle wore his high-tops; Huff, a pair of Riddells; and Erich Barnes, a pair of Spot-Bilt cleats. Others, like Shofner, King, and Jerry Hillebrand, wore white sneakers. Gifford wore low-cut black ones.

"It had gotten cold real quick, and the field was very rough and frozen in spots," Dick Haley said. "I can still remember we had fires built on the sidelines to try to keep warm. We didn't have the equipment we should have had. We wore regular football shoes. It was very difficult to maintain your footing and to make quick cuts."[65]

The day after the game, Fran Fogarty, the Steelers' business manager, said the team had bought sixty pairs of sneakers in August and routinely brought them to away games. "We kept them in a big box on the sidelines, and anyone could change who wanted to do so," Fogarty said.[66]

"There could have been," Russell said, "but they weren't offered to us."[67]

The temperature an hour before the 2:05 P.M. kickoff was 29 degrees, and there were 25 mph gusts of wind, creating a wicked wind chill.[68]

The Giants kicked off before a capacity crowd of 63,240. On the first play from scrimmage, Theron Sapp fumbled after being hit by end Andy Robustelli, and safety Jim Patton recovered for the Giants on the 25. Michaels was struggling with his kicking, but it didn't affect his defensive play. He dumped Tittle for a 6-yard loss on first down, and after an incompletion on third down, Chandler kicked a 34-yard field goal. It was an ominous start, but "This didn't bother us," Parker said later.[69]

Gary Ballman finally broke loose again, taking the kickoff on his 14 and racing 57 yards to the Giant 29. John Henry Johnson gained 6 yards over right guard, but Brown threw incomplete to Ballman on third-and-4. Michaels lined up for a 30-yard field goal attempt, the scenario Brown had imagined the night before while talking with Cordileone. The kick veered wide right.

Hanging onto the ball was bound to be a problem in the icy conditions. On the second play from scrimmage after Michaels's miss, Morrison fumbled and Clendon Thomas recovered at the 33. Katcavage broke through on first down to sack Brown and dislodge the ball, but Mike Sandusky fell on it for a 5-yard loss. After Sapp regained the 5 yards, Brown connected with Ballman, streaking toward the end zone. He had only Dick Lynch to beat, but the ball squirted out from inside Ballman's right elbow near the goal line and was recovered by Barnes in the end zone and returned to the 34. Ballman was a step away from a touchdown, it appeared, but the score would have been disallowed because of a holding call on the Steelers.

Still, the Steelers had squandered another opportunity. A holding call would have taken them out of field goal territory, but even if they had to punt, a good kick could have pinned New York inside the 10.

Instead, Tittle went to work. King gained 12 yards on a draw, and Aaron Thomas caught a 16-yard pass to put the Giants at the Steeler 41. Earlier, cornerback Willie Daniel had broken up a short sideline pass to Shofner. Mindful of the scouting report that Daniel played that route tight, Tittle had Shofner make the same quick cut to suck Daniel in and then streak down the sideline. Shofner, getting good traction from his sneakers, made a Willie Mays–like over-the-shoulder catch for a 41-yard touchdown. Chandler, the so-called master of the home elements, saw his kick glance off the left upright, à la Michaels, giving New York a 9–0 lead 7:12 into the game.[70]

On second-and-3 from his 38, Johnson ran 14 yards up the middle to put the Steelers on the Giant 48. Brown fired deep for Dial, but Lynch intercepted at the 5-yard line and returned the ball to his own 44. So far, Ed Brown was doing a better job as a prophet than as an NFL passer.

Tittle fumbled on the next play—the fifth time a player mishandled a ball in the quarter—but center Greg Larson recovered for a 13-yard loss. Tittle mixed in runs with passes—25 yards to Shofner on third-and-24, 18 yards to Thomas, a screen to Morrison for 7. King ran up the middle for 3 yards to give the Giants first-and-goal at the 5. Now it was New York's turn to waste a scoring opportunity. After the Giants were penalized 15 yards for pushing, Andy Russell picked off a pass at the 2-yard line as the first quarter wound down.

After the teams exchanged punts at the start of the second quarter, the Steelers reached midfield but had to punt again after Brown once more threw incomplete to Ballman on third down. Pittsburgh got a break when Eddie Dove fumbled Brown's punt, and Art Anderson recovered for the Steelers at the Giant 24.

Sapp gained a yard, and Ballman caught an 8-yard pass, but on third-and-1 John Henry Johnson was stopped for no gain. All season, Parker had faced fourth-and-short decisions. After Dick Hoak was dropped for a four-yard loss from the Redskin 2 on fourth-and-goal back in October, the Steelers coach declared, "You can bet your life I'm not going to get down that close again and come away with nothing."[71] So, on fourth down with a berth in the NFL title at stake, Parker passed up a field goal try and went for the first down. "We only had about a foot or so to go," Parker said later.[72] Sapp got the call over left tackle, and he was stopped by Robustelli and John LoVetere. The Steelers came away with nothing.

Pittsburgh forced a punt and took over on its 38. Dial caught an 11-yard pass, and Johnson and Sapp ground out yardage to the Giant 37 before Brown threw two more incompletions Ballman's way—sandwiched around a fumble by Johnson that Sandusky recovered. Patton had an interception but dropped the second throw. Michaels lined up for a 42-yard field goal attempt, but rookie quarterback Bill Nelsen, who had taken over as the holder a week earlier, fumbled the snap. New York took over on its 42.

"It looked to spectators that day as if the Steelers were thoroughly bewitched, for they either dropped the ball or gave it away again and again," wrote Robert Smith.[73]

Tittle had a little over two minutes left in the half. He hit Shofner with a 44-yard pass down to the Pittsburgh 14, but the ace receiver was injured on the play. Morrison gained 6 yards on a draw, and King picked up 5 to make it first-and-goal at the 3. The *Press's* Pat Livingston described Morrison as "a lumbering 195-pound back who never before had been anything but a minor annoyance to the Steelers."[74] On this day, he was becoming a major pain.

Tittle faked a handoff to King and tossed a pass to an open Morrison in the end zone. The Giants had a 16–0 lead with just 1:13 left in the half, a margin that could have been cut if the Steelers hadn't blown two shots at field goals and failed to capitalize on two other chances.

Brown got his team moving after Chandler's kickoff. He hit Dial for 25 yards down to the Giant 37 and then, out of the shotgun, hooked up with Carpenter for 8 more. Sapp ran around right end for 9 yards to give the Steelers a first down at the 20 with forty seconds left.

A lot of war stories were passed down to young Steelers over the years. As a rookie in '68, Rocky Bleier heard many of the tales, and Cope's account, suggested that because of Brown's abstinence from liquor the week leading up to the Giant game, "his system couldn't take the shock," in Bleier's words. "By kickoff, his hands were shaking visibly and he was feeling slightly irritable."[75]

"I think Brownie was a little nervous," Cordileone said. "I guess the game weighed on his mind a lot. He wanted to win it so bad."[76]

Despite having played eight years in Chicago, Brown, a native of California, hadn't seemed to adjust to playing in wintry conditions. At a practice at Yankee Stadium, Cordileone and Myron Pottios were photographed laughing as they pranced over the snow on the sidelines. Days earlier, Brown was photographed at practice in Pittsburgh as he held a snowball in his palm, surrounded by grinning teammates Hoak, Sapp, and Johnson. Brown was not smiling; he looked rueful at best. He hadn't been able to adjust to the elements. In its 1958 pro football preview, *Sports Illustrated* suggested that if the Bears could schedule games at the end of the season in California, where Brown played in high school and college, he might just lead the NFL in passing. "He has the arm and the eye but an inexplicable inability to coordinate the two when the weather turns cold," the report read.[77]

Whether it was nerves, the weather, or the time away from Dante's, Brown was having a rough go of it. From the 20, he tried three straight passes and misfired on all three. Twice he had receivers wide open for touchdowns but underthrew them, including a play on which Ballman had 5 yards on Lynch, the league leader in interceptions in both '63 and '61, at the goal line.

Brown had an arm powerful enough to counteract the wind and frigid conditions. "I'll tell you what," Cordileone said. "He threw a football, forget it. He'd throw it through your body."[78]

Brady Keys agreed. "Nobody could ever catch his balls," the defensive back said. "He threw the ball too hard. Only Buddy Dial could catch his balls."[79]

But the throw to Ballman nose-dived weakly into the frozen turf. Michaels kicked a 27-yard field goal with seven seconds left before halftime to cut Pittsburgh's deficit to 16–3.

The Steelers' offensive line was providing great protection, but "this had to be the overdue off-day that Ed Brown had coming to him," Robert Smith wrote. "He would throw to Gary [Ballman] and miss him by ten feet. Or he would ignore Gary running all alone and try to jam the ball through a trio of defenders."[80]

The score should have been closer. The Steelers had squandered scoring chances and made mistakes, but they didn't seem in awe of the two-time defending conference champs. "With wonderful protection for an inaccurate passer, a defensive line that savaged Y. A. Tittle, stout runners and receivers in the open, the Steelers seemed the clearly superior force in the first half," Red Smith wrote.[81]

The second half began "with the Steelers still hoping Destiny would throw down the thread."[82] The Giants received the kickoff but were forced to punt, and Pittsburgh took over on its 33. On third-and-1 from the 42, the Giants bunched together and braced for Johnson to ram the line or soar above it. Instead, he burst through the right side for a 48-yard run before Lynch dragged him down at the 10. A holding penalty on Johnson set the Steelers back, but on third down from the 21, Ballman beat Patton in the right corner for a touchdown to bring the Steelers within 16–10 with 4:16 elapsed in the third period. Thanks to Chandler's missed conversion, the Steelers could snatch the lead with one scoring drive.

The Giants had the ball; the Steelers had a defense that looked as if it was going to make a critical stand and give the offense good field position. Tittle had lost his most dangerous weapon, Shofner, who did not return to action in the second half. Sherman could feel the game shifting as abruptly as a gust of wind changed direction in Yankee Stadium. "I was most fearful in the third quarter," the Giant coach said later. "The Steelers were beginning to gain momentum."[83]

On first down from the Giant 21, Cordileone and Stautner hurried Tittle into an incompletion. King fought for 2 yards, leaving the Giants with third-and-8 at the 23. Stautner walked along the line, "slapping his teammates on the butt" as "wintry smoke poured out through the bars of his face mask." Chandler would average 43.6 yards on his five punts that day, so, depending on the wind, a good return would leave the Steelers close to midfield, putting the Giants literally on a slippery slope.[84]

"The worst of it," Sherman said, "was that they were driving toward the infield part of the gridiron where the underfooting was the worst and where pass coverage was tough. Then it happened."[85]

"It" had happened before—three weeks earlier, in fact. On that day, Pittsburgh had the Bears bottled up deep in their own territory, facing third down, when Mike Ditka came up with his thunderous catch and run. On a mid-December day in the Bronx, a third-down play would turn out to be no less miraculous.

The play was simple enough. Gifford, flanked on the right side, would run a post pattern—sprint straight ahead and then cut diagonally across the field—with Glenn Glass, the second-year defensive back, covering him. Both were wearing sneakers.

"Frank Gifford was 'a Sunday ballplayer,'" Tittle said four decades later. "He was a gamer. He didn't look flashy with the long runs, but the big plays, the times you needed something big, you go to Frank Gifford and you'd probably get success. That's what Frank was noted for: come through in the clutch."[86]

Glass was another pickup of Parker's. Parker's assistant, Buster Ramsey, had been on the staff of the Buffalo Bills and, while there, he pushed to select Glass, who had played tailback in the single wing at Tennessee, in the 1962 AFL draft. But frustrated at being stuck on the sidelines after an injury, Glass wanted out of Buffalo, so the Steelers, with Ramsey having joined their staff, traded with the Bears for the rights to sign him. Glass played defense in college, but it hadn't been much of a challenge for him, the way the college game focused on the running game in that era. "I was a safety man," he said, "but you know what that means: You just stand around in the middle of the field."[87]

The Steeler pass rush was pouring in on Tittle, but he managed "a clumsy sidearm toss." As Gifford streaked across the middle, the throw looked like one of Brown's passes: it would likely reach Gifford on a bounce. "I shouldn't have even thrown the ball," Tittle said.[88]

Russell, the left linebacker, had dropped back in pass coverage and, out of the corner of his eye, saw Gifford cutting across the field. Russell blamed himself for "a huge mistake," but he was only following the conventional defensive wisdom: drop back, watch the quarterback's eyes, and react to the ball. "Bullshit," Russell said forty-seven years later. "You can't do that, and I learned that the hard way in that game. Pro quarterbacks are too good, they're too quick, and they throw the ball too fast."[89]

Russell had made his third interception of the year that day, and he would get 15 more before he retired, but none of them by using that technique. "What I would do in the future," he said, "I'd just go cover him. I'd be all over Frank Gifford. I wouldn't even look at the quarterback. Anybody in your zone, you cover man to man. If I'd have covered Frank Gifford, he would not have caught that pass. From that point forward, I didn't play zone defense the way we were taught. I played it my way. And from that point forward nobody caught the ball in my zone—rarely."[90]

Gifford, with a step on Glass, "lunged and shot out his right hand like he was picking up the morning paper."[91] The ball "hit into his hand nose-first and snuggled there like a baseball."[92]

Dick Haley had a perfect view from his safety position. "I've seen that picture so many different places over the years," he said. "I was playing over the top of that and the corner was underneath, and the ball was thrown low and Gifford reached down, one hand—he's running full speed—and the ball stuck. The weather, the conditions, everything was terrible, and he had to do it with a ball that's half frozen and a field that's half frozen, with the wind blowing, and I said, 'You can't do that one out of ten times,' and yet that was the one time. It could have been one in how many, I don't know."[93]

More like, as Tittle said, "The odds of Frank catching it were about a thousand to one."[94]

"It was the biggest catch I ever made," Gifford said. "All I was trying to do was bat the ball up in the air and it stuck in my hand."[95]

Glass was close enough to Gifford that he had a handful of the flanker's jersey in his right hand while Gifford was still trying to gain control of the ball and grasp it with both hands. Glass dragged Gifford down at the Steeler 47—close to where Pittsburgh could have taken possession on an incompletion and a good punt return—for a gain of 30 yards. Tittle went right back to Gifford, this time for 25 yards to the 22. On the next play, as Gifford ran his post pattern again, Tittle hit Morrison out of the backfield, and he outran linebacker Myron Pottios to the end zone to make it 23–10 with 6:11 seconds gone in the third period.

There were still nearly twenty-four minutes of football left, time for the Steelers to score two touchdowns and pull off another comeback, but the sudden twist of fortune felt like a knockout blow. "You could feel everybody on the bench lift up with a now-we-got-'em emotional surge," said the scout Tunnell.[96]

"Gifford turned the game around," Parker said later. "If he doesn't hold that ball, we take over, and I think we would have won. Give the credit to Gifford. I thought we would win it with one of our late rallies until Gifford made that catch. It was a great play, the turning point."[97]

"We were a team that could have our back broken," Art Rooney Jr. said, "and that was the play that did it."[98]

The Giants got the ball right back, after Barnes broke up a pass intended for Ballman on third-and-2 from the Steeler 35. Tittle hit Aaron Thomas with a 31-yard pass, and an unsportsmanlike conduct call on Pittsburgh advanced the ball to the visitors' 15. A 14-yard throw to Gifford put the Giants on the 1, and Morrison plunged in for his third touchdown to make it 30–10 with 5:50 left in the quarter but no magic left in the Steelers' season. There would be no Ballman kickoff return to save them, no bomb to Red Mack to rescue them, no Dick Haley interception to pull the game out.

The Steelers reached the Giant 25, but Barnes intercepted Brown. Pittsburgh got the ball back, and with half a minute left in the quarter Brown hit Dial with a 40-yard TD pass to make it 30–17. Michaels and Chandler each missed field goal attempts in the fourth quarter, but Chandler connected from 41 yards with 2:25 left in the game to make the final Giants 33, Steelers 17. The Giants were headed to Wrigley Field to play the Bears for the NFL championship. The Steelers were about to tumble into fourth place at 7–4–3, with Cleveland in second place at 10–4, and St. Louis third at 9–5. It was an inglorious finish to a season that had sparkled with hints of destiny, a tease that Steeler history was about to be rewritten. And there were a few more insults to endure.

"The Steelers looked like a consignment of rusted corrugated iron roofing in their big chance for their first sectional title," Harold Rosenthal wrote for the *New York Herald Tribune*. "Their reputed hard noses were rubbed vigorously into the semifrozen turf, their vaunted ball control was a hollow mockery."[99]

The truth was, the Steelers weren't manhandled. Even Rosenthal conceded that Johnson "was a terror in the rushing department," totaling a game-high 104 yards. Tittle had a game worthy of an MVP, but the Steelers had sabotaged themselves. Michaels missed an early field goal, and a muffed hold cost Pittsburgh another attempt. Ballman's fumble cost the Steelers an opportunity. Pittsburgh could have gotten a field goal instead of running Sapp on fourth-and-1. Prime chances, no points. And, of course, there was Gifford, who had made the greatest one-handed catch in Yankee Stadium since Brooklyn's Sandy Amorós in the 1955 World Series. "Gifford was the guy who killed us," Parker said.[100]

But the player who bore the role of goat was Ed Brown. As tough as Tittle was on the Steeler secondary, the Giant defensive backs got a big break because of Brown's scattershot throws. "Ballman would have had five touchdowns if Brown had been able to hit him," Parker said.[101]

Parker would rue his decision to force the best field general he ever had into retirement. "I have no doubt we would have beaten the Giants with Layne at quarterback that day," he reflected later. "Ed Brown was never the leader Layne was, and that's what we needed that day—a leader."[102]

Ernie Stautner was so angry with Brown in the locker room that he was ready to take a poke at the quarterback. "I might have, except I was too tired," he said.[103]

If ever a team needed to win just one game, Layne had earned the reputation as the guy who could do it. "I don't know if Bobby would have made that great a difference on the season as a whole, but once we got to that final game, Layne would have been the difference between us winning and losing," Art Rooney told Ray Didinger years later, after the Steelers won their first Super Bowl. "A game like that, with everything riding on one roll of the dice, was Bobby's meat," Stautner reflected more than a decade later.[104]

Huff was right: The difference was Tittle. It wasn't just a case of Brown losing his touch; "many of his throws were so far off target as to appear ludicrous," wrote Tex Maule.[105]

"I think maybe the pressure got to the guy more than anything else," Art Rooney Jr. said. "Brown was a real good football player. He was not a great player. I don't think he had the confidence in himself."[106]

The Giants didn't miss Webster, but the Steelers could have used Brady Keys. "When we played the Giants I could always hold Del Shofner," Keys said. "He never scored on me. That was the difference in the game."[107]

"That's a lucky football team," Lou Michaels fumed in the locker room. "That's the story of their lives—L-U-C-K."[108]

And, of course, it wasn't the story of the Steelers. Their lot was the saga of a snake bitten team. Four years earlier, Jack Butler, who would finish his career as a Steeler defensive back with fifty-two interceptions, sustained a career-ending knee injury late in the season. As he lay in his bed at Mercy Hospital, he reflected, "Buddy Parker says you have to be lucky in this league. He's so right."[109]

The disappointment from that day would ease for some of the players who went on to play in championship games, but some of the dismay lingered over a lifetime. "I felt we were going to win the whole thing," Red Mack said. "I truly did. After all these years, I look back and say, 'I just can't imagine that we lost that game.'"[110]

There was plenty of room for analyzing and second-guessing. "You can hunt excuses," Clendon Thomas said forty-five years later. "Here I am talking about it at my age and remembering. You can't help but what-if yourself. What if we'd brought our ice shoes. What if we'd not had Brady hurt."[111]

Anyone could have gone back to the start of the season and started wondering. What if John Henry Johnson hadn't hurt his ankle and had been available to bust the Browns' goal line stands in Cleveland? What if the Steelers had been able to keep Charley Johnson from snatching away a victory in the final seconds in St. Louis? And if Lou Michaels hadn't hit a crooked upright on a point-after in the opener? If John Reger had been able to hang on to Bill Wade's mistake of a pass in the final minute, two days after the Kennedy assassination? And what if Gifford . . . ?

Buddy Parker had his own theory. He might have had regrets about not keeping Layne on the squad, but the team had gone into the season with a loss he felt was too hard to overcome. "One man cost us that championship. Big Daddy Lipscomb," Parker said three years later. "With Lipscomb, there is no doubt we would have won another game or two."[112]

Could the 1963 Steelers actually have gone 11–2–1 or 10–2–2 instead of 7–4–3? Or even 12–2? It would have taken a few breaks, but with a couple, Pittsburgh and Art Rooney wouldn't have had to wait another eleven seasons to get a shot at the franchise's first championship. But this was not the Steelers' day for even a tidbit of luck. Some aspects of the game can be defined with scientific precision, Timothy Gay demonstrates in *The Physics of Football,* but Gay is also well aware of one incontrovertible, inexplicable truth about football, which former Minnesota Vikings coach Bud Grant duly noted: "There are coaches who spend 18 hours a day coaching the perfect game and they lose because the ball is oval and they can't control the bounce."[113]

After the final gun, there was little from which the Steelers could draw consolation. "I feel kinda crushed," Dial told Rooney after the game. "I never felt so confident of winning a game in my life. I thought we had it."

"So did I," Rooney replied. "So did I."[114]

Two days later, George Halas, "a stubborn old codger," was named coach of the year by United Press International, drawing twenty-five of the forty-two votes cast. Parker and Wally Lemm of the Cardinals each got six votes. Halas's Bears and the Packers each placed six players on the first team of the '63 all-NFL selections, offense and defense, as voted by UPI and AP. The Giants had five players named to the squad; the Cardinals had two. The Steelers had none. What they had were a seldom-used halfback picked up in midseason, a rookie starting at linebacker and another playing regularly at defensive tackle, a cornerback who went undrafted and made the team after asking for a tryout, a defensive tackle unloaded by three other teams, and a bunch of other players nobody wanted and nobody believed in—a group that Parker assembled like a mad scientist and had battling for a berth in the NFL Championship Game right up until the final period on the final Sunday of the regular season.[115]

The Browns earned a berth in the Runner-Up Bowl against the 11–2–1 Packers, who finished second to the 11–1–2 Bears in the Western Conference. That was probably best for the Steelers. Another postseason exhibition would do nothing to ease the crush of falling short of the championship game—again. In a final bit of irony and a nod to the quirks of the system, the Cardinals, at 9–5, with one more loss than Pittsburgh, finished in third place by a few percentage points: .643 to .636. It's doubtful any Steelers noticed, let alone complained, the way some New York observers did when the Steelers were a threat to win the conference with fewer victories than the Giants.

The atmosphere on the flight back from New York to Pittsburgh was appropriately funereal. All flights are somber after a loss, but on this one, something really had died: the dream of a championship. Rooney sat slouched in a front seat. "We could have won it," he said repeatedly.[116]

A sequence of four photos on the front page of Monday morning's *Post-Gazette* showed the Giants' Barnes recovering the fumble Ballman lost in the end zone, then eluding Carpenter on the return. "You know Gary never forgot that?" Carpenter said forty-four years later.[117]

Surely only historians and the most diehard of fans would remember years later—or for merely weeks afterward. Any casual fan glancing through a press guide or a record book in the future would look at the 1963 standings and never imagine that this fourth-place team had stuffed Jimmy Brown in the end zone; come from behind to beat the Cardinals, Redskins, and Cowboys; slugged out a standstill with the eventual world champion Bears; and then let a conference title slip away, just like the ball that squirted out of Ballman's arms. The names on the Steeler roster may not have gotten the publicity that the Giant players enjoyed, but it could boast "an oldster or two who needed only to have the light turned his way to make people realize he had been a star for a long time"—players like Joe Krupa, Preston Carpenter, and Buzz Nutter.[118]

On Monday morning, the *Post-Gazette*'s banner headline, in all caps, read: "GIANTS END STEELER HOPES, 33–17." The italicized banner head at the very top of the page, above the *Post-Gazette*'s flag, was directed at another page 1 story. The headline read: "2 Below Zero Is Predicted for Today."

It looked as though it was going to be a long, cold winter in Pittsburgh.

EPILOGUE

The two teams that had battled for a berth in the NFL title game on the last Sunday of the '63 regular season seemed destined for another showdown the following year. Indeed, it came to pass, and in Yankee Stadium again. Only this time the game that took place on the first anniversary of the Kennedy assassination, and the battle between the Steelers and Giants, wasn't for first place in the Eastern Conference—it was to avoid last place.

The Giants were in the cellar, with a 2–6–2 record and, with a win, could drop the 3–7 Steelers into last place. Pittsburgh romped, 44–17. They had beaten the Giants, 27–24, in the second week, a game that produced an iconic photo in NFL history. Defensive end John Baker barreled into Y. A. Tittle, leaving him kneeling, dazed, and bloodied in the end zone. Yat's helmet was knocked off, and he was lucky his head wasn't, too. The image was immortalized by *Post-Gazette* photographer Morris Berman. Tittle retired at the end of the season. Big John Baker played his last season with the Steelers in 1967 and then spent a year with the Lions before returning to his hometown of Raleigh, North Carolina, where he served as sheriff for twenty-four years. He died at age seventy-two on October 31, 2007.

Buddy Parker's team was on its way to a 5–9 record with a new cast. The highlight of their year came in Cleveland on October 10, a Saturday night, when John Henry Johnson jitterbugged for 200 yards in a 23–7 win over the eventual NFL champs. It must have turned into another sad night for the "Gang at Sophie's Café." The victory gave Pittsburgh a 3–2 record, but the Steelers went on to lose their next five games, during which their proud defense gave up at least thirty points each week, before the rout of the Giants.

If there is a day that officially marked the team's descent back to the Steeler Ice Age of the thirties and forties, it was probably October 18, 1964, the afternoon of a 30–10 loss in Minnesota that started the slide. The team would not win more than five games in a season until 1971, Chuck Noll's third year. It would then take three more seasons—a total of six—for Noll to accomplish what Parker was confident he could do in five: bring Pittsburgh and the Rooneys an NFL title.

Cleveland, at 10–3–1, edged out 9–3–2 St. Louis for the Eastern Conference title in 1964 and routed Baltimore in the championship game, 27–0. The Bears had nearly as bad a fall as the Giants that year but avoided last place, with a 5–9 record.

The Steeler lineup that had challenged for the Eastern Conference title the year before unraveled quickly. This time Parker's moves did not pan out; they backfired with a vengeance. The Buddy Dial trade blew up, and first-round draft pick Paul Martha proved to be no replacement for the sure-handed Texan. Myron Pottios was injured in the preseason. In the aftermath of his tussle with Lou Michaels, Red Mack was dealt to Philadelphia, returned to Pittsburgh in '65, and in '66 became a member of the Packers during their Super Bowl I season.

Michaels's status was as shaky as Mack's. When Parker obtained kicker Mike Clark in a trade with Philadelphia, Michaels grew upset over ribbing about the deal, and KO'd teammate Jim Bradshaw. Michaels was suspended and then traded to Baltimore, and he would gain lasting notoriety for a confrontation with Joe Namath at a bar on the eve of Super Bowl III. "He stood there and he pointed to me," Michaels recalled, "and he said, 'We're going to kick the s-h-i-t out of you, and I'm going to do it.'" Namath taunted Michaels and poked fun at the Colts and Johnny Unitas. Michaels seethed, but no one was KO'd, and they parted amicably.[1]

The '63 season was the last in Pittsburgh for Frank Atkinson, Preston Carpenter, Glenn Glass, Lou Cordileone, and John Reger. Carpenter played two years with the Redskins, another with the Vikings, and one more with the Dolphins. "As long as I was playing football I didn't care where I went," he said.[2] Reger played for the Redskins for three more years as a teammate of Sam Huff.

Cordileone was out of football for a few seasons, then came back to play for two years for the Saints. He took a shot—a brief one—at the career as a mortician he had envisioned once his playing days ended. "I went to school for about a week," he recalled. "I said, 'You know what? I can't do this.'"[3] He found something more to his liking: owning a bar in the French

Quarter called the Huddle, where he installed two barber chairs instead of stools at one end of the bar. "I just thought they'd be more comfortable," he said.[4] It was there that Cordileone got as close as he could to landing in a championship game as a Steeler. When the Steelers made it to Super Bowl IX, their first title game, held at the Superdome, the former defensive tackle was there as saloonkeeper, greeting friends and fans from Pittsburgh in town for the game. He eventually moved to California.

Thomas's all-around skills helped the Steelers in '64 when injuries reduced their receiving corps. The former Oklahoma Sooner switched over to wide receiver and caught forty-two passes over two seasons before returning to safety. He retired after the '68 season.

When George Allen left the Bears to become head coach of the Rams after the '65 season, he obtained Pottios, and the linebacker played there through 1970. When Allen took over the Redskins for the '71 season, he brought over Pottios as part of the "Over-the-Hill Gang," which went to the Super Bowl in the next season and lost to the unbeaten Miami Dolphins. Pottios, who'd grown up in Charleroi, Pennsylvania, in the same county as Haley, retired after the '73 season.

Brady Keys concluded his eight-year NFL career with a half season in Minnesota and a final one with the Cardinals. Before leaving the Steelers, he embarked on an entrepreneurial career, beginning with his All Pro Fried Chicken franchises. "I want to be a model for black people who want to go into business for themselves," Keys said in a 1969 interview.[5]

Theron Sapp played two more seasons with the Steelers before retiring. He too went into the fried chicken business, back in his home state. He earned the nickname "Drought Breaker" for a touchdown he made for Georgia, but the one he scored in Dallas helped the Steelers keep alive a dream of breaking a drought of their own.

Bob Ferguson's NFL career ended after playing in just two games with the Vikings after his trade from Pittsburgh. He returned to Ohio State to earn a masters in sociology, got elected to the College Football Hall of Fame in 1996, and died on December 30, 2004.

Bob Schmitz's playing career ended after the 1966 season. He spent thirty-three years as an NFL scout with BLESTO, the Steelers and Jets. He was just days into his retirement in June 2004 when he died from an apparent heart attack. He was sixty-five.

Several players stayed in football after their playing days and excelled in new roles. Ernie Stautner coached for more than thirty years, prominently as defensive line coach and defensive coordinator for Tom Landry's

Cowboys. Dick Haley played one more year with the Steelers and then began a distinguished career in evaluating talent, becoming the director of player personnel and helping Art Rooney Jr. draft the kind of players who would make them perennial Super Bowl contenders. The '63 year was Hoak's last on a winning team as a player, but he would share in the franchise's glory years. When he retired after the '69 season, he ranked as the second-leading rusher in team history, behind John Henry Johnson. He returned to the team as coach of the running backs, a position he held for thirty-four years, and was on the staff for five Super Bowl victories.

One can only speculate about the toll that playing like human pinballs took on the players. Some, like defensive back Willie Daniel, eventually suffered from dementia, but he was able to count on the loving care of his wife, Ruth. There's no telling what nature dictated, or what price was exacted for playing kamikaze football in a meaningless exhibition against Detroit in January 1963, what the cost was for the players who "gave it all they had for the pride these steel-hard giants take in their battering profession."[6] Who knows what was driving these players to prove—like Red Mack back on a high school football field, or John Henry Johnson—that they could be better than the next guy, or good enough to become a pro, or maybe even good enough one day to play for the NFL championship. And at the end, when there were no more practices, no more Sundays to compete against Jimmy Hill of Sam Houston State or Joe Fortunato of Mingo Junction, Ohio, or Joe Walton of Beaver Falls, Pennsylvania, was it all worth it?

"I did my job and I walked away happy and I don't regret anything," Carpenter said. "And that's the best part." Carpenter died June 30, 2011; he was 77. The pay was mediocre and daily life less than glamorous, "but I loved every minute of it," Russell said. "I was so excited to be a pro. It didn't matter to me."[7]

Three marquee players from the early sixties were inducted into the Pro Football Hall of Fame: Bobby Layne in '67, Stautner in '69, and Johnson in '87. After being hospitalized for internal bleeding, Layne died of cardiac arrest on December 1, 1986. He was fifty-nine. Stautner watched the Steelers win the Super Bowl in February 2006 and then died a week and a half later. He was eighty, and he had been coping with Alzheimer's disease for eight years. John Henry Johnson died June 3, 2011, at age 81.

Ed Brown, who was named comeback player of the year by UPI a week after the season-ending loss to the Giants, retired after the 1965 season. In its account of his retirement, the AP called Brown "a rather unheralded starter." Maybe that was true. He didn't win a championship, and he flopped in the

1963 showdown against the Giants. But on one Saturday night in Cleveland, Ed Brown was good enough to leave Jim Brown in awe, and he threw game-winning passes to Red Mack and Gary Ballman, and for one unlikely season he carried the hopes of Steeler fans on his right arm. His playing days over, Brown went back to California. "My dad asked me, 'What are you going to do now?'" the quarterback recalled years later. "I said, 'I don't know. All I've ever done is play football.'" His father bought him a liquor store, and Brown ran it for twelve years. He died of prostate cancer in August 2007.[8]

Russell had to leave the team to serve two years of military service, which he completed in Europe. "That's a long time to be away from football," he said after the Giant loss. "What I hate about it is that I'll have to make the team all over again, just like a rookie."[9]

Russell was a lot more intent on resuming his pro football career than he had been starting it. "I was very motivated to return," he said. "I wasn't thinking about winning championships. I was just thinking, 'Can I make it back?'"[10] Russell returned and endured six straight losing seasons. But he wound up a twelve-year career with seven Pro Bowl appearances and two Super Bowl rings. He was the last active Steeler player from the '63 squad.

If there was one football team whose regrets and frustration could match the Steelers', it was the University of Pittsburgh. The Panthers went 9–1, their finest season since the 9–0–1 team of 1937, yet they wound up snubbed by all the bowls. Navy, the only team that beat Pitt, was invited to the Cotton Bowl to play Texas. Nebraska met Auburn in the Orange Bowl. The Gator Bowl matched North Carolina against Air Force. Pitt was left out.

The world had been shaken up and scarred in 1963, and not even the most optimistic forecasts for innovation and the economy were going to ease the pains of a chaotic, traumatic year. If *U.S. News & World Report* had been on target in its conclusion before the Kennedy assassination that the national attitude was "one of some uncertainty rather than one of full confidence," what in heaven's name was the state of mind of the American people in the aftermath of November 22, 1963?[11]

Sports had changed forever too. Pro football, with a rival league, more lucrative deals for coveted players, and the growth of television, was changing swiftly from the days when Art Rooney Sr. and Bobby Layne could simply shake hands on a new contract. "It's a new era," Rooney said days after the season-ending loss to the Giants. "Now it's really big business."[12]

Sports Illustrated named Pete Rozelle its man of the year, a departure from its practice of honoring athletes, and a nod to the "big business" that pro football had become, as Rooney noted.[13]

Buddy Parker resigned during the first week of September 1965 after four consecutive preseason losses. Upset that his authority had been usurped when Dan Rooney balked at a proposed trade with Philadelphia, Parker finally made good on his threat to quit. He returned to Texas to run a business. Two years later, he said in an interview, "No, I don't miss football really."[14] That sentiment is believable, on one hand; anyone who suffered so mightily after a loss might feel immense relief to be unburdened by the weight of coaching responsibilities and the dread of one more loss. On the other hand, how could someone who practically mortgaged his soul and sanity to win football games for fifteen years not feel the lure of his raison d'être? And how could he have undergone such a change of heart after declaring a year earlier, "I'll listen to any job, head coach or assistant"?[15]

Parker's abrupt decision to quit the Lions lingered as one of his regrets. Surely there were others. In the fall of '75, about nine months after the Steelers won their first Super Bowl, Parker praised Rooney and said, "I would have liked to have won a championship for him. I guess I was about a decade too soon."[16] But he was right on time in Detroit.

Parker died on March 22, 1982, from kidney failure, two weeks after being hospitalized for a ruptured ulcer. "The charge that I was in too big a hurry to give the Steelers a championship is true," Parker was quoted as saying in his obituary. "The charge that I gave away too many draft choices for veterans I thought could help us win is true."[17] He was sixty-eight.

Noll took over the Steelers in 1969—Hoak's last year as a running back—and, after winning the opener, lost the next thirteen games. In 1974, he took the Steelers to the Super Bowl and brought home the franchise's first championship, eleven seasons after Buddy Parker and a blood-'n'-guts team of renegades came mighty close to doing it themselves.

But what if Y. A. Tittle's third-down pass had glanced harmlessly off Frank Gifford's hand and fallen onto the frozen field at Yankee Stadium? What if Don Chandler had been forced to punt and Brown had led the Steelers on a scoring drive that put them ahead, 17–16, and they had hung onto the lead? "Maybe take the game. Who knows?" Parker said afterward.[18] What would have happened in a rematch with the Bears two weeks later on the frozen turf at Wrigley Field? "I don't know. I think we could have beat 'em, but who knows?" Cordileone said forty-seven years later. "You don't know what's going to happen."[19]

"We would have beat them," Russell said with no hesitation. "I think we did beat 'em in Pittsburgh."[20]

Rooney made the trip to Chicago to watch his friend George Halas coach the Bears to a 14–10 victory over the Giants. After the game, Rooney said, "Yeah, the Steelers could have beaten both of them, only we weren't in there."[21]

After all the second-guessing, the analyzing and reflection, sometimes there's no room for logic. Sometimes you're left with the quirks of the game, like a crooked upright on a goalpost, or the volleyball bounces of a pass that gave St. Louis a touchdown in the Cardinals' victory. The '63 season looked like it could have been the year the Steelers had been waiting for since 1933.[22]

"I put it down in the book as it wasn't meant to be," Michaels said. "That's the way it happened. And that's the way it worked. What can you say about it? There are things that sometimes happen for you, sometimes don't happen for you."[23]

AFTERWORD

The eleven-year-old kid who watched the Steelers cling to a championship dream bounced back, too. Days after the 33–17 loss to the Giants, he even made the front page of the *Youngstown Vindicator,* standing in a sleigh driven by Santa Claus and pulled by a couple of donkeys wearing fake reindeer antlers. Sitting in a sleigh pulled by donkeys was probably the Christmas equivalent of playing in the Runner-Up Bowl. The headmistress of the school had arranged the event and alerted the newspaper to a good photo opportunity. It was no Morris Berman photograph of Y. A. Tittle for eternity, but it was good enough for a sixth-grader. And he had a broad grin despite the frigid weather and the aftermath of the Steeler loss.

Christmas was a week away, and four days after the holiday, the NFL title game between the Bears and Giants was held at Wrigley Field on another frozen field, with temperatures in the single digits. If you were a Steeler fan, it was tough to resist watching and imagining how Pittsburgh would have done in a rematch with Wade and Ditka. Hampered by an injured knee, Tittle threw five interceptions, and Del Shofner dropped a pass in the end zone. For a Steeler fan, it figured that such lapses couldn't have happened against Pittsburgh two weeks earlier. The Bears won, 14–10. The winner's share, per player, was $5,899.77, the loser's share $4,218.15, a much better payday than the Steelers got playing in the Playoff Bowl the year before.[1]

With little off-season coverage, the draft over, no such thing as sports talk radio shows, and no 24-7 sports on TV, football practically went into hibernation until the College All-Star Game in the first week of August in '64—which brought one more reminder that it could have been the Steelers playing George Mira, Carl Eller, and Charlie Taylor instead of the Bears. But there were other diversions to keep a young Steeler fan from dwelling on disappointment.

The Beatles were only weeks away from appearing on *The Ed Sullivan Show,* opening up a whole new world of transistor radio, rock 'n' roll, and 45 rpm records to a sixth-grader. The Beatles would even play at the Civic Arena, the same venue Leonard Bernstein had condemned for its acoustics. Later, there would be a school dance with Beatles songs playing on a record player, and the discovery that a girl's hand in yours could feel as soft and comfortable as a nicely broken-in baseball glove. And probably smell better.

And there would always be reminders of life and death. At the end of July, during training camp, Willie Galimore, who had scored the opening touchdown in the Steelers-Bears 17–17 tie, and teammate John Farrington, whose 54-yard reception set up Galimore's score, died in a car crash. The kid, now twelve, went with his dad to see Barry Goldwater, the Republican presidential candidate, speak at Idora Park in the summer. Maybe it was the memory of Kennedy or just a disinterest in politics, but the kid probably would have had a better time there riding the Wildcat or hearing the Human Beinz in concert.

The wait for a good Steeler team would seem as interminable as the last week of school before summer vacation—magnified a hundred times. Seasons of 2–12 . . . 5–8–1 . . . 2–11–1 went by—and so did the coaches. In that time, the rival Browns won a championship and so did the New York Mets; Forbes Field was torn down and the Beatles disbanded—just as easily as the '63 Steelers were disassembled. Tucked inside those events was a lesson about how brick and mortar could be crushed, but you could hang on to the smell and sights and sounds of a Sunday afternoon, and the spectacle of John Henry Johnson running with a football like a man dashing out of a burning building could become imbedded in your memory as securely as a tattoo on your arm. And if the Mets could win a World Series, well, how could anyone doubt that we could land a man on the moon, even if it wasn't Big Daddy Lipscomb? And who would dare scoff that even the Steelers could win a championship?

At last, seeing black-and-gold uniforms in a playoff game on TV made you feel the way you do when your lungs give thanks as you explode to the surface after holding your breath underwater for as long as you can. As the clock ticked off the final seconds on January 12, 1975, to make it official that the Steelers were, indeed, after forty-one seasons, champions of the NFL, it felt as if all the noisemakers, confetti, and cheers on New Year's Eve in Times Square were fluttering inside your stomach.

At some point, another lesson seeped into the kid's subconscious, where it would linger like some valuable tool or device that had been neglected and forgotten in a corner of a garage or attic, then discovered with the exclamation, "I've been looking for this!" No one articulated and described that lesson better than Pat Conroy in *My Losing Season*. "Winning is wonderful in every aspect, but the darker music of loss resonates on deeper, richer planes," Conroy wrote. "Loss is a fiercer, more uncompromising teacher, coldhearted but clear-eyed in its understanding that life is more dilemma than game, and more trial than free pass." And there could hardly be a more fitting performer to applaud Conroy's tale than Andy Russell, who went from a player on a 1–13 team to a Super Bowl champion. Conroy's contention that loss teaches us more is "absolutely true," Russell wrote in "A Letter to Pat Conroy," one of the chapters in Russell's book, *Beyond the Goalpost*.[2]

Forty-one years after two uncles, Big Daddy Lipscomb, Ernie Davis, John F. Kennedy, and the '63 Steelers' dream died, I returned to Rosewae Drive and the front yard where I once wore away the grass diving after footballs. It was a sunny, balmy spring afternoon, but there were no kids outside playing catch, no mothers tending their gardens. There was an addition on one end of the house—our house—and the trees had grown a lot bigger. But mostly I was surprised at how small the yard was compared to how I remembered it. Maybe the whole world looked bigger back then—bigger with hope and dreams. As big as Big Daddy, as big as New York.

The one thing that hadn't changed over four decades was the rich sheen of the grass, and I didn't have to close my eyes to see my neighborhood pals playing tackle football on it, or to picture an overcast, late fall Sunday afternoon long ago, on a day the flag dangled limp at half-mast, along with our spirits, and the sight of Mike Ditka ricocheting through a half-dozen defenders as Clendon Thomas gave chase and the eleven-year-old kid in the stands at Forbes Field clenched his fists and pleaded, "Catch him. Catch him."

NOTES

PREFACE

1. John Kobler, "Crime Town USA," *Saturday Evening Post,* March 9, 1963, 71.
2. Jack Sell, "Last-Minute Layne Deflates Browns," *Pittsburgh Post-Gazette,* Nov. 23, 1959.
3. Al Abrams, "The Comeback Kids," *Pittsburgh Post-Gazette,* Nov. 23, 1959.
4. George Strickler, "Packers Win; Bears Tie, Retain Lead," *Chicago Tribune,* Nov. 25, 1963; Pat Livingston, "Steelers Warned," *Pittsburgh Press,* Sept. 21, 1963.
5. Art Rooney Jr., conversation, March 10, 2008.
6. Bill Conlin, "Bears 'Lucky' to Tie Steelers," *Philadelphia Evening Bulletin,* Nov. 25, 1963.
7. Al Abrams, "A Bear of a Tie," *Pittsburgh Post-Gazette,* Nov. 25, 1963; Lou Cordileone, conversation, Aug. 13, 2008; Lou Michaels, conversation, Aug. 29, 2007; Conlin, "Bears 'Lucky.'"
8. Robert Riger, *Best Plays of the Year 1963: A Documentary of Pro Football in the National Football League* (Englewood Cliffs, N.J.: Prentice-Hall, 1964), 69.

PRESEASON

1. Ray Didinger, *Pittsburgh Steelers* (New York: Macmillan, 1974), 21.
2. Jack Sell, *Pittsburgh Post-Gazette,* "Steelers Hire Buddy Parker for 5 Years," Aug. 28, 1957.
3. Art Rooney Jr., conversation, April 29, 2010.
4. Didinger, *Pittsburgh Steelers,* 21.
5. Jack Goodwin, "Fran Watches Layne in Awe and in Desperation," *Minneapolis Star,* Nov. 5, 1962.
6. Steve Hubbard, "Destiny's Derelicts," *Pittsburgh Press,* Jan. 3, 1988.

7. Myron Cope, "Pro Football's Gashouse Gang," *True,* Sept. 1964, 106; Andy Russell, conversation, April 19, 2010; Frank Atkinson, conversation, Oct. 10, 2007.

8. Cope, "Pro Football's Gashouse Gang," 106; Lou Cordileone, conversation, Aug. 13, 2008.

9. Andy Russell, interview, April 19, 2010.

10. Richard Sandomir, "Little Consolation in Third-Place Game," *New York Times,* Feb. 5, 2011.

11. Sandy Grady in Didinger, *Pittsburgh Steelers,* 22.

12. Lou Cordileone, conversation, Aug. 13, 2008.

13. "Parker Slated to Remain as Steelers' Coach But Layne's Career Nears End," *Youngstown Vindicator,* Jan. 8, 1963 (United Press International, published in *Vindicator*).

14. Lou Cordileone, conversation, Aug. 13, 2008.

15. Ibid.

16. Mike Shropshire, *The Ice Bowl: The Dallas Cowboys and the Green Bay Packers Season of 1967* (New York: D. I. Fine Books, 1997), 59.

17. Tarasovic was listed as defensive end that year; he played linebacker in '63.

18. Jack Sell, "Eagles Top Steelers in Wild Fray, 35 to 24," *Pittsburgh Post-Gazette,* Dec. 4, 1961.

19. Didinger, *Pittsburgh Steelers,* 29.

20. Michael Richman, "Eddie LeBaron," *Coffin Corner,* 25, no. 3 (2003): 1.

21. Tex Maule, "Pro Football Scouting Reports," *Sports Illustrated,* Sept. 9, 1963, 54; Andy Russell, interview, April 19, 2010; Bobby Layne with Fred Katz, "Pro Football's 11 Meanest Men," *Sport,* Nov. 1964, 16.

22. Jimmy Brown with Myron Cope, *Off My Chest* (Garden City, N.Y.: Doubleday, 1964), 44–45.

23. Stephen Norwood, *Real Football: Conversations on America's Game* (Jackson: University Press of Mississippi, 2004), 109.

24. "Packers Picked to Lead the Pack," *Pittsburgh Press,* Sept. 1, 1963.

25. Tex Maule, "The Cowboys Can Ride High on Better Defense," *Sports Illustrated,* Sept. 9, 1963, 52.

26. Joe Falls, "NFL Predictions: New Threats, Old Champions," *Sports All-Stars 1963 Pro Football,* 44.

27. William N. Wallace, "Steelers: A Lot of Discards Seeking a Jackpot," *New York Times,* Dec. 10, 1963.

28. Arthur Daley, "The Great Untangling," *New York Times,* Dec. 10, 1963.

29. "The Way People Live Today," *U.S. News & World Report,* Nov. 11, 1963, 56.

30. Ibid.

31. Ibid., 56–57.

32. Ibid., 58.

33. Ibid., 59.

34. Ibid., 59.

35. *Pittsburgh Press,* Sept. 7, 1963.

36. Al Abrams, "Monday Morning's Sports Wash," *Pittsburgh Post-Gazette,* Dec. 11, 1961.

37. Robert Gordon, "Hate Bomb Kills 4 Girls at Negro Church," *Philadelphia Inquirer,* Sept. 16, 1963 (UPI).

38. "Fiery Deaths of 3 Laid to Race Insult," *Pittsburgh Post-Gazette,* Sept. 16, 1963.

39. Geoffrey Gould, "Valachi Will Resume Crime Expose Tuesday," *Pittsburgh Post-Gazette,* Sept. 30, 1963 (AP).

40. UPI, "Luciano Aide Reveals Story of U.S. Mafia," *Pittsburgh Press,* Sept. 19, 1963.

GAME 1

1. Timothy Gay, *The Physics of Football: Discover the Science of Bone-Crushing Hits, Soaring Field Goals, and Awe-Inspiring Passes* (New York: Harper, 2005).

2. Al Abrams, "Monday Morning's Sports Wash," *Pittsburgh Post-Gazette,* Dec. 3, 1962; Lou Michaels, conversation, Aug. 29, 2007.

3. Jack Sell, "Steelers, Bears Battle to 17–17 Deadlock," *Pittsburgh Post-Gazette,* Nov. 25, 1963.

4. Al Abrams, "Steelers Ooze Confidence," *Pittsburgh Post-Gazette,* Sept. 11, 1963.

5. Ibid.

6. Buck Jerzy, "They Don't Make 'Em like Lou Anymore," National Polish-American Sports Hall of Fame, http://polishsportshof.com/inductees/football/lou-michaels.

7. Lou Michaels, conversation, Aug. 29, 2007.

8. John Steadman, "Sub's Life No Role for Michaels," *Baltimore News American,* Dec. 30, 1964.

9. Richard G. Hubler, "Hollywood's Frightening Lover," *Saturday Evening Post,* Nov. 13, 1954, 44.

10. Pat Livingston, "Lou Michaels Went to College to Get Grid Education," *Pittsburgh Press,* Nov. 8, 1962.

11. "Lou Michaels, Brother of Walt, Spurs Rams Hopes," *Proball,* July 1958.

12. Steadman, "Sub's Life No Role."

13. Bill Wise, *1963 Official Pro Football Almanac* (Greenwich, Conn.: Fawcett, 1963), 65.

14. Jack Sell, "Steelers Win, 16 to 7, on Michaels' Toe," *Pittsburgh Post-Gazette,* Sept. 9, 1963.

15. "Steel Shuffle Bringing Jobs to City," *Pittsburgh Press,* Sept. 19, 1963.

16. Johnny Sample with Fred J. Hamilton and Sonny Schwartz, *Confessions of a Dirty Ballplayer* (New York: Dial Press, 1970), 97.

17. Bob Barnett, "Profile: Ray Kemp," Pro Football Hall of Fame, Jan. 18, 2005, http://www.profootballhof.com/history/release.aspx?release_id=1379.

18. Richard Goldstein, "Lowell Perry, 69, Football Star and Ford Aide," *New York Times,* Jan. 11, 2001.

19. Ibid.

20. "Rooney Rates with Rickey, Brown as Benefactor—Kemp," *Pittsburgh Courier,* Aug. 31, 1963.

21. Al Abrams, "Parker's Best Team," *Pittsburgh Post-Gazette,* Jan. 8, 1963.

22. Al Abrams, "Is Parker on Way Out?," *Pittsburgh Post-Gazette,* Dec. 4, 1962.

23. Abrams, "Parker's Best Team."

24. Jack Sell, "Raymond K. Parkers Host Arthur J. Rooneys of the Steelers," *Pittsburgh Post-Gazette,* Jan. 11, 1963.

25. Abrams, "Steelers Ooze Confidence."

26. Al Abrams, "The Best Is Yet to Come," *Pittsburgh Post-Gazette,* Oct. 3, 1960.

27. Michael MacCambridge, *ESPN College Football Encyclopedia: The Complete History of the Game* (New York: ESPN Books, 2005), 710.

28. Pat Livingston, "Apathy, Not Team, Discourages Rooney as Season Nears," *Pittsburgh Press,* Aug. 27, 1963.

29. Ibid.

30. Pat Livingston, "Show Great But Gate Flops As Steelers Whip Eagles, 31–0," *Pittsburgh Press,* Nov. 30, 1959.

31. Pat Livingston, "Ernie Stautner Raps Booing Fans and Small Crowds," *Pittsburgh Press,* Nov. 29, 1961.

32. Roy Blount Jr., *About Three Bricks Shy of a Load: A Highly Irregular Lowdown on the Year the Pittsburgh Steelers Were Super but Missed the Bowl* (Boston: Little, Brown, 1974), 102.

33. Charles Danver, "Travelin' Judge," *Pittsburgh Post-Gazette,* Sept. 24, 1963.

34. Myron Cope, "Pittsburgh's Patient Whipping Boy," *Sports Illustrated,* Dec. 19, 1966, M3.

35. Mitzi Michaels in Al Abrams, "Who Are the Animals?," *Pittsburgh Post-Gazette,* Dec. 13, 1963.

36. Joe Tucker, *Steelers' Victory after Forty* (New York: Exposition Press, 1973), 156.

37. Livingston, "Apathy, Not Team."

38. Ray Didinger, *Pittsburgh Steelers* (New York: Macmillan, 1974), 136.

39. "D.C. Steelers' Fan Pin-Points Parker's Problems," *Pittsburgh Courier,* Aug. 31, 1963.

40. Pat Livingston, "Steelers Hope to Rebound with Giants," *Pittsburgh Press,* Sept. 18, 1963.

41. Didinger, *Pittsburgh Steelers,* 23–24.

42. Pat Livingston, "Eagles Ready Attack, Fans for Steelers," *Pittsburgh Press,* Sept. 13, 1963.

43. John Underwood, "The Magnificent Squirt," *Sports Illustrated,* Oct. 8, 1962, 48.

44. Sandy Grady, "Nice Old Lady Meddles and Hexes," *Philadelphia Evening Bulletin,* Dec. 10, 1962.

45. Hugh Brown, "Best Defense in Years Saves Eagles 21–21 Tie with Steelers," *Philadelphia Evening Bulletin,* Sept. 16, 1963.

46. Ibid.

47. Steadman, "Sub's Life No Role."

48. Underwood, "The Magnificent Squirt," 50.

49. Roy McHugh, "Is Tommy McDonald Pro Football's Piersall?," *Sport,* Nov. 1962, 84.

50. Gay, *The Physics of Football,* 161.

51. Pat Livingston, "Steeler Star's Kick Hits Post," *Pittsburgh Press,* Sept. 16, 1963.

52. John Dell, "Michaels Had Cross to Bear," *Philadelphia Inquirer,* Sept. 16, 1963.

53. Livingston, "Steeler Star's Kick Hits Post."

54. Good, "Choking Steeler Saved from Death," *Philadelphia Inquirer,* Sept. 16, 1963.

55. Ibid.

56. "Fast Action Saved Reger from Choking," *Pittsburgh Press,* Sept. 16, 1963.

57. "Bears' Defense Halts Packers," *Pittsburgh Press,* Sept. 16, 1963 (UPI).

GAME 2

1. AP, "Big Daddy Happy, Has Big Day," *Pittsburgh Post-Gazette,* Jan. 14, 1963.

2. Clendon Thomas, conversation, Aug. 30, 2008.

3. Preston Carpenter, conversation, Sept. 8, 2007.

4. "Steeler Star Lipscomb Dies, Dope Hinted," *Pittsburgh Press,* May 10, 1963.

5. "Requiem for Big Daddy," *Esquire,* Sept. 1963, 89.

6. Ibid.

7. Al Abrams, "The Big Pro Trade," *Pittsburgh Post-Gazette,* July 20, 1961.

8. Johnny Sample with Fred J. Hamilton and Sonny Schwartz, *Confessions of a Dirty Ballplayer* (New York: Dial Press, 1970), 339.

9. Pat Livingston, "Lipscomb's Death Shock to Steelers," *Pittsburgh Press,* May 10, 1963; UPI, "Sports Stars Join Drive for Kennedy," *New York Times,* Oct. 18, 1960.

10. Jimmy Miller, "Big Daddy Flying High," *Pittsburgh Post-Gazette,* Aug. 8, 1962.

11. Ibid.

12. Al Abrams, "Monday Morning's Sports Wash," *Pittsburgh Post-Gazette,* Sept. 9, 1963.

13. "Steelers High on Curry as West Liberty Camp Starts," *Pittsburgh Courier,* July 20, 1963.

14. "D.C. Steelers' Fan Pin-Points Parker's Problems," *Pittsburgh Courier,* Aug. 31, 1963.

15. Lou Cordileone, conversation, Aug. 13, 2008.

16. James F. Lynch, "New Cheers for an All-American," *New York Times,* Feb. 2, 1960.

17. William N. Wallace, "'It's Not Magic,' Says Tittle," *New York Times,* Nov. 10, 1963.

18. Y. A. Tittle, conversation, Sept. 8, 2008.

19. 1964 Steeler press guide.

20. Lou Cordileone, conversation, Aug. 13, 2008.

21. Ibid.

22. Ibid.

23. Jim Sargent, "Frank Varrichione: All-American and Pro Tackle," *Coffin Corner,* 21, no. 5 (1999), 2.

24. Lou Cordileone, conversation, Aug. 13, 2008.

25. Pat Livingston, "Apathy, Not Team, Discourages Rooney as Season Nears," *Pittsburgh Press,* Aug. 27, 1963.

26. Al Abrams, "A Day We Won't Forget," *Pittsburgh Post-Gazette,* Sept. 17, 1963.

27. Arthur Daley, "Savoring a Rare Treat," *New York Times,* Sept. 22, 1963.

28. Y. A. Tittle, conversation, Sept. 8, 2008.

29. Ibid.

30. Ben Thomas, "Glynn Griffing's Passing Sparks Rebs in Sugar Bowl," *Youngstown Vindicator,* Jan. 2, 1963 (AP).

31. At the time, a team could draft a player if his class had graduated even though he had not used up his eligibility. If the player had been redshirted or sat out a year after transferring, he could be drafted after his fourth year, and the rights to him would remain with the team that picked him even if he didn't sign for a year. Jim Campbell, "1936–37 NFL Draft," *Coffin Corner,* 7, no. 5 (1985).

32. Thomas, "Glynn Griffing's Passing."

33. Y. A. Tittle, conversation, Sept. 8, 2008.

34. "What's Wrong with the Civil Arena?," *Pittsburgh Press,* Sept. 20, 1963.

35. "Steelers to Stay Here—Rooney," *Pittsburgh Press,* Sept. 17, 1963.

36. Herbert G. Stein, "Big Crowds at Pitt Hear Meredith," *Pittsburgh Post-Gazette,* Sept. 19, 1963.

37. Al Abrams, "Monday Morning's Sports Wash," *Pittsburgh Post-Gazette,* Dec. 11, 1961.

38. Jimmy Miller, "Steelers Brush Up on 'Pressure' Tactics," *Pittsburgh Post-Gazette,* Sept. 19, 1963.

39. Pat Livingston, "Tittle Ready? Giants to Wait for Kickoff," *Pittsburgh Press,* Sept. 22, 1963.

40. "Tittle Is Still Ailing for Steelers' Game—42,000 Expected," *New York Times,* Sept. 22, 1963.

41. William N. Wallace, "Sherman Adds It Up," *New York Times,* Sept. 24, 1963.

42. Gene Ward, "Giants in 31–0 Pitt Shocker," *New York Daily News,* Sept. 23, 1963.

43. Pat Livingston, "Steelers Sub Team Play for Lipscomb," *Pittsburgh Press,* Sept. 1, 1963.

44. "Steelers High on Curry as West Liberty Camp Starts," *Pittsburgh Courier,* July 20, 1963.

45. Livingston, "Steelers Sub Team."

46. Jack Sell, "JHJ Makes a Suggestion," *Pittsburgh Post-Gazette,* Sept. 26, 1963.

47. Pat Livingston, "Steelers Turn Giant-Killers before 46,068," *Pittsburgh Press,* Sept. 23, 1963.

48. Al Abrams, "It Was a Great Day," *Pittsburgh Post-Gazette,* Sept. 23, 1963.

49. Gordon S. White Jr., "Losers Helpless without Tittle," *New York Times,* Sept. 23, 1963.

50. Livingston, "Steelers Turn Giant-Killers."

51. Ibid.

52. Y. A. Tittle, conversation, Sept. 8, 2008.

53. "Tittle Wanted to Play but Sherman Said No," *Pittsburgh Press,* Sept. 23, 1963.

54. Ward, "Giants in 31–0 Pitt Shocker."

55. Wallace, "Sherman Adds It Up."

56. Y. A. Tittle, conversation, Sept. 8, 2008.

57. UPI, "Packers Win the 'Big One,'" *Pittsburgh Press,* Sept. 23, 1963.

GAME 3

1. Andy Russell, conversation, Oct. 4, 2007.
2. Ibid.
3. Ibid.
4. Ibid.
5. AP, "Baker, Oregon State QB, Drafted by Rams," *Pittsburgh Post-Gazette,* Dec. 4, 1962.
6. Jack Sell, "Question Mark Buddy Parker Still ? Mark," *Pittsburgh Post-Gazette,* Dec. 5, 1962.
7. Andy Russell, conversation, Oct. 4, 2007.
8. Ibid.
9. Andy Russell, interview, April 19, 2010.
10. Jack Sell, "Steelers Play Annual Alumni Game Tonight," *Pittsburgh Post-Gazette,* Aug. 3, 1963.
11. Jack Sell, "Steelers (6) Favorites Over Cards," *Pittsburgh Post-Gazette,* Sept. 25, 1963.
12. Pat Livingston, "Steelers Face Cards, Problem," *Pittsburgh Press,* Sept. 29, 1963.
13. Murray Olderman, "Two Careers for Charley Johnson," *Sport,* March 1964, 86.
14. Pat Livingston, "Steelers Wary of Cardinals," *Pittsburgh Press,* Sept. 27, 1963; Pat Livingston, "Cards' Lemm Protégé of Conzelmann," *Pittsburgh Press,* Sept. 28, 1963.
15. Livingston, "Steelers Wary of Cardinals."
16. Olderman, "Two Careers for Charley Johnson," 25.
17. Dave Anderson, "Toughest Guy in Pro Football," *Sport,* Dec. 1966, 81.
18. Pat Livingston, "Card Blitz Worries Parker," *Pittsburgh Press,* Sept. 26, 1963.
19. Livingston, "Steelers Wary of Cardinals."
20. Jimmy Miller, "Steelers, Cards 'Stuck' with Battle Plans," *Pittsburgh Post-Gazette,* Sept. 26, 1963.
21. Robert Riger, *Best Plays of the Year 1963: A Documentary of Pro Football in the National Football League* (Englewood Cliffs, N.J.: Prentice-Hall, 1964), 17.
22. Ibid., 18.
23. Ibid., 18.
24. Ibid., 17.
25. Ibid., 17.
26. Gordon S. White Jr., "4th-Period Rally Tops Cards, 23–10," *New York Times,* Sept. 30, 1963.
27. John Kuenster, *Chicago Daily News;* Dick Kaplan, ed., *1961 Football Yearbook Kick-Off* (New York: Popular Library), 10.
28. AP, "'I Have to Show Them I Can Play Pro Ball,' Says Fullback," *Pittsburgh Post-Gazette,* Aug. 8, 1963.
29. Pat Livingston, "Steelers Find Title High-Priced," *Pittsburgh Press,* Sept. 30, 1963.
30. AP, "'I Have to Show Them.'"
31. Ibid.
32. Al Abrams, "'Larrupin' Lous" to Rescue," *Pittsburgh Post-Gazette,* Sept. 30, 1963.

33. Ibid.
34. Official game play-by-play account.
35. Livingston, "Steelers Find Title High-Priced."
36. Ibid.
37. Al Abrams, "'Larrupin' Lous' to Rescue," *Pittsburgh Post-Gazette,* Sept. 30, 1963.
38. Livingston, "Steelers Find Title High-Priced."
39. "Never Threw a Punch—Michaels," *Pittsburgh Press,* Sept. 30, 1963.
40. Ibid.
41. Ibid.
42. Ibid.
43. Andy Russell, interview, April 19, 2010.
44. Livingston, "Steelers Find Title High-Priced."
45. Ibid.
46. Riger, *Best Plays of the Year 1963,* 18.
47. Jack Sell, "Cards Bow to Steelers by 23 to 10," *Pittsburgh Post-Gazette,* Sept. 30, 1963.
48. Riger, *Best Plays of the Year 1963,* 22.
49. "Never Threw a Punch," *Pittsburgh Press.*
50. Chuck Heaton, *Cleveland Plain Dealer,* Sept. 30, 1963.

GAME 4

1. Jimmy Miller, "Steelers Get Brown, Deal Bobby Joe Green," *Pittsburgh Post-Gazette,* April 5, 1962.
2. Jack Sell, "Steelers' New Passer Here for 'Schooling,'" *Pittsburgh Post-Gazette,* June 13, 1962.
3. Jack Sell, "Parker Irked—Seeks Trades," *Pittsburgh Post-Gazette,* Aug. 20, 1962.
4. Joe Tucker, *Steelers' Victory after Forty* (New York: Exposition Press, 1973), 156.
5. Al Abrams, "A Play-Off Classic," *Pittsburgh Post-Gazette,* Jan. 7, 1963.
6. Pat Livingston, "Parker Tells Bobby Layne to Retire," *Pittsburgh Press,* Jan. 8, 1963.
7. Arthur Daley, "The Leader," *New York Times,* March 28, 1963.
8. Gary Cartwright, "Layne Was Toughest," *Dallas Morning News,* Feb. 19, 1967.
9. Ray Didinger, *Pittsburgh Steelers* (New York: Macmillan, 1974), 135.
10. "Parker Unruffled by Steeler Loss," *Pittsburgh Press,* Aug. 12, 1963.
11. "Steeler Boss Cautious but Happy," *Pittsburgh Press,* Aug. 18, 1963.
12. "Steeler Coach Disgusted by Defeat," *Pittsburgh Post-Gazette,* Aug. 26, 1963.
13. Didinger, *Pittsburgh Steelers,* 136.
14. Lou Cordileone, conversation, Aug. 13, 2008; B. Faye, "Meanest Man in Pro Football," *Collier's,* Nov. 25, 1950, 17.
15. Lou Cordileone, conversation, Aug. 13, 2008.
16. Cope, "Bobby Layne: I Have No Regrets," *Sport,* Jan. 1963, 77; Bobby Layne as told to Murray Olderman, "This Is No Game for Kids," *Saturday Evening Post,* Nov. 14, 1959, 97.

17. Jim Wexell, *Pittsburgh Steelers: Men of Steel* (Champaign, Ill.: Sports Publishing, 2006), 47.
18. Lou Cordileone, conversation, Aug. 13, 2008.
19. Michael MacCambridge, *America's Game: The Epic Story of How Pro Football Captured a Nation* (New York: Random House, 2004), 79.
20. Preston Carpenter, conversation, Sept. 8, 2007.
21. Shelby Strother, *NFL Top Forty: The Greatest Pro Football Games of All Time* (New York: Viking, 1988), 42.
22. Red Mack, conversation, Aug. 8, 2007.
23. Ibid.
24. Brady Keys, conversation, Sept. 4, 2007.
25. Carlton Stowers, "Life with the Fast Layne," n.d., newspaper clipping on file with the author.
26. Alex Karras and Herb Gluck, *Even Big Guys Cry* (New York: Holt, Rinehart and Winston, 1977), 124.
27. Preston Carpenter, conversation, Sept. 8, 2007.
28. Arthur Daley, "The Leader," *New York Times,* March 28, 1963.
29. Paul Hornung, *Football and the Single Man* (Garden City, N.Y.: Doubleday), 152.
30. Myron Cope, *The Game that Was: An Illustrated Account of the Tumultuous Early Days of Pro Football* (New York: Thomas Y. Crowell, 1974), 257.
31. Lou Cordileone, conversation, Aug. 13, 2008.
32. Charley Feeney, "Odds and Ends," *Pittsburgh Post-Gazette,* Nov. 26, 1971.
33. "Trolley Intercepts Bobby Layne's Pass," *Pittsburgh Press,* Dec. 12, 1961.
34. "2 Killed as Auto Slams into Trolley," *Pittsburgh Press,* Dec. 16, 1961.
35. AP, "Boy Steals Trolley in Philadelphia," Dec. 17, 1962.
36. Karras and Gluck, *Even Big Guys Cry,* 124–25.
37. Bob St. John, *Heart of a Lion: The Wild and Woolly Life of Bobby Layne* (Dallas: Taylor, 1991), 108–11.
38. Karras and Gluck, *Even Big Guys Cry,* 126.
39. Dick Haley, conversation, May 14, 2008; Red Mack, conversation, Aug. 8, 2007.
40. Al Abrams, "'Larrupin' Lous' to Rescue," *Pittsburgh Post-Gazette,* Sept. 30, 1963.
41. Jimmy Miller, "Ex-Steeler Helps Locals with Phone," *Pittsburgh Post-Gazette,* Sept. 30, 1963.
42. Andy Russell, conversation, Oct. 4, 2007.
43. Pat Livingston, "Genius QB Ryan Next for Steelers," *Pittsburgh Press,* Oct. 1, 1963.
44. Jack Hand, "Inside Football's Biggest Brains—Frank Ryan and Charley Johnson," *Pro Sports,* Jan. 1966, 20.
45. Livingston, "Genius QB Ryan Next for Steelers."
46. AP, "Paul Brown 'Shocked' by Firing," *Pittsburgh Post-Gazette,* Jan. 11, 1963.
47. Pat Livingston, "New 1–2 Punch Browns' Weapon," *Pittsburgh Press,* Oct. 3, 1963.
48. Livingston, "Genius QB Ryan Next for Steelers."
49. Pat Livingston, "Bob Ferguson May Start at FB," *Pittsburgh Press,* Oct. 4, 1963.
50. Pat Livingston, "Dick Hoak Gets Steeler Starting Job," *Pittsburgh Press,* Aug. 15, 1961.
51. Pat Livingston, "Steelers Facing Last Big Test," *Pittsburgh Press,* Sept. 8, 1963.

52. Pat Livingston, "Defense Keeps 'Heat' on Thomas," *Pittsburgh Press,* Sept. 24, 1963.

53. Roy McHugh, "Brady Keys Talk of the Town," *Pittsburgh Press,* Oct. 15, 1964.

54. Pat Livingston, "Steelers Find 'Buoyancy' in Title Bid," *Pittsburgh Press,* Oct. 2, 1963.

55. Al Abrams, "About Great Promotions," *Pittsburgh Post-Gazette,* Aug. 21, 1962.

56. Jack Sell, "Steelers Tried Field Goals as Browns Went for TDs," *Pittsburgh Post-Gazette,* Oct. 7, 1963.

57. Pat Livingston, "Parker Defends Strategy against Brown," *Pittsburgh Press,* Oct. 8, 1963.

58. Sell, "Steelers Tried Field Goals."

59. Chuck Heaton, "84,684 Watch Browns Win, 35 to 23," *Cleveland Plain Dealer,* Oct. 6, 1963.

60. Andy Russell, interview, April 19, 2010.

61. Sell, "Steelers Tried Field Goals."

62. Edward Chay, "Browns' Defense Cheered," *Cleveland Plain Dealer,* Oct. 7, 1963.

63. Heaton, "84,684 Watch Browns Win, 35 to 23."

64. Pat Livingston, "Steeler QB a Standout in Defeat," *Pittsburgh Press,* Oct. 7, 1963.

65. Jimmy Miller, "Odds Favor Steelers to Lose First," *Pittsburgh Post-Gazette,* Oct. 2, 1963.

66. Jimmy Brown with Myron Cope, *Off My Chest* (Garden City, N.Y.: Doubleday, 1964), 212.

67. Livingston, "Steeler QB a Standout in Defeat."

68. Sell, "Steelers Tried Field Goals."

GAME 5

1. Stephen Norwood, *Real Football: Conversations on America's Game* (Jackson: University Press of Mississippi, 2004), 90.

2. Tex Maule, "Why Oklahoma Is Unbeatable," *Sports Illustrated,* Nov. 18, 1957, 73.

3. Ibid.

4. Gary T. King, *An Autumn Remembered: Bud Wilkinson's Legendary '56 Sooners* (Norman: University of Oklahoma Press, 2005), 137.

5. Deane McGowen, "Oklahoma Star Back Is Rushing toward More Records," *New York Times,* Nov. 2, 1957.

6. Pat Livingston, "Defense Keeps 'Heat' on Thomas," *Pittsburgh Press,* Sept. 24, 1963.

7. AP, "Oklahoma Crushes Kansas State and Sets Record with 32nd Straight Triumph," *New York Times,* Oct. 7, 1956.

8. UPI, "Oklahoma Overwhelms Texas to Tie Pitt's Record of 33 Victories in Row," *New York Times,* Oct. 14, 1956.

9. Joseph M. Sheehan, "Oklahoma Trounces Notre Dame, 40 to 0," *New York Times,* Oct. 28, 1956.

10. AP, "Thomas Scores Twice as Oklahoma Eleven Bests Oklahoma State," *New York Times,* Dec. 1, 1957.

11. Deane McGowen, "Sooners Are Better with Thomas," *New York Times,* Nov. 2, 1957.

12. Pat Livingston, "Defense Keeps 'Heat' on Thomas," *Pittsburgh Press,* Sept. 24, 1963.

13. Ray Didinger, *Pittsburgh Steelers* (New York: Macmillan, 1974), 20.

14. Gabe Essoe, *Tarzan of the Movies: A Pictorial History of More than Fifty Years of Edgar Rice Burroughs' Legendary Hero* (New York: Cadillac, 1968), 182, 184.

15. Jack Sell, "Steelers Obtain Thomas in Deal," *Pittsburgh Post-Gazette,* Sept. 4, 1962.

16. Pat Livingston, "Steelers Sub Team Play for Lipscomb," *Pittsburgh Press,* Sept. 1, 1963.

17. Clendon Thomas, conversation, Aug. 30, 2008.

18. Pat Livingston, "Steeler QB a Standout in Defeat," *Pittsburgh Press,* Oct. 7, 1963.

19. Robert Riger, *Best Plays of the Year 1963: A Documentary of Pro Football in the National Football League* (Englewood Cliffs, N.J.: Prentice-Hall, 1964), 17.

20. J. Kirk Sale, "The Man to Watch Is . . . the Middle Linebacker," *New York Times,* Dec. 10, 1967.

21. Pat Livingston, "Steelers Find Title High-Priced," *Pittsburgh Press,* Sept. 30, 1963.

22. Pat Livingston, "Cardinals 'Hungry' for Steelers' Victory," *Pittsburgh Press,* Oct. 11, 1963.

23. "Bob Ferguson Glows in Steelers' Victory," *Pittsburgh Post-Gazette,* Sept. 30, 1963.

24. Pat Livingston, "No Fumbles," *Pittsburgh Press,* Oct. 1, 1963.

25. Pat Livingston, "Steelers Review Feud with Cardinals," *Pittsburgh Press,* Oct. 12, 1963.

26. Pat Livingston, "Parker Playing Hunch with Sapp," *Pittsburgh Press,* Oct. 9, 1963.

27. Pat Livingston, "Vengeful Cards Battle Steelers," *Pittsburgh Press,* Oct. 13, 1963.

28. Ric Roberts, "Fans Still Optimistic about Snake-Bitten Steelers," *Pittsburgh Courier,* Oct. 12, 1963.

29. Pat Livingston, "Excitement Cowboys' Commodity," *Pittsburgh Press,* Oct. 23, 1963.

30. Livingston, "Vengeful Cards Battle Steelers," *Pittsburgh Press,* Oct. 13, 1963.

31. Jack Sell, "'Bomber' Obtained from Eagles, Will Be Ready for Cards Sunday," *Pittsburgh Post-Gazette,* Oct. 8, 1963.

32. Ibid.

33. Jack Sell, "Fullback John Henry Johnson Sidelined for Sunday Action," *Pittsburgh Post-Gazette,* Oct. 10, 1963.

34. Bill Nunn Jr., *Pittsburgh Courier,* Nov. 9, 1963.

35. Pat Livingston, "Steeler Plum Turns into Lemm-on," *Pittsburgh Press,* Oct. 14, 1963.

36. Al Abrams, "Suddenly, It Was a Loss," *Pittsburgh Post-Gazette,* Oct. 14, 1963.

37. Robert Morrison, "Late, Late Show Puts Steelers to Bed, Ends Big Nightmare," *St. Louis Post-Dispatch,* Oct. 14, 1963.

38. "Pottios Picks up Steelers on Defense," *Pittsburgh Press,* Aug. 26, 1963.

39. Livingston, "Steeler Plum Turns into Lemm-on."

40. Morrison, "Late, Late Show Puts Steelers to Bed."

41. Livingston, "Steeler Plum Turns into Lemm-on."

42. Pat Livingston, *Pittsburgh Press,* Oct. 14, 1963.

43. Al Abrams, "Suddenly, It Was a Loss," *Pittsburgh Post-Gazette,* Oct. 14, 1963.

44. "Can Steelers' Line Finally Chain Brown?," *Pittsburgh Courier,* Nov. 9, 1963; Al Abrams, "Card Strategy Misfires," *Pittsburgh Post-Gazette,* Oct. 14, 1963.

45. Don Smith, *Coffin Corner* 16, no. 6 (1994).

46. Norwood, *Real Football,* 106.

47. Bill Wise, *1963 Official Pro Football Almanac* (Greenwich, Conn.: Fawcett, 1963), 66.

48. Livingston, "Steeler Plum Turns into Lemm-on."

49. Pat Livingston, *Pittsburgh Press,* Sept. 24, 1963.

50. Pat Livingston, "'Prevent Defense' Defies Football Theory," *Pittsburgh Press,* Oct. 15, 1963.

51. Pat Livingston, "The Volatile Mr. Ramsey," *Pittsburgh Press,* Oct. 14, 1963.

52. Pat Livingston, *Pittsburgh Press,* Sept. 10, 1963.

53. Al Abrams, *Pittsburgh Post-Gazette,* Oct. 15, 1963.

54. Livingston, "Steeler Plum Turns into Lemm-on."

55. Riger, *Best Plays of the Year 1963,* 38.

56. "Johnson's Stock up as Steelers Stagger," *Pittsburgh Courier,* Oct. 19, 1963.

57. Didinger, *Pittsburgh Steelers,* 24.

58. Livingston, "Steeler Plum Turns into Lemm-on."

59. Ibid.

60. AP, "Browns Batter Giants by 32–24," *Pittsburgh Post-Gazette,* Oct. 14, 1963.

61. Riger, *Best Plays of the Year 1963,* 29.

62. Jimmy Cannon, *Nobody Asked Me, But: The World of Jimmy Cannon,* ed. Jack Cannon and T. Cannon (New York: Holt, Rinehart and Winston, 1978), 226.

63. Pat Livingston, "Steelers Find 'Buoyancy' in Title Bid," *Pittsburgh Press,* Oct. 2, 1963.

GAME 6

1. "Dry Spell—and Autos—Make It Tough on Sam," *Pittsburgh Post-Gazette,* Oct. 17, 1963.

2. Al Abrams, "Buddy Hasn't Given Up," *Pittsburgh Post-Gazette,* Oct. 15, 1963.

3. Howard Whitman, "Make Friends with Your Nerves," *Pittsburgh Post-Gazette,* Sept. 9, 1963; Howard Whitman, "You Must Release Inner Tension," *Pittsburgh Post-Gazette,* Sept. 10, 1963.

4. Al Abrams, "Buddy Hasn't Given Up," *Pittsburgh Post-Gazette,* Oct. 15, 1963.

5. Pat Livingston, "Redskins Tilt Crossroads for Steelers," *Pittsburgh Press,* Oct. 17, 1963.

6. Pat Livingston, "Snead's Passes Pose Threat for Steelers," *Pittsburgh Press,* Oct. 19, 1963; Pat Livingston, "'Prevent Defense' Defies Football Theory," *Pittsburgh Press,* Oct. 15, 1963.

7. UPI, "McPeak Hits Criticism of QB Snead," *Pittsburgh Press,* Oct. 15, 1963.

8. Dick Haley, conversation, May 14, 2008.

9. Ibid.

10. Ibid.

11. Joseph M. Sheehan, "Pitt Bows, 29 to 13," *New York Times,* Oct. 20, 1957.

12. Michael Strauss, "Gerlick's Field Goal Puts Orangemen on Top, 24–21," *New York Times,* Nov. 3, 1957 (Strauss reports that the ball was on the Pitt 35-yard line).

13. Joseph M. Sheehan, "Panthers Rally," *New York Times,* Oct. 26, 1958.

14. Dick Haley, conversation, May 14, 2008.

15. Jack Sell, "Castoffs Spark Steelers to Upset, 17–13," *Pittsburgh Post-Gazette,* Nov. 6, 1961; Bridget Wentworth, *Newark Star-Ledger,* Jan. 25, 2009.

16. Pat Livingston, "Wrong Guesses Disturb Haley," *Pittsburgh Press,* Aug. 21, 1962.

17. Dick Haley, conversation, July 23, 2010.

18. Art Rooney Jr., interview, Oct. 4, 2008.

19. Dick Haley, conversation, May 14, 2008.

20. Bob Thomas, "Vinton Is Big Time—Earns $25,000 a Year," *Pittsburgh Post-Gazette,* Oct. 16, 1963.

21. Vince Johnson, "Racket Raiders Nab 31 Here," *Pittsburgh Post-Gazette,* Oct. 17, 1963.

22. Al Abrams, "A Teammate of Jim Brown," *Pittsburgh Post-Gazette,* Oct. 16, 1963.

23. Jack Sell, "Steelers Turn Cards, 19–7, Regain Second," *Pittsburgh Post-Gazette,* Dec. 3, 1962.

24. Jack Sell, "Steelers Deal Ferguson for Draft Choice," *Pittsburgh Post-Gazette,* Oct. 16, 1963.

25. Pat Livingston, "Sapp to Take over as Steeler Fullback," *Pittsburgh Press,* Oct. 16, 1963.

26. Ibid.; "Big Daddy of the Big Ten," *Stanley Woodward's Football,* Nov. 1960; Sam Huff and Leonard Shapiro, *Tough Stuff: The Man in the Middle* (New York: St. Martin's Press, 1988), 168.

27. Jimmy Brown with Myron Cope, *Off My Chest* (Garden City, N.Y.: Doubleday, 1964), 195.

28. Pat Livingston, "Johnson Was Given OK to Pass Up Drills to Help Heal Ankle," *Pittsburgh Press,* Oct. 21, 1963.

29. George Barrett, *New York Times,* "The Mirror Is Closed by Hearst Corp.," Oct. 16, 1963.

30. "Time of Change for the Nation's Newspapers," *U.S. News & World Report,* Nov. 4, 1963, 44–45.

31. "Doghouse Blues! Injured JHJ Slow Healer, Says Parker," *Pittsburgh Post-Gazette,* Oct. 17, 1963.

32. Al Abrams, "Pros' Lure Intriguing," *Pittsburgh Post-Gazette,* Oct. 17, 1963.

33. Jimmy Miller, "1,000 Nuns to See Game with Redskins on Sunday," *Pittsburgh Post-Gazette,* Oct. 17, 1963.

34. Ed Kiely, "A Man Nobody Knows," Steelers game program, Oct. 29, 1961.

35. Pat Livingston, "Steelers Dial New TD Strategy," *Pittsburgh Press,* Oct. 21, 1963.

36. Pat Livingston, "Snead's Passes Pose Threat for Steelers," *Pittsburgh Press,* Oct. 19, 1963.

37. Bill Wise, *1963 Official Pro Football Almanac* (Greenwich, Conn.: Fawcett, 1963), 75.

38. Jack Walsh, "Redskins Beaten on Two Miscues," *Washington Post,* Oct. 21, 1963.

39. William N. Wallace, "Barnes Aims to Step Less Lively," *New York Times,* Oct. 2, 1963.

40. Pat Livingston, "Steelers Muffed Chance for 2nd Week in Row," Oct. 14, 1963.

41. Pat Livingston, "Johnson Was Given OK," *Pittsburgh Press,* Oct. 21, 1963.

42. Lou Cordileone, conversation, April 30, 2010.

43. Jimmy Miller, "Steelers Have Special Rooters," *Pittsburgh Post-Gazette,* Oct. 17, 1963.

44. Livingston, "Johnson Was Given OK."

45. Ibid.

46. "Haley Big 'Thief,'" *Pittsburgh Post-Gazette,* Oct. 21, 1963.

GAME 7

1. Roy Blount Jr., *About Three Bricks Shy of a Load: A Highly Irregular Lowdown on the Year the Pittsburgh Steelers Were Super but Missed the Bowl* (Boston: Little, Brown, 1974), 17.

2. Art Rooney Jr., *Ruanaidh: The Story of Art Rooney and His Clan* (n.p.: Author, 2008), 115.

3. Ibid.

4. Red Mack, interview, Oct. 11, 2008.

5. Ibid.

6. Ibid.

7. Ibid.

8. Ibid.

9. Mervin Hyman, Morton Sharnik, and Herman Weiskopf, "Big Men of the Midwest," *Sports Illustrated,* Sept. 16, 1960.

10. "Stanley Woodward's All-Sectional Team for the Midwest," *Stanley Woodward's Football,* Nov. 1960, 40.

11. Red Mack, interview, Oct. 11, 2008; Ed Fay, conversation, Sept. 24, 2008.

12. Red Mack, interview, Oct. 11, 2008.

13. Red Mack, conversation, Aug. 8, 2007.

14. Ibid.

15. Ed Fay, conversation, Sept. 24, 2008.

16. "Mack Shows Speed in Steeler Scrimmage," *Pittsburgh Post-Gazette,* Aug. 6, 1961.

17. "Red Mack Starts in Steeler Drills," *Pittsburgh Press,* Aug. 6, 1961.

18. "Military Status Steeler Concern," *Pittsburgh Post-Gazette,* July 28, 1961; Tom Landry, "Ex-Steeler Moegele Big Help to Dallas," *Pittsburgh Post-Gazette,* Aug. 22, 1961.

19. Chester L. Smith, "Rooney U. Hopes Red Mack's Knees Can Stand Strain," *Pittsburgh Press,* Aug. 10, 1961.

20. Bobby Layne with Fred Katz, "Pro Football's 11 Meanest Men," *Sport,* Nov. 1964, 14.

21. Ed Fay, conversation, Sept. 24, 2008.

22. Ibid.; Red Mack, interview, Oct. 11, 2008; Ed Fay, conversation, Sept. 24, 2008.

23. 1962 Steeler press guide.

24. Red Mack, interview, Oct. 11, 2008.

25. Jack Sell, "The Two Seasons," *Pittsburgh Post-Gazette,* Oct. 15, 1963.

26. Tom Landry, "The Cowboys Figure to Ride a Little Harder This Year," in *Pro Football The Pros Football '63, 1963,* ed. Herbert M. Furlow (New York: Counterpoint, 1963), 55.

27. Tex Maule, "A Shuttle Shakes Up the Pros," *Sports Illustrated,* Nov. 5, 1962, 16.

28. Don Schiffer, *Pro Football 1963* (New York: Pocket Books, 1963), 32.

29. "'God of Heavens' Rites Revived," *Pittsburgh Post-Gazette,* Oct. 23, 1963.

30. Roger Lane, "Steel Firms Tell of Bright Profits," *Pittsburgh Post-Gazette,* Oct. 24, 1963 (AP).

31. Lee McInerney, "Berle, Smith Top 2 Bills," *Pittsburgh Post-Gazette,* Oct. 21, 1963.

32. Mel McKeachie, "Joey Heatherton Finds Pittsburgh 'Beautiful,'" *Pittsburgh Post-Gazette,* Oct. 23, 1963.

33. Jack Sell, "Steelers Made 8-Point Picks," *Pittsburgh Post-Gazette,* Oct. 23, 1963.

34. Ibid.

35. Pat Livingston, "Johnson Faces Fight to Regain Fullback Job," *Pittsburgh Press,* Oct. 24, 1963.

36. Sell, "Steelers Made 8-Point Picks."

37. Pat Livingston, "Johnson Faces Fight to Regain Fullback Job"

38. "Steeler Foes Prefer Games at Stadium," *Pittsburgh Press,* Oct. 22, 1963.

39. Al Abrams, "Good Seating Big Help," *Pittsburgh Post-Gazette,* Dec. 5, 1962.

40. Lou Cordileone, conversation, April 30, 2010.

41. Pat Livingston, "Steelers Win Race to Stay in Race," *Pittsburgh Press,* Oct. 28, 1963.

42. Al Abrams, "Done Up Red and Brown," *Pittsburgh Post-Gazette,* Oct. 28, 1963.

43. Bill Wise, *1963 Official Pro Football Almanac* (Greenwich, Conn.: Fawcett, 1963), 38.

44. Sam Blair, "Cowboys Lose Again," *Dallas Morning News,* Oct. 28, 1963; Al Abrams, "Cowboys Fight Back," *Pittsburgh Post-Gazette,* Oct. 28, 1963.

45. Livingston, "Steelers Win Race to Stay in Race."

46. Blair, "Cowboys Lose Again"; Livingston, "Steelers Win Race to Stay in Race."

47. Red Mack, interview, Oct. 11, 2008.

48. Al Abrams, "Done Up Red and Brown."

49. Ibid.

50. Pat Livingston, "Brown Unloaded Long 'Bomb' and Hoped Mack Would Nab It," *Pittsburgh Press,* Oct. 28, 1963.

51. Ibid.

52. Peter Golenbock, *Landry's Boys: An Oral History of a Team and an Era* (Chicago: Triumph Books, 2005), 149.

53. Livingston, "Steelers Win Race to Stay in Race."

54. Abrams, "Done Up Red and Brown."

55. Livingston, "Steelers Win Race to Stay in Race."

56. UPI, "Giants Pull Browns Down with Crowd," *Pittsburgh Press,* Oct. 28, 1963.

57. Livingston, "Brown Unloaded Long 'Bomb.'"

GAME 8

1. Tommy Devine, "Parker Keeps It Simple," *Sports Illustrated,* Nov. 15, 1954, 29.
2. Tommy Devine and Bob Latshaw, "The Man Who Stirred up the Lions," *Sport,* Oct. 1954, 82.
3. Ibid., 80.
4. Devine, "Parker Keeps It Simple," 29.
5. Stanley Frank, "He Dies for Detroit Every Week," *Saturday Evening Post,* Nov. 13, 1954, 109.
6. Dick Haley, conversation, May 14, 2008.
7. Arthur Daley, "Another Abrupt Departure," *New York Times,* Sept. 8, 1965.
8. Frank, "He Dies for Detroit," 109.
9. "A Pride of Lions," *Time,* Nov. 29, 1954, 58.
10. Frank, "He Dies for Detroit," 109.
11. Ibid., 112.
12. AP, "Slashing Centenary Halfback: Centenary Has Edge on Texas," *Spartanburg (S.C.) Herald Journal,* Oct. 21, 1934.
13. "Lions on the Loose," *Newsweek,* Aug. 26, 1957, 90.
14. Ibid.
15. Jack Sell, "Steelers Hire Buddy Parker for 5 Years," *Pittsburgh Post-Gazette,* Aug. 28, 1957.
16. Art Rooney Jr., *Ruanaidh: The Story of Art Rooney and His Clan* (n.p.: Author, 2008), 172.
17. Johnny Sample with Fred J. Hamilton and Sonny Schwartz, *Confessions of a Dirty Ballplayer* (New York: Dial Press, 1970), 104–5; Rooney, *Ruanaidh,* 183.
18. Bobby Layne on "The Detroit Lions vs. the Cleveland Browns," *The Way It Was,* April 1, 1976; Dick Haley, conversation, May 14, 2008.
19. Sample with Hamilton and Schwartz, *Confessions of a Dirty Ballplayer,* 104–5.
20. Art Rooney Jr., conversation, April 29, 2010.
21. Preston Carpenter, conversation, Sept. 8, 2007.
22. Rooney, *Ruanaidh,* 167.
23. "Negro Gridders Won't Boycott Charity Event," *Pittsburgh Post-Gazette,* Aug. 10, 1961.
24. "Steeler-Colt Game Skirts Racial Block," *Pittsburgh Press,* Aug. 10, 1961.
25. "Card Passing Whiz Misses Steeler Fray," *Pittsburgh Press,* Aug. 26, 1961.
26. Francis Stann, "What's Wrong with the Washington Redskins?," *Sport,* Aug. 1961, 47.
27. UPI, "Redskins, Udall End Discrimination Feud," *Pittsburgh Press,* Aug. 15, 1961.
28. Sample with Hamilton and Schwartz, *Confessions of a Dirty Ballplayer,* 102.
29. Roy Blount Jr., *About Three Bricks Shy of a Load: A Highly Irregular Lowdown on the Year the Pittsburgh Steelers Were Super but Missed the Bowl* (Boston: Little, Brown, 1974), 172.
30. George Tarasovic, conversation, Nov. 28, 2007.
31. Pat Livingston, "Bob Ferguson May Start at Fullback," *Pittsburgh Press,* Oct. 4, 1963.
32. Jimmy Miller, "Tarasovich Tracy Cut by Steelers," *Pittsburgh Post-Gazette,* Nov. 7, 1963.

33. Lou Cordileone, conversation, Aug. 13, 2008.

34. Lou Cordileone, conversation, April 20, 2010.

35. Preston Carpenter, conversation, Sept. 8, 2007.

36. Dan Rooney, *Dan Rooney: My 75 Years with the Pittsburgh Steelers and the NFL,* as told to Andrew E. Masich and David F. Halaas (Cambridge, Mass.: Da Capo Press, 2007), 83.

37. Ibid.; Art Rooney Jr., conversation, April 29, 2010.

38. Rooney, *Dan Rooney,* 119.

39. Frank, "He Dies for Detroit," 109.

40. Pat Livingston, "The Longer Season," *Pittsburgh Press,* Oct. 23, 1963; Clendon Thomas, conversation, Aug. 30, 2008.

41. Art Rooney Jr., conversation, April 29, 2010.

42. Devine and Latshaw, "The Man Who Stirred up the Lions," 81; Rooney, *Ruanaidh,* 128.

43. Andy Russell, conversation, Oct. 4, 2007.

44. Preston Carpenter, conversation, Sept. 8, 2007; Murray Tucker, *Screamer: The Forgotten Voice of the Pittsburgh Steelers* (Lincoln, Neb.: iUniverse, 2007), 132.

45. Red Mack, conversation, Aug. 8, 2007.

46. Andy Russell, conversation, Oct. 4, 2007.

47. Jim Bradshaw, conversation, Dec. 10, 2007.

48. Robert Riger, *Best Plays of the Year 1962: A Documentary of Pro Football in the National Football League* (Englewood Cliffs, N.J.: Prentice-Hall, 1963), 37.

49. Ibid.

50. Bill Wise, *1963 Official Pro Football Almanac* (Greenwich, Conn.: Fawcett, 1963), 99.

51. Clendon Thomas, conversation, Aug. 30, 2008.

52. AP, "Sherman Says Giants Played Their Top Tilt," *Pittsburgh Post-Gazette,* Oct. 30, 1963.

53. Al Abrams, "Steelers—'Alley Cats,'" *Pittsburgh Post-Gazette,* Nov. 1, 1963.

54. "City's Future Painted in Glowing Colors," *Pittsburgh Post-Gazette,* Oct. 29, 1963.

55. Andrew Bernhard, "Growth of Cities Is World Problem," *Pittsburgh Post-Gazette,* Oct. 28, 1963.

56. "Meet Challenge of Growth, Papers Told," *Pittsburgh Press,* Sept. 23, 1963.

57. "Voters Can Force Reform; Why Wait for Grand Jury?," *Pittsburgh Post-Gazette,* Oct. 30, 1963.

58. Sherley Uhl, "Firemen, Teamsters Tangle," *Pittsburgh Press,* Nov. 2, 1963.

59. Brute Kramer, "Football Has Strong Hold on Fans," *Pittsburgh Post-Gazette,* Oct. 30, 1963.

60. Jack Sell, "Long Bomb by Steelers Could Upset Green Bay," *Pittsburgh Post-Gazette,* Oct. 31, 1963.

61. Wise, *1963 Pro Football Almanac,* 19; Vince Lombardi with W.C. Heinz, *Run to Daylight!* (Englewood Cliffs, N.J.: Prentice-Hall, 1963), [PG]; "After Tough Rookie Year, Ferguson Eyes Grid Comeback," *Pittsburgh Courier,* Aug. 3, 1963.

62. Lee Remmel, "Pack 'a Little Flat' in Victory, Vince," *Green Bay Press-Gazette,* Nov. 4, 1963.

63. Pat Livingston, "Parker Tries to Relax Steelers," *Pittsburgh Press,* Nov. 5, 1963.

64. Ibid.
65. Remmel, "Pack 'a Little Flat.'"
66. Lee Remmel, "'I'm Getting My Legs under Me,' Happy Taylor Concedes," *Green Bay Press-Gazette,* Nov. 4, 1963.
67. Al Abrams, "Close for One Half," *Pittsburgh Post-Gazette,* Nov. 4, 1963.
68. Don Schiffer, *Pro Football 1963* (New York: Pocket Books, 1963), 46.
69. Remmel, "'I'm Getting My Legs under Me.'"
70. Jack Sell, "Fifteen Irish Backs," *Pittsburgh Post-Gazette,* Nov. 5, 1963.
71. Remmel, "Pack 'a Little Flat.'"
72. Al Abrams, "Run to Oblivion," *Pittsburgh Post-Gazette,* Nov. 4, 1963.
73. Remmel, "Pack 'a Little Flat.'"
74. Remmel, "'I'm Getting My Legs under Me.'"
75. Remmel, "Pack 'a Little Flat.'"
76. Pat Livingston, "Steelers Find Taylor Crawls—All over You," *Pittsburgh Press,* Nov. 4, 1963.
77. Remmel, "Pack 'a Little Flat.'"

GAME 9

1. UPI, "How Do Bears Do It?," *Chicago Sun-Times,* Nov. 7, 1963.
2. Steve Snider, "Pro-Football Has Become a Craze," *Chicago-Sun Times,* Nov. 3, 1963.
3. "Can Steelers' Line Finally Chain Brown?," *Pittsburgh Courier,* Nov. 9, 1963.
4. Pat Livingston, "Steelers May Reactivate Womack," *Pittsburgh Press,* Nov. 7, 1963.
5. Snider, "Pro-Football Has Become a Craze."
6. Pat Livingston, *Pittsburgh Press,* Oct. 10, 1963.
7. "Steelers Discover Why Huff Piled On," *Pittsburgh Press,* Nov. 4, 1963.
8. Sam Huff, conversation, July 9, 2008.
9. Dick Haley, conversation, May 14, 2008.
10. Myron Cope, "Kiss the Guy or Tackle Him?," *Saturday Evening Post,* Oct. 26, 1963, 77; Jack Sell, "JHJ Makes a Suggestion," *Pittsburgh Post-Gazette,* Sept. 26, 1963.
11. Jimmy Brown with Myron Cope, *Off My Chest* (Garden City, N.Y.: Doubleday, 1964), 186; Sam Huff and Leonard Shapiro, *Tough Stuff: The Man in the Middle* (New York: St. Martin's Press, 1988), 143.
12. Jim Murray, *Los Angeles Times,* Feb. 1, 1970, from microfiche (headline illegible).
13. Ron Borges, "John Henry Was a Hard-Driving Man," *Game Day,* pro football program, 1983 (full date illegible).
14. Myron Cope, "Kiss the Guy or Tackle Him?," 77.
15. AP, "Wolfner, Cards, Hits 49er Eleven," *New York Times,* Oct. 14, 1955.
16. Ibid.
17. Ray Didinger, *Pittsburgh Steelers* (New York: Macmillan, 1974), 18.
18. Cope, "Kiss the Guy or Tackle Him?," 75.
19. Didinger, *Pittsburgh Steelers,* 21.
20. Louis Effrat, "Bears Win Western Title by Besting Lions in Rough Football Game," *New York Times,* Dec. 17, 1956.

21. AP, "Parker Threatens to Quit as Pro Football Coach," Dec. 18, 1956.
22. Red Mack, interview, Oct. 11, 2008.
23. AP, "Lions Extended as They Defeat Packers in Rough Game, 21 to 17," *New York Times,* Nov. 22, 1954.
24. AP, "Texas Defeats Oklahoma, 34–14, as Fans Fight and Pop Bottles Fly," *New York Times,* Oct. 12, 1947.
25. Otto Graham, "Football Is Getting Too Vicious," *Sports Illustrated,* Oct. 11, 1954, 26, 50–52.
26. Tex Maule, "Giants Killer," *Sports Illustrated,* Nov. 24, 1958, 44.
27. Sam Huff, conversation, July 9, 2008.
28. Chris Tomasson, "John Henry Got Better with Age," *Canton Repository,* Oct. 6, 1986.
29. Borges, "John Henry Was a Hard-Driving Man."
30. Red Mack, interview, Oct. 11, 2008.
31. AP, "Taylor Claims Huff Was Piling On, Had 'Words' with Pro Rival," *Youngstown Vindicator,* Jan. 29, 1963.
32. Norman Miller, "Violent World Crashes on Gridder," *Youngstown Vindicator,* Jan. 29, 1963.
33. Hal Lebovitz, "Jimmy Brown Picks His Five Greatest Games," *Sport,* Dec. 1964, 78.
34. Jack Sell, "Rudy or Bobby for the Steelers?," *Pittsburgh Post-Gazette,* Nov. 7, 1961.
35. Gordon Cobbledick, "Suspensions without Pay Would Curb Brutality of Football's Hatchet Men," *Cleveland Plain Dealer,* Nov. 24, 1963.
36. Cope, "Kiss the Guy or Tackle Him?," 77.
37. Tomasson, "John Henry Got Better with Age." Bryan W. Winfrey, Arizona State University Athletic Department, from a Tempe (AZ) *Daily News* article, 1980 (Winfrey constructed a bio for the department from assorted clips).
38. Cope, "Kiss the Guy or Tackle Him?," 77.
39. AP, "Johnson, Back after Ban, Leads Lions' 23–17 Victory over Rams," *New York Times,* Nov. 16, 1959.
40. UPI, "Lions Fullback Suspended," *New York Times,* Nov. 3, 1959.
41. AP, "Johnson, Back after Ban."
42. Brown with Cope, *Off My Chest,* 162–63, 165.
43. Steve Snider, "Pro Football Has Become a Craze," *Chicago-Sun Times,* Nov. 3, 1963.
44. Brown with Cope, *Off My Chest,* 163.
45. "Citizens Committee Planned for Solving Problem," *Pittsburgh Post-Gazette,* Nov. 7, 1963.
46. Cope, "Kiss the Guy or Tackle Him?," 77.
47. Jack Olsen, "In the Back of the Bus," *Sports Illustrated,* July 22, 1968, 30.
48. Pat Livingston, "Brown Unloaded Long 'Bomb' and Hoped Mack Would Nab It," *Pittsburgh Press,* Oct. 28, 1963.
49. Jack Sell, "Hoak to Be Honored by Jeanette Fans, among 54,490 Expected," *Pittsburgh Post-Gazette,* Nov. 5, 1963.
50. Jack Sell, "Stautner, Thomas Uncertain for Browns Tilt," *Pittsburgh Post-Gazette,* Nov. 8, 1963.
51. Lou Cordileone, conversation, Aug. 13, 2008.
52. Brown with Cope, *Off My Chest,* 194.

53. Cope, "Kiss the Guy or Tackle Him?," 76.

54. Lou Cordileone, conversation, Aug. 13, 2008.

55. Brown with Cope, *Off My Chest,* 43; Clair Young, "The Raging Moods of John Henry Johnson," *Pro Sports,* Jan. 1966, 9.

56. "Ballman Took Risk on 92-Yard Run," *Pittsburgh Press,* Nov. 18, 1963.

57. Brown with Cope, *Off My Chest,* 191.

58. "Benny Plays Seriously—for Laughs," *Pittsburgh Post-Gazette,* Nov. 4, 1963.

59. Pat Livingston, "Parker Tries to Relax Steelers," *Pittsburgh Press,* Nov. 5, 1963.

60. Ibid.

61. Pat Livingston, "Steelers May Reactivate Womack," *Pittsburgh Press,* Nov. 7, 1963.

62. Pat Livingston, "Steelers Must Adjust Defense for Brown(s)," *Pittsburgh Press,* Nov. 6, 1963.

63. Ibid.

64. Brady Keys, conversation, Sept. 4, 2007.

65. Pat Livingston, "Warfield to Get Treatment," *Pittsburgh Press,* Oct. 6, 1966.

66. *Pittsburgh Press,* Sept. 1, 1962.

67. Brady Keys, conversation, Sept. 4, 2007.

68. Livingston, "Steelers May Reactivate Womack."

69. "Grid Fans Have Selves to Blame," *Pittsburgh Post-Gazette,* Nov. 9, 1963.

70. Alvin Rosensweet, "No Joy in Mudville (Cleveland) Tonight," *Pittsburgh Post-Gazette,* Nov. 11, 1963.

71. Al Abrams, "Back in the Running," *Pittsburgh Post-Gazette,* Nov. 11, 1963.

72. Rosensweet, "No Joy in Mudville."

73. Jimmy Jordan, "57,331 Sellout for Pitt-Penn State Tilt," *Pittsburgh Post-Gazette,* Nov. 22, 1963.

74. Sam Sciullo Jr., *Pitt Stadium Memories* (Pittsburgh: University of Pittsburgh, 2000), 68.

75. "Ex-Steeler Tackled as Traffic Scofflaw," *Pittsburgh Press,* April 16, 1975.

76. Tommy Holmes, "Browns Lose, Giants Tie for Lead," *New York Herald Tribune,* Nov. 11, 1963.

77. Chuck Heaton, "Parker Says Added Pressure Hit Ryan," *Cleveland Plain Dealer,* Nov. 11, 1963.

78. Ed Bouchette, "Bob Schmitz / Former Steeler Who Tackled Jim Brown for a Safety," *Pittsburgh Post-Gazette,* June 10, 2004.

79. Mike Rathet, "Finds Brown All Alone," *Youngstown Vindicator,* Nov. 11, 1963 (AP).

80. Pat Livingston, "Rooney U. Unties Itself to Shackle Cleveland, 9–7," *Pittsburgh Press,* Nov. 11, 1963.

81. Sciullo, *Pitt Stadium Memories,* 69.

82. Livingston, "Rooney U. Unties Itself."

84. Pat Livingston, "Ed Brown 'Loses' Receiver, then Finds Him for TD Toss," *Pittsburgh Press,* Nov. 11, 1963.

84. Jack Sell, "54,497 See Steelers Win, 9–7," *Pittsburgh Post-Gazette,* Nov. 11, 1963.

85. Myron Cope, "Pittsburgh's Patient Whipping Boy," *Sports Illustrated,* Dec. 19, 1966, M3.

86. Ibid.

87. Official game play-by-play account.

88. Rathet, "Finds Brown All Alone."

89. Livingston, "Ed Brown 'Loses' Receiver."

90. Rathet, "Finds Brown All Alone."

91. Livingston, "Rooney U. Unties Itself"; Sell, "54,497 See Steelers Win, 9–7."

92. Al Abrams, "About a Man in a Slump," *Pittsburgh Post-Gazette,* Nov. 13, 1963.

93. Tommy Holmes, "Browns Lose; Giants Tie for Lead," *New York Herald Tribune,* Nov. 11, 1963.

94. Pat Livingston, "Steelers Find 'Buoyancy' in Title Bid," *Pittsburgh Press,* Oct. 2, 1963.

95. Pat Livingston, "Extra Holiday for Steelers," *Pittsburgh Press,* Nov. 12, 1963.

96. Livingston, "Ed Brown 'Loses' Receiver."

97. Bouchette, "Bob Schmitz."

98. Jack Sell, "Hobbling the Horse," *Pittsburgh Post-Gazette,* Nov. 12, 1963.

99. Jack Sell, "Rest Cure for Browns Game Pays Off; Buddy Tries Again," *Pittsburgh Post-Gazette,* Nov. 12, 1963.

100. Rosensweet, "No Joy in Mudville."

GAME 10

1. Arthur Daley, "Another Abrupt Departure," *New York Times,* Sept. 8, 1965.

2. Art Rooney Jr., *Ruanaidh: The Story of Art Rooney and His Clan* (n.p.: Author, 2008), 212.

3. Tom Danyluk, *The Super '70s: Memories from Pro Football's Greatest Era* (n.p.: Mad Uke, 2005), 3.

4. Rooney, *Ruanaidh,* 179.

5. Alfred Wright, "If There's Time, There's Hope," *Sports Illustrated,* May 23, 1960.

6. Pat Livingston, "Steelers Sign MSU's Ballman," *Pittsburgh Press,* Dec. 13, 1961.

7. Judi Ballman, conversation, Oct. 8, 2008.

8. Al Abrams, "The 'Goose,' Talks Up," *Pittsburgh Post-Gazette,* July 26, 1962.

9. "Steelers to Start Second Week of Drills," *Pittsburgh Post-Gazette,* Aug. 6, 1962.

10. "Tracy OK, to See Action against Browns," *Pittsburgh Post-Gazette,* Aug. 17, 1962.

11. Ray Kelly, *Camden (N.J.) Courier-Post,* April 25, 1973.

12. Johnny Sample with Fred J. Hamilton and Sonny Schwartz, *Confessions of a Dirty Ballplayer* (New York: Dial Press, 1970), 275.

13. Pat Livingston, "Training Paid off for Gary Ballman," *Pittsburgh Press,* Nov. 19, 1963.

14. Pat Livingston, "Steelers Are Really Having a Ball, Man!" *Pittsburgh Press,* Nov. 18, 1963.

15. Judi Ballman, conversation, Oct. 8, 2008.

16. Livingston, "Training Paid off for Gary Ballman."

17. Ibid.

18. Lou Cordileone, conversation, April 30, 2010.

19. Judi Ballman, conversation, Oct. 8, 2008.

20. Ibid.

21. Jim Bradshaw, conversation, Dec. 10, 2007.

22. Ibid.

23. Bill Wise, *1963 Official Pro Football Almanac* (Greenwich, Conn.: Fawcett, 1963), 50.

24. Ruth Daniel, e-mail interview, Jan. 12, 2008.

25. Arthur Daley, "A Profitable Punch," *New York Times,* Nov. 19, 1961.

26. Ibid.

27. Ray Didinger, *Pittsburgh Steelers* (New York: Macmillan, 1974), 21.

28. Ruth Daniel, e-mail interview, Jan. 12, 2008.

29. Daley, "A Profitable Punch."

30. Ibid.

31. Ruth Daniel, e-mail interview, Jan. 12, 2008.

32. Al Abrams, "Mad, Mad Football Whirl," *Pittsburgh Post-Gazette,* Nov. 12, 1963.

33. Joseph P. Browne, "Pittsburgh No Longer Haven for Murderers," *Pittsburgh Post-Gazette,* Nov. 11, 1963.

34. Al Abrams, "Mr. Stichweh Volunteers," *Pittsburgh Post-Gazette,* Nov. 14, 1963; "Irma the Body Casino-Bound," *Pittsburgh Post-Gazette,* Nov. 14, 1963.

35. Vince Johnson, "Jayne Mansfield Show Banned by Officials Here," *Pittsburgh Post-Gazette,* Nov. 14, 1963.

36. AP, "Cleveland Suburb Bans Mansfield Movie," *Pittsburgh Post-Gazette,* Nov. 11, 1963.

37. AP, "Bear-Packer Skirmish Has Chicago Agog," *Pittsburgh Post-Gazette,* Nov. 14, 1963.

38. "Spies Beware!," *Chicago Sun-Times,* Nov. 13, 1963.

39. Pat Livingston, "Extra Holiday for Steelers," *Pittsburgh Press,* Nov. 12, 1963.

40. Wise, *1963 Official Pro Football Almanac,* 71.

41. UPI, "McPeak Denies Dissension," *Pittsburgh Press,* Nov. 12, 1963.

42. Pat Livingston, "Budd (9.2) May Join Mitchell in Backfield," *Pittsburgh Press,* Nov. 14, 1963.

43. Pat Livingston, "Relaxed Steelers Ready for 'Skins," *Pittsburgh Press,* Nov. 15, 1963.

44. Pat Livingston, "McPeak Stays Calm for Steeler Battle," *Pittsburgh Press,* Nov. 17, 1963.

45. Fran Zimniuch, *Eagles: Where Have You Gone? Catching up with Chuck Bednarik, Tim Rossavich, Jeff Kemp and Other Eagles of Old* (Champaign, Ill.: Sports Publishing, 2004), 44.

46. Livingston, "Relaxed Steelers Ready for 'Skins."

47. Lester J. Biederman, "Saints & Sinners to Honor Rooney," *Pittsburgh Press,* Nov. 16, 1963.

48. UPI, "AFL 'Too Inferior' for Title Playoff with NFL—Retzlaff," *Pittsburgh Press,* Nov. 12, 1963.

49. UPI, "NFL-AFL Title Tilt Far Off—Rozelle," *Pittsburgh Press,* Nov. 16, 1963.

50. "The Outlook for Kennedy," *Pittsburgh Post-Gazette,* Nov. 15, 1963.

51. Ibid.

52. Al Abrams, "Justice in Photo Finish," *Pittsburgh Post-Gazette,* Nov. 18, 1963.

53. Jack Walsh, "Steelers Collar Redskins, 34–28," *Washington Post,* Nov. 18, 1963.

54. Ibid.

55. Robert Riger, *Best Plays of the Year 1962: A Documentary of Pro Football in the National Football League* (Englewood Cliffs, N.J.: Prentice-Hall, 1963), 50.

56. Edwin Pope, "The South," Dick Kaplan, ed., *1961 Football Yearbook Kick-Off* (New York: Popular Library, 1961), 19.

57. "Ballman Took Risk on 92-Yard Run," *Pittsburgh Press,* Nov. 18, 1963.

58. Walsh, "Steelers Collar Redskins, 34–28."

59. Steve Guback, "Double Damage in Dual Role," *Washington Evening Star,* Nov. 18, 1963.

60. Pat Livingston, "Somebody up There Likes 'Em," *Pittsburgh Press,* Oct. 29, 1962.

61. Livingston, "Steelers Are Really Having a Ball, Man!"

62. Walsh, "Steelers Collar Redskins, 34–28."

63. Al Abrams, "About a Man in a Slump," *Pittsburgh Post-Gazette,* Nov. 13, 1963.

64. Jimmy Miller, "Real Cliff Hanger," *Pittsburgh Post-Gazette,* Nov. 18, 1963.

65. Abrams, "Justice in Photo Finish."

66. Livingston, "Steelers Are Really Having a Ball, Man!"

67. *Pittsburgh Press,* "Ballman Took Risk."

68. Livingston, "Steelers Are Really Having a Ball, Man!"; Abrams, "Justice in Photo Finish."

69. Livingston, "Ballman Took Risk."

70. Don Schiffer, *Pro Football 1963* (New York: Pocket Books, 1963), 107; Livingston, "Steelers Are Really Having a Ball, Man!"

71. *Pittsburgh Press,* "Ballman Took Risk."

72. Livingston, "Steelers Are Really Having a Ball, Man!"

73. UPI, "McPeak Wants to Build Winner," *Pittsburgh Press,* Nov. 19, 1963.

74. Miller, "Real Cliff Hanger."

75. Jack Sell, "The Substitute Speaker," *Pittsburgh Post-Gazette,* Nov. 19, 1963.

76. Miller, "Real Cliff Hanger."

77. Ibid.

GAME 11

1. "500,000 to See Kentucky," *Chicago Sun-Times,* Nov. 2, 1963.

2. *Chicago Sun-Times,* Nov. 12, 1963.

3. Steve Snider, "Pro-Football Has Become a Craze," *Chicago-Sun Times,* Nov. 3, 1963.

4. Arthur Daley, "Too Much Enthusiasm," *New York Times,* Dec. 8, 1959.

5. Gordon S. White Jr., "Rioting Fans Halt Giants-Browns Game 20 Minutes," *New York Times,* Dec. 7, 1959.

6. "Football—Another Business That's Really Booming," *U.S. News & World Report,* Nov. 18, 1963, 103–4 (the American Professional Football Association was formed in 1920; it was repackaged as the NFL in 1922).

7. Jack Sell, "The Substitute Speaker," *Pittsburgh Post-Gazette,* Nov. 19, 1963.

8. Ibid.

9. Bruce Morrison, "Bears Go to the Top 26–7!" *Chicago Sun-Times,* Nov. 18, 1963.

10. Al Abrams, "Papa Bear on the Prowl," *Pittsburgh Post-Gazette,* Nov. 20, 1963.

11. AP, "Bears Favored over Steelers," *Pittsburgh Post-Gazette,* Nov. 20, 1963.

12. Tex Maule, "Down Go the Packers," *Sports Illustrated,* Nov. 25, 1963, 31.

13. Joe Agrella, *Chicago Sun-Times,* Nov. 22, 1963.

14. Shirley Povich, "Bears Winning with Old Stuff," *Washington Post,* Nov. 10, 1963.

15. Bruce Morrison, "Ability to Make Big Play Has Offset Weak Offense," *Chicago Sun-Times,* Nov. 15, 1963.

16. "Ball Control Won Says Wade," *Chicago Sun-Times,* Nov. 18, 1963.

17. "Bears Defenses Same—Parker," *Pittsburgh Press,* Nov. 21, 1963.

18. Joe Agrella, "Why Steelers Worry Halas," *Chicago Sun-Times,* Nov. 21, 1963.

19. "Bitter Brown Anxious to Defeat Bears," *Chicago Sun-Times,* Nov. 21, 1963.

20. Ibid.

21. Ibid.

22. Jeff Davis, *Papa Bear: The Life and Legacy of George Halas* (New York: McGraw-Hill, 2008), 327.

23. AP, "U.S. Space Program Necessary, Says JFK," *Pittsburgh Post-Gazette,* Nov. 22, 1963.

24. "A Pride of Lions," *Time,* Nov. 29, 1954, 60.

25. Art Rooney Jr., conversation, April 29, 2010.

26. Dan Rooney, *Dan Rooney: My 75 Years with the Pittsburgh Steelers and the NFL,* as told to Andrew E. Masich and David F. Halaas (Cambridge, Mass.: Da Capo Press, 2007), 103–4.

27. Art Rooney Jr., conversation, April 29, 2010.

28. Sherley Uhl, "Fearless Kennedy Braved Bone-Crushing Crowds," *Pittsburgh Press,* Nov. 23, 1963.

29. "President's Death Hits City like Bomb," *Pittsburgh Press,* Nov. 22, 1963.

30. "Dipping Flag Told City Tragic News," *Pittsburgh Press,* Nov. 23, 1963.

31. Art Daley, "Five Texan Packers 'Go Home,' Claim 'That's Not Dallas,'" *Green Bay Press-Gazette,* Nov. 23, 1963.

32. AP, "NFL Crowds Somber but Stands Are Filled," *Green Bay Press-Gazette,* Nov. 23, 1963.

33. Sam Huff, conversation, Sept. 9, 2008.

34. AP, "NFL Crowds Somber."

35. AP, "Sonny Wept about JFK," *Pittsburgh Post-Gazette,* Nov. 23, 1963.

36. "NFL Games to Be Played 'in Tradition,' Rozelle Says," *Green Bay Press-Gazette,* Nov. 24, 1963.

37. Dick Haley, conversation, May 14, 2008.

38. Leonard Koppett, "Sports Schedule Drastically Cut as Nation Mourns," *New York Times,* Nov. 24, 1963.

39. John Rendel, "Dog Show Begins Despite Criticism," *New York Times,* Nov. 24, 1963.

40. Al Abrams, "Whirl around the World of Sports," *Pittsburgh Post-Gazette,* Nov. 23, 1963.

41. Gordon Cobbledick, "Suspension without Pay Would Curb Brutality of Football's Hatchet Men," *Cleveland Plain Dealer,* Nov. 24, 1963.

42. "20 Calls a Minute," *Chicago Tribune,* Nov. 24, 1963.

43. Lou Michaels, conversation, Aug. 29, 2007.

44. Red Mack, conversation, Aug. 8, 2007.

45. Andy Russell, conversation, Oct. 4, 2007.

46. Joseph M. Sheehan, "N.F.L. Games Today Stir Fans' Anger," *New York Times,* Nov. 24, 1963.

47. Ibid.

48. "Attendance about Normal," *New York Daily News,* Nov. 25, 1963.

49. Y. A. Tittle, conversation, Sept. 8, 2008.

50. Pat Livingston, "Hard-Nosed Krupa Underrated Tackle in Steeler Defense," *Pittsburgh Press,* Oct. 19, 1961.

51. Ron Cook, "Rozelle Blew Call in '63," *Pittsburgh Post-Gazette,* Sept. 14, 2001.

52. Murray Olderman, "Two Careers for Charley Johnson," *Sport,* March 1964, 86.

53. AP, "NFL Crowds Somber," Nov. 25, 1963.

54. Davis, *Papa Bear,* 391.

55. AP, "NFL Crowds Somber."

56. Ibid.

57. Matt Mosley, "No Heart for This Game," *Dallas Morning News,* Jan. 27, 2004.

58. Ibid.

59. Bill Wise, *1963 Official Pro Football Almanac* (Greenwich, Conn.: Fawcett, 1963), 41.

60. Mosley, "No Heart for This Game."

61. Ibid.

62. Dick Young, "They Came with Mixed Emotions—but They Came," *New York Daily News,* Nov. 25, 1963.

63. Ibid.

64. Red Smith, *New York Herald Tribune,* Nov. 25, 1963.

65. Sandy Grady, "Doors Never Close in Toyland," *Philadelphia Evening Bulletin,* Nov. 25, 1963.

66. Frank Atkinson, conversation, Oct. 10, 2007.

67. Fred Remington, "Nets Cancel Scheduled Programs," *Pittsburgh Press,* Nov. 23, 1963.

68. Art Rooney Jr., conversation, April 29, 2010.

69. Dick Young, "Does One Grieve More than the Other?," *New York Daily News,* Nov. 24, 1963.

70. AP, "334,892 See NFL Despite Protests," *Youngstown Vindicator,* Nov. 25, 1963.

71. Ruth Daniel, e-mail interview, Jan. 12, 2008.

72. Mosley, "No Heart for This Game."

73. AP, "NFL Crowds Somber."

74. Lee Remmel, "First Half 'Sharp as I've Seen,' Vince," *Green Bay Press-Gazette,* Nov. 25, 1963.

75. Art Daley, *Green Bay Press-Gazette,* "Packers Battle 49ers—with Heavy Hearts," Nov. 24, 1963.

76. "Renfro Given New Car, Trips; Fete Canceled," *Youngstown Vindicator,* Nov. 25, 1963.

77. Milton Gross, "NFL Teams Play with Mixed Emotions, amid Protests," Nov. 25, 1963.

78. Bill Lyon, *When the Clock Runs Out: 20 NFL Greats Share Their Stories of Hardship and Triumph* (Chicago: Triumph Books, 1999), 223.

79. Grady, "Doors Never Close."

80. Jim Becker, "Giants' Loss No Tragedy for Fans," *Green Bay Press-Gazette,* Nov. 25, 1963.

81. Sam Huff, conversation, July 9, 2008.

82. Hugh Brown, "Eagles Stumble into NFL Cellar," *Philadelphia Evening Bulletin,* Nov. 25, 1963.

83. AP, "NFL Crowds Somber."

84. Grady, "Doors Never Close."

85. George Strickler, "Packers Win; Bears Tie, Retain Lead," *Chicago Tribune,* Nov. 25, 1963.

86. Cooper Rollow, "We'll Settle for Tie, Says Halas (Still in First Place)," *Chicago Tribune,* Nov. 25, 1963.

87. Jack Hand, "Cards Tip Giants, Forge Three-way Deadlock in East," AP, Nov. 25, 1963.

88. Art Rooney Jr., conversation, April 29, 2010.

89. Frank Atkinson, conversation, Oct. 10, 2007.

90. Strickler, "Packers Win."

91. Ibid.

92. Pat Livingston, "Steelers Miss Win . . . Just Bear-ly," *Pittsburgh Press,* Nov. 25, 1963.

93. Strickler, "Packers Win."

94. "Steelers High on Curry as West Liberty Camp Starts," *Pittsburgh Courier,* July 20, 1963.

95. "Football Roundup: Tan Stars Stand Out in Both Leagues," *Ebony,* Nov. 1963, 70; "Steelers High on Curry," *Pittsburgh Courier,* July 20, 1963.

96. Strickler, "Packers Win."

97. Ibid.

98. Jack Sell, "Freezing the Bears," *Pittsburgh Post-Gazette,* Nov. 22, 1963.

99. Jack Sell, "Rooney U. Hopes to Retain Title Chances!" *Pittsburgh Post-Gazette,* Nov. 30, 1963.

100. Livingston, "Steelers Miss Win."

101. Jack Sell, "A Good Joe," *Pittsburgh Post-Gazette,* Oct. 24, 1963.

102. Robert Smith, *The Great Teams of Pro Football* (New York: Dell, 1965), 228.

103. Strickler, "Packers Win."

104. Jim Wexell, *Pittsburgh Steelers: Men of Steel* (Champaign, Ill.: Sports Publishing, 2006), 35–36.

105. AP, "Parker Threatens to Quit as Pro Football Coach," *New York Times,* Dec. 18, 1956.

106. Davis, *Papa Bear,* 9, 31, 18.

107. Pat Livingston, "4 Steelers Added to Casualty List," *Pittsburgh Press,* Dec. 7, 1959.

108. Wexell, *Pittsburgh Steelers,* 57.

109. Davis, *Papa Bear,* 393.

110. Pat Livingston, "'Silent Whistle' Cost Steelers TD, Helped Bears Gain," *Pittsburgh Press,* Nov. 25, 1963.

111. Strickler, "Packers Win."

112. Red Smith, *New York Herald Tribune,* Dec. 30, 1963.

113. Roy McHugh, "Mike Ditka: Pro Football's Ty Cobb," *Sport,* Dec. 1964, 66.

114. Mike Ditka with Don Pierson, *Ditka: An Autobiography* (Chicago: Bonus Books, 1987), 90.
115. Rollow, "We'll Settle for Tie."
116. Riger, *Best Plays of the Year 1963,* 69; Strickler, "Packers Win."
117. Bill Conlin, "Bears 'Lucky' to Tie Steelers," *Philadelphia Evening Bulletin,* Nov. 25, 1963.
118. Armen Keteyian, *Ditka: Monster of the Midway* (New York: Pocket Books, 1992), 88.
119. Jack Sell, "Bears Save Skin When Unexpected Pass Hits Steeler," *Pittsburgh Post-Gazette,* Nov. 25, 1963.
120. Strickler, "Packers Win."
121. Sell, "Bears Save Skin."
122. Strickler, "Packers Win."
123. Sell, "Bears Save Skin."
124. Ibid.
125. Rollow, "We'll Settle for Tie."
126. Strickler, "Packers Win."
127. Rollow, "We'll Settle for Tie."
128. Davis, *Papa Bear,* 393.
129. Rollow, "We'll Settle for Tie."
130. Davis, *Papa Bear,* 392.
131. Grady, "Doors Never Close."
132. Becker, "Giants' Loss No Tragedy for Fans."
133. Arthur Daley, "NFL Fans Give Heavy Hearts Lift," *New York Times,* Nov. 25, 1963.
134. Al Abrams, "Monday Morning's Sports Wash," *Pittsburgh Post-Gazette,* Dec. 11, 1961; Al Abrams, "Pro Football at Its Toughest," *Pittsburgh Post-Gazette,* Nov. 25, 1963.
135. "Visitors to Family Were Advised to Be Ready for Football Games," *New York Times,* Nov. 23, 1963.
136. Leonard Koppet, *New York Times,* Nov. 25, 1963.
137. David Condon, *Chicago Tribune,* Nov. 25, 1963.
138. Remmel, "First Half."

GAME 12

1. Jimmy Brown with Myron Cope, *Off My Chest* (Garden City, N.Y.: Doubleday, 1964), 192.
2. Dave Eisenberg, "Buddy Slippery Receiver," *New York Journal-American,* Dec. 11, 1963.
3. Kevin Sherrington, "Football Took Its Toll on Ex-Dallas Cowboy Buddy Dial," *Dallas Morning News,* March 28, 2008.
4. AP, "Pittsburgh's Dial Could Be Top NFL Receiver," *Chicago Sun-Times,* Nov. 3, 1963.
5. Don Schiffer, *Pro Football 1963* (New York: Pocket Books, 1963), 94.
6. Lou Prato, "Sing-Along Football Star," *Sport,* July 1963, 64.

7. Ibid., 64.

8. Ibid., 65.

9. David Barron, "Former Rice, Steelers Receiver Dies at 71," *Houston Chronicle,* March 1, 2008.

10. Dahleen Glanton, "In Seconds, Killer Stole Untold Years," *Chicago Tribune,* July 31, 1999.

11. Barron, "Former Rice, Steelers Receiver."

12. Prato, "Sing-Along Football Star," 65.

13. Arthur Daley, "Rice for the Sailors," *New York Times,* Jan. 1, 1958.

14. Arthur Daley, "A Matter of Luck," *New York Times,* Dec. 7, 1958.

15. Joseph M. Sheehan, "Four Giant Draft Choices Excel in All-Star Football Workouts," *New York Times,* Aug. 13, 1959.

16. Milton Gross, "Steelers' Buddy Dial at Home on Field, on Stage, in Pulpit," *North American Newspaper Alliance* (published in *Pittsburgh Press*), Dec. 13, 1963.

17. Prato, "Sing-Along Football Star," 65.

18. UPI, "Dial Makes Good without Giants," *Detroit News,* Dec. 13, 1963.

19. Prato, "Sing-Along Football Star," 55.

20. Ibid.

21. Ibid.

22. Ibid.

23. Peter Golenbock, *Landry's Boys: An Oral History of a Team and an Era* (Chicago: Triumph Books, 2005), 113.

24. AP, "Judge Rules Pact with Club Invalid," *New York Times,* June 21, 1960.

25. AP, "Oilers Sign Appleton to $104,000 Pact," *New York Times,* Feb. 2, 1964.

26. John Clayton, "Appleton's Haunting Past Slowly Healing," *Pittsburgh Press,* May 5, 1986.

27. Ibid.

28. Steve Marantz, *Boston Globe,* Dec. 12, 1982.

29. Preston Carpenter, conversation, Sept. 8, 2007.

30. UPI, "Dial Makes Good without Giants," *Detroit News,* Dec. 13, 1963.

31. Will Doerge, "Steelers Leave Ex-Mate Dial Limp with Bruised Feelings," *Pittsburgh Press,* Sept. 28, 1964.

32. Marantz, *Boston Globe,* Sept. 12, 1982.

33. Sherrington, "Football Took Its Toll."

34. Ed Asher, "Ex-Rice Star Thrown for Loss over Pension," *Houston Chronicle,* May 11, 1999.

35. Dahleen Glanton, "In Seconds, Killer Stole Untold Years."

36. Alvin Rosensweet, "City Pours Out Its Grief in Services Today," *Pittsburgh Post-Gazette,* Nov. 25, 1963; Harold V. Cohen, "No Column Today," *Pittsburgh Post-Gazette,* Nov. 25, 1963.

37. Jack Sell, "Blow the Whistle (or Don't)," *Pittsburgh Post-Gazette,* Nov. 26, 1963.

38. Jack Sell, "Steelers 13-Point Picks over Eagles," *Pittsburgh Post-Gazette,* Nov. 27, 1963.

39. Jack Sell, "Better than Roger," *Pittsburgh Post-Gazette,* Nov. 27, 1963.

40. Jimmy Miller, "Coach Parker Warns Title Contenders Eagles Could Be Spoilers Here," *Pittsburgh Post-Gazette,* Nov. 28, 1963.

41. Pat Livingston, "Eagles Aim at Steeler Title Bid," *Pittsburgh Press,* Dec. 1, 1963.

42. Ibid.

43. Milton Gross, "Epithet Triggered Violent Fist Fight of Eagles Players," *Pittsburgh Press,* Dec. 12, 1963.

44. "Scotti, Mellekas Hurt in Hotel-Lobby Fight," *Philadelphia Inquirer,* Nov. 25, 1963.

45. Gross, "Epithet Triggered Violent Fist Fight."

46. Ibid.

47. Ibid.

48. H. D. Quigg (UPI), "A Town in Torment," *Pittsburgh Press,* Dec. 1, 1963.

49. Harry J. Stathos, "The Beatles . . . Britain's Latest Craze," *Pittsburgh Press,* Dec. 1, 1963; Pat Livingston, "Parker's Title Plan Simple, Steelers 'Just' Win Three," *Pittsburgh Press,* Nov. 29, 1963.

50. Miller, "Coach Parker Warns"; Hugh Brown, "Interference Call Helps Steelers Deadlock Eagles," *Philadelphia Evening Bulletin,* Dec. 2, 1963.

51. "'Nobody but Us Hurts Us,' Says Steeler Coach," *Pittsburgh Post-Gazette,* Dec. 2, 1963.

52. Ibid.

53. Jack Sell, "Steelers, Eagles Keep Old 'Ties,' 20 to 20," *Pittsburgh Post-Gazette,* Dec. 2, 1963.

54. Bill Wise, *1963 Official Pro Football Almanac* (Greenwich, Conn.: Fawcett, 1963), 54.

55. Dick Haley, conversation, May 14, 2008.

56. "Stayed in Bounds, Buddy Dial Says," *Pittsburgh Press,* Dec. 2, 1963; "Steelers Admit They Were Bad Against Eagles," *Philadelphia Inquirer,* Dec. 2, 1963.

57. "Stayed in Bounds," *Pittsburgh Press.*

58. "'Ridiculous Game,'" *Philadelphia Inquirer.*

59. Brown, "Interference Call Helps."

60. Pat Livingston, "Rally for Tie Saves Hopes of Rooney U.," *Pittsburgh Press,* Dec. 2, 1963.

61. Brown, "Interference Call Helps."

62. Ibid.

63. "'Ridiculous Game,'" *Philadelphia Inquirer.*

64. "Stayed in Bounds," *Pittsburgh Press.*

65. Brown, "Interference Call Helps."

66. "'Nobody but Us Hurts Us,'" *Pittsburgh Post-Gazette.*

67. "'Ridiculous Game,'" *Philadelphia Inquirer.*

68. Ibid.

69. "'Nobody but Us Hurts Us,'" *Pittsburgh Post-Gazette.*

GAME 13

1. Jack Sell, "Much-Traveled Rookie Tackle Roamer—from Far East to West (Liberty)," *Pittsburgh Post-Gazette,* Aug. 9, 1963.

2. Ibid.

3. Andy Russell, conversation, Oct. 4, 2007.

4. Frank Atkinson, conversation, Oct. 10, 2007.

5. Roy McHugh, "Atkinson Finds Rare Richness in Hardness of Pro Football," *Pittsburgh Press,* July 28, 1964.

6. Ibid.

7. Ibid.

8. Sell, "Much-Traveled Rookie Tackle Roamer."

9. Frank Atkinson, conversation, Oct. 10, 2007.

10. "Steelers' Coach Says 'Team Wasn't Ready,'" *Pittsburgh Post-Gazette,* Aug. 12, 1963.

11. Frank Atkinson, conversation, Oct. 10, 2007.

12. Ibid.

13. McHugh, "Atkinson Finds Rare Richness."

14. Frank Atkinson, conversation, Oct. 10, 2007.

15. Ibid

16. Andy Russell, *An Odd Steelers Journey* (Champaign, Ill.: Sports Publishing, 2002), 13; Frank Atkinson, conversation, Oct. 10, 2007.

17. Jerry Green, *Detroit News,* Sept. 17, 1966.

18. Al Abrams, "Farout Steeler Fan," *Pittsburgh Post-Gazette,* Feb. 16, 1976.

19. Ibid.

20. Dan Fitzpatrick, "A Gold Rush That Ended," *Pittsburgh Post-Gazette,* March 19, 2003.

21. Pat Livingston, "Steelers Risk Title Hope with Cowboys," *Pittsburgh Press,* Dec. 6, 1963.

22. Pat Livingston, "Win Over Cowboys Must for Steelers," *Pittsburgh Press,* Dec. 8, 1963.

23. Tex Maule, "A Shuttle Shakes Up the Pros: How Landry Made a Virtue out of Weakness," *Sports Illustrated,* Nov. 5, 1962, 18.

24. Bill Wise, *1963 Official Pro Football Almanac* (Greenwich, Conn.: Fawcett, 1963), 36.

25. Livingston, "Steelers Risk Title Hope."

26. Pat Livingston, "Steeler Ties Okay—but, No More Please," *Pittsburgh Press,* Dec. 4, 1963.

27. "Dallas: Too Soon for Success," *Sports Illustrated,* Sept. 10, 1962.

28. Pat Livingston, "Steeler Recalls Colts' Experience," *Pittsburgh Press,* Dec. 7, 1963.

29. Al Abrams, "Impressions and Reflections," *Pittsburgh Post-Gazette,* Dec. 5, 1963.

30. Pat Livingston, "Win Over Cowboys Must for Steelers," *Pittsburgh Press,* Dec. 8, 1963.

31. Ibid.

32. UPI, "Detroit Set to Put Hex on Cleveland," Dec. 8, 1963 (*Pittsburgh Press*).

33. Jack Sell, "Steelers Corral Four Draft Picks," *Pittsburgh Post-Gazette,* Dec. 6, 1963.

34. Frank Atkinson, conversation, Oct. 10, 2007.

35. Art Rooney Jr., conversation, March 10, 2008.

36. Frank Atkinson, conversation, Oct. 10, 2007.

37. Pat Livingston, "Steelers, Giants Face Showdown," *Pittsburgh Press,* Dec. 9, 1963.

38. Gary Cartwright, "Steeler Rally Hobbles Cowboys, 24–19," *Dallas Morning News,* Dec. 9, 1963.

39. Preston Carpenter, conversation, Sept. 8, 2007.

40. Ibid.

41. UPI, "Dial Makes Good without Giants," *Detroit Press,* Dec. 13, 1963.

42. Preston Carpenter, conversation, Sept. 8, 2007.

43. Armen Keteyian, *Ditka: Monster of the Midway* (New York: Pocket Books, 1992), 111–12.

44. Cartwright, "Steeler Rally Hobbles Cowboys, 24–19."

45. Ibid.

46. "Parker Wins Two Gambles," *Pittsburgh Press,* Dec. 9, 1963.

47. Frank Atkinson, conversation, Oct. 10, 2007.

48. "Parker Wins Two Gambles," *Pittsburgh Press.*

49. Ibid.

50. Ibid.

51. Ibid.

52. Al Abrams, "About a Man in a Slump," *Pittsburgh Post-Gazette,* Oct. 13, 1963.

53. "Parker Wins Two Gambles," *Pittsburgh Press.*

54. Adam Van Brimmer, "Fullback Forever Known as the Drought Breaker," *Augusta (Ga.) Chronicle,* Nov. 22, 2007.

55. Livingston, "Steelers, Giants Face Showdown."

56. Robert Riger, *Best Plays of the Year 1963: A Documentary of Pro Football in the National Football League* (Englewood Cliffs, N.J.: Prentice-Hall, 1964), 44–45.

57. Livingston, "Steelers, Giants Face Showdown."

58. Cartwright, "Steeler Rally Hobbles Cowboys, 24–19."

59. "Parker Wins Two Gambles," *Pittsburgh Press.*

60. Rick Dorsey, "The Battle of Georgia Tells Old Tale," *Augusta (Ga.) Chronicle,* Nov. 26, 1999.

61. UPI, "Giants Eye Revenge Next Week," *Pittsburgh Press,* Dec. 9, 1963.

62. UPI, "Detroit Crushes Browns' Dreams," *Pittsburgh Press,* Dec. 9, 1963.

63. Livingston, "Steelers, Giants Face Showdown."

64. UPI, "Giants Eye Revenge."

GAME 14

1. Robert Oates Jr., *Pittsburgh's Steelers: The First Half Century* (Los Angeles: Rosebud Books, 1982), 41.

2. Arthur Daley, "Aerial Circus," *New York Times,* Aug. 25, 1958.

3. Stephen Norwood, *Real Football: Conversations on America's Game* (Jackson: University Press of Mississippi, 2004), 109.

4. Frank Atkinson, conversation, Oct. 10, 2007.

5. Andy Russell, interview, April 19, 2010.

6. Ray Didinger, *Pittsburgh Steelers* (New York: Macmillan, 1974), 82.

7. Pat Livingston, "Tittle Ready? Giants to Wait for Kickoff," *Pittsburgh Press,* Sept. 22, 1963.

8. Sam Huff, conversation, July 9, 2008.

9. "A Pride of Lions," *Time,* Nov. 29, 1954, 61–62.

10. Ruth Daniel, e-mail interview, Jan. 12, 2008.

11. Pat Livingston, "Steelers Find 'Buoyancy' in Title Bid," *Pittsburgh Press,* Oct. 2, 1963.

12. Matt Schudel, "Buzz Nutter," *Washington Post,* April 18, 2008.

13. Pat Livingston, "Giants Cautious for Steeler Clash," *Pittsburgh Press,* Dec. 12, 1963.

14. Pat Livingston, "Rozelle Stays Neutral in Hassle over Tie Tilts," *Pittsburgh Press,* Dec. 11, 1963.

15. "NFL May Review Standings Ruling," *New York Times,* Dec. 10, 1963.

16. Livingston, "Rozelle Stays Neutral."

17. Ibid.

18. Jack Sell, "Speaking of Ties," *Pittsburgh Post-Gazette,* Dec. 11, 1963, in Andy Piascik, "Old and New Style: Winning Percentages," *Coffin Corner,* 27, no. 5 (2005), 21–22.

19. Livingston, "Rozelle Stays Neutral."

20. Joe Williams, "Michaels vs. Chandler FG Duel Shaping Up," *Pittsburgh Press,* Dec. 12, 1963.

21. Livingston, "Rozelle Stays Neutral."

22. Al Abrams, "Giants 'Welcome' Steelers," *Pittsburgh Post-Gazette,* Dec. 12, 1963.

23. Al Abrams, "Whirl around the World of Sports," *Pittsburgh Post-Gazette,* Dec. 14, 1963.

24. Jack Sell, "Steelers Bear out Parker's Prophecy," *Pittsburgh Post-Gazette,* Dec. 12, 1963.

25. Didinger, *Pittsburgh Steelers,* 80.

26. *New York Daily News,* "Pressure's on Giants: Steelers," Dec. 12, 1963.

27. Ibid.

28. Sam Huff, conversation, July 9, 2008.

29. Ibid.

30. Huff in J. Kirk Sale, *New York Times,* Dec. 10, 1967.

31. Pat Livingston, "Ernie Admits Injury May Stop Him but Vows to Play while Health Lasts," *Pittsburgh Press,* n.d., microfiche, Pro Football Hall of Fame, Canton, Ohio.

32. Rick Morrisey, *Rocky Mountain News,* Feb. 24, 1991, Pro Football Hall of Fame archives.

33. Bud Shrake, "Toughest Steeler of Them All," *Dallas Morning News,* Dec. 8, 1963.

34. AP, "Giants' Word on Steelers: They're Tough," Dec. 10, 1963.

35. Joe Trimble, "Giants Tabbed 7-Point Pick over Steelers in Title Tilt," *New York Daily News,* Dec. 10, 1963.

36. Joe Williams, "Eerie Steelers Minute Men of Pros," *Pittsburgh Press,* Dec. 13, 1963.

37. AP, "Joe Morrison, 51, Former Giant," *New York Times,* Feb. 5, 1989.

38. Arthur Daley, "The Last Hurrah," *New York Times,* Dec. 15, 1963.

39. William N. Wallace, "Steelers Pit Brown, 35, against Tittle of Giants, 37," *New York Times,* Dec. 15, 1963.

40. Johnny Sample with Fred J. Hamilton and Sonny Schwartz, *Confessions of a Dirty Ballplayer* (New York: Dial Press, 1970), 308.

41. Jimmy Hill, "The Toughest Job in Football," *Sport,* Jan. 1965, 51.

42. Roy Terrell, "The Day the Boys Scared the Men: The Spirit Was Willing," *Sports Illustrated,* Dec. 18, 1961, 17.

43. Wallace, "Steelers Pit Brown."

44. Pat Livingston, "Brown Credentials Make Steelers Threat for Title," *Pittsburgh Press,* Aug. 23, 1963.

45. Wallace, "Steelers Pit Brown."

46. Joseph V. Rieland, Steelers game program, Dec. 1, 1963; Livingston, "Brown Credentials."

47. Al Abrams, "An Artisan at Work," *Pittsburgh Post-Gazette,* Oct. 30, 1963.

48. UPI, "Dial Makes Good without Giants," *Detroit Free Press,* Dec. 13, 1963.

49. Jim McCulley, "Don's Big Toe Is Giant Edge in Stadium's Whirly Winds," *New York Daily News,* Dec. 13, 1963.

50. Williams, "Michaels vs. Chandler FG."

51. Ibid.

52. Pat Livingston, "Parker Favors Dry, Fast Field," *Pittsburgh Press,* Dec. 14, 1963.

53. McCulley, "Don's Big Toe."

54. Myron Cope, "Pro Football's Gashouse Gang," *True,* Sept. 1964, 37.

55. Lou Cordileone, conversation, Aug. 13, 2008.

56. Myron Cope, "Pro Football's Gashouse Gang," 37.

57. Lou Cordileone, conversation, Aug. 13, 2008.

58. Arthur Daley, "Steelers Title Bid Poses Problem!" *New York Times,* Dec. 13, 1963.

59. Didinger, *Pittsburgh Steelers,* 80.

60. Cope, "Pro Football's Gashouse Gang," 37.

61. Didinger, *Pittsburgh Steelers,* 81.

62. Clendon Thomas, conversation, Aug. 30, 2008.

63. UPI, "Taylor Declares: 'I Never Took Worse Beating,'" *Youngstown Vindicator,* Jan. 1, 1963.

64. Jack Sell, "28,000 to See Steelers in Exit," *Pittsburgh Post-Gazette,* Dec. 13, 1958.

65. Dick Haley, conversation, May 14, 2008.

66. Jack Sell, "Future Steeler Stars Meet in Hotel Roosevelt, Look to Bowl Activity," *Pittsburgh Post-Gazette,* Dec. 17, 1963.

67. Andy Russell, interview, April 19, 2010.

68. Didinger, *Pittsburgh Steelers,* 82 (play-by-play indicates winds west/northwest, 15–25 mph).

69. Joe Bradis, "Parker Blames Both Offense and Defense," *Pittsburgh Post-Gazette,* Dec. 16, 1963.

70. Didinger, *Pittsburgh Steelers,* 82.

71. Pat Livingston, "Johnson Was Given OK to Pass up Drills to Help Heal Ankle," *Pittsburgh Press,* Oct. 21, 1963.

72. Bradis, "Parker Blames Both Offense and Defense."

73. Robert Smith, *The Great Teams of Pro Football* (New York: Dell, 1965), 187.

74. Pat Livingston, "Gifford Turns Tide for Giants," *Pittsburgh Press,* Dec. 16, 1963.

75. Rocky Bleier with Terry O'Neil, *Fighting Back* (New York: Warner Books, 1976), 64–65.
76. Lou Cordileone, conversation, April 30, 2010.
77. Tex Maule, "Y. A. Tittle Starts Another Season," *Sports Illustrated,* Oct. 6, 1958.
78. Lou Cordileone, conversation, Aug. 13, 2008.
79. Brady Keys, conversation, Sept. 4, 2007.
80. Smith, *The Great Teams of Pro Football,* 227.
81. Red Smith, "Winner-Take-All," *New York Herald Tribune,* Dec. 16, 1963 (published in *Youngstown Vindicator*).
82. Riger, *Best Plays of the Year 1963,* 85.
83. Arthur Daley, "Watchful Waiting," *New York Times,* Dec. 17, 1963.
84. Didinger, *Pittsburgh Steelers,* 84.
85. Daley, "Watchful Waiting"; Daley, *New York Times,* Dec. 17, 1963.
86. Y. A. Tittle, conversation, Sept. 8, 2008.
87. Pat Livingston, "Glass Solid Gold in Steeler Defense," *Pittsburgh Press,* Sept. 25, 1963.
88. Didinger, *Pittsburgh Steelers,* 84.
89. Andy Russell, interview, April 19, 2010.
90. Ibid.
91. Riger, *Best Plays of the Year 1963,* 85.
92. Smith, *The Great Teams of Pro Football,* 188.
93. Dick Haley, conversation, May 14, 2008.
94. Didinger, *Pittsburgh Steelers,* 84.
95. Gordon S. White Jr., "Everyone Agrees Gifford Held Victory in Palm of Right Hand," *New York Times,* Dec. 16, 1963.
96. Daley, "Watchful Waiting."
97. Joe Trimble, "'Bald Eagle' Clicks on 17 out of 26 Aerials Good for Three Touchdowns," *New York Daily News,* Dec. 16, 1963.
98. Art Rooney Jr., conversation, April 29, 2010.
99. Harold Rosenthal, "Giants, Bears Score Impressive Triumphs, Play for NFL Crown Dec. 29," *New York Herald Tribune,* Dec. 16, 1963, (published in *Youngstown Vindicator*).
100. Livingston, "Gifford Turns Tide for Giants."
101. Joe Trimble, "'Sweetest Year,' Tittle Says," *New York Daily News,* Dec. 16, 1963.
102. Didinger, *Pittsburgh Steelers,* 85.
103. Ibid.
104. Ibid., 124, 136.
105. Tex Maule, "The Giant Story: Tittle Takes Dead Aim on a Title," *Sports Illustrated,* Dec. 23, 1963.
106. Art Rooney Jr., conversation, April 29, 2010.
107. Brady Keys, conversation, Sept. 4, 2007.
108. Leonard Shecter, "Lou Michaels Takes a Last Crack at Title," *New York Post,* Dec. 16, 1963.
109. Al Abrams, "A Good Man Bedded Down," *Pittsburgh Post-Gazette,* Dec. 10, 1959.

110. Red Mack, conversation, Aug. 8, 2007.

111. Clendon Thomas, conversation, Aug. 30, 2008.

112. Gary Cartwright, "Layne Was Toughest," *Dallas Morning News,* Feb. 19, 1967.

113. Timothy Gay, *The Physics of Football: Discover the Science of Bone-Crushing Hits, Soaring Field Goals, and Awe-Inspiring Passes* (New York: Harper, 2005), 128.

114. Didinger, *Pittsburgh Steelers,* 85.

115. UPI, Dec. 17, 1963.

116. Jack Sell, "The New Era," *Pittsburgh Post-Gazette,* Dec. 19, 1963.

117. Preston Carpenter, conversation, Sept. 8, 2007.

118. Smith, *The Great Teams of Pro Football,* 227.

EPILOGUE

1. Lou Michaels, conversation, Aug. 29, 2007.

2. Preston Carpenter, conversation, Sept. 8, 2007.

3. Lou Cordileone, conversation, Aug. 29, 2010.

4. Roy McHugh, "Ex-Steeler Cordileone Tackles Zany Bar in French Quarter," *Pittsburgh Press,* Jan. 7, 1975.

5. Keys Group Company, "The Early Years," http://www.keysgroup.com/read_the_history.html.

6. UPI, "Parker Slated to Remain as Steelers' Coach But Layne's Career Nears End," Jan. 8, 1963.

7. Preston Carpenter, conversation, Sept. 8, 2007; Andy Russell, interview, April 19, 2010.

8. AP, July 22, 1966; *Game Day,* pro football program, Dec. 19, 1996.

9. "'Pressure' Talk Sparks Giants," *Pittsburgh Press,* Dec. 16, 1963.

10. Andy Russell, conversation, Oct. 4, 2007.

11. "The Way People Live Today," *U.S. News & World Report,* Nov. 11, 1963.

12. Jack Sell, "The New Era," *Pittsburgh Post-Gazette,* Dec. 19, 1963.

13. *Sports Illustrated,* Jan. 6, 1964.

14. *Detroit Free Press,* Jan. 1, 1967.

15. Jack Gallagher, *Houston Post,* Feb. 28, 1966.

16. *Game Day,* pro football program, Nov. 23, 1975.

17. "'Buddy' Parker, 68, Dies; Former Coach of Steelers," *Pittsburgh Post-Gazette,* March 23, 1982.

18. William N. Wallace, "Steelers Pit Brown, 35, against Tittle of Giants, 37," *New York Times,* Dec. 15, 1963.

19. Lou Cordileone, conversation, April 30, 2010.

20. Andy Russell, interview, April 19, 2010.

21. Jack Sell, "A Bear Rooter," *Pittsburgh Post-Gazette.*

22. Al Abrams, "Steelers Might Have Won," *Pittsburgh Post-Gazette,* Dec. 31, 1963.

23. Lou Michaels, conversation, Aug. 29, 2007.

AFTERWORD

1. Roger Treat, *The Official Encyclopedia of Football* (New York: A. S. Barnes, 1964), 494.
2. Pat Conroy, *My Losing Season* (New York: Doubleday, 2002), 14; Andy Russell, *Beyond the Goalpost* (n.p., 2009), 123.

INDEX